The Susskind Interviews:
Legal Experts in Changing Times

AUSTRALIA
Law Book Co.
Sydney

CANADA and USA
Carswell
Toronto

HONG KONG
Sweet & Maxwell Asia

NEW ZEALAND
Brookers
Wellington

SINGAPORE and MALAYSIA
Sweet & Maxwell Asia
Singapore and Kuala Lumpur

The Susskind Interviews:
Legal Experts in Changing Times

Edited by
Richard Susskind

THOMSON

SWEET & MAXWELL

Published in 2005 by Sweet & Maxwell Limited of
100 Avenue Road
London NW3 3PF
www.sweetandmaxwell.co.uk

Typeset by Servis Filmsetting Ltd, Manchester
Printed in England by
Athenaeum Press Ltd

No natural forests were destroyed to make this product; only farmed
timber was used and replanted

A CIP catalogue record for this book is available from the British Library

0421 91260 X

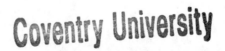

DEDICATION

This book is dedicated by his fellow contributors to Lord Woolf, Lord Chief Justice of England and Wales, 2000–2005.

FOREWORD

The time is ripe and the cast list stellar. This book—the transcript of a series of public conversations in Gresham College—makes a substantial contribution to some of the key legal, social, and political questions of this decade.

The place of law, the role of our legal system and its complex interactions with the public, the profession, the judges, and the Executive, has risen dramatically on political and public agendas. The driving forces behind this are various—the interest of the Government in the reform of the legal system, the debate about the adequacy of the system to deal with serious crime and the threat of terrorist activity, and continuing public and media concern over "law and order".

To that flux of thought, discussion and potential legislation, Richard Susskind brings a rich tapestry of informed opinion and comment from a group of the major players on the legal side of the debate. His skill as an informed interviewer in eliciting comment of both provenance and experience is a delight to encounter. It demonstrates beyond contradiction that there is an alternative to the Paxman school of interrogation.

Sir Thomas Gresham, whose will made provision for the education of those who live and work in the City of London, would surely be more than content with this latest publication from the lecture and conversation series of Gresham College.

Lord Sutherland of Houndwood KT FBA PRSE
Provost, Gresham College

ACKNOWLEDGMENTS

This book contains the revised and edited transcripts of a series of public interviews that I conducted at Gresham College from 2001 to 2004. I tell the story behind the discussions in the introductory chapter that follows. My purpose here, and it is a very pleasant one indeed, is to thank the many people who helped me bring this book together.

Above all, I am enormously grateful to my interviewees for agreeing to participate, for doing so with such enthusiasm and good humour, and for reviewing and revising their respective chapters in so timely a fashion. I therefore extend my warmest of thanks (in order of their appearance at Gresham) to Lord Woolf, Tony Williams, David Pannick QC, Lord Justice Auld, Michael Bray, Lord Irvine, Lord Bingham, Lord Goldsmith QC, David Lock, Oliver Letwin MP, Dame Elizabeth Butler-Sloss, Cherie Booth QC, Lord Saville, Sir Hayden Phillips, Professor John Gardner, Lord Mackay, Lord Falconer and Professor Vernon Bogdanor. It was a privilege and a lot of fun to have the opportunity to meet and talk with them. I was sorely conscious as I prepared the book that my interviewees are amongst the busiest people in the land. Their collective efficiency in reviewing the manuscripts and returning the chapters was remarkable. I am especially grateful to Lord Woolf and Lord Irvine, who were the first to agree to be interviewed and who, in turn, gave early credibility to the venture.

I should make just one further observation about the revisions: other than in three short postscripts, we did not seek to update the chapters in the light of relevant events that had occurred since the interviews. Statements of the law are therefore intended to have been accurate and current as at the dates of the respective interviews. The three exceptions were the postscripts to the interviews with Tony Williams (Chapter 2), Lord Irvine (Chapter 13) and Lord Woolf (Chapter 20).

My friends and colleagues at Gresham College were hugely supportive: Sally Bunyan and Geoff Pavitt excelled on the organisational front, Helene Murphy was superb on the public relations side and Duncan Burbidge was our indispensable audio-visual specialist. The Provost of the college, Lord Sutherland, was tremendously supportive throughout, as were the Council and our patrons and sponsors, the City of London Corporation and the Mercers' Livery Company. Gresham College Council member, Jack Wigglesworth, merits particular mention for attending the lion's share of the conversations and offering friendly feedback on the train journeys home. More generally, it is a pleasure to thank all my fellow professors at Gresham for their camaraderie over the last few years. Most of all at the college I thank our Registrar, the redoubtable Barbara Anderson—she was an invariable source of encouragement, attended all the interviews, charmed the guests, helped with the manuscripts and, behind the scenes, was instrumental in bringing this book into existence.

We have never met or spoken (having communicated entirely by email) but I must acknowledge the fine work of Alison McPherson of Premier Typing, who produced the first drafts of the manuscripts from the audio recordings we had made. For sponsoring the interviews, I am most grateful to *The Times* and, in particular, to Frances Gibb who made this possible. Dominic Hartley, of the Department for Constitutional Affairs, kindly read the entire book in manuscript. I very much valued his support and observations. I must also say how much I appreciated the ongoing encouragement of members of audience, both from the occasional attendees and from the frequent flyers.

The staff at my publisher, Sweet & Maxwell, have been helpful throughout. Peter Lake kindly set the project in motion; and, thereafter, I was ably assisted by Susan Lewis, Caroline Shaw, Samantha Siddle, Amanda Strange and Dick Greener.

Lastly, I thank my family: Daniel, for helping me keep my study intolerably messy; Jamie, for his invaluable critique of the introductory chapter; Ali, for lighting up our home; and my wife, Michelle, for her unwavering confidence in my work and her preternatural tolerance of my working habits.

Richard Susskind
Radlett, England
May 2005

CONTENTS

INTRODUCTION—EDITOR'S PERSONAL IMPRESSIONS

Gresham College is a remarkable little institution. It was founded in 1597, further to the last will and testament of Sir Thomas Gresham, the great merchant and Royal Agent. Sir Thomas passed away at a time of major turmoil and upheaval—in Government and religion, certainly; but nowhere more so than in the academic world. This was an era, as was so frequently said, of "new learning", and scholars were wrestling with the emergence of scientific thinking and method. Sir Thomas worried, however, that the discoveries and insights of these thinkers in the great universities were not reaching ordinary people in the City of London. Accordingly, it is widely held, he left provision for a group of professors to be retained and given the task of raising public awareness amongst the citizenry of London in their respective disciplines. Thus, Gresham College was born.[1]

Today, there are eight Gresham professors, one in each of divinity, music, rhetoric, physic, commerce, geometry, astronomy and law. And the college is enjoying something of a rebirth. It can be found by travelling to High Holborn, a busy street in the heart of London. A little alley, no more than 30 paces long and easy to overlook, leads to a small cluster of rooms around a courtyard. This is Barnard's Inn, and here lies the college. Readers of Dickens will recall that it was here that Pip lived and worked in much of *Great Expectations*. The focal point of the hotch-potch of rooms is the hall of the college, Barnard's Inn Hall. It dates from the late 14th century and was restored by the Mercers' Company in 1931. The high, beamed ceiling is of old scraped timbers, the rich oak panelled walls have been lovingly cleaned and restored, the leaded windows now provide adequate natural light, and two handsome stone Tudor fireplaces stand at each end of the hall. It is here, in unarguably pleasant surroundings, that today's Gresham professors give their public lectures.

From lectures to interviews

I was appointed Gresham Professor of Law in September 2000. In my first academic year, I presented six lectures in my main area of interest—the impact of

---

[1] For a fascinating historical introduction to Gresham College, see Richard Chartres and David Vernont, *A Brief History of Gresham College, 1597–1997* (St Edmundsbury Press, Bury St Edmunds, 1997).

information technology on the law, lawyers, judges and courts. These lectures were attended by a faithful, enthusiastic but smallish audience and it struck me then that I was a long way from fulfilling Sir Thomas's aspiration of edifying the great body of people of the City of London. Historically, Gresham law lectures had always been relatively poorly attended, but the cocktail of law and IT was failing even more remarkably to draw the crowds. As I pondered my dilemma at a typically good-humoured academic board meeting in the Spring of 2001 (the academic board is the body on which all the professors sit), I heard of a recent event at the college which had involved a fellow professor holding a discussion with a distinguished guest. This gave me an idea. Instead of delivering further lectures on legal technology, why not forget about IT and instead hold a series of public discussions, each an hour or so in length, with leading lawyers and judges? I could think of no better way to intro-duce the law to a lay audience than to get its most illustrious exponents along to the college for an extended public conversation. I guessed also, rightly in the event, that many eminent lawyers would welcome the opportunity to speak publicly and at greater length than is normally possible when interviewed on television, radio or for newspapers.

So I set about organising a series of interviews for my second academic year at Gresham. To kick-start the programme of interviews, I felt sure that I should secure the involvement of one or two very major figures from the legal world. Their par-ticipation would lend the initiative some gravitas and gravitational pull, some cred-ibility when I approached others. In Lord Woolf and Lord Irvine, then the Lord Chief Justice and the Lord Chancellor respectively, I found my first champions. With very little persuasion they agreed to be my guests—with Lord Woolf to open the series and Lord Irvine to close. I had worked with them both in various ways over the years, so they were not committing to an entirely unknown quantity. That said, the concept and approach was new, so I was (and remain) enormously grate-ful that they took the leap with me. With such eminent support, securing the remain-ing four guests for the rest of the series was no doubt an easier job. And, because the first series was generally thought to have gone rather well, I decided to host a further series the following year. Better still, Gresham College extended my tenure for a year, enabling a third series. In all, I held 20 discussions with 18 legal experts (Lords Woolf and Irvine each appearing twice).

Selecting the interviewees

How did I go about selecting the guests? I wanted to hold discussions with individ-uals who represented all main aspects of the legal world—judges, barristers, solici-tors, academics, politicians, with a civil servant thrown in for good measure. Only one of my guests (Oliver Letwin) had I not met before. In fact, most were, variously, friends, colleagues, and people I had advised.

Looking back, I ask myself if there were any significant omissions from the final line-up. Two spring to mind. First, it would have been good to have invited a client to talk about being on the receiving end of legal service. A General Counsel from a major international organisation would have served well for that purpose. Secondly, someone from the voluntary legal sector, from the Citizens Advice Bureau perhaps, would have completed the jigsaw—a good deal of practical legal guidance is imparted to individuals on a daily basis not by lawyers but by many good-spirited lay volunteers. To have had a specialist or practitioner from this corner of the legal world would have widened our horizons. If I run another series, I will make sure to patch these gaps.

When planning the format for the interviews, I recalled the marvellous television discussions that Bryan Magee held with some leading philosophers and broadcast in the late 1970s and early 1980s. The series was called *Men of Ideas*[2] and Magee managed to get his guests to cover some very complex terrain in ordinary, everyday language. The dialogues appeared to be informal and relaxed, although it transpired that huge effort was expended in advance and afterwards in achieving the conversational tone.[3] I liked the effect, and a similar approach began to form in my mind's eye: I would sit with each of my guests at the front of the hall at Gresham; our chairs, with a coffee table between us, would be set at an angle such that we would be turned to one another and yet also facing the audience; we would be on a slightly raised dais but not on a substantial stage; and we would chat for an hour or so. It would be as though the audience was eavesdropping on, but not participating in, what I hoped would be some fascinating discussions. My job would be to create a relaxed atmosphere that would encourage my guests to speak naturally and conversationally.

I had also been much influenced by the success of some so-called "gold-fish bowl" discussions that I had encountered at various commercial and Government conferences. These discussions brought a group of people together at an event to discuss, amongst themselves, some issue of great moment or controversy. They were observed keenly by the audience but there was no audience participation. When well moderated, I had been amazed at how uninhibited the participants had become, how freely they had spoken, as though they were gathered in private rather than being so thoroughly observed. The trick seemed to have been to engage them in topics about which they felt strongly. In relation to my interviews then, ideally my guests would almost forget that there was an audience and would be lost in a stimulating chat. That was the idea, in any event, and I like to think that we often achieved the desired effect. Certainly, almost all guests noted how remarkably quickly the hour passed. As with the gold-fish bowls, I was never keen to have audience participation. I felt it would break the conversational spell and, to be blunt, all too often those who ask questions are much less interested in listening to the response than being seen to have posed the question in the first place. Also, the issues we were discussing were often sensitive and highly charged and I feared rude or aggressive or inappropriate questions from the floor.

Conducting the interviews

How did we prepare for the interviews? I was reluctant to ask my guests to undertake much preparation in advance. I was not inviting them to give lectures. Indeed, when enticing them to come to the college, I emphasised precisely that they would need to do very little beforehand. But neither would it have been fair not to have given advance warning of the subjects that I hoped to explore. With most of my interviewees, we met face-to-face for an hour so, perhaps a fortnight before the event. I came to these meetings with a list of questions that I intended to ask. We

---

[2] Bryan Magee, *Men of Ideas* (Oxford University Press, Oxford, 1982).
[3] Bryan Magee, *Confessions of a Philosopher* (Phoenix, London, 1997), Ch.22.

talked about these, refined them and I determined whether there were no-go subjects or sensitive topics that they wished me to avoid. I was keen not to embarrass my guests with inappropriate questions. With these preliminary meetings under our belts, all that remained was for the interviewees to turn up on the night (all the sessions were held at six o'clock in the evening). Some guests were unable to meet before the day and so, for all but one of these, we resorted to an exchange of emails, covering the same ground. The exception was Oliver Letwin, a trusting man—we had not met before and yet he was happy to arrive with no prior warning of what was to happen to him. For the rest, I hoped that our initial interchanges would encourage them to ponder our discussion topics and gather some thoughts (and anecdotes) in advance. As for my own preparation, my background and current activities are such that I was acquainted with most of the general issues we would discuss. But for each, I also had to immerse myself in further material—ideally a book or some speeches written by the individual in question.

The idea of publishing a book of transcripts was not in my mind at the outset. It came to me after the first series. In the early days, we hoped we might have an archive of webcasts from the interviews, and so we audio- and video-recorded each discussion. For a variety of reasons, however, I concluded the webcasts did not capture or reflect the tone and content of the interviews. In contrast, when the Lord Chancellor's Department provided me with a transcript they had produced of my first conversation with Lord Irvine, I felt that a collection of transcripts, if suitably revised, might work. In the end, we revised the transcripts lightly. I was keen to maintain the informality and the flow and did not want any heavy editing to stultify the very natural and unscripted responses that guests had made. As I mentioned in my acknowledgments, other than in the three short postscripts to the interviews of Tony Williams (Chapter 2), Lord Irvine (Chapter 13) and Lord Woolf (Chapter 20), we did not seek, in revising the chapters, to update them in the light of relevant events that had occurred since the interviews.

But, to repeat, the publication of the interviews was not in our minds when I sat down with my guests. We were keen, if we could, to provide an hour of interesting, accessible and entertaining insights into the law. By and large, I am told we succeeded in this. However, whilst the feedback from the audience was generally very positive, I should confess, in the interests of honesty, that some of my journalist and litigator friends grew a little impatient with my interviews over the years. They felt I was not persistent or even combative enough to stretch my guests and to explore the defects in their arguments. Worse, they said, I lacked the killer instinct when (as rarely happened) an answer was weak or unjustifiably equivocal. Quite apart from the unlikelihood of my catching out, say, the Lord Chief Justice or the Attorney General on a fine point of law, to view the interviews as debates or confrontations was to fail to understand the thrust of the exercise. Gresham College is an academic institution. Its professors are charged with the task, as has been said, of raising public awareness of certain disciplines, in my case of the law. The academic dimension requires discourse that is balanced, systematic, rigorous and comprehensive. I was not in pursuit of sound-bites or oral smoking guns. This was not a media opportunity, nor the chance to capitalise on an unguarded throwaway remark. I was keen to offer a platform for some great legal figures to present their views in a more extended and yet informal manner than media interviews or cross-examinations ordinarily allow. In any event, I also believe—if I might complete my defence—that a friendly, conversational and relaxed tack is more likely to lead to penetrating response and insight than a confrontational approach, which is one that so often encourages the recipient to be less, rather than more, forthcoming.

In summary, I opted for a style that was more Parkinson than Paxman.

What were the guests like?

When I speak to friends and colleagues of my interviews at Gresham College and tell them the range of formidable individuals who have been my guests, I am most commonly asked not what they said, but what were they like. I have found a considerable curiosity about the personalities of those I interviewed at Gresham. While many are household names, it is not clear from their brief media appearances and edited highlights what kinds of human beings these people are. With this in mind I thought it might be interesting in this introduction to offer, albeit briefly, my personal impressions of the interviewees.

Readers looking for gossip, intrigue or scandal will be disappointed by my reflections in the next few pages. It will become clear that I admired all my guests and enjoyed their company. While my reflections may seem like an exercise in sycophancy, it should hardly be surprising that I like and think highly of those who joined me at Gresham, because I selected them personally and never felt inclined to spend the evening with anyone for whom I had low regard, no matter how eminent or influential. As I said, I knew all but one personally and had worked alongside many in one capacity or another. And quite a few I counted as friends. But it was not just I who liked my guests. Barbara Anderson, the Registrar of the College, faithfully attended all the interviews and indeed joined me in meeting and greeting the interviewees prior to each session. Without fail, she described each and every guest as a "sweety" and my guess is that if someone had not been a sweety, Barbara would not have been slow in saying so.

So what, if anything, do these leading lawyers have in common? In repose, I think it fair to say, they present as regular human beings. If you saw them wandering along the road or eating a sandwich or hitting a tennis ball, you would not immediately conclude that they house the finest legal minds of their generation. When we sat together at the start of our discussion on the raised dais at the front of the main hall, before a word had been uttered, the audience could not have guessed how the coming hour might unfold. Without exception, however, these lawyers came to life within a few words of their responses to my first questions. Their eyes lit up. They became animated. They effused an energy, born no doubt of a clear fascination, if not love, for the work that they do. They were invariably good humoured, articulate, committed, engaged and, of course, expert, authoritative, intelligent and compelling. It was a privilege to spend extended time with them. None took himself or herself too seriously. None was too defensive or precious or unjustifiably circumspect. They spoke freely, frankly and confidently of the past, present and future.

It may be far from diplomatic to say so, but many of my guests were quite advanced in years, by which I mean in their mid-60s and more. I know that this is not a great age by today's standards, but it is surely remarkable when it is considered that they are still working well in excess of 80 hours each week and they hold some of the most senior positions in the land. The vitality of senior judges has always interested me. When most citizens have comfortably retired, there are over 40 judges in England (in the Court of Appeal and the House of Lords) who are approaching or past retirement age and are just warming up. They often have their best working years in their late 60s, operating with the energy of people one-third their age. I have never been sure if this high age-to-energy ratio is a cause or effect of judicial work. Is it that working as a judge on the most challenging of cases keeps the mind active and alert? Or is it, as a matter of judicial evolution, that only the most active and alert survive and are able to progress to the top of the profession? I did not ask any of my guests to address this conundrum.

With these preliminary observations made, let me now introduce you to my interviewees, as I found them.

Personal impressions

My first guest was **Lord Woolf**, who had been appointed the Lord Chief Justice of England and Wales in the previous year. From the bang of the starter's pistol he embraced the spirit of the occasion and seemed to relish the opportunity of chatting at length before a public audience. He exuded the verve and optimism that often accompanies the initial assumption of a great office; and the audience could not help but be struck by his warmth and sincerity, by his generosity of spirit. Here was an evidently good man who discussed and cared deeply about a range of vital social issues—the reform of civil justice, human rights, terrorism, the role and reputation of judges, and trial by jury. He spoke compellingly but not in legal jargon. His commitment in many directions was beyond question. I do not think I have ever met anyone with such strength of purpose. Whether in arguing or defending his position or in driving through some initiative or other, Lord Woolf applies his will determinedly and yet with such a lightness of touch, that supporting him on all fronts seems entirely natural. He is a man of both reflection and action and this blend was apparent in his answers to my various questions. I could not have wished for a more prominent guest or a better start to the series. The hall overflowed. The audience had sat with the Lord Chief Justice and had, I hoped, gained greater insight to the man and his role than had been possible in the past.

Tony Williams was my next guest. At that time, as global managing partner, he was in charge of Andersen Legal, the massive legal business of the international accounting and consulting firm. Previously he had been managing partner of Clifford Chance, another vast law firm. With such heavy-hitting jobs under his belt, the audience might have expected a ruthless and uncompromising rottweiler of a solicitor. Instead we enjoyed the company of a pleasant, mild-mannered and affable man who took us tolerantly and with considerable clarity through a variety of subjects, including the work and future of major international law firms, lawyers' pay and methods of charging, quality of life for the lawyer, multi-disciplinary practice, information technology, and the challenges facing the legal profession. He was good-humoured, insightful and natural. I can say in retrospect that he was yet to have his finest hour—this came when, after the Enron scandal, the global empire of Andersen collapsed. In these dark times he stayed resolutely with the ship, he wound up Andersen Legal and personally secured jobs for almost all his partners and employees. He looked after others before himself and has been widely respected for that. It is typically generous of him that he added a postscript to his interview, explaining what must have been an agonising episode in his working career.

From a solicitor, I moved to a barrister, **David Pannick QC**. One of the country's top silks, David Pannick is blessed with the gift of clarity. He says what he means and his meaning is clear. Regular readers of his column in *The Times* will know this, as do judges and fellow advocates who meet him in the upper courts. At Gresham, David Pannick's arguments were clearly structured and signposted, his premises were unambiguously laid out, so that he carried me (and the audience) inescapably to his conclusions. There was no waffle or sophistry nor evasion nor dissemblance. He was youthful and lively and his pleasant voice fortified still further the strength of his positions. Sadly, we had a technical glitch that night, so that not all of our discussion was captured. However, we managed to reconstruct most of the lost portion and so the transcript is almost faithful to the evening's meeting. We considered at length the issue of terrorism and human rights and talked also about judicial review. David Pannick dealt with these so ably that I remember pondering how unenviable a task it must be to appear against him in the courtroom.

My fourth guest was another member of the Judiciary, **Lord Justice Auld**. A judge in the Court of Appeal, Sir Robin Auld was very much in the news when we met, having recently completed his monumental report as chair of the Criminal Courts Review. He was a strong physical presence on the dais and throughout I found him to be a man who thinks deeply about difficult issues, a thoughtful person whose views were never hastily formulated. He appeared balanced and entirely plausible even when his views were at odds with many in the legal profession. He talked about his review, how he was appointed, and his main recommendations. He spoke at length and with great insight about juries, the doctrine of double jeopardy, the problems of retrials, the rules on the admissibility of evidence, the peculiarities of serious fraud cases and the challenges of dealing with young defendants. Sir Robin is relatively unusual amongst judges in having completed a doctorate as a younger man. I found this background in scholarship infused not just his analysis of the criminal courts but also the way in which he spoke to me at Gresham. His arguments were tight and well grounded in research. Had he not chosen the life of a barrister and then that of a judge, he could, without any doubt, have been a pre-eminent teacher of the law.

Next was the second and final solicitor of the series. This was **Michael Bray**, Chief Executive of Clifford Chance—on a number of measures the largest law firm in the world. Michael Bray had succeeded Tony Williams. Like his predecessor, he challenged the stereotypes of law firm leaders that we have come to know from popular novelists such as John Grisham and Scott Turow. Far from the Machievallian despot, Michael Bray came across as an avuncular and engaging man. He seemed entirely comfortable in the chair and spoke with easy-going authority about running and working in a major law firm, orchestrating a transatlantic merger, the work of a banking lawyer, the earnings of solicitors, how partners are selected, training, and the relocation of his firm from the City to Canary Wharf. He was at his most animated, I felt, when talking about his work as a banking and finance lawyer. Although an accomplished chief executive, the "deal junkie" was never far from the surface.

My final guest in the first year of discussions was the then Lord Chancellor, **Lord Irvine**. We played to a packed house that evening. Lord Irvine had featured regularly in the media around that time and I suspect many visitors were curious to see what the man was like. Neither for the first nor the last time at Gresham, popular preconceptions were found to be misconceptions. Lord Irvine was affable, open and often humorous. The setting and format suited him well. He had ample opportunity to build his arguments, lay out his evidence and demonstrate his complete mastery of the Lord Chancellor's brief. He was not constrained by the usual demands for quotable quotes nor concerned that some prejudicial sound-bite might appear the next day, torn tendentiously from its context. In turn, he was relaxed, friendly and forthcoming. His was a most accomplished appearance and, interestingly, when it came to be edited, the transcript needed almost no revisions at all. His fluency in speech translated comfortably into first rate prose. I had wanted the series to end on a high and, according to my friends in the audience, it did just that. Lord Irvine also seemed pleased, so much so that, not long afterwards, he agreed to come back for a second helping.

The summer of 2002 flashed by and it seemed just days (although it was months) after sitting with Lord Irvine that I began my second year of interviews. The Senior Law Lord, **Lord Bingham**, was the first to take the seat. His reputation preceded him. The only person in English legal history to have been Master of the Rolls, Lord Chief Justice and Senior Law Lord, even amongst senior judges Lord Bingham is something of a legend. There is a tale that the great philosopher, Bertrand Russell, said of the equally great economist, John Maynard Keynes, that speaking to him was like standing at the edge of a precipice. So it feels with Lord Bingham. At the risk of offending the rest of my guests, if asked to say whom I regard as the most brilliant of all, I would have to say Lord Bingham. Although unfailingly polite, witty and indeed very good to me during my time as his adviser on IT matters, I always have the sense that Lord Bingham clearly and immediately sees all the sloppiness and confusion in my thinking. At Gresham, he seemed a little hesitant in the first few minutes, as though he was securing his bearings. Once warmed up, he spoke with peerless gravitas and authority about the possibility of a new Supreme Court to replace the Appellate Committee of the House of Lords, the nature of judicial decision-making, the relationship between the Judiciary and the Home Office, human rights, the appointment of judges, jury trials, judicial inquiries and judicial independence. On all of these matters, and most are controversial, I felt that evening that the answers we heard were, quite simply, right.

From the Senior Law Lord the baton was passed to Her Majesty's Attorney General, **Lord Goldsmith**. This is a man who appears to have moved seamlessly and to good effect from being a successful commercial QC to taking on the job of being the Government's most senior legal adviser. I could see quickly, after but a few minutes of discussion with him, how he made the transition so smoothly—he was open, friendly, balanced, intelligent and, unusual amongst the eminent, a good listener. He treated the audience to a wide-ranging trip across many topics including the office of the Attorney General, the prosecution agencies in Government, the criminal justice system, the jury system, his move from the Bar into the heart of the public sector, pro bono legal work, the Attorney General's role in foreign affairs and his public interest function. It was hard not to be impressed with his range, his vitality and the modesty with which he described his job. He answered my questions (save for one ill-judged query) directly and elegantly, organising and presenting his thinking with the clear head of a leading silk.

Next up was **David Lock** who visited Gresham as his bruises were beginning to fade from the experience of being a Government minister (at the Lord Chancellor's Department) and a Labour MP who lost his seat under difficult circumstances. A point of principle had been at issue, he had maintained his ground and kept his integrity when others might have wavered; but he left Westminster in the process. He had bounced back deservedly to become the Chairman of the National Criminal Intelligence Service and the National Crime Squad and it was largely in these capacities that he talked to me. One of my more youthful-looking guests, David Lock came across as intelligent, focussed, principled and industrious. His answers were full and frank, a robust mix of theory and action, of ideas and practice. He talked candidly about how he lost his seat, the training of MPs, the role of the National Criminal Intelligence Service, organised crime, drugs, illegal immigration, surveillance and human rights, jury trials and the trappings (wigs, gowns, and so forth) of the courtroom. The discussion of serious crime was disturbing and yet not at all melodramatic. In all, it felt reassuring to know someone of David Lock's calibre was involved in countering the dark side of our society. Westminster's loss, it was natural to conclude, was the criminal justice system's gain.

The appearance of **Oliver Letwin** at Gresham needs a little bit of explanation. I was keen to have a senior politician in the seat to talk about law and order and so, originally, I invited the then Home Secretary, David Blunkett. He had the audacity to resist the temptation to join me and so I turned, quite naturally, to his then opposite number, Dr Letwin MP. From his television appearances, I had always thought him to be an intelligent and articulate man, and so I looked forward to meeting him and chatting with him. Even though I had not met him before, he was happy to come along without any prior meeting or interchange about the questions I might ask. On the evening, his performance was one of the consummate politician. He had the air—natural and not affected, I felt—of someone who could settle well in some high office. And yet, I also had the sense that he was but a visitor to the legal world, that he was passing through law and order rather than being a lifetime exponent. With most of my guests, if their arms were chopped off, I would not be surprised to find "law" etched in the cross-section. With Oliver Letwin, in contrast, I did not feel that law was an integral part of his very being. Yet he was an undoubted master of the brief. He spoke, at breakneck speed and with gusto and authority, on the roles of the Home Secretary and the Home Office, on sentencing policy, burglary, and asylum, and he perorated with conviction on terrorism and human rights. He was a credit to his party and a pleasure to interview.

Next came the first of only two women with whom I held interviews. This was **Dame Elizabeth Butler-Sloss**, the President of the Family Division. More than most of the judges who came to Gresham, Dame Elizabeth's work on the bench, most notably in relation to divorce law, has clear implications for much of the general public. Tackling a controversial area like divorce was, for me, what these interviews were all about—discussing difficult issues, that touch the lives of many, with the leading legal figures. With her strong voice and clear intellect, Dame Elizabeth may at first have seemed to those who did not know her to be a rather formidable woman, but I and others could see very quickly her empathetic side. She spoke with great compassion and insight about some of the very difficult issues upon which she is called to judge—custody, consent to medical treatment, fathers' rights, delays in child care cases. She peppered her responses with examples from real cases. There was good humour there as well. It is hard to think that anyone has thought more deeply about the social, ethical and legal dimensions of these matters and I felt comforted that it was someone of Dame Elizabeth's stature who was presiding over this aspect of the administration of justice. She also offered some fascinating insights into the remarkably wide scope of the work of the Family Division, medical law, judicial decision-making, medical expert witnesses and her conduct of the Cleveland Inquiry into child abuse.

Then came **Cherie Booth QC**, and with her a sizeable audience, many of whom I presumed were curious to find out what the Prime Minister's wife was like in real life. However, I was determined to steer well clear of any personal or political issues concerning Number 10 and to focus exclusively on her experience as a barrister and her insights into life at the Bar. In the end, this was one of my favourite interviews. Cherie Booth seemed completely at ease and entirely unassuming. She was chatty and informal and, in turn, I felt more relaxed than during any other interview. She spoke engagingly about the work of the barrister, the challenges facing female lawyers, the future of the Bar, human rights, judicial decision-making and appearing before the Court of Appeal and the House of Lords. She was more than willing to banter light-heartedly and was as far from the stereotypical, stuffy QC as could be imagined. The interview seemed to fly by and I sensed disappointment in the audience when I drew the discussion to a close.

During his second visit to Gresham, at the end of April 2003, **Lord Irvine** was even more ebullient than at his first. He knew the format now, was at apparent ease with it, and addressed various issues of the day with characteristic authority and confidence. He spoke about the drawbacks of a Ministry of Justice, the relationship between the Judiciary and the Home Office, the accountability of judges, likely plans for the tribunal system and about the future of QCs. We also discussed the role of the Lord Chancellor, the separation of powers doctrine and the appointment of judges. Lord Irvine was up-beat and persuasive. We were neither of us to know that but 44 days later the Prime Minister would announce the abolition of the role of the Lord Chancellor and that a range of major constitutional changes would follow. That announcement lends poignancy to Lord Irvine's remarks. To some extent, the announcement also set the agenda for many of my later discussions.

Under normal circumstances, my interview with Lord Irvine would have marked the end of my term as Gresham Professor of Law. I had held the appointment for the standard three years and my job might have been thought to be coming to end. However, the college had kindly extended my tenure by one year, so that I might conduct one further year of interviews. I was delighted to have this chance because there was unfinished business. Government proposals for the elimination of the Lord Chancellor, the establishment of a new Supreme Court to replace the Appellate Committee of the House of Lords, and a new regime for the appointment of judges deserved considerable public discussion—I was keen to have the chance to talk through the implications of these matters with some uniquely qualified individuals. More, there were other dimensions of the law that I believed merited coverage at Gresham. I began, therefore, to assemble an array of guests for my final year.

The first of these, in late September 2003, was **Lord Saville**, a judge with whom I have worked closely over the years. He is a judge in what is formally known as the Appellate Committee of the House of Lords, the highest court of appeal in the land. In the jargon, he is one of the Law Lords. The audience might have expected a representative from this elite coterie of judges to have been aloof or even other-worldly. I knew otherwise. Lord Saville is as natural and unaffected a human being as one could hope to find. He has a wide range of interests well beyond the law (vegetable gardening, squash, flying and horse riding, for example) and he tackles these with verve. He is best known, however, not for his judicial, aviating or equestrian activities, but as Chairman of the long-running and often controversial Bloody Sunday Inquiry. When we met, he discussed the inquiry at length and did so with such clarity and balance that no-one listening could doubt that the hearing is in excellent hands.

He also spoke of his career, his work in the Court of Appeal, judicial review of public inquiries and the Supreme Court. Of particular interest to me, he also told of the remarkable use of IT in his inquiry. Lord Saville challenges conventional and clichéd stereotypes of the senior judicial figure. Where the popular perception may be one of detached and elderly individuals, Lord Saville is entirely contemporary in outlook and youthful in spirit and activity.

Fans of the television comedy series *Yes Minister* were entertained by my discussion with **Sir Hayden Phillips**, the Permanent Secretary (that is, the top civil servant) at the Department for Constitutional Affairs (formerly the Lord Chancellor's Department). When we met, Sir Hayden was the most experienced civil servant in Whitehall, and so here was a rare glimpse of the quintessential mandarin-in-motion. I probed in a number of directions and we learned, from the coal-face of policy-making, about the work of the civil service and of his department. We spent some time on the vexed issues of the abolition of the Lord Chancellor, the establishment of the new Supreme Court, the future of QCs and judicial appointments. He parried my more penetrating queries with little difficulty. He almost made me feel, for example, that the Government's attempt to abolish the office of the Lord Chancellor had been handled well. Well, not quite. It was clear, though, that Sir Hayden was a very quick and incisive thinker; more than that, he was charming, urbane, entirely at ease with himself and the occasion. I thought at the time how much he seemed to be enjoying the discussion. I suppose senior civil servants are rarely exposed to the public, so it may be that he welcomed this rare chance to air some of his own thinking.

Next to take the seat was **John Gardner**, Professor of Jurisprudence at the University of Oxford. John Gardner is a philosopher and as such might have been expected to be an ageing, eccentric and pleasantly detached armchair theorist. Not a bit of it. First of all, he was the youngest of my interviewees by a fair margin, the only one in his or her 30s in fact; and, I feel bound to say, the only one younger than me. Also, he came over as a man with both feet firmly planted on the ground, even though we discussed more abstract issues than I explored with my other guests. We started by reflecting on the nature and scope of jurisprudence (broadly, legal philosophy), and then talked about the legendary debate between his two distinguished predecessors, Ronald Dworkin and Herbert Hart. We moved from there to chat about judicial decision-making, the relationship between law and morality, his own work on complicity, and about causation. Throughout, John Gardner was assured, pleasantly sardonic, very likeable and not at all obscure. He talked amusingly and with self-deprecation about his own working methods. In short, he was a fine ambassador for the groves of academe.

On only one occasion did I venture beyond the hall at Gresham College to conduct an interview. This was with **Lord Mackay** who was the Lord Chancellor from 1987 to 1997. We met at the hall of the ancient, indeed the premiere, livery company—the Mercers'. And in these splendid surroundings we were treated to a marvellous blend of wisdom and erudition. Lord Mackay had originally trained as a mathematician and I wondered then, as I had done in the past, whether or not I might be interacting with a super-computer, one of remarkable processing speed and storage capacity. His ability to get to the heart of any issues and to draw upon his encyclopaedic knowledge was fine to behold, all the more remarkable because Lord Mackay speaks softly and in an unassuming manner. He spoke about matters that were close to his heart—the constitutional reforms, the abolition of the role of

Lord Chancellor, the establishment of a new Supreme Court, the appointment of judges, and judicial inquiries. He also covered some vexed issues arising out of immigration and asylum, explaining the widespread discomfort that the Government's then draft bill had engendered. He was uninhibited and conversational, and walked us through complex matters in a fashion with which the man on the Clapham Omnibus would have been entirely at home.

From a previous Lord Chancellor, we passed at my next meeting to the current Lord Chancellor, although the incumbent was by then also called the Secretary of State for Constitutional Affairs. This was **Lord Falconer**, who had become the first person to lead what is now known as the Department for Constitutional Affairs (no longer the Lord Chancellor's Department). My strongest memory of the evening is not of the interview itself but of an incident prior to it. In her ongoing quest to find out exactly what daddy's job is, my nine-year-old daughter, Alexandra, had come along to hear me interview Lord Falconer. She had joined us in the room in which we tended to gather before the discussions. Upon entering, as I effected introductions, Lord Falconer headed straight for Alexandra, bent down to her level and nattered with her for a while. This was the spontaneous reaction of a kind family man. During our discussion he remained extremely friendly and open, tackling difficult issues nimbly, with conviction and, I sensed, great honesty. We chatted—for that is how it felt—about the role and abolition of the Lord Chancellor, the independence of judges, plans for the proposed Supreme Court, the appointment of judges, the constitutional reforms generally, the future of QCs and the new Freedom of Information regime. This was the third Lord Chancellor I had interviewed at Gresham and those who had heard each in action could not but conclude how unlike one another they were and how impressive they were in quite different ways.

By this stage in the series of interviews, my successor as Gresham Professor of Law had been appointed. I was delighted to learn that it was to be **Vernon Bogdanor,** the Professor of Government at the University of Oxford and the doyen of constitutional matters. Given that many of my discussions had focussed on major constitutional issues, I thought it would therefore be doubly appropriate to have him as a guest. As I began to prepare, I realised it would be triply appropriate because he would be the first interviewee on the subject of constitutional reforms who was not himself an active participant in the changes. I had spoken to various judges and politicians and indeed a top civil servant, but each had a vested interested in the matter or even an axe to grind. As social scientists rightly tell us, however, you cannot objectively evaluate a phenomenon of which you are part. I welcomed the chance, then, to speak to an independent, objective expert. I was not disappointed. With the precision and assurance of a surgeon, Vernon Bogdanor dissected the various issues that I addressed with previous guests. We covered the full range of old chestnuts—the constitutional reforms, the appointment of judges, terrorism, human rights, the new constitutional settlement, and freedom of information. He analysed and disposed of each with quiet authority and placed them in the wider context of classic debates such as whether the UK should have a written or unwritten constitution. This was the leading constitutional theorist, at the peak of his powers, putting the various reforms in their wider context. It was an education.

And so we came to the final session and to the return of **Lord Woolf**. I felt it pleasingly symmetrical that he should have been at Gresham for the first and last interviews. It was remarkable how much had happened since we had last convened. Indeed, much of his own energy since we had first met in Barnard's Inn had been directed at securing the Judiciary in the face of the array of proposed constitutional reforms that had been the focus of many of my discussions with other guests. Not least among the threats of the reforms was that to the independence of the Judiciary. No-one had been better placed, psychologically and politically, to argue the judicial corner and Lord Woolf had done so forcefully in negotiating a concordat with Lord Falconer; a constitutional settlement of historic dimensions. And so it was a somewhat battle-weary Lord Woolf who joined me for the finale. We talked about the constitutional reforms generally, the proposed abolition of the office of the Lord Chancellor, the concordat that he had agreed with the Lord Chancellor, the setting up of the new Supreme Court, QCs, and prison reform. Once again, his conviction and determination were plain for all to see, delivered in his fatherly and reassuring way. Not for the first time, Lord Woolf had been central to fundamental change in the legal system and his first-hand rendition of the fascinating constitutional tale was riveting. Legal upheaval was afoot and Lord Woolf made us all feel a part of it.

This was a fitting end to what had been, for me at least, a hugely enjoyable experience. The interviews had started rather speculatively but they gathered force, grew in stature and now, as I hope readers will discover, constitute a compelling set of thoughts, observations and arguments from a remarkable collection of individuals. I conclude from my discussions at Gresham that the law is not simply in safe hands, it is under the stewardship of some outstanding human beings, people of great intellect and integrity. I am left in no doubt that our society is well served by these dedicated lawyers.

The Rt Hon The Lord Woolf of Barnes
Lord Chief Justice of England and Wales

Tuesday October 30, 2001

My guest this evening is Lord Woolf, a man who has enjoyed an immensely distinguished career in the law. He is perhaps best known for his work, while a Law Lord, in reviewing the civil justice system—his Access to Justice Inquiry of the mid-1990s. He later became Master of the Rolls, and last year, in 2000, was appointed Lord Chief Justice. He has had a huge impact on the development of the civil and criminal systems in this country, and my plan, in this discussion, is to explore a number of the major legal issues with which he has been involved.

We first met, formally, about seven years ago. Since then, I have had the good fortune to work with Lord Woolf on a number of initiatives. But, as I was reminding myself earlier, in fact we almost met twenty-two years ago, when I was a law student living in Glasgow. Late one afternoon I was at my closest friend's house. We were in his attic bedroom when his mother came rushing into the room in some considerable state of excitement. She was organising some kind of party in the house and told me that the main guest was Sir Harry Woolf. She said to me, "You're a law student. You'll have to come and speak to him and ask him some questions." Then she looked at me. I was a second-year law student, very long of hair, and fairly dirty of jeans and looked generally unkempt. After a moment's reflection, she said "Well, maybe not!" She wandered off and there followed all sorts of pleasant noises from below. About two hours later she came back and she said, "It was such a pity you didn't meet him. He's a marvellous man. Hopefully, some time in the future you'll get an opportunity to ask him some questions." That opportunity, ladies and gentlemen, has arisen for me tonight.

Welcome, Lord Woolf.

As I said in my introductory remarks, perhaps you're best known for your work on access to justice, on civil reform. I think that might be the most useful place for us to start. Can you give us a crisp summary of the context, the background and the nature of that review?[1]

---

[1] See Lord Woolf, *Access to Justice—Interim Report* (Woolf Inquiry Team, June 1995) and *Access to Justice—Final Report* (HMSO, July 1996). Also available at *www.dca.gov.uk*

Well, its name really gives you the lead into it. It was designed to help the citizen to be able to take advantage of civil justice. I thought, especially at a time when we were introducing the idea of human rights being part of our domestic law, it was a mockery to give the citizen more rights if the citizen was not in a position to enforce those rights. So that really was the key theme to the reforms.[2]

We had at that time a very good legal system, if you were content that it should serve only a minority of the population. If you were able to afford to use the system, either because you were eligible for legal aid—and only a small section of the public was eligible for legal aid—or because you were extremely wealthy, then the system served you very well; though even then it was run really for the convenience of the lawyers rather than the convenience of their clients.

It took a long time and, implicit in what I've said already, it was expensive. It was also very complex. The idea was to try and devise a system which was much more comprehensible to the ordinary citizen; which was able to provide the ordinary citizen with the form of justice which was proportionate to the dispute which he or she had. If it was a small, simple dispute, then it had to be a small, simple procedure. If it was a more complex dispute, then it justified more complex treatment. If it was very complex, then of course you could have the whole Rolls Royce panoply of services the system could provide. But the idea was to make it proportionate, and it was felt that if that was achieved, that would help. Above all, we tried to identify what was the purpose of civil justice, and the purpose of civil justice was to resolve disputes.

The trouble with the court system as it was, was that instead of bringing people together to resolve their disputes, once they got in the litigation process, what might have been a small dispute became a bigger and bigger dispute. So we wanted to try and get over that.

One of the big changes that occurred was that we devised ways of trying to avoid people having to get involved with the courts at all in order to resolve disputes, because the best way and the cheapest way of doing it was to do it without getting involved in litigation. So that was another aim that we were trying to achieve.

You produced an interim report and then a final report. How did people respond? By people, I mean on the one hand the legal profession, as well as consumer groups and the public more generally.

Timing is everything, and I was very, very fortunate. I think that both the legal profession and ordinary people really recognised that we had to do something about our system. So, although there were lots of people who had tried to achieve what I was seeking to achieve before, they were not going with the tide, and I just happened to be very lucky; I came in at the right time, when the institution of the law was ready and realised it had to change. So I did not have the opposition which you can often have from the legal profession and the Judiciary, who are very comfortable with the system they know. That is hugely understandable. Why change it if it seems to be doing all right, especially if they do not appreciate that it is doing all right only for the few?

---

[2] The civil reforms are also discussed by Lord Irvine (Ch.6).

Six years down the road, are you pleased with progress?

Well, of course it is very difficult to gauge success, and I am probably the least suitable person to ask whether it is a success because it is much better that others judge it. But there's no doubt that one of the main aims that I was seeking to achieve, which was a cultural change, has been achieved. It is quite significant. There are signs of the change.

First of all, the way the judges are doing their job has changed. The judges have realised that we're no longer able just to sit back and leave it to the two parties to bring the litigation forward. They realise they've got to take charge.

Secondly, there has been a drop in the volume of litigation right across the board, except for the very simple procedure which exists for small claims, where business is booming, and the response when there is a survey indicates that the public find that the system serves them well, although it is very rough and ready and one might almost describe it in some ways as a rough justice. But that is what you need for a small dispute. Above all, you want a decision, and it does not matter necessarily whether the decision is entirely as polished as it might be. The critical thing is that you get a quick result so that the whole thing does not start festering like a sore and taking over the lives of those who are involved in the dispute, which could very easily happen in the old system. There are some horror stories I used to tell at conferences which I was attending when I was trying to crusade for the changes I wanted to see.

Looking back at the review and then the implementation, if you had your time again, is there anything you would do differently? We see other reviews emerging: Lord Justice Auld's, Sir Andrew Leggatt's; Auld's on criminal,[3] Sir Andrew's on tribunals.[4] What lessons have you learned in making things happen, in moving from document to action?

What lessons have I learned? I was undoubtedly engaged in a learning process during the time I was conducting the review because we were feeling our way. I think one of the very important lessons that I learned, which does not necessarily answer your question, is that you have got to take people with you if you are going to try and change the system. It is no use bringing out excellent recommendations if they fall on ground which is not fertile, so you have got to prepare the ground well. I do not suppose I always did that as well as I should have done.

The other thing that one learns is you must never take anything for granted. Particularly you can never take it for granted that you are always going to have the resources you need, and perhaps I was optimistic in thinking that more could be achieved than was possible with the resources which were then available. But I think one must be courageous and have a go! That was what we did.

---

[3] Lord Justice Auld, *Review of the Criminal Courts of England and Wales* (The Stationery Office, London, October 2001). Also available at *www.criminal-courts-review.org.uk*

[4] Sir Andrew Leggatt, *Tribunals for Users: One System, One Service, Report of the Review of Tribunals* (The Stationery Office, London, March 2001). Also available at *www.tribunals-review.org.uk*

There was a time, which Richard knows about well. He was advising us on IT with regard to the changes we were bringing about. The IT was really central to the whole way we were thinking about the system, because it did enable us to achieve so many things that we did not think would be able to be achieved. There came a crunch period when it looked as though we were in a position where we would have to stop the implementation of the reforms because unfortunately the IT had lagged miles behind. I was very, very pleased that the present Lord Chancellor, who initially was sceptical about the whole exercise but became convinced, took the decision to go ahead without the IT. I think Richard in fact advised me, correctly, that to try and introduce a new system of civil justice, a new philosophy of civil justice, and new IT together at the same time was a recipe for disaster, but a lot of siren voices were saying "play safe" and "wait until the IT is ready".

Because of course technology is never ready, as we all know! Because the theme was access to justice, there is a potential tension between offering greater access to justice on the one hand and people's fears of creating a more litigious society on the other. I was recently reading a book by Charles Handy and he was telling the story of an American family who refused to have their child visit another friend's home because they realised this friend's parents were under-insured in the event of an accident. It's a grotesque example, but we've heard more local examples of people suing others for food poisoning after a dinner party. How do we offer greater access to justice but at the same time not create this kind of claims culture in which everyone wants to have a go?

I am afraid this is almost an insoluble problem but I can just tell you my simplistic response to it. I think that as long as the claims are bona fide, genuine and proper claims, then the citizen should be entitled to have means of getting that to which they are entitled. If on the other hand they are not bona fide claims, then the system must be able to ensure that those unjustified claims get no further than they should do and are moved out of the system as early as possible. This was one of the things we've tried to do and I think we have to some extent succeeded. So to that extent we can reconcile the two issues. I must say that it is one of the things that does concern me.

We are now in an era of human rights, and I am a great believer that we did the right thing in making the European Convention on Human Rights part of our domestic law. I think that the public will become more and more attracted to that event as time passes. Until that time, the way that this country had worked was not so much to enforce rights but to enforce duties. So the focus was on whether the Government or another local body of a public nature had done its duty. The courts were there to make sure that it did its duty; above all that it obeyed the law. Now once you get to talk about human rights, you're turning it round. You are saying what we are doing is enforcing the individual's right rather than enforcing the public duty. In many ways, it is just the obverse, but there is a fundamental difference.

We are becoming a rights culture and so everybody is conscious of their rights. It is very important that, in that culture, the courts do what is their responsibility, which is to keep the balance between the individual and those who have the responsibility for performing their duties. I hope we are getting the balance right. We have got to learn how to do it better and better, and of course we will get some cases wrong. Fortunately we have appeals and the appeals system should make sure that where judges get it wrong to begin with, it is put right.

I have no doubt we are going through a learning experience and we will get more used to it as we get more accustomed to it. You do see things in the papers sometimes which rather surprise you when you see it is attributed to the fact that we have now got human rights, and I think we have got to make sure that we do not get things out of proportion.

Let's move on to a different but not unrelated issue—access to justice but from a financial point of view. One of the criticisms that was levelled at your inquiry was that it did not include a review of the legal aid system. There was parallel work going on, however, and when the then new Lord Chancellor (Lord Irvine) came in, as I recall, he appointed Sir Peter Middleton to make sure that the reforms of the legal aid system, as being proposed, sat comfortably with your own reforms. It does still seem to me and to many others, however, that access to justice may not actually be provided to people simply because they can't afford access to justice; they can't afford legal representation. There is a growing concern that there is lack of public funding for people who have meritorious claims and yet don't have the wherewithal to pursue them. What is your response to that?

Well, you're quite right. My responsibilities were not in relation to the public funding of the costs of litigation. I think, and I hope, that the Lord Chancellor will not mind me saying this, and even if he does, I am going to say it, so we won't worry about that! I think he took a great leap into the dark and we are in a period of experiment there. I hope it is going to work all right, but I think it is too early yet to say it is all right.

If I may I will just take up a little bit of time to explain, because I think this very important. I think it is actually critical. Our system of legal aid for civil proceedings was one of the most developed forms of legal aid that you could find anywhere. The way that it worked was that if you had a case with a reasonable prospect of success, and you were below the line for getting legal aid, then, so far as your financial position was concerned, you got legal aid. The only trouble with this is that although the Government extended the amount of money that it was putting into legal aid, fewer and fewer people—a smaller and smaller proportion of the population—were eligible. Because if the cost was going up, the way that the Government tried to control it was by cutting down those who were eligible. And so if you were a person with a reasonable amount of money, but by no means wealthy so you could not afford to get involved in litigation, you found you could not get legal aid.

Perhaps the classic situation where this occurred that illustrates the point was in relation to actions against the medical profession and the health service. Those actions were brought almost exclusively for negligence by those who were eligible for legal aid. There were a handful of cases brought by the majority of the public who were not eligible for legal aid and just could not afford to bring those proceedings. There was too much at risk, even though they might have a good case. And at that time, under the old procedure, they were normally contested; they just could not take the risk. That really demonstrates the shortcomings of the system as it was before.

The Lord Chancellor was therefore faced with what do we do about this inability to get resources, and so he made changes which were contrary to the whole culture and traditions of this country, bringing in a type of contingency fee like they had in America. Now, it is not the same as the contingency fee in America; we call it a conditional fee. In America, lawyers take a percentage of the winnings, and so they may have done very little work but if you have a very large claim, they get a very large fee. They can be very large indeed and there are some very wealthy lawyers in America who fly around chasing up business in their own aeroplanes.

What happened in England was the conditional fee, and they put in an uplift, so that if the case was a success, the lawyer would get his ordinary fees and a percentage more which he had agreed with the clients. That has been changed again so that if you win, the defendant has to pay that uplift. That has, for a defendant, the result that they are in the end paying an awful lot of money if they lose. They are paying their own costs, they are paying the other side's costs, and they are paying this uplift, and I am worried about that balance.

I am also worried that it does give the lawyer an interest in the outcome. The Lord Chancellor was in favour of that, and in a sense it is very good, because it will make the lawyer strive harder. But it does mean that the lawyer is in a less objective position than they were previously. And they are in a position where, unless they win the case, they do not get paid anything. That could be worrying because they have got to resist the temptation of agreeing, for example, to a settlement which might not be as good as it should be for their clients so as to ensure they get paid, and things of that sort. So this is a very bold experiment and I think it may certainly result in people who could not afford otherwise to bring cases doing so now.

There is a second possible very real advantage. What the Lord Chancellor is saying that he's doing is taking the money which would otherwise have gone in providing legal aid and community legal services and spreading that money through doing that to a wider audience than before. And of course if he achieves that, that will be a very good thing. But we are in the early days and I would just like to see how it goes. Some say they are worried by the fact that they could be put in a situation of conflict, and there's no doubt that they are put in a situation of conflict, but if they are acting in a professional way they should be able to cope with that, and I hope they will be able to.

In terms of the "new landscape" for civil justice, as you called it, would it be fair to summarise this by saying that you are confident that the new system seeks to achieve proportionality, that is to say the cost of pursuing an action should be in some sense proportionate to the amount at issue but, if I can use the metaphor, the jury's still out as to whether or not the changes in legal aid will mean that genuine access to justice is achieved?

I do not think I can say we have achieved proportionality, but what I do think is the system now is more proportional than it was before. I am afraid the dreadful thing is that there are no reforms which will make being involved in litigation other than an expensive business, not only in what it costs but what it demands of the people who are involved. It is so easy for them to get sucked into it and for it to take control. My advice to everybody is to try and avoid getting into a litigation process, and that is why I am a great believer in alternative ways of resolving disputes and only using the courts as a last resort. I think one of the good things that is happening is that this is much more the position that we are in now; people are using alternatives and the lawyers are beginning to see what they can do. Clients are now saying, "We do not want to get involved in a complex case. Cannot we have some mediation and sort it out?". Take a neighbours' dispute where there's two people who live alongside and they are fighting over a boundary, perhaps because one of them wants to have a garage and there is only room for one garage, not two garages. They can get into a situation where, first of all, they cannot speak to their neighbour and they are daggers drawn, so they are never going to be able to go on living together because the sight of the neighbour is something which they just cannot accommodate. Secondly, there were cases where, under the system as it was, where they finished up both having to sell their homes to pay the costs of the litigation, and nobody won! That is a dreadful indictment of the system and it is really something that one cannot find acceptable.

I hope that sort of extreme disproportionality is much less likely to happen now than it was before, but I do not say that we have achieved proportionality. I think we have gone towards it and we have got to do more. Reforming is not a once-performed exercise, you have got to carry on all the time. There is a long way to go. As for the second part of the equation, I think you're absolutely right in what you said.

You mentioned human rights. There has been much media coverage and interest in potential conflicts between human rights on the one hand and measures being taken to counter terrorism on the other. Before we delve into that particular issue, for those who are not familiar with the Human Rights Convention and what it means for our legal system, could you offer a quick overview of the topic of human rights? Then we can explore some of the particularly difficult issues that are being thrown up today?[5]

I have already given an indication of the difference between a system which has got a Human Rights Convention as part of its law, and a system which has not, such as we had before. It gives the citizen rights and that is extremely important; rights which the courts can enforce when it is appropriate to do so; that is a secondary thing which is appropriate.

One never knows when they are going to be of value to an individual, or for that matter a commercial enterprise. Things can happen suddenly, out of the blue, which affect the individual. The individual can be wrongly arrested. The Human Rights Act will lead to their position being better than it was previously—there will be more protection. There can be a situation where, unfortunately, you become the subject of media attention in a most inappropriate way. Again, human rights may help you in that situation.

The law was already moving in the direction of that. Human rights, although they have just recently become part of our domestic law, are no novel feature of our law. It must not be forgotten that we were a country that was largely responsible for

---

[5] Human rights are also discussed by David Pannick QC (Ch.3), Lord Bingham (Ch.7), David Lock (Ch.9), Oliver Letwin (Ch.10), Cherie Booth QC (Ch.12) and Professor Bogdanor (Ch.19).

drafting the Convention that we were to make part of our law so many years later. Also we were the first country to sign the Convention, but only as part of our international obligations, not as part of our domestic law. We had to take another step, which Parliament only took recently, but there are many ways in which the Human Rights Act, as I can see it, is of benefit to the citizen.

The position normally is one where it is when the citizen's rights are really being undermined that he or she needs protection, and it may be that the Human Rights Act is the only protection they have. Sometimes they are in a position where, but for human rights, they would feel very vulnerable indeed because they are, for example, being victimised or demonised, and they need protection from what would otherwise be an intolerable situation. So I think we all are in a better position as a result of the introduction of the Human Rights Act. Without seeking to be political in any way, I think that, when history comes to be written, one of the things this Government will be able to claim, if it cannot claim anything else, is that it took this step right at the beginning of its first term of office.

One right conferred, crudely, the right not to be detained without some kind of trial, is potentially prejudiced today. Sitting in your seat in a few weeks will be David Pannick, a human rights barrister, and a specialist in many other areas too. In a recent Times *article, he was warning against cherry picking (although he didn't use that phrase). He was talking about the notion of being able to pick and choose when to apply human rights. There's a debate about the extent to which, in the light of threats from terrorism, those protections afforded to people being detained might actually be removed or prejudiced. Have you thoughts on that?*

Yes, this is something that is extremely important. Any nation, where its interests are under attack, wishes to protect itself, and naturally it wants to do what it sees is in the interests of the public good as a whole. But it must act in accordance with the law, and if, in the process of doing that, it is going to infringe the human rights of the individual, then that has to be justified.

One of the important things about human rights is that most of them, apart from two most important ones, are not unqualified. You are allowed to infringe them as long as you act in a proportionate and legitimate manner, and there has got to be a balance. So when a country's national interests are involved, we all, as members and citizens of that country, have to be prepared for our rights to some extent to give way to the national interest, and that is recognised in the human rights legislation.

A balance has to be drawn, and that is where the courts come in. The judges are meant to be very skilled at deciding the balance, and they have to decide whether what is being done is justified. Now, if you are responsible for governing the country, then sometimes that becomes rather irritating because it gets in the way of doing things that you feel should be done for the benefit of the public as the whole. And my response as a judge would be that that is exactly the situation when the Human Rights Act is most important because it does enable the courts to give protection in those cases where it is appropriate. It also provides a standard against which the Government has to judge what it is doing.

When it comes to make decisions, it has to take into account and balance, in the way I was suggesting, the rights of the individual and the interests of the public. It is my belief that in the great majority of cases there is not a problem. If the Government is acting in a responsible way, which I am sure it would want to do, then human rights do not get in the way because it would have taken into account the rights of the citizens in deciding what action it is taking. And it is, it seems to me, very important that you should then have that protection because it is when you have a situation of pressure that we know from experience that it is so easy to get things wrong if you are in a position of power. The more powerful you are, the easier it is to get it wrong, and the human rights legislation is a break which ensures that there is the proper consideration given to the interests of the individual, albeit that it may be a little bit inconvenient to do that. Normally, the individual's rights can be accommodated. But it does mean that issues will come before the courts and there will be decisions from time to time where the courts will say to the Government, "You've got it wrong". That can be very frustrating to the Government and that is unfortunate, but it does not mean that the courts should not do their duty, and it does not mean that the Human Rights Act is not playing its proper role.

To look at that in practical and particular terms, the Legislature is introducing tighter laws relating to detaining suspected terrorists indefinitely, where there is good cause, but doing so without trial. These individuals may bring their cases before the courts to consider whether or not that particular piece of legislation justifiably contravenes, or derogates from, the European regulations. Is it conceivable that the body of law going through just now could be challenged in the courts in due course?

Certainly, but there is one very important provision in the Human Rights Act, which I think fits in with our constitutional law of tradition. This is very important. This country is a democracy. Our freedoms, which we value so highly, are in the care of Parliament. What the courts will invariably be doing is trying to give proper effect to what Parliament has done. The fact remains that, under the Human Rights Act, all that the courts can do if Parliament has actually contravened the Human Rights Act is to grant a declaration of incompatibility. Then it is for the Government to put that matter right, and there is a special speedy process by which you can do so.

Now, before human rights were part of our domestic law, you could go off to Strasbourg and get a decision from the European Court of Human Rights, and we can still do that. I think something which we can take pride in is this country's reputation for putting right infringements of human rights. It is second to none, even when they were not part of our domestic law. This country has always respected the decisions of the European Court of Human Rights, although they sometimes expressed rather forcibly that they disagreed with the decision, but when it came to the final push, we did put the law right in accordance with the requirements of the decision.

Do you see a distinction between the position in the US which, in a sense, has been the direct recipient of terrorist activity, on the one hand, and the UK, which is just potentially so? There does seem to be an exception or a justification in human rights terms where, in times of war or great public emergency, human rights may, I hesitate to say be diminished, but the reality is they are set to one side in favour of the greater good.

9

Well, as I indicated, I think that there needs to be scrutiny of this. In the States, the Supreme Court has got very wide powers to scrutinise legislation and decide whether it is constitutional or not. Their freedoms are dependent upon a written constitution and they will have the same problems that we have. The bigger the danger, the bigger the emergency, the more it is reasonable for the Government to say to the public, "We're very sorry, in this particular situation you, and the whole public, have to accept intrusions into what would otherwise be your rights. We would not expect this to happen in other situations".

Anybody who, like myself, is old enough to have lived through the last World War, knows that at those times there were very considerable infringements, but nobody objected to these because it was realised this was in the national interest. We hope that we won't have the same sort of danger to this country that was then existent. We hope we do not have the sort of tragedy here that occurred in the States on the 11th of September. But there were some decisions in the last war which I do not think the courts now would be particularly proud of, where citizens' rights were unnecessarily infringed, and I think that is something that we should remember. There are very famous dissenting judgments in decisions given during the wartime period by the courts—by judges who are now revered—which were very unpopular with their colleagues. That just illustrates the fact that there are stresses in those times and you do not always get it right, and I do not say for a moment that we would always get it right today either, but we would try.

On a lighter note, but not unrelated, I used to teach legal philosophy and legal theory. One of the big issues that students and scholars and lecturers all discussed (and indeed still discuss) is the question of how judges come to decisions. It is one of these interesting areas of what is known as jurisprudence and innumerable textbooks have been written on the matter by non-judges. Having you here allows me to test some of the academic theories. So, I want to ask you a set of questions. What is it you are doing when you are judging? At a crude level, is this a question of the extent to which you are making the law or deciding according to the law? Are you applying it? Do you feel you are bound by a body of rules? Or are you making decisions according to some kinds of principles or policies or purposes? I often refer in this connection to Professor Ronald Dworkin, who was the Professor of Jurisprudence in Oxford for many years. He developed an idea that he called "the chain novel", whereby someone writes Chapter One of a novel and they hand that chapter to someone else to write Chapter Two; and this second author has to maintain a consistent style, tone, theme and story-line. In turn, the second author would hand the two completed chapters to a third author—and so on, until the novel was completed. He then likened this process to the development of the Common Law.[6] If I can put it this way—it's partly a psychological point, it's partly a structural point—what does it feel like to be faced with major issues in the court? Again, do you feel you have got major discretion or are you substantially bound by the past?[7]

---

[6] See Ronald Dworkin, *Law's Empire* (Fontana, London, 1986).
[7] Judicial decision-making is also discussed by Lord Bingham (Ch.7), Dame Elizabeth Butler-Sloss (Ch.11), Cherie Booth (Ch.12) and Professor John Gardner (Ch.16).

Well, perhaps I could start off by saying, so far I have not had to decide a case by tossing a coin! The day may yet come . . . ! The great majority of cases that judges are deciding up and down the country are ones where they are really not engaging legal skills or there are not difficult legal problems, but they are being tried object-ively. That is very important. Because the judges are independent and they are objec-tive; they identify which side they think is accurate in the case that is put forward. Judges are not given—and do not even acquire—an ability to see somebody give evi-dence and automatically say, "Well, that person is speaking the truth, and that other person is not speaking the truth".

The situation can be that the person who is speaking the truth is sometimes very hesitant, very worried, and gives a lot of the symptoms that might popularly be thought to indicate they are not speaking the truth. This is because they are so worried about getting it right and being accurate that they are not glib. Then the person who is not speaking the truth can be very glib. Fortunately, in the great majority of cases, there are almost certainly various factors that help the judge. There may be documents that have been written at the time. There may be a witness who is independent, who can say what he or she saw. So you are very, very much helped. Factual issues for determination are—or can be—extraordinarily difficult to resolve and you can only do your best. In civil cases, the position is you say which is more probably right. In criminal cases, before the jury, the situation is rather different. The person is entitled to be treated as being innocent unless the jury is sure of the person's guilt, so the burden is very heavily upon the prosecution. The reason for that is it is obviously much better that a person who is guilty, or so we would say, gets off, than the person who is innocent is found guilty. That is absolutely funda-mental to our legal system. Now, I do not think Richard is actually talking to me about those sorts of cases, but that is what we are doing day in and day out: decid-ing where the truth lies.

There are cases where you have to decide where the law lies, and one of the great benefits that we have is that our law is our oldest institution and it has been devel-oped and built with experience. In the majority of cases which have legal points, all you need to do is find the answer, by looking at the cases or looking at the legisla-tion for what the law says, but there are situations, and one can easily give examples, where the law has never visited the situation before, and the judge is not entitled then to say, "Well, I am afraid there's no answer here provided by the law, so I am going home. I cannot help you"! What the judge must do in that situation is try and find the way forward, and in the course of trying to find the way forward, the judges do make law. They do not legislate, but in relation to that particular case, what they do is they try and find the underlying principles which are reflected in the development of the law and apply them to the new situation.

If I may just take one sort of case, as an example of how difficult that can be, a case which I was not in so I can talk about it. It is the case with those conjoined Siamese twins. That was a wholly new problem that the courts were faced with and with which they had to grapple to try and find a solution. If you look, as I have, at the judgments, which were given in that case, which were very long, the different judges gave judgments, but they were all trying to find principles which would guide them to what was the right answer. They were looking at different situations entirely and trying to draw analogies, and that is the way we work in developing the law. Society is changing very rapidly, and the number of cases coming before the courts where new issues are arising is accelerating. That is one of the reasons why it is a hugely rewarding job, being a judge now, but it is also a reason why actually I think it is more difficult to be a judge than probably it has ever been. I suspect if you ask a judge whether that was the position at any time in our history, they would have answered exactly the same way. I hope that gives a sort of picture; those cases where the law is not clear are the ones that keep the judge awake at night and worry the judge about what the answer should be.

It does pose an enormous burden on the judge. I have a quotation here I would like to, as some Americans would say, share with you. It is from Professor Hazel Genn, whose work I know we both admire, in her book Paths to Justice. *One of the questions she asks is in the context of a major survey she undertook about people's attitudes to pursuing disputes. Respondents were asked whether or not they agreed with the statement that most judges were out of touch with ordinary people's lives. About two-thirds, 66 per cent, agreed or strongly agreed with that statement; 13 per cent disagreed or strongly disagreed; and a relatively sizeable proportion, 21 per cent, felt unable to agree or disagree. There's a little quotation in italics: "Well, it's that whole glasses on the end of the nose sort of thing"! I think there is a serious issue here. As you've described it, some of the largest decisions in society are made by judges, and rightly so under our legal system. However, according to this research, the level of confidence in judges is not as high as I am sure you would want. You know the statistics, but how do you react?*[8]

I think I had better put my glasses on in order to answer that question! Actually, relying on props, I think that is another question in the survey, because I was very kindly given a copy of her book, which I read with interest. A question of the same sort was asked, first of all, of a section of the public who had never been involved in cases, and they really did have a rather bad impression of the Judiciary. Then there was the same question given to those who actually sampled the system. Without being able to quote the precise percentage, the second sample was much more favourable.

But having made that remark, I accept that one of the things that is probably the biggest challenge that we have today, as the Judiciary, is to increase the public's confidence in our system. I do not think that on the whole the public think badly of judges. I think actually most of the public, if they were asked seriously to sit down and talk about judges, would have a high regard for them. I know that when there is a problem like medical malpractice or a situation where there is foot and mouth disease or mad cow disease, the public, I think, are reassured when a senior judge is given the job of making a report. I think the public are reassured by that because they know at least that the judge will be independent and objective and he or she won't mind saying anything to anyone. They can be independent, and I think that is a very, very important asset of our society.

On the other hand, and I do not know and quite frankly do not think it is important, but I just wonder sometimes whether we would be not so obviously characterised as being out of touch if we did not wear the fancy dress that we wear in court. I am afraid it does enable us to be mocked and the subject of humour of the

---

[8] Hazel Genn, *Paths to Justice* (Hart Publishing, Oxford, 1999).

comedian and others. But where there are public surveys, when we ask, "Do we get rid of our wigs?", the public say, "No", they want us to keep them, and so we seem to have this difficulty.

I think that we've got to do all that we can to explain to the public what we are doing. That is why I am delighted to be here with you this evening. I am probably being totally arrogant in thinking that perhaps you do get an insight, which if you are not a lawyer you would not otherwise have, in what we do every day when we sit in court and we try hard to do justice, in the case that is in front of us. We think we are doing something worthwhile because we think the public needs justice and we have got to get over to the public that that is what we are doing. Actually, I've the most marvellous bunch of colleagues who are really devoted to the job and work extremely hard. You might think that they're only in court from 10.30am to 4.15 in the afternoon, but if you saw them at their home when they're working away on the papers, not only in the evenings but nearly every weekend, you would see that they really do deserve to be appreciated by the public. I think it is very hard to get the message across, but we try.

In many ways it is a public relations issue. I remember when I was involved, as you were, in reviewing the Civil Division of the Court of Appeal, we did ask judges about their working habits and working hours. And I can say that Court of Appeal judges work as hard as the hardest working of City lawyers. That would not generally, I think, be perceived, so it's a perception rather than a reality issue perhaps.

Moving on, there has been a debate recently, in light of Sir Robin Auld's review of the criminal courts, about the role of juries. I would be very interested to hear your views on Sir Robin's recommendations. One of his suggestions is that we need to be far stricter in relation to people finding excuses for not sitting on juries; otherwise we simply aren't assembling juries that are genuinely representative of society. Sir Robin also identifies some circumstances in which he feels juries should not sit in the future, in very complex fraud trials for example. I do not think these and other views have been fairly represented in the media but what are your thoughts on his recommendations?[9]

Well, Sir Robin Auld has tried to do for the criminal justice system that which my report was meant to do for the civil justice system: take a look at the whole thing and make some sensible recommendations. He has made over 300 recommendations. I do not say that anybody would agree with all his recommendations but, speaking for myself, I agree with a substantial number of his recommendations, the great majority, and I think that they are well designed to achieve a better criminal justice system, and I think that is very important. What I do believe must happen is, I think, there must be general discussion with the public about the virtues of what he is talking about.

We have, it seems to me, two great advantages already in our criminal justice system. One is our jury trial. It is a huge protection for the individual who is coming

---

[9] The criminal justice system is also discussed by Lord Justice Auld (Ch.4), Lord Irvine (Ch.6) and Lord Goldsmith (Ch.8).

before the courts. I talked a few moments ago about it—the burden of proof and the fact that you're being judged by ordinary people. It is very easy for a judge who is sitting in a court day in, day out, having one villain brought before him after another, to think everybody who is brought before him is a villain. We're all human, and I think that the jury therefore is a huge protection. But, again, I am concerned that we do have proportionality and we have speedy justice. I am afraid that sometimes we do not get proportional or speedy justice.

We have another great virtue in this country, and we are unique in this. 30,000 magistrates are members of the public who without pay administer justice for 95 per cent of the criminal cases, and anybody can be a magistrate. They want to broaden the range of people becoming magistrates, they want to broaden the racial mix of magistrates, and the Lord Chancellor has done his very best to encourage this to happen. They are ordinary members of the public and for small cases, they have provided high quality justice. There are a very low number of appeals from decisions of magistrates. The question is, should they be given to sit with judges, so there are two magistrates and a judge and a more extended jurisdiction with the object, not of taking very serious cases, not even taking medium serious cases, but taking cases which are a bit more serious than they hear now and disposing of them more cheaply and more quickly than happens at the present time? I think that is something which we should really consider very seriously. Sir Robin knew when making this recommendation that it was a controversial recommendation, but he thought it was necessary to make that recommendation, which is one which has been made before.

I indicated that I think timing, if you're making recommendations for reform, is extremely important. When similar recommendations were made in the past, they hit the rocks and have never been implemented. We value our jury system so much that we think even if a defendant may be guilty, we must not interfere with his right to a jury, even in the sort of case that I am talking about. Sir Robin is not saying that he should not be able to go to a jury; what he's saying is it should not be for the defendant in this band of cases to decide whether he goes to a jury, but it should be for a judge to decide, who is subject to appeal, because we all know, who are in the courts trying criminal cases, that the right to trial by jury in some of the cases I am referring to is being abused at the present time.

You can understand it. If you're a defendant, you want to put off the evil day. Again and again, it happens time after time, somebody says, "I want to go to a jury", and indicates therefore that he is going to plead not guilty—when he gets to court, he pleads guilty. Huge expense is incurred, a lot of trouble is taken, statements being taken from witnesses and procedures being gone through. Now, if you're experienced, you know the sort of cases where really it is delay that is the reason why sometimes a defendant is electing to go to trial. It does not really serve him any purpose. Often they spend their time as remand prisoners in custody when they'd be much better off getting their punishment, whatever it is, over and not waiting for the time it takes to get to the trial. But it is a highly sensitive issue, it is highly controversial, and I know there's a lot of very distinguished lawyers who would say that what is proposed is the thin end of the wedge, and whatever happens we must not allow that wedge to intrude into our very important right. Again it is a question of individual judgment, I think it is a matter to be debated. We should try and get a result which most people think is the right result. That is what I think we should do.

One of Sir Robin's recommendations is that when juries come to, and I quote, "per-
verse decisions", there may be grounds for these to be overturned by a judge. Is that
another thin end of the wedge?

Well, it could be described as a thin end of the wedge. I think, myself, that it is a
basic right of a jury sometimes to say, "We do not care what the law says, we do not
care what that judge says, we're going to find this person not guilty because we just
think the result otherwise would be deeply unjust". Now, if a jury as a matter of
principle does that, then I would not interfere with their verdicts, speaking personally. Sir Robin would argue to the contrary, and I would not agree with him. I think
we have got to debate that issue. I do not encourage you to take my view. I encourage you to read the careful arguments that Sir Robin has advanced.

But there is another category of case where you can see where the explanation for
the jury's verdict is not because of any point of principle; the case is not one of those
sorts of cases. It is not the liberty of the subject case, but it is clear that somebody
who has committed perhaps a very serious crime is going away free because the jury
have come to a perverse decision, an absurd decision. Why we cannot tell, because
they do not give reasons, but the evidence can be overwhelming that somebody has
committed a very serious crime and they might recommit the same sort of crime
again if justice is not done. In that sort of situation, as long as there are real safeguards—and I would want the Attorney General to be involved as the guardian of
the public interest—and for there to be other safeguards, including the involvement
of judges, then in a very small minority of cases, even though it would mean somebody being retried, I would myself personally think that this is justified. After all, if
a judge comes to a perverse decision, that is a decision that the High Court will
immediately put aside. I am not saying that the courts should then say that the
person is guilty, I am merely saying that they should be retried before a different jury.

Lord Woolf, we've crossed a lot of quite difficult terrain. Alas, we come to an end. I feel
I could go on all night asking you all sorts of questions, but I do want to conclude with
one. What would you say to pupils in schools, to students in university, those who are
contemplating a career in the law? We live in times of immense change. Do you feel
optimistic about the future of the legal profession and the Judiciary as a place for a
rewarding career, or vocation or calling?

Very. I think it is a wonderful career. I do not think I would do anything different
from what I have done if I had my life over again. I regard myself as extremely fortunate in being able to practise law and hold a judicial appointment.

On behalf of Gresham College, Lord Woolf, very many thanks.[10]

---

[10] Lord Woolf returned to Gresham College for the final interview of the series. This is reproduced in
Ch.20 of this book.

CHAPTER TWO

Tony Williams
Global Managing Partner, Andersen Legal

Tuesday November 6, 2001

*It is my great pleasure tonight to welcome Tony Williams to Gresham College. Tony
is Global Managing Partner of Andersen Legal and previously was Managing Partner
of Clifford Chance. Tony therefore manages a law firm of a particular type—a major
commercial concern that handles large (often very large) transactions and disputes.
Tonight I hope to find out from Tony what it is like to be in his position—organising,
managing and directing the kind of firm he works within. I also want to gain some
insight into the part of the legal marketplace with which he is occupied.*

*I should say at the outset that Tony has been a client of mine for a number of years
and we have worked quite closely together, but he has agreed that tonight I need show
none of the deference that I normally reserve for him.*

*Tony, I wonder if we could begin by talking about the kinds of work that major inter-
national law firms do. Some people in the audience will be familiar with the range and
scope of these businesses, but others, when they think of law firms, may have in mind
the high street lawyer. Can you therefore give us a flavour of the work of the large international law firm.*[1]

Yes, I think there is an increasing distinction, and it has been developing over the
last 20 years or so. The larger international firms are really operating in two main
areas of work, which tend to be the larger corporate acquisitions—flotations,
capital raising, either debt or equity, often involving not just one country but a
group of countries around the world—or acting for financial institutions on
banking and other major transactions. What you read in the business pages of the
press is the sort of work that the firms by and large will be doing. In addition to that,
it tends to be larger and more complex, perhaps litigation work—protecting intellectual property rights, working for pharmaceutical companies, that sort of thing.
So it tends increasingly to be much more corporate or finance work for institutional
clients rather than individuals, although there is some private client work.

---

[1] The workings of an international law firm are also discussed by Michael Bray (Ch.5).

17

You don't practise law now, but you did in the past, of course. For example, you ran the Moscow office of Clifford Chance. To give us a sense of the work of a lawyer in a major law firm, can you say a little about the kinds of services with which you might have been involved there?

A range of things, from, say, somebody like Merrill Lynch setting up in Moscow; or a big joint venture between Atlantic Richfield (a big American oil company) and Luk Oil, which is the big Russian oil company, to explore for and exploit oil in Russia; including anything those clients want including getting their flats in Moscow or their work permits.

The current recession—how does that affect big law firms, because clearly there is less corporate activity?

Yes, clearly within the legal market and generally in professional services, their performance is based on activity in the market. It's not a matter of how stable or otherwise the market is; it's the fact that the market is going up or down. At the moment, we've seen a downturn of corporate activity and a slowdown in lending activity, quite dramatically so this year. So the likelihood is that it's probably down something like a third in its activity levels of last year, which admittedly was an exceptional year.

What size are the very large law firms?

Well, they will vary. My firm, for example, worldwide, has about 3,000 lawyers, but the larger firms around the world would be, in most cases, 1,000 lawyers plus. Not particularly because you want to be that big, but because of the depth and breadth of services that you need, and because you need specialists in a range of different areas. Just acting for one client on a large transaction can monopolise 30, 40 or 50 different lawyers—it seems unbelievable, but it can happen.

And their organisation? Most people know that law firms tend to be partnerships, but for that size of organisation, a partnership might, on the face of it, seem a rather bizarre and inappropriate structure?

It is quite bizarre because by and large law firms do operate as partnerships, and partnerships were classically animals of three, five or 10 people. Increasingly firms have tried to maintain a feeling of partnership and a sense of belonging in a partnership, while accepting a more corporate decision making structure, and to try to balance those two competing pressures. The other issue obviously that arises in a partnership is that partners are personally liable for all of the liabilities of the business, so if one of their colleagues makes a mistake, they have everything at risk.

There must be a bit of a tension there, because on the one hand, one is being asked as a partner in a big firm to hand over responsibilities for management and control to a small number of individuals; while, on the other hand, you are sharing the liability often with people you barely know or perhaps have never met. I presume there are many reactions to this, but how well do partners respond—essentially—to being told what to do?

Managing a law firm has been described as herding cats. I think that's unkind to cats! You do it by persuasion and by encouragement, and by a clear mutual interest. If people see it is in their interests to be within the organisation and they are excited by what they are seeing, they will stay. The liability issue, if you looked at it and worried about it all the time, you would be paralysed with fear. But when you really analyse it, it comes back to trusting the people who are your partners and trusting the arrangements you have. Within the larger law firms you have fairly massive amounts of insurance to cover those sorts of eventualities. In the UK, I don't think there has been a case in recent years of a larger firm suffering major problems because of these sorts of claims.

I think it's true to say that accounting firms have been subject to more claims. Is it because lawyers are better at covering themselves, at managing their exposure?

Lawyers are the ones who are suing, which adds to the advantage! The particular peculiarity with the accounting profession is because of the clear statutory audit role. People assume that auditors are guaranteeing the financial statements, whereas in effect what they are doing is a review of them. But that gives them a higher degree of liability. In other words, when a company fails, one of the first organisations you look to, because they're still around whereas the directors may have disappeared, are the auditors. In legal services, it's more difficult because there is not a black and white audit-type opinion in the advice you're giving to show that there has been a clear mistake, although it is fair to say the number of claims overall have been reasonably stable over the last few years. But there is a growing trend of people looking at professionals to sue.

Most people are familiar with the distinction between barristers and solicitors, but from what you are saying, you can draw what may be an equally significant distinction between lawyers who undertake work for major corporations and institutional clients, as against law firms that really concentrate on the individual. Indeed, what we have seen emerge in some jurisdictions is what might be termed rather unfairly "a premier league" of law firms. And even amongst, say, the top 30 or 50 firms in the City of London, many people would go further and refer to the top five as belonging, as is said, to the "Magic Circle".

You have to be very careful when looking at the professions overall because although you've got very different businesses, you are trying to retain certain common standards and common values. My initial experience was in a very general high street

19

type firm. But yes, what we have seen over the last 10 years in particular—around the world, it's not just a UK phenomenon—is a smaller group of firms tending to monopolise the larger transactions and the higher value transactions. That tends to become a virtuous circle, in that they have done the last deal and therefore people feel comfortable that they have the experience and therefore they get the next one and, as a result, pull away. In the London market in particular, we have a Magic Circle. Ten years ago people would have argued who was or was not in it. Now you would clearly say there is a Magic Circle of five firms in the London market—with many of the others aspiring to get in.

And is that realistic without a merger? If you were asked to jump five years ahead, leaving analysis of the accounting firms and their legal divisions for later in the discussion, do you think these five firms will remain in that position or do you think others will come through?

In the legal profession in Europe, five years is a long time to look ahead, but they are in a very strong position at the moment. They would have to do something silly, or be very complacent, to drop out. Others clearly are trying to knock at the door. As each year goes by it gets more difficult for them to do so, and they would probably need to do some sort of merger or some sort of major leap up to get the attention of the market.

And what about international mergers leaving aside the regulatory issues? Clifford Chance, when you were Managing Partner, was one of the first to enter into a major merger with a US firm, but do you predict a major move towards transatlantic mergers and, if so, could that upset the balance of the leaders in the local, City market?

If there was a major move across the Atlantic, yes. What we haven't yet seen, although a lot of people are looking at it, is what I would describe as a first tier London firm merging with a first tier New York firm.

A Magic Circle firm?

A Magic Circle firm with its equivalent in New York. I suspect we will see at some stage but not yet. The imperatives are much stronger on the English firms to do that. Fundamentally the London market is much smaller. Those London firms, five, 10 or 20 years ago, had to become more international. They went initially to Europe and also to Asia-Pacific because the London market wasn't big enough and because much of the European market was being serviced by professional services and investment banking services out of London. But the New York firms don't have that imperative. The US market is a massively deep market. Any major transaction in the world comes to New York and has a significant piece in New York, so you can be very successful, very effective, with your main focus in New York, that's the big difference.

20

I've also heard it said that there's a sufficient gap in the level of profitability of the New York firms as compared with the London firms, that even the highly profitable London firms would be unattractive merger candidates.

Yes, there certainly used to be. But between what I would call the Magic Circle London firms and the major New York ones, there's less now than there ever has been. Ten years ago it would probably be two or three times in New York what it was in London; I suspect now it varies between the same or 20, 30 or 40 per cent higher, but not dramatically out of line. It will be interesting to see how that works through with the downturn, because obviously the United States went into a downturn probably four, five or six months before the UK, so you may see that trend changing. But the advantage the American firms have is that the New York market is a very specialised and very profitable market, and much deeper than the equivalent London market.

Staying with the issue of profit for now, last week, when Lord Woolf was in your chair, he was talking about the system of litigation in the United States whereby litigation lawyers can get, as it were, a slice of the action. So, a very successful and large claim, as he put it, would give rise to some very wealthy lawyers. Even putting these litigation lawyers to one side, I think, when they hear, for example, that New York lawyers are earning many millions of dollars each year, many people think they're overpaid. What is your feeling about the fat cat lawyer argument, both here and abroad?

It's there. It is an argument. One has to bear in mind, certainly looking at the UK, that you have about 100,000 lawyers in the UK, of which probably about three-quarters of them are in private practice. The range of income varies from £20,000 up, but the average, certainly for those doing legal aid work, is probably only late 20s or 30s, and it ranges through the spectrum. As always, it's very easy to pick out big numbers and there are some people earning a lot of money. Overall in the profession, the earnings level has changed quite dramatically over the last 20 years in the more successful firms.

I mentioned I was in a general practice as a trainee. I moved house a couple of years ago. In 1975, in the firm I was in then, for buying an equivalent house to the one I bought four years ago, in cash terms in 1975 the legal fees for that conveyancing were more than they were in 1997. Now when you think of inflation through the 70s and 80s—there are two things that proves. The scale of fees in the 70s was ridiculous, and there has been a major level of change in the competitiveness of those providing legal services.

The high street firms have some real issues, particularly in how they respond to address new technology and changing client expectations. But yes, you have many very successful lawyers, making a lot of money. I don't think we should be ashamed about that. One of the great success stories of England is that our legal profession is a major international export. Our English legal services are used internationally on a major scale. We made a net contribution to the balance of payments last year of over a billion pounds, and we are pleased about that.

What about quality of life? It is the case that many of the very highly paid lawyers to whom you are presumably referring work enormously hard, often at the expense of their health and their families. They have a different view of retirement and the future, do they not?

It is a lot more relentless exercise. One has the view of the solicitor going out and playing golf three days a week and I think the answer to that is "I wish". Certainly at the higher end of the profession, it is a very, very pressurised business. I was in New York a couple of weeks ago, and talking to one partner of a law firm—and this man is probably certifiably mad, but there we are! But let me explain how this man worked: he was in the office seven days a week; he was always in the office for at least 12 but normally 16 hours a day. One of his colleagues said, "His son got married earlier this year, and do you know he only managed 10 chargeable hours on the day of his wedding?" I thought, you very sad man! And it *was* very sad.

This is a big issue, particularly in New York, despite the very high salaries being awarded—and in fact partly because of the very high salaries. Many lawyers are working hard for a number of years and then saying, "I want a life; I'm getting out", and that's an issue that the profession in New York is having to come to terms with. Increasingly in London, the issue is one of people saying, "Yes, it's great to get a decent income, etc., but I don't have time to see my family", or "The friends I've had for the last 10 years or so, I've lost contact with", etc., and the pressures are real. I'm not just speaking about the legal profession. This is a feature across many parts of working life in the UK and in the US. The pressures are very, very high and it is resulting in far too many good quality people leaving the profession too early.

To what extent do you think the pressures are linked to the way that lawyers charge? Lawyers basically charge by the hour; you might want to discuss or challenge that, but that's my perception. If you contrast this model with bankers on a big deal, they'll be getting a share of the deal. Do you want to talk a little bit about that, and then we can go on and see what the implications are for how hard one works?

By and large, lawyers operate on the chargeable hour basis. In reality, charging by the hour is a cost plus basis—it must be. I think it's unfortunate because it militates against being more efficient, it militates against effective use of technology, and it militates against doing things differently.

The problem is that for some General Counsel that's the only buying method they understand. I would very much like to see the profession go to a fixed fee approach, and in many areas it is already going this way; perhaps to a fixed fee with the success element, but on a basis that is clear and understood from the start.

Certainly at the more "retail" end of the market, that is what the clients want too. A friend of mine has just been involved in a divorce and last week was sitting down with her lawyer and the lawyer said, "Well, the bill is X". Now that was a very significant amount—I'm sure it was the right amount because I know it had been a very unpleasant and acrimonious dispute, but had the level of fees been more managed and better communicated up front, it may well have influenced the parties' behaviour to settlement. So the hourly basis may be right for certain types of work,

but it does need to move on. It has moved on when you look at, say, residential conveyancing, which is increasingly on a fixed basis.

*Do you think it encourages longer working hours? It seems to me that if you are
working for a fixed fee, the incentive to be efficient is greater.*

Yes, it certainly is. In fact, in my old firm, there was one office in Europe that always
produced a relatively poor level of profitability, and they said, "Look, in this market
we just cannot charge more per hour". Interestingly enough, without any urging
from me, the relevant partners decided to go to clients with fixed price deals, and
these were genuinely the fixed price. They then used new technology, they reorgan-
ised their practice, and they actually improved their performance, and also their
quality of life. So the hourly fee approach is an impediment to the move to efficiency.
   One of the interesting parallels is the defence industry. Since the war, until the
early 80s, the defence industry worked on a "cost plus" basis. You can develop anything—the Government would always pay you that plus 10 or 20 per cent. When it
all then went out to fixed price tendering, there was massive restructuring in the
industry, and the client got a cheaper service but the industry changed and adapted
to it and our profession needs to do that as well.

*And then there is competitive tendering. Could you speak a little about that, because
the so-called beauty parades actually occupy huge amounts of senior management time
in firms.*

Yes, it's quite bizarre. Lawyers are one of the last of the professions that is still
embarrassed talking about fees and money, while clients are saying, "We want you
to tell us what it's going to cost" etc. The old idea of the little pocket in the back of
a barrister's gown so that you could put the fee in there without him actually having
to see or touch the filthy money is a rather antiquated concept.

*Let's move on to what is perhaps a more controversial issue. In many people's minds,
in a sense, you sold out the legal profession by becoming the first very high profile senior
lawyer to move from leading a major law firm to leading the legal practice of one of
the "Big Five" global accounting firms. We've talked about the Magic Circle in the
legal world in the UK. Similarly, there are these five very, very substantial accounting,
tax and consulting firms that dominate their particular markets around the world,
although the imperatives that are driving them are different.*

I had been at Clifford Chance for 19 very enjoyable years. It was time for me to move
on, and I was looking at a range of options. I must say this one was nowhere near
my horizon at the time. I started discussions with Andersen and it became more and
more interesting. I had been, as you mentioned earlier, living in Moscow for a
number of years. It was in Moscow that the first idea of putting the services together

came to me, because a major investment bank was devising some horrendously complex financial products in Russia. I was doing the legal and exchange control side of that deal, and we were using accountants to do the tax and accounting side of it and then putting it together. The client said, "I want opinions from you on this", and we said, "Right, we'll do ours and they will do theirs", and he said, "No, we want you to do one joint opinion, and how you deal with it behind the scenes, that's your problem". Well, being typical lawyers, we said, "Oh no, that's not the sort of thing we do", and the client said, "Yes it is, I'm paying, and you're doing it"—a fairly compelling argument!

So we did it, and it got me thinking, because that was a very uncertain market—in England or France they wouldn't have thought of it in that way, but this was a very new market. This was a major value product—there was over a billion dollars invested through this—and they needed to know that there was no crack between the advice at all, so they wanted something comprehensive.

And within six months we hired into the law firm the head of tax in that accounting firm. Being a law firm, we couldn't actually hire him in as a partner, so we had to call him a Director of Tax, which was the wonderfully inventive name we came up with. We rewarded him like a partner, he came to partners' meetings, and he received all partner information but could not be called a partner. That got me thinking how silly that was.

Andersen are obviously very strong on the audit and the tax and the accounting side, growing in business consulting, growing a corporate finance practice and now with an established legal practice. I liked the opportunity of bringing together a very strong legal practice; ratchetting that up internationally to be a very strong legal player, but combining that with other services, not on just a simplistic one-stop shop, but on a quality "this is your issue; how can we deal with it?" basis.

Many clients don't care whether it is a legal or a tax or an accounting issue. They know they have business problems and they want people to deal with them. It was putting the advice you give in a much more business-like context and actually doing it in a way that worked with your colleagues to solve a problem rather than standing in a legal ivory tower that made it interesting to me.

Why is it that commentators and lawyers alike, not all but some, find this offensive?

There are a number of reasons. Firstly, certainly in the States, less so in the UK, there is still an element there that lawyers traditionally have been what I've described as members of the flat earth society—something can't be done, shouldn't be done, until it is done, in which case it was a good idea and they are glad they thought of it!

There are some real issues. There is a nervousness about how you blend those services together, these are important issues. It is essential that your legal advice is genuinely independent of other commercial considerations, you must preserve your client's confidentiality, you must not create a position of conflict in relation to your other clients with the advice you are giving. These are very important issues and they need to be dealt with.

Personally, I believe that they can be dealt with within a broader organisation by very strict controls and very strict organisation. Others believe that they can only be dealt with by rigid divorce. There are legitimate consumer protection issues here. I believe they are dealt with by appropriate rules and regulations. I am concerned that in some cases some of the rhetoric we see is more about protectionism than it is about consumer protection.

There are some regulatory issues here though, aren't there? Different jurisdictions have reacted in different ways to proposals for accounting and law firms to come together.

Yes, in New South Wales in Australia, for example, over a number of years they have reformed the law to permit full multidisciplinary partnerships. Here in England, they are not permitted at the moment. I work in a separate legal partnership. We work very closely with our colleagues within Andersen but we are quite separate in a legal and regulatory sense.

Other countries are going in different ways. Spain has effectively adopted a concept of allowing different businesses to be associated and work closely together. In America the American Bar Association has come out against the idea of working together, but they are not the regulator, individual states are, and we are seeing different states take different views, which will be a bit of a mess actually in the United States. But you are seeing a more informed debate going on now than we perhaps had in the past. There was too much of the "this is the end of civilisation as we know it" sort of discussion. It's now a much more mature debate people are having on how credibly to protect the client's interest, how to make the client aware of what might be the differences on client confidentiality in one structure as opposed to another, and those are legitimate things to address.

What about clients? What's your experience of clients' responses?

Well that, to my mind, is the most important one. The question is what do clients want and do clients feel adequately protected, and indeed are they adequately protected? The fact that we number, amongst our clients in the UK for example, 15 or 16 of the FTSE 100, that we have a large number of international clients that are comfortable to use us on larger and larger transactions is an important sign that we are winning people round.

We were told a couple of years ago there would be no demand for our services at all, and yet last year our turnover was almost $600 million. If that's no demand, I'd like to be around when there *is* a demand for our services! But it's a process. We often have to get in to a client doing relatively small transactions and convince them that we are competent, that we do have the right professional standards, that we can deliver. As we have been developing our international operations, people have felt more comfortable and it has been moving up. Developing a reputation and developing a practice is a long, slow process and there are no short cuts.

What differences do you see between leading a law firm and leading an accounting firm—culturally and in working style?

In a legal environment, at Clifford Chance, I was in what was, and what still is, one of the world's largest law firms. I thought that was a pretty large organisation, and indeed it is, and there were around 2,000 lawyers, and a total staff of say 4,500. I'm now part of an organisation of 85,000 people. It is the sheer scale and the different nature of the businesses that is different. You realise that lawyers are much more fiercely independent thinkers—not always terribly functional thinkers, but fiercely independent in the way in which they operate.

Within a larger organisation it is very interesting, for me certainly, to understand the way in which other businesses work, the way in which other people interact, and realising the good and bad in that. There are some elements where I believe a legal practice does better, but there are also other areas where you see the sort of best practice that we could really learn from. But they are a much bigger organisation, they are much more corporate in structure—they have to be. When you are 20 times bigger than Clifford Chance, you just have to run yourself differently.

But, in Andersen, you recently held a global partners' meeting?

Yes, we get together. It's meant to be about every 18 months to two years, all partners around the world. It was slightly depleted this year because of the September the 11th events, but we had about 2,500 partners together out of about 4,500. And it was fascinating because obviously within the Andersen organisation the lawyers are a relatively small part. But it's a firm that has a very, very strong sense of partnership, and you were meeting many people for the first time. Spending time getting to know those people, getting to work together, makes you realise the opportunities there are within an organisation of that size.

Tell us about how you are growing the business, because your challenge is, as I understand it, within a decade, say, to be one of the world's premier law firms.

Yes, it's always nice to have a manageable target! As I've said, we're already, in numbers terms, one of the largest players in the world. That's not really the challenge. You can always go out and hire plenty of people. The issue every year is to keep ratcheting up the quality of all the lawyers you have, the quality of the work you are doing for the clients, the client's confidence in you and the market perception of you. This is a long and difficult process. That requires growing younger lawyers up through the organisation, which is the classic way of growing a firm, but that won't be quick enough for us, so we are quite actively hiring individual partners and indeed looking to merge with other firms in other parts of the world.

You were uncomfortable, I think, about making a five-year prediction, so let's try a 10-year prediction instead! Within 10 years, how many of the top 10 law firms do you think will actually be from the accounting world?

It's always a difficult one. The pace of change will depend on when, going back to your earlier question, a top tier UK and a top tier US firm get together, because that will shift the whole game to a large extent. But I think within that 10-year period it clearly will happen. I don't know exactly what the numbers will be and how quickly the market will consolidate. I suspect that at a truly international level, by which I mean firms with very strong operations in 10 or 15 countries around the world and strong international reputations, you will probably be talking of no less than six and not more than 12 firms at the absolute top level. I suspect that one and possibly two of those will be linked to the big five accounting firms.

You were talking about merger and looking for a merger. You spend a lot of time travelling—talk us through your trips and how you go about growing.

As you can see, a lot of it is lunches and dinners with other firms! Before you do any visit, the good thing about the Web now is you can get so much information on firms. There's a lot of gossip—there's almost too much—published about law firms, so you pull together as much of that as you can. You look and see what sort of firms are likely to fit with what you want. You try and find out where there are firms having difficulties so that either you will talk with the entire firm or a spin-off group. And, quite frankly, it's like any dating game; you go up and try your chat-up lines, some more inventive than others. Normally you would have an initial discussion, often over a dinner or a general meeting, where you will just explore the world as both firms see it.

You will be told a lot of lies during those discussions, just like a normal first date, and you will decide how beautiful or ugly your partner is and decide whether you want to go forward, and they will do the same! From there, you are effectively building the case, how confident you feel, because you are talking about a people business, and you have to feel comfortable with the relationship you are building. It will take any number of months to develop that and feel comfortable.

I've been having discussions recently with one group of lawyers, and my first meetings I thought went horribly. I spoke to one of the partners at the firm a few weeks ago and I said, "I'd really rather we stopped now. We've been good friends for quite some time, but if your other partners aren't interested, fine". "No, no, no, you have very much misunderstood. We do love you really!". You will have misunderstandings, you will have miscommunications, and it's a matter of working through them. But really, in the end, for something to work, you have to do something as quickly as you possibly can, you have to produce some real excitement and enthusiasm about it, and sometimes you have got to make two plus two make five or more. If it makes less than four, you're in trouble.

To what extent is it secretive? You hear cloak-and-dagger tales about the way in which people meet and conspire when major mergers are contemplated.

Yes, in typical lawyer style, you have silly little code names. I was in discussion with one firm when I was in my former role a few years ago, and we rented a funny little flat, in Middlesex Street. I was just very pleased there were no *News of the World* photographers around, because it was not entirely one of the best districts but it was a cheap flat, where we had all our meetings. A load of boring old suits went in, stayed a number of hours, and sometimes in the middle of the night, turned up on the street again. Fortunately it was a part of town where we wouldn't find any journalists or anybody else, so we got away with that!

But yes, you do have all those sorts of cloak-and-dagger games because one of the key things is to gradually bring your partners on board. It's quite important not to give them too much of a surprise because, particularly in law firms, if you surprise a lawyer, the first reaction is "no". So you've got to warm them to it, to a stage where they will be asking you, "Why don't you bloody well get on with this deal?", in which case you know you have sufficient oomph to go forward.

But it's quite a long game. This is not the kind of artifice you engineer overnight.

Oh no, it's a long process. In Andersen Legal, we did a strategic review last year. We gave a copy of that—sorry, we gave a sanitised version of that—to everybody in the firm, and had copies on our website, setting out our direction and what we're trying to achieve. It's quite clear what we plan to do in relation to the UK as well as other parts of the world. We wanted to make sure everybody was aware, and comfortable with that, so that now whatever we do we can link back and say it's consistent with, and it's implementing, part of the programme. You gradually widen the circle. You get people to feel more comfortable. But there is a very strong legal press, and you've got to be very careful of news getting out at the wrong time.

How do you see technology having an impact on the delivery of legal services? And why is it that you feel, as presumably you do, that the accounting firms are better placed to exploit technology than law firms?

Until quite recently, technology in law firms has been, and you've heard me say this before, about automating the quill pen. The processes have been the same: the drafting processes, the documentation processes and the negotiation processes. You talk to lawyers and they say something along the lines: "Nothing of ours could be organised, nothing of ours could be systematised, it's all original work". When you analyse it, you know that's bull. There is a significant amount that *does* rely on their judgment and their experience, and that's a very, very valuable part of their advice, no doubt about it at all, but a lot of what lawyers do is pure process.

One of the questions and one of the challenges will come back to the pricing model. Clients will increasingly demand access to a certain degree of legal advice online. But there will be much more intelligent drafting tools; the sweat of that will be taken out of it. It comes back to the point we were making earlier on lawyers' quality of life as well. We cannot continue to drive profitability in law firms by increasing the hours people do because they will just fall by the wayside in increasing degrees. IT will transform it dramatically because the legal profession, by and large, has not embraced technology and the opportunities of technology that are there.

Our knowledge and precedent systems have not changed much over the years. The way we make our services available to our clients has not changed much. And, both of us know from discussions with General Counsel and other buyers of our services that they want relevant and helpful advice readily available to them, not just thrown at them in the form of brochures. Are the accounting firms more likely to do elements of that? Much of their business has already gone down that route, and indeed increasing amounts are.

Take my own organisation, for example. If you are a US expatriate, you still have to file a US tax return. That traditionally was done in the country wherever that expat was based, and it was done in England for those based here. That has now been changed in that we have reformatted the information they have to provide. They can now provide that information online. Those reports are then prepared and prepared for filing in India—at a fraction of the price, and to a much better standard. People here didn't want to do it; in India, they were very keen to do it. The client, all he does is email his form, he doesn't care where you are, providing it is done properly. That has been a major change.

Another aspect relates not just to your Windows system and your time recording system, but the sheer investment required to get a knowledge system running effectively to organise your documentation, to organise your litigation files, etc., because increasingly the courts will operate online, and that is a major investment. Firms such as Andersen probably invest more in IT per year than the turnover of all but the top 20 law firms in the world, and that spending power, if used effectively, is a major competitive advantage.

Reflecting on our earlier discussion, do you see that technology may establish an even greater divide between those leading commercial law firms on the one hand and smaller practices, high street firms, on the other, between those who can afford the technology, who can engage in R & D, who can get major systems up and running, and those who feel it's beyond them?

That is the risk, and actually the shame is that a lot of the smaller firms have not actually embraced that in the way they could, because it could give them a major opportunity and a major advantage. You will recall, a couple of years ago, we were on a panel judging some legal awards, and one of them was for the use of IT. I remember one of the projects was by a very small law firm that specialised in personal injury claims but on the defendants' side, so by and large acting for insurance companies. That, over the last 10 years, has become a commodity business. They produced for their clients a secure web site where they had details; only about a paragraph on every case: who it was, the amount they had advised them to reserve, the costs to date, the likely cost, any novel items, etc. The clients, rather than playing telephone tag with a lawyer who by definition was in court a lot, could email specific instructions on individual matters, saying "settle this" or "do that". The responsiveness was there and built in. The cost of that technology was very, very cheap, and certainly getting cheaper by the day.

But they had thought even beyond that, in that the client could mine that information and do a lot of claims analysis work—how many of these cases are motor accidents, how many involve milk floats, how many involve back injury, etc. So not only was the client getting a better service, they could probably—by mining this information—dispense with or re-allocate to more valuable work, some of their claims analysts back at head office. So they had changed the value of their service and they had given themselves a real competitive advantage.

Now that was on a very small scale. You will see the same with firms, for example, doing a lot of residential property work. Increasingly over the next few years we will move to a stage where the Land Registry and local authority searches, are all online, so there will be no excuse for not moving electronically. I made the mistake in London of selling a flat a year or so ago. I always make a point of not using lawyers within my own firm. I was in a rush to exchange and complete because I'd bought another flat so I wanted the money! I said to my lawyer, "Why haven't the other side responded? You'd given them 10 days to get on and do everything". He sent me this wonderful correspondence, which was a spat between the two law firms as to the date upon which the documents had been sent and received. Rather than forget that and get on with it, they'd had three exchanges of correspondence on it. I asked, "given the urgency, why wasn't it faxed, or better still, why wasn't it emailed?". Using the post was inexcusable in the circumstances.

But it does require, in individual firms, large or small, the commitment of people like you who are leading the firms. I have to say that it's fairly rare to meet a managing partner who speaks enthusiastically and knowledgeably about technology. As you go round and about and meet your equivalents, are you finding increasing enthusiasm for technology or do you think lack of uptake is a generational issue?

There is to some extent a generational issue. And quite frankly, until now, in the profession, if every minute of your day can be spent serving clients who will pay you your full dollar, your incentive to look at change is limited. Now, any consultant will tell you that is the time you should be looking at change, but of course you never do. Also, in some traditional firms there is a concern that by using technology more widely, particularly if you are tied to an hourly rate approach, you will be destroying value the more you spend on technology which is a quite bizarre idea. So of course the model only works if you change your whole approach to pricing and the whole approach to your business.

There are relatively few either individual lawyers or law firms that necessarily have the confidence to embrace that change. That being said, it's as important for the retail end of the market, because we are at a position, as legal aid is increasingly being withdrawn for a wide range of legal services, where there is a massive middle income and lower income market not being served by legal services. Many people have Web access. A lot of legal advice and assistance could be provided which is otherwise just being completely unserviced at the moment. I know you have written about the so-called latent legal market many times, but I believe it's there in the business world and in the private world as well.

A couple of concluding questions. Leaving aside particular firms, what major challenges do you think, over the next decade, the legal profession face?

30

There are a number. The first one is, coming back to the pressures of work issue, recruiting and retaining the most able lawyers, and this will become an increasing issue unless there is a change in the way lawyers work. The pressures are causing a lot of people to go. Indeed, I remember having a meeting with some lawyers in the States and them saying, "We can't understand it, we've increased our lawyers' earnings by 20 per cent a year, and the more we increase earnings, the more they go". And I say, "Well, surely you understand, particularly in the States, once they've paid off their loans for their law college and they have got their deposit on their flat and their car, they have options, and people are exercising those options". That is an increasing issue, for the profession.

The big one is actually identifying what clients we will be serving and how we will be servicing them going forward, because, certainly in the commercial world, the client base has gone through dramatic change. Just look at the companies that were members of the FTSE over the last few years. I suspect in and out of the FTSE over the last five years have probably been 300 companies. That is the level of transformation that the market has gone through. We need to understand what our clients will want, and how will they want it delivered. The idea that we will carry on providing our services in precisely the same way as we've done before—is naïve. Why shouldn't we go through that fundamental level of change? The difficulty our profession faces is that we do not know exactly what format change will take, and that's unsettling.

What about the public's perception of lawyers? Do you feel there's work to be done there?

Well, we need to move more to the centre of business and to show we understand our clients' business, and not be a bunch of pompous over-charging farts. If we move to the centre of business, we have a great future. If we let other professionals, either investment advisors or whoever, take the role that traditionally lawyers have had, we will be increasingly marginalized to legal draftsmen.

I have a final question for you and one I'm going to ask everyone I interview. I have in mind the pupil at school or the student at university who is contemplating a career in the law. What would you say to them?

Well, my daughter is desperately keen to pursue a career in law, and my son is desperately keen not to! It comes back to my previous answer. It's unclear what the profession will be like. Change is one of two things, it's either a threat or a great opportunity. I believe it is a fantastic opportunity for the legal profession to become much more relevant again to people, to society and to business. So I think it's a great opportunity.

The work pressures will not change dramatically, but it can be a very, very exciting career. My son's preference is to play cricket, and therefore the chances of him doing that as a lawyer are pretty slim, so I think I'm right to steer him—well, he's already steering himself—away from it.

When I was a student, I turned to the person who actually became my principal. He was a wonderful lawyer, actually *is* a wonderful lawyer, and he turned to me and said: "Don't go into the law. Two things happen: first you get dandruff and then you get fat!". So all I can say is, Head & Shoulders took care of the dandruff, but I lost on the fat!

I cannot think of a less suitable note to end on. Tony Williams, many thanks.

Postscript

A few months after the above interview, in the aftermath of the collapse of Enron, and under remarkable and unprecedented conditions, Andersen ceased trading. With the death of Andersen came also the demise of Andersen Legal. As said in my Introduction, Tony Williams distinguished himself in winding up the affairs of Andersen Legal and personally striving to find new homes for all partners and employees. He kindly agreed to supplement this chapter with a personal account of the events just described.

If only I had 20:20 foresight. Within three months of my talk Andersen in the US admitted to shredding Enron related documents. This resulted in the rapid collapse of an organisation employing 85,000 people. Although no part of Andersen Legal was involved in any Enron work the impact on the legal business was devastating. In 2001 we were a top 10 global law firm in terms of turnover, by June 2002 Andersen Legal had ceased to exist. The stronger Andersen Legal firms opted to go independent, some joined EY Law or other law firms. The English legal practice was dissolved with the firm scattered amongst about a dozen law firms. Subsequent laws adopted in the US and across Europe caused the accounting firms to abandon their legal aspirations. Accordingly the threat of the accounting-linked law firms evaporated by early 2004.

However the trends of globalisation and consolidation in the legal industry have continued. Clients are becoming more astute and demanding buyers of legal services. We are still at an early stage of transformation in the legal market. In the next 10 years the legal market will change beyond recognition, and I now appreciate you have to expect the unexpected!

On May 31, 2005, the US Supreme Court unanimously overturned Arthur Andersen's conviction.

CHAPTER THREE

David Pannick QC
Barrister, Fellow of All Souls College, Oxford[1]

Tuesday November 27, 2001

My guest this evening, David Pannick, is widely acknowledged within the legal profession as one of the country's top barristers. Beyond the legal world he is also well known—as a fortnightly columnist for The Times. *His contributions there show remarkable range and not infrequently bring a smile to the face. David studied law at Hertford College, Oxford and was appointed a Fellow of All Souls in 1978. He was called to the Bar in 1979, and became a QC at the remarkably youthful age of 36. His clients have included the Lord Chancellor, the Chief Rabbi, Princess Diana and the Human Fertilisation and Embryology Authority. Since 1998, on a part-time basis, he has sat as a Deputy High Court judge.*

I would like to start our discussion this evening, David, with the difficult and highly controversial questions that arise in relation to terrorism. In the news just now, of course, is a Government Bill that would permit the detention of certain suspected terrorists without trial. Before we delve into the details of the particular Bill, can you put the general issue in context for us?

Certainly. Some history might help. In November 1943, the Home Secretary, Herbert Morrison, decided to release the fascist Sir Oswald Mosley and his wife Diana from detention. The Prime Minister, Winston Churchill, was in Cairo, meeting President Roosevelt. Churchill cabled to express his approval. He observed that "the power of the Executive to cast a man into prison without formulating any charge known to the law, and particularly to deny him the judgment of his peers, is in the highest degree odious and is the foundation of all totalitarian Government whether Nazi or Communist". I would like to suggest that our Parliament should

---

[1] This chapter is different from all others in the book for two reasons. First, on the evening of the interview, there was a problem with the audio facilities, such that almost half of the interview was not recorded. With the help of David Pannick, however, and an article written by him on relevant topics in *The Times* on October 23, 2001, much of the missing portion was recreated, although the end result is still a little shorter than the rest of the interviews. The second difference is that this interview, unlike the others, includes direct questions from the audience.

33

have given the same response to the proposals by the Home Secretary, David Blunkett, for detention without trial of terrorist suspects, and for suspending Article 5 of the European Convention on Human Rights.[2]

What are Mr Blunkett's concerns?

The Home Secretary is concerned that, because of Article 3 of the Convention (protection against torture, and inhuman or degrading treatment or punishment), he cannot remove from this country foreign nationals suspected of associations with terrorism who have a well-founded fear of persecution in the countries to which they might be sent. However bloody their hands may be, we are obliged to give them asylum here. The Home Secretary wishes to take power to detain such individuals, rather than allow them to live in the community. Mr Blunkett has obtained Parliament's approval to the suspension (or derogation) of the United Kingdom's obligations under Article 5 of the Convention because that provision prohibits detention in these circumstances.

This must surely have profound implications for the liberties of the individual.

Indeed. But Mr Blunkett has made it very plain that he is not concerned by criticism from those who are worried about, as he puts it, "airy-fairy civil liberties". But it is nevertheless the case that to confer power on the State to detain objectionable people without trial is wrong in principle, of dubious legality, and also highly undesirable for pragmatic reasons. It is wrong in principle because, as Churchill suggested, people should only be imprisoned when specific crimes can be proved, or pending a criminal trial. If there is evidence on which the individuals concerned can be prosecuted for terrorism offences in the past or for conspiring to assist terrorism offences in the future, here or abroad, then the Convention is no bar to lengthy prison sentences. But mere suspicion cannot suffice, any more than it can provide a basis for locking up suspected murderers or rapists without trial. Some of us retain an old-fashioned preference for imprisoning people only if their criminality can be proved. As Norman Birkett KC, Chairman of an advisory committee considering cases of administrative detention, wrote in his diary in December 1939, it is necessary to keep "justice alive in a world in which we were supposed to be fighting for it". We are battling against terrorism precisely so that we can maintain a society in which we enjoy individual autonomy, the rule of law, and the right to dissent; goals which we cherish and which the terrorists abhor. To discard those values, even temporarily, and confer a power on the State to detain those of whom it disapproves, devalues all of us. A liberal democracy must confront the difficult question of what rights it should accord to those whose aim is to destroy the civilisation which confers those very freedoms. Can western society protect itself without abandoning the

---

[2] Human rights are also discussed by Lord Woolf (Ch.1), Lord Bingham (Ch.7), David Lock (Ch.9), Oliver Letwin (Ch.10), Cherie Booth QC (Ch.12) and Professor Bogdanor (Ch.19).

values which define its identity and so make it worth protecting? Or, as the Home Secretary suggested in his speech to the Labour Party Conference earlier this month, has judicial review "become a lawyers' charter" which prevents the State from "protecting the majority from the minority"?

You said a few minutes ago that the Home Secretary's proposals are also of dubious legality. Can you expand upon this?

"In time of war or other public emergency threatening the life of the nation", Article 15 of the Convention allows states to derogate from their obligations "to the extent strictly required by the exigencies of the situation". The European Court has stated that the words "threatening the life of the nation" refer to "an exceptional situation of crisis or emergency which affects the whole population and constitutes a threat to the organised life of the community of which the State is composed". This was so stated in 1961 in the case of *Lawless v Ireland*.[3]

The European Court is unlikely to accept that current problems are "threatening the life of the nation". There have (happily) been no terrorist incidents in this country associated with the 11 September attacks in New York and Washington, far less incidents of such gravity as to threaten civil society which cannot be addressed by existing laws. Indeed, there have been grave terrorist outrages in England in recent years (such as the Brighton bombing and the Canary Wharf bomb) which did not lead the Government to conclude that detention without trial was appropriate.

In any event, the Government will not be able to establish that indefinite detention is "strictly required" in relation to people against whom no criminal charges are being brought, especially when no other European State is contemplating such measures. All other countries are proceeding on the traditional basis that a person may not be detained without trial by reason of suspicion, but must either be charged with a criminal offence or released from custody. It is very difficult to understand why detention without trial is "strictly required" in the United Kingdom alone.

What are your pragmatic objections?

If Parliament confers broad powers of detention without trial, it will contribute nothing to our safety and cause substantial misery to innocent victims, as the experience of regulation 18B of the Defence Regulations during the Second World War demonstrates. The obligation to produce evidence for a criminal trial is an essential discipline for otherwise unaccountable and inefficient security services in which it is difficult to have great confidence when they failed to identify the dangers pre-11 September. In his study of detention without trial in wartime Britain, Professor Brian Simpson concluded that: "MI5's main achievement in the early part of the war was to secure the detention, at huge cost, of somewhere over 30,000 people, amongst whom there were virtually no spies at all". Simpson describes how, in 1940,

---

[3] (1961) 1 E.H.R.R. 15, 31 (para.28).

a large number of entirely innocent Italians living in London were unjustifiably detained, including the Head Chef of the Cafe Royal and two clowns who had been employed by the Bertram Mills Circus for 15 years.

Hundreds of Jews of German origin were detained, the security services being incapable of appreciating that they had no sympathy with the policies of Adolf Hitler which had caused them to flee to this country.

There is also a more fundamental, pragmatic concern about the Home Secretary's approach. One of the main achievements of this Government has been to introduce the Human Rights Act 1998 which aims to inspire all sections of our community to understand that a harmonious society depends on shared, core values which protect the interests of all. By abandoning those principles as soon as the going gets tough, the Government is sending a very clear message that the values are, in truth, nothing more than a statement of political expediency, to be dumped whenever convenient. If that is the approach adopted by the State, it cannot seriously expect the rest of the community to adopt a different approach. That message will be received not just by people in this country but also by repressive regimes in other parts of the world, who will seize upon the Government's action as justifying a denial of civil rights for their people because of what the Governments of those countries will insist are emergency situations. Parliament and the Government will regret allowing basic human rights to become the first casualty of the war against terrorism. Lord Woolf, the Lord Chief Justice, has pointed out that "in times of national danger people can lose their sense of proportion". Parliament should introduce a note of realism and remind the Home Secretary about principle and legality.

Turning back to your arguments about legality, is it not sometimes possible that the approach being advocated by senior members of the Government is based on intelligence that they have seen, intelligence that could not be released to the general public because doing so might endanger the lives of operatives in the field?

But then, you see, you are down to the question of whether you depart from civil liberties on the basis that politicians are telling you, as they will always tell you, that they know best. We have never in this country, for a hundred years, proceeded on that basis. And let me stress again that this country has traditionally seen it as part of its role to encourage the promotion of human rights in other parts of the world which are not so fortunate as we are. There is a very real danger that repressive regimes throughout the world are pointing to this country; they are already doing it. They are saying that what David Blunkett is doing, what Parliament is approving, is a validation of their approach, of Mugabe's approach and other people's approach; that civil liberties are all very well in their place, but they must bow to concerns about terrorism, about people who want to disrupt society, about information from security services, and they are saying, and will say, how can you, the European Community, how can you, the United States, lecture us on civil liberties? How can you tell us that we must respect civil rights when you, at the first sign of danger in your country, abrogate, cancel, suspend your own commitments? And I find that a very troubling feature of this, and I don't know what the answer is to those countries.

Dwelling on another legal issue that you raise, is it really only through escalation of terrorist activities that the Government could be justified, in terms of the Convention on Human Rights, in suspending its obligations? Might there be any other set of circumstances that might entitle the UK to derogate?

Under Article 15 of the Convention, the Government has to show that there is a public emergency of a very serious nature, in this country, not elsewhere, not in Afghanistan, not in the United States on the 11th of September—here. And they have to show that the measures that they are taking are proportionate. The history in this country is that we have faced very serious terrorist threats. We faced the terrorist threat of the most awful nature with the Brighton bombing. We faced the Canary Wharf bombing. We faced circumstances in which many people were killed in outrages that led to the wrongful conviction of the Birmingham Six. And at none of those times, despite what was going on in this country from terrorists, did the Government think that it was appropriate or necessary to suspend our obligations under the European Convention. I am recognising in principle that it may come to the situation that we all agree that there are exceptional circumstances, but thankfully they are not occurring.

But something nags at me in all of this. Is it not disconcerting that it would only be on the occurrence of certain awful events that the Bill before Parliament could be justified in the minds of many. By then, however, it would be too late. In the field of risk management, we talk about whether or not one wants to put a fence at the top of a metaphorical cliff or an ambulance at the bottom. In many ways what we are wanting here, presumably, is some form of fence at the top of the cliff. The fence that Mr Blunkett is erecting is one with which many people are uncomfortable. But I could imagine, in the aftermath of some kind of major terrorist atrocity in this country, that people would ask why indeed there weren't pre-emptive measures in place. In retrospect, people would be clear we needed pre-emptive measures. Prospectively, people are understandably hesitant.

I've read the debate in the House of Commons. The Home Secretary is not saying that there is evidence that these people who he wishes to detain are otherwise going to be promoting or instigating bombings in this country. That, as I understand it, is not his position. His concern is that we have in this country a number of specific individuals who are responsible for funding the al Qaida network and they are responsible for giving support of various sorts to terrorism abroad, either terrorist incidents that have already occurred in the United States on the 11th of September or they are planning further actions, matters of this sort.

I just cannot see why, if there is such information, it is not right and proper to bring that information before a court. There is no difficulty about having a trial at the Old Bailey of the most secret material. We have had many high profile cases, criminal cases, in the past where people have been convicted on the basis of evidence from the security services that these individuals have been traitors or they have committed other acts of espionage. What happens is that the Old Bailey trial is held either completely or in part in camera, that is, in private—the public are not admitted—but the evidence is heard and the jury determines whether or not these individuals are guilty as charged, and if they are they are sent away for a long time.

Nor can there be the objection that we simply don't have a category of criminal offence that will cater for people who are here plotting or financing terrorism abroad. First of all, there is the Terrorism Act 2000 that contains a large number of such criminal offences. Secondly, no sensible person would dispute that if there are gaps in our criminal law, then it is entirely right, indeed highly desirable, that those gaps be closed so that what these people are accused of doing should be a criminal offence in this country, even if what they are plotting to do is to carry out terrorism abroad. The only question is whether it is proper for the determination of their guilt to be carried out in a criminal trial by a jury with the evidence being tested, or whether it should be done on the say-so of the Home Secretary outside the criminal process.

There is a standard of proof issue, I would imagine, in the sense that a criminal case has to be proven beyond reasonable doubt. What is the standard of proof in the tribunal? Do we know that?

Yes, the standard of proof is a lower standard—it's whether or not there is proper evidence upon which a suspicion can be established. It would either be on a balance of probabilities or something even less than that. But that in itself raises difficulties.

Fundamental issues. What I have in mind is whether one could retain a quasi-criminal trial process but, even though this might offend all manner of legal principles, lower the standard of proof for these difficult terrorist cases. Could this be a possible approach?

It could.

Let me ask a different sort of question. Imagine you were instructed to make the argument, as it were, for the other side. What is the strongest argument you could give?

Well, the strongest argument, the argument that you have given already, is that we are facing risks, we are facing threats. It's essential in relation to a limited number of people who after all are not British citizens; they have no right to be here. They are people who we are only keeping here because we can't remove them to a safe third country, and there is protection in that they can go to the Special Immigration Appeal Commission and the matter will need to be reviewed every six months, and you're an airy-fairy civil libertarian if you suggest to the contrary! Those are the arguments.

We don't normally do this but I know you are interested to hear any thoughts or questions from the floor. Do we have any questions from the audience?

[From a member of the audience] Will the people who are threatened with being locked up have the opportunity to argue that they are at no risk if deported and so opt out, as it were?

Oh certainly, yes. They can say, "I would prefer to go abroad—send me to Saudi Arabia. I'm perfectly happy there may be concerns that I will be tortured here, there or everywhere, but rather than remain in Pentonville, I'd rather go there". Sure— that's entirely an option, and you are right, that's one of the points that the Home Secretary would make. The problem, though, is that in reality we are dealing here with people who will assert, and the Government will accept, that they will be tortured wherever they might be sent abroad to a country that will have them. We are talking about people in respect of whom there are very few countries that will have them, and they will have them because they want to ill-treat them, and the problem arises because the European Court of Human Rights has said that in no circumstances can you remove a person from this country to face torture or ill-treatment abroad. That arose in the Chahal case in 1996, where the Government said, well, this man may be tortured or ill-treated in India, but he is a danger to national security and we are entitled to put our national security above his individual interests and so we are going to remove him. And the European Court in Strasbourg said, no, you can't do that.

[From a member of the audience] So the question being articulated there is that the term "locked up" is, as was said, odious. But I think what is being suggested is perhaps an alternative, that is to say that the liberty of those individuals suspected could be restricted in some other way.

Yes, well, "locked up" I think is accurate because what the Home Secretary is proposing is that they should be detained in a prison. They are not going to be told "you can't leave your village in Somerset", or "you're going to be restricted in your movements". It is possible you are right in principle that the Home Secretary may be persuaded that an appropriate way to proceed is to confine these people to house arrest, the equivalent of what people used to have in South Africa, and you will take away from them their phones and their laptops and everything else so that they can't communicate with anyone else. But that poses difficult questions of surveillance, particularly if, as we are told by the security services, these are sophisticated terrorists who are devious and clever. Therefore what he is proposing is indeed to lock them up. They will go to Pentonville or Parkhurst, no doubt the maximum-security wing because they are so dangerous, and they will be there two or three to a cell, slopping out. So "locked up" I think is accurate.

[From a member of the audience] So the question is what happens if, as you put it, doubtful Governments protest and say people are safe to come back, that allegations about cruelty are lies, and that they will welcome the individuals back and treat them fairly?

That is a standard problem in asylum law. Very often the individual will say, "I want to stay in this country because I'm at risk of being tortured or badly treated if I'm returned to country X", and the Home Secretary will consult with country X and he will be persuaded that there is no danger at all. Under immigration and asylum law, the individual has a right of appeal to a special adjudicator, someone who is experienced in looking at issues of asylum law. There is a judicial determination on the evidence produced on both sides as to whether there is a real risk of persecution, and that may well happen in some of these cases, because the issue of detention only arises if it is established that you cannot remove these people to a safe third country. The Government may try to remove some of them but it is enacting the legislation through Parliament because it believes that there will be at least some people who it cannot remove and who therefore either will remain at liberty in this country or will have to be detained.

You have to have a reasonable basis for suspecting that this individual is involved either in financing terrorism or being involved in terrorism, but the important point, as I've said, is not that you need to prove their involvement, but you have a proper, reasonable basis for suspecting. So you would have to adduce material that would justify your suspicion. The problem, as I've indicated, is that often the material will be based upon confidential source material from the security services and therefore the individual concerned will not be told what it is that is held against him, and therefore he will have considerable difficulty in responding to those allegations; indeed, it would be impossible for him to respond.

[From a member of the audience] Would you hold the same position if the European Convention really allowed us to take account of risks to other jurisdictions and not just our own?

My position would be exactly the same because I don't see any logical or policy reason why this country should at the moment be more of a safe haven for people to conduct these types of awful activities than any other country that subscribes to the European Convention. What I have difficulty understanding is why, whether one looks at the question from the point of view of danger to this country or danger to other countries from the presence of people in this country, the risks and the dangers are so much greater for the United Kingdom than they are for France, Germany, Italy and all of our European partners. That's the difficulty I have.

[From a member of the audience] So, the question suggests that we are facing here risks that we've never had to confront before, and so grave are these risks, or poten- tially these risks, that graver measures than we've ever had to rely upon before should be invoked?

It's obviously a pragmatic assessment how great you think the risks are. We can dis- agree about that. We have also got to assess the difficult question of assessing the risks when we don't know and we are not being given by the politicians the infor- mation, and whether we are prepared to accept their assessment. But there is also a question of principle, isn't there? There's a question of principle that we are battling against terrorism surely precisely because we regard it as absolutely vital to maintain our sort of society. And the difference between us and the terrorists is that we believe in a society that respects individual liberty and pluralism and all those other values that we take for granted. It seems to me that if you readily accept that you are going to abandon, even in part, an important aspect of your individual liberties, you are handing a victory to the terrorists and you are failing to uphold that for which you are at root fighting. That's the position that I adopt, and I'm willing perhaps more than you are to wait a bit longer before we take these dramatic steps in relation to locking up people without trial.

I would need to be persuaded that there really are events occurring in this country that justify the exceptional measures that the Home Secretary is taking. I can see that if tragically there were to be appalling events that echo what happened on the 11th of September in New York and Washington occurring here, then that would put a different perspective on things, but I am wholly unpersuaded that at the moment the risks and the threats are so grave, two months after those awful events, that the Home Secretary and Parliament are justified in departing from the values and the principles that we have hitherto adopted in awful times that have occurred in the past. I gave the example of the bombings in Birmingham in 1974, and the blowing up of the Grand Hotel, the attempt to assassinate the Cabinet in the Grand Hotel in Brighton in the 1980s. You know, I'm not persuaded that times now in this country are any worse than they were then, and I fear that what is being done is being done because it is convenient for the security services not to have the obligation to adduce evidence to establish their case against individuals, to prove their case, and then to lock them up for a long, long period of time.

The reputation of the intelligence and security services is low, and one of the features of September 11th that I think strikes home again and again to most of us, is that the US Government, for example, spends $4 billion a year on intelligence and yet intelligence about these particular events did not seem to have filtered through. The evidence suggests that the intelligence services are not as geared up as we would want, and yet the whole process upon which the new measures are to be based is actually information and intelligence gathered by these very security services.

[From a member of the audience] One of your arguments was that other countries would question our right to lecture them on civil liberties. Is there not another side to that coin in that we have actually been criticised quite heavily by a lot of countries overseas—like Egypt and Saudi Arabia, who are crucial to our coalition—for being too soft and harbouring terrorists or people who are suspected of terrorism in their countries?

I'm not persuaded at all that we should tailor our approach to civil liberties and human rights by reference to the attitude that is adopted in Egypt and other countries not known for their tolerance of civil liberties. It seems to me we should be saying to countries like that it is vital and important that we recognise freedom of speech, individual liberty and autonomy. If you believe that we have in our country individuals who are responsible for promoting or financing terrorism in your country, please supply us with the evidence; and if you supply us with the evidence, we will be absolutely delighted to bring proceedings against these individuals, to have them convicted, to have them imprisoned and detained by reason of that for a very long time.

Many thanks to members of the audience for these questions. Can we talk now, David, about where the Government Bill to detain certain terrorists without trial goes from here? It is going through the House of Lords just now. Have you any sense, from what you have heard, about what is likely to happen in the Lords?

It got through the House of Commons yesterday. It is going to the House of Lords where it is being debated tonight, and the passage through the House of Lords I think will take all of this week and part of next week. The likelihood, and the over-whelming probability, is that the Home Secretary, or rather the Government, will face a much more difficult task in the House of Lords. I think what is likely to occur is that the House of Lords will not adopt the approach that I'm suggesting of throwing out these measures in their entirety. I think what is likely to happen is that the House of Lords will introduce greater judicial controls in relation to the circumstances in which the Home Secretary can exercise these powers; that is to introduce judicial review, which the Home Secretary does not want, to confine the length of time these individuals can be detained before the matter must go back to a judicial authority, perhaps toughen up the standard of proof in relation to these matters, perhaps introduce greater procedural rights so that the individuals are told what the case against them is. All of that I would expect the House of Lords to introduce. It is then for the Home Secretary, who has been fairly uncompromising on this matter so far, to decide whether or not speed is so important that he is prepared to agree with the House of Lords and grant concessions or whether he is prepared to take a bit longer and override, as he's perfectly able to do with the Government's majority in Parliament, the approach of the House of Lords and get the Bill through essentially in its existing form.

Imagine that happens, and so the Bill goes through, as is. What legal recourse, what remedies, would a client (perhaps a client who comes to you) have in this situation? And what's the formal process here?

Well, okay, you are locked up, you are detained, you are told that you are suspected of terrorist activities, and the Government accepts that you cannot be removed to any other country because you would be persecuted there. You would have the right to go to the Special Immigration Appeal Commission, as I mentioned. You wouldn't know the evidence against you. Let's assume you lose. You would then need to ask the Court of Appeal and the House of Lords to rule on whether the criteria in Article 15 of the Convention—that's the one that limits when there can be a suspension of human rights—are satisfied. If you failed in the English courts, you would need to apply in the European Court of Human Rights in Strasbourg. That court is not known for the speed of its deliberations.

The issue for the European Court would be whether or not there really is a public emergency which justified the suspension of your human rights and whether the measures taken are proportionate to that emergency. I think, on current evidence, you would win, but you would not win for some time. When you did win it is quite probable, one hopes, that current concerns would have been dissipated; that the world will again be a happier place. You would receive some compensation, and next time round there would be a precedent that would make it more difficult for the Government to act in this way.

Can I move to what I think is a related issue? The current Home Secretary's attitude to judicial review generally. There is a tension, it seems to me, between the current administration and the Judiciary in relation to judicial intervention in Executive decisions. I perceive that tension as being greater than it has been over the last decade. Could you introduce the notion of judicial review, say a little bit about it for our audience, and then run through your views on this tension?[4]

Judicial review is the legal procedure by which anyone who is the subject of an administrative decision made by Government—for example, an immigration decision or a decision in relation to prison treatment, matters of that sort—it's open to the individual to go to court and to say to the High Court judge that the decision is either illegal, there's no lawful basis for making this decision; or it's procedurally unfair, the person didn't have the right to have their say before the decision was made; or it is irrational or disproportionate. It's not an appeal on the merits of the decision but it is a review of whether the decision falls within the proper scope of the discretion of the decision-maker. Home Secretaries traditionally have not liked the exercise of judicial review. All Home Secretaries lose judicial reviews. They also win a lot of them, but the ones they lose get the publicity, and the ones they lose cause them to be upset.

Could you give us a couple of examples of high profile losses?

High profile judicial reviews that the Government has lost in recent times—it lost a judicial review in relation to the content of the Criminal Injuries Compensation Scheme. It regularly loses immigration and asylum cases.

The Saville Inquiry: that's been subject to judicial review?

Yes, the Saville Inquiry in Northern Ireland relating to Bloody Sunday, a case in the High Court last week relating to whether or not the soldiers who are giving evidence to the Bloody Sunday Inquiry should be required to give their evidence in person in Northern Ireland, and the High Court quashed the decision of the Saville Inquiry that, no, they could give evidence either by video link from England or that the Inquiry would come to England to hear their evidence.

---

[4] Judicial review is also discussed by Lord Saville (Ch.14).

All Home Secretaries, all administrative bodies, don't like losing those cases, and they get cross. This Home Secretary is no different; he has given a number of speeches in which he has described judicial review as a lawyers' charter, and he suggested that lawyers really ought to ask themselves whose side are they on. Now, this is unfortunate because it fails to recognise, again, that individuals are entitled to put their cases and if the decision is unlawful in some respect, then the court should say so. It is, I think, one of the most valuable controls on arbitrary decision making, one of the most valuable means of ensuring high quality in Government decision-making, that those decisions are subject to review by an independent Judiciary. Lord Woolf, Lord Chief Justice, in an interview in the *Sunday Times* about a month ago, made those points more eloquently, and emphasised how vital it is to uphold those principles, particularly in difficult times.

David Pannick, on that note, on behalf of everyone here, many thanks indeed for joining us.

CHAPTER FOUR

The Rt Hon Lord Justice Auld
Lord Justice of Appeal
Chairman of the Criminal Courts Review (1999–2001)

Tuesday February 26, 2002

I am delighted today to welcome Sir Robin Auld to Gresham College. Sir Robin is a Court of Appeal judge. After a distinguished career at the Bar, he was appointed to the High Court in 1987 and to the Court of Appeal in 1995. He was the Senior Presiding Judge for England and Wales from 1995 to 1998. He is perhaps best known today for the work he undertook, from 1999 until 2001, as Chairman of the Criminal Courts Review, a Government initiative—or an initiative launched by the Government— inviting Sir Robin, as he will tell us, to review the criminal courts system.[1]

A very warm welcome to you, Sir Robin, and a warm welcome also to all our guests this evening.

Sir Robin, your report extends to almost 700 pages and contains 328 recommendations, so I think we will need to be selective tonight. I think it would help the audience, in the first instance, if you provided a little bit of context; if we understood how you came to be appointed and, broadly, your terms of reference.[2]

Well, I came to be appointed as a result of a telephone call asking me to go and see the Lord Chancellor. I was a bit anxious because I wasn't quite sure what I had done wrong! When I arrived he pushed a piece of paper under my nose, which were the terms of reference for the Review, as it came to be, and asked me would I prepared to do it. And it was as brief as that. I said that I would like a little time to think about it. I did, and I agreed to do it. It was an extraordinarily broad job, which I don't think I appreciated at the time. It was a review, with the terms of reference into the workings and the procedures of the court at every level. It involved consideration not only of the way in which the courts worked and the jurisdiction they exercised, but also the structure of the criminal justice system as a whole: the relationship of

[1] Lord Justice Auld, *Review of the Criminal Courts of England and Wales* (The Stationery Office, London, October 2001). Also available at *www.criminal-courts-review.org.uk*
[2] The criminal justice system is also discussed by Lord Woolf (Ch.1), Lord Irvine (Ch.6) and Lord Goldsmith (Ch.8).

the courts to the other criminal justice agencies, the funding, the way in which central management, such as there was, managed, and then of course procedure, evidence, use of information technology. It was all to be conducted with quite a broad brush and all to be done within a year.

In the event, you were appointed in December 1999. I suppose you didn't get fully up and running until early 2000; and you reported, finally, in October 2001. I say "finally" because clearly drafts were ready at an earlier stage. It turned out to be a massive exercise.

Yes it did. I think everybody realised at the beginning that a year was optimistic, especially given the inclusion in the terms of reference of the rules of evidence. Once you start looking at other systems, which I tried to do, with some visits abroad talking to judges and jurors from other countries and different jurisdictions, the whole thing clearly became much larger than I think anybody had expected. I tried to keep it within a fairly narrow range as far as I could, subject by subject, but the totality of it was something that required more than one man and more than one year. I say one man—I had 12 consultants, of whom Richard was one, and I had a great deal of help from them, and I had a good secretariat of lawyers and administrators. But a year was too short a time I think, and 18 months was just about enough.

Just for clarification, during the course of your work, a Government policy paper came out. It was entitled "Criminal Justice: The Way Ahead".[3] What was the relationship between your report and that document?

Well, there was no relationship. This paper was on its way to being published towards the end of my year, when I think the Lord Chancellor and the Home Secretary were hoping that they would see my report fairly soon. They had been, as Governments do, gearing up for the report in anticipation of what they thought I was going to say. They didn't know what I was going to say.

I think the timing was just wrong. It looked as if it were going to be a pre-emption of my report, and there were a few exchanges over that. Eventually the Government produced its document, which was called "The Way Ahead" I think. It was quite a detailed document referring to what I was doing and half-alluding to what the Government thought I might be going to recommend, while I at the same time was distancing myself from it as hard and as fast as I could. But I understand the Government's problem over this: they had a programme, I wasn't keeping to it, and they had a momentum, which I imagine was difficult to stop by the time they had got to that stage.

Can we turn to some of the recommendations? There was a remarkable amount of debate about a number of them, but perhaps none more so than in relation to juries and

---

[3] *www.dca.gov.uk*

the jury trial. For many people, the jury is the heart of the justice system of England and Wales. In this context, you really put down a number of challenges. Can you talk through, first of all, your perception of the current state of the jury system and then can we go on and reflect upon your recommendations?[4]

The current state was made raw I think by the two mode of trial Bills that the Government had introduced, which were flawed in all sorts of fairly obvious ways, and so that by the time I was appointed I was asked to look at the system as a whole. Nobody said anything to me about juries, although clearly they were within my terms of reference. I thought that I ought to look at them in the light of the attempts at reform by the Government, and also to look at them afresh from my own point of view. I had spent years addressing juries and had loved it. I think if you were to ask me when I enjoyed my time at the Bar most, it would have been addressing juries. But as a judge, and with the Judicial Studies Board, I had become increasingly conscious that a great many cases were going to juries that, because they lacked seriousness or because of the circumstances of the alleged offence of the offender, simply did not deserve to be there. With that in mind, I began to look at the divide between the jurisdiction of the magistrates' court and the crown court.

This country is pretty well unique in the way in which the bulk of its crime is tried by lay justices. No other country in the world depends on lay justices as we do to try up to 90 per cent, 95 per cent in terms of numbers of offences, of all our criminal work. Other countries have different systems, but they have different dividing lines too between jury trial and lower courts. In Canada, you don't get a jury until the conviction attracts a sentence of five years. In America, it is six months. There are other differences and other divides in other countries. So that's how I came to look at the true need for jury trial in some of the lesser of the middle range cases. I suggested, as you know, an alternative. Not one which would deprive people of the right to trial by jury in the sense of making it an automatic denial, but leaving it to the court to decide in middle ranking cases whether, by reason of the offence itself and/or the circumstances of the offender, it was a case that should be tried by jury, or by the other form of fair trial that we have in this country, by magistrates.

I think if you were to ask me to justify it, as I can and as I did in the report, it seems to me that a court should decide, whatever the criteria are and wherever the line is drawn, the court should decide how a defendant should be tried in accordance with the law, on an objective basis. It should not be for a defendant to choose his court of trial on the subjective basis of where he thinks he has the best chance of acquittal. That's to skew the system it seems to me. That is not everybody's view, I know that. But that's how I ended up after a good deal of agonising.

One point that arises here is a generic one that bears on your entire report but, I think, comes sharply into focus in relation to juries: did you have enough time to undertake detailed empirical research in relation to the criminal justice system? Many have asked, in relation to your findings and recommendations, if we really know what juries do.

---

[4] The jury system is also discussed by Lord Irvine (Ch.6), Lord Bingham (Ch.7), Lord Goldsmith (Ch.8) and David Lock (Ch.9).

Surely if we are going to come to a definitive view about the appropriateness of juries, the argument runs, we should see how effectively they work, we should understand how they come to their decisions, we should evaluate their performance and so forth. Did you feel hampered by the lack of opportunity to undertake detailed investigations?

No, I didn't feel hampered, for two reasons. There are two sorts of research into juries. One is to teach you how the system works and the way in which it presents cases to juries; in the way in which it assists them to make their decisions; how it looks after them and their domestic worries and concerns when they are taken away from their life in this way. The other is to enquire, if you can, how juries reach their verdicts individually. That latter form of research is not permitted here.

It struck me, looking at intrusive research of the latter kind, that there were limits to what you would derive from it. You might, if you could conduct a form of research that would be illuminating. That is to say you would not have self-conscious juries either telling you what they had done afterwards or having you present in their retiring room while they were considering their verdict. If you could get over that practical difficulty, you would learn possibly one of three things. You might learn—you might—that juries are not doing their job properly, they are not reaching verdicts in accordance with the directions of law and the evidence put before them and in accordance with their oath. Or you might find out that they are doing a terrific job. Or, more likely, you might find that juries in their makeup are infinitely variable, that they respond in different ways to different circumstances, the personalities of the judge or the barrister, domestic irritants of their own, and that you can't draw any general conclusions at all.

It seemed to me that the prospect, even if I could conduct it in the time, of learning much from intrusive research of that sort would be minimal and at worst damaging, because you would damage the integrity of verdicts being reached while the research was under way by the simple question mark put over the exercise of doing it.

More interesting was research of the first sort, as to how you can help juries reach their verdicts, and the circumstances and conditions in which they have to work. There is much research on this. Penny Derbyshire, who compiled one of the pieces of work for my study, produced an appendix for my report which chronicles immense research on jury trial all over the world, mostly in common law countries, telling us what they had learned, sometimes decades ago, about reforming the way in which juries can be assisted to reach their verdicts in a more civilised way than is presently the case in this country. I would have been, it seemed to me, reinventing the wheel if I had tried to embark upon some sort of research of that sort. The New Zealand Law Commission, the most recent on the scene, had conducted the most impressive piece of research, with 10 years work behind them, while I was in mid-course of the review. I was able to draw a great deal on that work and other pieces of work like it. So I did not think there would have been much benefit in my trying to set up some research project of my own, given the limited time and resources that I had.

So that we understand this clearly, because I think it was quite widely misunderstood or perhaps not reported accurately: you are saying you remain strongly in favour of trial by jury; you question its appropriateness or proportionality, presumably in certain kinds of cases; you want to maintain it for particular classes of case; you believe whether or not there should be trial by jury is an objective issue to be decided by the court; and, finally, you have some concerns about the extent to which juries themselves are representative and whether or not it is reasonable that people are at times excused (for a variety of reasons) from sitting on a jury. Is my summary right? I think you are often associated with the proposition: "Lord Justice Auld is in favour of abolishing the jury". Is this vastly mistaken?

I think your summary is spot on. I hope one of the principles that underlies my report is the retention and strengthening of lay justice, at both levels, through the jury, in cases appropriate for them in the crown court, and through the wider use of lay magistrates in the summary and, maybe enhanced, summary jurisdiction of the magistrates' courts.

There have been great complaints about the lack of representativeness of the magistrates. A lot has been done recently, but this is a matter of great concern. If you look at the way in which juries are made up at the moment, there is an equal concern about how well they reflect the community. At the moment, the one source for selection of jurors is the electoral rolls. You can see why there is concern if you confine yourself to that source—people who are itinerant, people who have only recently arrived in this country, people who have no homes of their own for one reason or another, simply never get on a jury list. So you have jurors which are not at all representative from that point of view of the ethnic minorities in the country and of the young. And the facility that those who are required to attend jury for getting out of it is notorious. If you are a hard working man, self-employed or employed, it may be difficult for you to get away from your job to do jury service, and employers are increasingly reluctant to permit it. Sometimes in long fraud cases this can be a terrible burden. It can amount to months of absence from your work. And so those who serve on these cases very often are those who, at the other end of the scale, do not reflect the community well in all its various skills.

So juries are terribly unrepresentative. I sought in my review, and the report of it, to try to do something about that, recommending that other sources be put together with the electoral roll to find a true cross section of society for juries: those on the driving licence registrar, those on the telephone directory, and various other public registers of that sort. Nothing new about it—it has been done in the States. Most of the states of the United States and in Australia and Canada have been doing this for years, and as a result are getting a very much more representative jury than we have been able to achieve so far. In addition, cutting out all the various opportunities there are for claiming exemption, excuse and so on, and being tough with people to make sure they do their jury service. What's the result? In the States now, where jury service is far more intrusive than it is here, people regard it as an important civic duty. It is part of their routine. The conditions under which they serve are much more sensitive to the needs of potential juries and jurors than the ones we have in operation here. On the whole, efforts are made to ensure that they don't sit for too long, that they are properly rewarded in terms of appreciation and financially. And so the whole exercise there has become a far more reflective microcosm of society than we have so far achieved here. That's how I sought, principally, to ensure that lay justice through juries, in cases appropriate for them, would be strengthened. I think that is not one of the controversial aspects of my recommendations.

What about categories of people who should be automatically excluded?

Again, not with any originality, I took the view there should be no automatic categories of exclusion, save possibly for those who are mentally ill and also, with some
limit of time, those who have been convicted of offences. I do not see why members
of the church, who are presently exempt, why people involved in the court service,
why police officers, why barristers and solicitors and even judges, should not as a
matter of principle be eligible for jury service and required, unless there is some
good reason in the instant case, to do it. Why should a policeman be regarded as
ineligible because of his job when those of us who have been burgled might find ourselves asked to sit on a jury and might have equally strong feelings about crime from
that particular vantage point? Clearly there would be difficulties with those involved
in the law if they know the counsel or they know the solicitor, or the judge is called
to a court where he sometimes sits. That would be an occasion for seeking excusal
for that reason.

As a matter of principle, I think everybody should be eligible and required to do
jury service. Judges who have done it in other common law jurisdictions have found
it educational and hard work to be on the receiving end of the sort of gibberish that
sometimes judges have to deliver to juries. And the lack of help that they have is
quite educative. Far from being in a position to dominate juries, they have found that
they have sat in there and usually somebody else has been the foreman. They have
enjoyed it and it has helped them in their own jobs when they return to the bench
or to the counsel's role or to the witness box.

*What about jury selection? Anyone who has read John Grisham's novels or seen a
variety of feature films, courtroom dramas from the US, will be familiar with the notion
of teams of psychologists digging up the backgrounds of the various candidates. How
do you feel about this?*

Well, that's a regular mystery, isn't it? I've sat in on a number of these procedures
in the States. It is, I think, something which is just so alien to our culture of a
random selection of jury, that it was not even a starter here, putting aside all
the administrative difficulties that it would involve. But there are also basic faults
in the system it seemed to me. If you are selecting a jury by cross-examination
and investigation, relying on specialists in the field, the end result is not going to be
a random jury. It is going to be a pretty ineffective attempt to get a so-called
balanced jury, and the scope for avoiding jury service through that means
is quite considerable on a case-by-case basis. You have only got to volunteer,
when you are being examined in the witness box, that your house was burgled
last week and, yes, you do have very negative feelings about burglars and you will
be off that panel. Farmers and businessmen will use this as a way—understandable, perhaps—of making sure that they are unacceptable to one or other side in
the process. The practicalities of this, and the colossal expense and delays that
it would involve to a system like ours, which is simply not used to it, seemed to
me too great. So I did not take a lot of time over deciding that we should not try
that here.

And appeals from juries? There are circumstances surely when, in defiance of the facts and the evidence, a jury may come to a perverse decision. Is that a phenomenon we should preserve as a feature of the legal system or do you believe there should be opportunities for appeal from perverse decisions like these?

Well, you already can, as a convicted defendant, appeal to the Court of Appeal against a perverse conviction if you can identify it as being perverse. Sometimes you can do so on the strength of the evidence or weakness of it, as it was deployed in the court below or on the directions of the judge, where the jury have clearly not listened to him or taken notice of directions which should have led to an acquittal. So, to an extent, we already have it in our system.

The real problem, both from the point of view of an appeal against the perverse conviction, and which we have not, a prosecution appeal against a perverse acquittal, is you simply do not know how the jury reached their verdict. This is not a matter which, as I think I said earlier, you can discover by some general piece of intrusive research into the system. You could only discover it if there was some way in which jurors, without too much clutter and palaver, were invited to give more of an indication of how they reached a decision than they do at present. The strength of the jury, traditionally, is the inscrutability of its verdict. The unanimity or near unanimity and the inscrutability gives it an amazing authority in our system. But as Sir Louis Blom-Cooper QC said recently, it is a curiosity in our democratic society today that in the criminal justice system those responsible for determining guilt in the most serious cases, jurors, are the only bodies who are not required to give reasons for their decisions. Magistrates have to give reasons for their decisions; judges do; judges when acting as fact finders do. Only the jury is immune from this requirement, at a time when, increasingly, people regard it as a right, part of the Article VI entitlement, to know why they have been convicted, or a prosecution to know why somebody has been acquitted. So if you introduced a system in appropriate cases by which a jury, through a series of staged questions, could be required, following the judge's directions, to say "yes" or "no", question by question, logically leading at the end either to an acquittal or a conviction—not elaborate questions, maybe just a few, in the right sort of case—you would have a better opportunity than you have now for detecting where verdicts are truly perverse, whether they are verdicts of conviction or verdicts of acquittal. Why, if you can detect, in that or in any other way, a perverse acquittal, should that not be subject to challenge by appeal?

The criminal justice system is not there just to protect the defendant who is facing a charge, it is there to protect society and the victims of society who may have been seriously injured and damaged. They too have an interest in seeing the right result where it can be obtained. So I see a case for perhaps extending the way in which jurors now give their verdicts, in some cases maybe a return to the special verdict, so as to enable the Court of Appeal to exercise an effective review, to know a little more than they do now about how a jury reaches its verdict. That works both ways.

It's a potential can of worms, though, because the skilled lawyer, whose craft is both formulating and destroying arguments, could have a field day when a jury put together its arguments, a jury generally not skilled in structuring and presenting arguments in the way that lawyers do. People would argue that the black box is better: that is to say, there is input and there is output, and one of the features of injecting lay involvement into the criminal justice system is precisely that it is not to generate formal legal arguments; rather, it is to apply non-technical emotions, reactions and perceptions in deciding guilt or innocence.

Jurors are required by their oath—they swear an oath—to return a true verdict according to the evidence. If that is what they are there to do, then they should do it. It is not a question, I think, of asking jurors to justify and reason their decision by argument. They tried that in Spain recently, and it was chaos. Of course juries could not formulate reasons in any sensible way, or most of them could not, in complex cases. What I have in mind is something far simpler. The judge might ask five or six questions, which, as I have said, will call for only an answer "yes" or "no", and the end question of which will lead logically through the sequence to a verdict of either guilty or not guilty. So nothing much is required of the jury more than doing what they are asked to do already, but to articulate stage by stage how they reached the end.

In cases mostly of any consequence, judges now give jurors a series of staged questions. If the answer to question one is yes, members of jury move on to question two, and if the answer to question two is no, then ask yourself the alternative question three. So they are given this exercise to do but you never know how they have done it. Of course the Old Bailey hand, and I'm not so far removed from that, will say well, this could be terrible because you will find that at question three, seven of the jury went one way and five went the other, but when they all ended up at question six they reached the same verdict, and so the verdict would be shown to be unsound. But if that is so—*if* it is so—and it happens on any great scale, then it would show that the system is not working. We would not be receiving truly unanimous verdicts. You can—and many do—say, as you've just done, it is a question of feel, it is the ordinary man bringing to the process his experience of life, a mix of prejudices that can rightly be brought to bear on the merits of the case. Lord Devlin called it a little Parliament. Lord Elwyn Jones used to say that Welsh juries had a great sense of fairness but that they were not dogmatic about it.

So, you have this contrary view of the human factor as against pure legalism. But it seems to me if that is what we want out of the system, we should be honest about it. We should not require juries to give a true verdict according to the evidence. We should not subject them to almost unintelligible directions of law and sometimes interminable summaries of the evidence if that's not what we have in mind. We should require them to give a verdict according to their conscience. That would be nice and neat and convenient, and it would fit many people's views of the jury system, but that is not what we purport to do now.

In two states in the US they have that in their constitution but there is very little recourse to it. So I think if we want an honest system we have got to do something about the way we operate it now with our system of jury trial—change it. If we don't want to do that, then we should make some effort to reach a system by which we can at least determine, in cases that require it, how juries have reached their verdict.

So—definitely keep jury trials, ensure that we have full representation of the community sitting on juries, and offer some, or ensure some, greater transparency, at least in the structure and flow of arguments of the juries. One final issue on juries before we move on: previous convictions. One reads so regularly in the newspapers of cases in which juries are told after coming to a finding of guilty that indeed the accused has committed some very disturbing offences in the past. A very common reaction in the press, and amongst lay people as well, is that surely the matter of previous convictions is relevant information that should be brought before the court. You looked at this?

I have always thought it was a pretty poor prosecution case that needs to rely on a defendant's previous convictions to prove his guilt. If the case is that poor and that weak, it should not be proceeded with. And if it is strong, it should not need it anyway. At the Bar, I both prosecuted and defended for many years. As a prosecutor, I never applied to put in a defendant's character when one of the permitted exceptions arose. As a judge, sitting as a recorder and then as a High Court judge for some 20 years or so, I always exercised my discretion against allowing a defendant's character to be put in evidence when one of the statutory exceptions arose. All my instincts were against it, *are* against it.

But the practicality is a problem. Anybody knows—if they don't already know by the time they first serve on a jury, they'll know by the time of their second trial—that if a defendant's character, a good character, is not mentioned as part of the case, the likelihood is that he has a bad character, and wonder what it is. And so this lurks in the background. It also makes for fragility of jury trials. The mere mention of a previous conviction can unseat weeks of work on a long fraud case and require it to be retried.

It seemed to me, as a result of work done by the Law Commission among others and by Professor John Spencer, who was one of my consultants, that if the reality is that if a man has a bad character all those determining his guilt or innocence are likely to know of it, for the reason I have just given, ought we to try to be a little more low key about the whole thing? On the Continent, it would be a matter of course for a man or a woman's record to be on the dossier as a matter of reference, no great point being made about it unless in the particular circumstances of the case it had a relevance to propensity or similar facts. It is there a matter taken for granted and not used as a weapon by the prosecution in all but the most exceptional circumstances as a means of proof. I am not saying that that is the answer for us, because it seems to me that it is a very difficult question. But I do think that all the concern we have about not knowing a man's previous convictions has to be tested against the reality of what happens in courts every day.

Let me move on to something entirely different. Some of you may have detected in me the trace of a Scottish accent. I am indeed Scottish and a Scots lawyer to boot. There is in Scots Law, although it has never been entirely clear to me why, a source of pride in the "not proven" verdict. Whereas in England you are guilty or innocent, in Scotland there is this intermediate phenomenon referred to as "not proven". Is that something you considered or had views on?

I certainly did. But, like the Runciman Commission, I spent some time in Scotland looking at their system. They are amazing, the Scots! They have juries of 15 and they have majority verdicts of what—eight to seven? Eight to seven is enough for a finding of sureness of guilt in Scotland! How they have got away with it for all this time, I simply do not know. And how, on top of that, they have this intermediate verdict of "not proven" when you could not persuade eight out of 15 that a man was guilty, just strikes me as amazing!

I'm sensing you are not a fan!

They seem to very content with it up there and it obviously works very well for the Scots, but I didn't think it would go down a bomb here.

Well, let's move swiftly on then! Let's turn to the issue of double jeopardy. Again this is a subject that comes up again and again in fiction (which just shows the kinds of books I read and films I watch). Can you explain the double jeopardy rule and then talk us through your thinking on this?

If you have been acquitted once of a crime, the rule is that you should not be in danger of being prosecuted and convicted of it thereafter. If you have been convicted of a crime, you should not be in danger of being prosecuted for it again. Where you have been acquitted—it is really a return to our subject of the perverse decisions—and if there were a mechanism, why should not a prosecutor challenge what is demonstrably a perverse acquittal, a serious murderer who has been acquitted in the teeth of evidence which has subsequently become available, the use of DNA for example? It can be conclusive proof in cases, sometimes against the back-cloth of a defendant boasting about having committed the offence but of being immune from the process of law by reason of his acquittal.

There are victims in the background, there are people whose lives have been ruined. Society is humiliated by this present possibility. Why shouldn't you have the opportunity to re-open an unjust acquittal where the evidence is sufficiently strong to demonstrate, within a reasonable time, that you were unjustly acquitted? It requires a mechanism for dealing with unjust acquittals, perverse acquittals of the sort that we were talking about before.

How strong would the evidence need to be? I can see difficulties in the notion of someone who has been judged innocent nonetheless feeling at any stage that their case might be reopened because of some new evidence.

That is an important point. There would have to be safeguards. One of the safeguards proposed is that the second prosecution should only take place on the authority of the Attorney General or the Director of Public Prosecutions, so that there would be a filter for only the most obvious cases requiring it. Secondly, the evidence would have to be of a very compelling nature even to initiate the prosecution a second time. I have in mind the sort of DNA cases where incontrovertible evidence appears connecting a man to a particular offence for which he has been acquitted.

Just putting aside all our traditions—and I know we must not do too much of that—what justification can there be for a violent killer or a rapist, or a robber, who has wrecked people's lives, not being brought to justice if the evidence demands it? I can't see any.

It seems to me there is none, but it is of course the wide range of innocent people who have been wrongly accused who would understandably not want to have to stand trial again.

Well, they should not be if the system is properly operated, if the filter through the Attorney General or the Director of Public Prosecutions operates in such a way that only evidence of a compelling kind would be relied upon to reprosecute somebody. The Court of Appeal would be a further filter, and the courts would be alive to the need to avoid abuse. If applications were made that the court considered were not strong enough, or if they were made too many years after the event, there would be a jurisdiction to prevent the reprosecution taking place. And it would only be for offences—I think this was what the Law Commission had in mind, certainly I did—of either murder, which was the Law Commission's view, or, as I suggested, cases involving sentences of life imprisonment or maybe sentences of up to 14 years in prison; the most serious cases where it is an affront to society if the defendant has clearly been wrongly acquitted.

Can we move now to yet another topic, that of retrials? They often seem such a dreadful waste of public funds and people's time. If in some way a case is prejudiced, do you feel a retrial is sometimes too radical a mechanism, or do you think there are ways in which one could finesse the situation without having to incur the expense, the delay, the uncertainty and the trauma of starting again?

One of the reasons for retrials in major cases is, as I have said, the fragility of our jury trial procedures. The mere mention of a previous conviction or unfortunate publicity in the middle of a case may bring a trial to a halt. The jury are apparently such delicate souls that they are not given credit for dealing with such information for what it's worth and ignoring it if they consider it irrelevant. Judges are credited with being able to do that. If we were more robust in the way in which we treat jurors, give them credit for some intelligence, approach the rules of evidence not on the basis of admissibility and inadmissibility but on a basis of allowing jurors to give evidence the weight it deserves rather than artificial rules of keeping it from them, you would reduce the scope for many of the retrials, which are such a scourge, not just for the defendant but for the prosecution witnesses and victims and for jurors who may have sat for weeks to no point save a retrial.

Another way round this, which I saw in Canada and in the United States and I know is a feature of many of the other Commonwealth countries, would be to allow defendants to opt for trial by judge alone in these cases where there are difficulties of that sort. In some of those jurisdictions there has been an enormous take-up of this form of procedure.

In Philadelphia, it is called "the slow plea of guilty": if you can't get a decent deal out of a prosecutor there, you can opt for trial by judge alone, on the basis that the judge will take an impartial, objective view, both as to the issue of guilt and the level of sentence required. In states in the Union—it varies from state to state—up to 70 per cent in some cases of serious criminal work is dealt with by defendants opting for trial by judge alone. When I was in Canada, the take-up there was high too— cases of murder, armed robbery, serious sexual offences, defendants opting for trial by judge alone. Why? The trial is quicker; there is no messing around with rules of evidence and juries being asked to go in and out while counsel engage in arid disputes before the judge about admissibility; the judge is not as horrified as a new jury might be about allegations that could affront and prejudice them. The whole process is more clinical and snappier, which, it seems, appeals to defendants in very serious criminal cases in newer common law jurisdictions than ours.

So, a combination of those features—giving juries more credit than they are given at the moment for being able to determine what is worth listening to and what is not, and also to giving defendants the option, if they want, of trial by judge alone—would remove, I think, about 80 to 90 per cent of unnecessary retrials at a stroke.

You mentioned admissibility. Your views on admissibility are, I think, quite radical, moving away from a very strict approach that would be the current approach to a less formal, touchy-feely approach. Could you say a little bit about this? I am reminded in this context of the phenomenon in United States that Professor Alan Dershowitz of Harvard refers to as "testilying".[5] According to this idea, generally well intentioned policemen sometimes fabricate evidence, not in an indiscriminately dishonest way, but when they passionately believe that someone is guilty and yet, because of the strict rules of inadmissibility, they are not able to bring the evidence that would lead to a conviction. They therefore invent the evidence. Clearly, we would not want to justify that, but it does rather provocatively raise a set of important issues about admissibility and about people getting off on what is regarded as a "technicality".

I do not think there is anything radical about my ideas on this. Jeremy Bentham said in the early part of the 19th century that we should move away from rules of evidence and trust juries to give all evidence the weight it deserves. The only test of admissibility should be relevance. A number of distinguished judges and jurors have been saying it for the last 175 years.

Bentham was quite radical himself!

In Scotland they have moved now to a system of greater admissibility, of written statements. Written statements, witness statements, are now admissible in Scotland as evidence for or against the maker, in contradiction or in support of his statement.

---

[5] Alan Dershowitz, *Reasonable Doubts* (Simon & Schuster, New York, 1996).

In many of the Commonwealth states, the same rule obtains. America is a bit different because they have a more extreme view of due process than we do.

We may be getting it as a result of human rights. But the problem you speak of would be less likely here if we moved away from strict rules of inadmissibility and due process as to evidence, and took a much more matter-of-fact approach, similar to that in our daily life, without the rule of hearsay intruding all the time on our conversation and our consideration of matters. There would not be the same need for police officers to fabricate material as admissible evidence to get over inadmissibility of other material if hearsay were admissible and could be treated for what it's worth by intelligent men and women of a better represented jury than is presently possible.

We talked a bit about police. You made recommendations about a re-allocation of responsibility for the progression of a case as between the police and the prosecution. Could you say just a few words about that?

We have developed, rightly, our rules of prosecution disclosure over the years. The prosecution are obliged to draw to the attention of the defence any documents that may be of relevance—may be of assistance—to the defence, although the prosecution do not intend to use them in evidence. The problem of this correct duty of disclosure is that in many cases it involves a vast exercise for the police in searching out and making available to defence solicitors documents, and files of all sorts, which may have some relevance, or may have no relevance at all. It is a particular problem in child abuse cases, where several social security agencies and local authorities can be required to produce lorry loads of documents as to the care of a child or a group of children over a period of years in various care homes. All this has to be read. It has to be read by the prosecutor (the police officer now) and scheduled. Those documents that are thought to be possibly relevant to the case have to be indicated, and then the defence solicitors and counsel have to spend hours reading them too, all at vast expense and time.

Sometimes there are nuggets there, sometimes there are vital documents there and it is a necessary exercise. But police officers, in my view, are not the right people to conduct the initial trawl. It seems to me, whilst they should be responsible for collecting together all the information which they consider might be of relevance, it should be done under the close guidance of a prosecuting solicitor or barrister, somebody from the Crown Prosecution Service.

And certainly when it comes to deciding from the rich harvest of documents that are gathered together what is disclosable, what is material to an issue in the case, that is clearly the job of a lawyer, the prosecutor, not of a police officer, who very often is quite junior, has had little training and does not regard the job as a particularly good career prospect. The Kent Police have become so concerned about this that they have engaged their own solicitors to do what presently the Crown Prosecution Service cannot do for them. And so my view is that the Crown Prosecution Service should be strengthened, and they should take the lead role in deciding what is truly disclosable to the defence, so as to avoid some of the miscarriages and false starts and unnecessary adjournments that we now have in our criminal trial process. It is a real clog on the system.

I suppose one of the Continental answers to the clog is the investigative magistrate. Did you look at that?

I did—the *juge d'instrucion*. But just as we are looking at it, Europe is abandoning him, and in most of the jurisdictions they are moving away from it. Germany abandoned, and I think Italy did. In France, the *juge d'instrucion* is confined to comparatively few cases, and he lacks the seeming impartiality of our courts. He is part investigator, part prosecutor and part judge—he is neither one thing nor the other, and the whole process is interminably slow. There was a collection of papers written about 10 years ago called "The Gradual Convergence" in which a French judge wrote in astonishment that we were considering even looking at the *juge d'instrucion* just when they were getting rid of him.

Two final issues. One—serious fraud; and the other—young defendants. I was conscious when we were discussing juries that we did not mention the use of jury trials in relation to serious fraud trials. You take the view, don't you, that some serious fraud trials are of such complexity that involvement of juries is inappropriate?

Well, some say that however complex the case, usually the issue is one of dishonesty, who better to decide dishonesty than a jury? That, so far as it goes, is fine. But some of the cases now are just *so* complex. Some of them involve highly specialised disciplines—accounting mechanisms, scientific formulae—which are extremely difficult for lawyers and the judges to follow, never mind juries, who are sitting in their jury box without half the aids and written cribs that the professionals have, trying to follow, sometimes for weeks on end, extremely complex evidence. I do not think people realise until they have done it how physically exhausting court work is, particularly for jurors, who are not used to this sustained concentration all day long at work, sometimes with the evidence moving very quickly, and having to pick the bones out of it at every stage, if not at the very end of a three or four month trial. It just seems to me a terrible burden to place on people, to take them away from their normal lives for such an onerous and difficult task, and expect to turn them into forensic experts of varying ability for the duration of the case. So, it seemed to me, as it seemed to Lord Roskill when he reported on these matters over 15 years ago, that it should be open to judges either to try such complex cases themselves or to try them with assessors who are experts in the field.

There are difficulties in assessors because they could be up-to-date or they could be out-of-date. They could have prejudices and hobbyhorses of their own, which could intrude in a much more pronounced way when there is only one of them on each side of the judge. Another option would be for defendants, who also find these trials a great burden, to opt for trial by judge alone. Many of them, I think, would welcome that, because it would quarter the time of trial and ease the burden that they have of presenting their case. Some of them, if they have a good defence, would want to put it to a judge and maybe to assessors, who might be more likely to see its merits than a jury blinded by prejudice might be. These are some of the thoughts that went through my mind. So, in general it seemed to me that we should move towards a situation where, either through option by defendants or giving judges the power to decide for themselves, in very heavy and complex cases, that such cases could be tried without a jury.

And, finally, to youth defendants. You have in mind a different sort of hearing for the young offender?

I've been very affected by the way in which young offenders are subjected to the panoply of the crown court. Even if they are sitting in front of the dock nowadays, as they sometimes are with their parents nearby, the formality of the hearing can be very intimidating to an adult, never mind to a child.

We require, in the magistrates' courts, magistrates to be quite significantly trained before they are allowed to deal with the youth list. We require them to have some knowledge of the law affecting children, and of their special needs and vulnerability in a courtroom setting. Yet in the more serious cases, cases involving murder or maybe drugs of some sort, children are left to the mercy of a jury who may be not only untrained, other than as parents perhaps, in the ways of children who face criminal offences, but also untrained in the way of balancing the evidence on one side or the other.

Why do we require the tribunal in the less serious cases to have some training themselves in the way in which youth justice works in this country, but not a random selection of jury men and women brought into court very often for the first time? It seemed to me that it might be a good idea—as you have already magistrates and stipendiary magistrates with the jurisdiction over young offenders up to the maximum of two years' custody—to give them unlimited jurisdiction, with the judge sitting with them. It could be a district judge, it could be a recorder or a circuit judge; or it could be a High Court judge, depending on the seriousness of the offence. And let that tribunal, in a much more matter-of-fact and informal way, deal both with the issue of guilt in the case of young offenders and with what to do with them if and when they are found guilty. That is why I think there is scope for some improvement there too.

Lord Justice Auld, thank you very much for sharing your ideas about criminal courts and their reform. It has been a great pleasure to have you with us at Gresham College.

CHAPTER FIVE

Michael Bray
Chief Executive Officer, Clifford Chance

Tuesday March 5, 2002

Michael Bray is the Chief Executive Officer of Clifford Chance; and Clifford Chance, on a number of measures, is the largest law firm in the world. During the next hour, Michael and I will be discussing a variety of issues arising in the world of legal practice and in the business of law.

Michael, you run the biggest law firm in the world. I thought we might start off by exploring some of the challenges facing someone in your position. It's often said that managing a partnership is a bit like herding cats. What's it actually like in practice?[1]

Herding cats is a pretty good description, although one of my partners brought to my attention the other day a description that he had seen, which was that running Clifford Chance had been described as rather like trying to keep 650 frogs in a wheelbarrow! Actually it is a bit like that! But I think it is very important in a law firm to keep the partnership ethos. It is trying to find a balance between having a management team that is agile enough to move, keep the direction, keep the firm moving forward—and at the same time giving partners a sense of ownership and involvement.

So that means a great deal of consultation. Do you think there is more consultation in a major law firm than you would find in a large company?

Communication is the most difficult thing in a partnership, and consultation. You cannot consult on every decision but you have to have a mechanism and a structure in place—and I don't think we have found the ideal yet—that enables partners to feel that they know what the issues are; that they have had an opportunity at least to give some input (which may be taken into account or not); and that decisions are taken by the people that they have elected to take decisions. But there

---

[1] The workings of an international law firm are also discussed by Tony Williams (Ch.2).

has to be openness and transparency, and a feeling that partners are somehow involved.

To give a sense of the practical challenges, in how many countries does your firm have offices and, in light of this, how do you run the business organisationally?

At the moment we are in, I think, 23 different jurisdictions. We run the business effectively on a matrix. We have six global practice areas: Corporate and M&A (Mergers and Acquisitions); Finance; Capital Markets; Litigation; Tax; and Real Estate. These are run as global businesses. In each case there is a global practice area leader, and then we have regional management. We have regional managing partners in London, in Europe, in Asia and in the States, and those regional managing partners and practice area leaders are the core management team which forms the Executive, which I chair, and that is supported by some very high level professional management. We have a Director of Finance, a Director of Knowledge and Information, a Director of Human Resources. We also have a Deputy CEO (Chief Executive Officer), and a COO (Chief Operating Officer); one shadows me and the other looks after professional standards and professional ethics. That forms the management group; it is a matrix really.

Walk us through the history of the firm because it is interesting. Although you are now a global giant, around 15 years ago it was very different.

It has changed a great deal. I joined Coward Chance, as it then was, in 1970, straight from university. I'm a banking lawyer. I became a partner in Coward Chance in 1976. I think there were only 18 partners in the firm then, and the total number of lawyers was about 60.

How many partners do you now have?

Today we have got about 650 partners and 3,600 lawyers.

It's grown a bit!

Yes, if we had the same degree of growth in the next 15 years as we have had in the past, we would be something like 20 million lawyers, but I don't think we are going to get there! So in 1976 I became a banking partner, and I have always been a banking partner. I'm a deal junkie really, by training—that's my history! I grew up at a time when the banking markets were taking off in London. There weren't many banking lawyers around in those days. In fact, they hardly existed; we were creating it as we went along. I was dispatched on aeroplanes to go and negotiate loan agreements with foreign Governments and major corporates, and acquired my negotiating skills that way.

We should come back to that later.

The real seminal moment was in 1987 when Coward Chance merged with Clifford Turner. That's when the vision that we have today was really created, because that brought together a banking firm and a corporate firm, but it also brought together two firms who genuinely believed in international expansion, and both firms had started to grow internationally. That merger was created on a vision—an international vision. At the time of that merger, in 1987, there were, immediately after the merger, about 170 partners. So in 1987, 170; today, 650—the growth is still enormous.

During the early years, during the late 80s and 90s, the strategy was very much centred around building the firm as a European-based operation: growing out the practice specifically in Continental Europe, in France, in Germany, Italy, Spain, and really forming a strong European-based practice. At the same time, we were continuing to grow organically in Asia. We were doing that all through the 90s. But we knew that the two very, very large markets which were going to be key to what we were trying to achieve were Germany and the United States. We did have a global vision.

We're going back into the late 80s. We could see the forces of globalisation and we wanted to create a global firm. There were two markets where we would not be able to do that—Germany and the United States. We could not grow organically to the right sort of level in those markets, so we knew that at some point we were going to have to do mergers in both of those countries. We were able to bring those together at the same time. A merger in Germany and a merger in the US. At that point, we took a quantum leap forward. That was the strategy I suppose that I was very much involved in. I led the team that negotiated those mergers, and then, for my sins, got asked to be CEO to implement it afterwards. It's much easier to put a deal together; actually to make it work is more difficult.

So how do you plan for the future? How do you formulate your strategy? You mentioned that the first formulation of the strategy was in the late 1980s. Looking back, have your attempts at formulating strategy borne fruit? Or does the market evolve in ways you can't imagine?

I think we've been good on strategy. How do you formulate strategy? I think you need to have a group of partners who are leading the firm, who just happen to be good strategic thinkers. The firm has always had a level of ambition. We successfully pulled off the merger between Coward Chance and Clifford Turner in 1987— that was transformational. That gave us the courage to do it again. But I think having a strategy is critical particularly with a partnership, where it is difficult to make decisions because you have to build consensus, and you have got to get partners behind something.

If you have a strategy and you think it through, and you think these are the moves we want to make and this is where we want to get to, then it becomes much easier to spot the opportunities. Life is about taking advantage of opportunities at the end of the day, so it is spotting the opportunities and working to create the opportunities that fit the strategy, and then once you see them, if they fit with the strategy and you have agreed the strategy, it is much easier to go to partners and say, look, this is the proposal, this is why we want to do it, this is what we've agreed, so let's do it.

I think because we have always had a vision of being very much an international firm, going back to 1987, we have always had a pretty clear idea of what we thought that meant in terms of where the firm should be and the type of practice it should have, the level at which it should have it, and the type of clients we should be acting for.

And what kind of clients are they?

They are major financial institutions and major corporates. Our strategy, in every place where we practise, is to try to be in the very top tier in all our chosen areas of practice—in the top three—which means that we have to have local credibility, local critical mass. That in turn means we have to have a client base that is fairly carefully shaped. It is shaped by the local market but it is shaped by the global market as well. So we will have local and regional clients who we would want to be market leaders in their particular sectors: a high level client base locally and regionally; and, on top of that, the big global clients: the big global financial institutions and some of the big global corporates.

In 1987, you were moving into the major league, and you were, if you will, the new kid on the block. You continue to have substantial energy and ambition. Do you think you are more aggressive, and perhaps more ambitious, than your competitors because you are the new kid on the block?

We did have a high level of ambition. I think we have a high degree of energy. I suppose there is an element of truth in that, but certainly the 1987 merger catapulted two firms—neither of which was in the top tier then—into a firm which got up into the Magic Circle, as it's called. So yes, I think you're right. There is a lot of energy there, and it's still there today.

The Magic Circle is the (quite contentious) name given to the five leading firms in the City of London. But of the five, you were the first, a couple of years ago, to undertake and bring about a major multi-national merger—simultaneously with Rogers & Wells in the United States and Pünder in Germany. And in so doing, you assembled what is often said to be the first, genuinely integrated, global law firm. Personally, you were a, if not the, key player in engineering the merger. How did you go about it? To what extent is it cloak-and-dagger activity? How secretive does one need to be?

It is almost impossible to conduct anything in a cloak-and-dagger fashion today. The difference between the merger in 1987 and the merger in 2000 is just amazing. When we merged Coward Chance and Clifford Turner, it was conducted in almost absolute secrecy. We started with relatively small groups of partners in each of the two firms being involved and we gradually expanded the groups.

In secret meeting places?

Secret meeting places, yes. We hired a flat in Hay Hill, and all the meetings were held there. It was an extraordinary place! We had full partners' meetings to approve the merger, and still it had not got out into the public domain. I think it was just beginning to break in the wine bars the day we announced it. Now, 13 years later in 2000, it was just impossible to do that.

Clearly, we had a strategy. We have always been pretty open about what our strategy is, and people were always speculating in general terms that there would be a transatlantic merger at some point. I think people focused on Clifford Chance as being likely to be the first firm to do that.

We had talked regularly to a number of law firms in Germany, the States and elsewhere, and of course we now have to live with this hugely active and aggressive legal press which is looking to report on anything that affects the big firms. But almost as soon as we had got into serious discussions with Punders and Rogers & Wells, it hit the press, and we had to cope with that. And it makes it very difficult if you are in a situation where the press find out about something and start to write about it, somehow creating an impression that they know more than a lot of partners know. So you have to manage that process, and that can be very difficult.

And equally, I know it's public knowledge that your firm was also in discussions with Australian firms but a merger in that direction did not come off. It must be hard in such circumstances to manage expectations, both internally and externally. There clearly must be commercial synergy between the firms, and the business case needs to be made, and the merging firms must enjoy roughly similar levels of profitability, I would have thought. But how tricky is it trying to match up the cultures of different firms because, for example, the culture of both US lawyering and German lawyering is quite different from the UK? How do you determine whether or not these firms are likely to be as good a cultural match as you would want? That seems to me to be terribly hard.

You can never be sure. You never find the perfect situation, so you have to look at what the opportunities are, what you've got, then make some decisions and judgments. There are real issues there. I suppose I would start from the proposition that, even before the merger with Rogers & Wells and Punders, Clifford Chance was a firm that was in probably 23 countries. We still had something like 80 lawyers of our own in the US, I think, and a similar number in Germany. These would be American lawyers and German lawyers. So we were a culturally diverse firm.

One of the differences between us and some of our key competitors has been that we embrace cultural diversity more than they do, and we treat it as a strength. So we try to come at it from that position. Having said that, there are real cultural differences, I think, particularly between the Americans and British, and also indeed between the Brits and Germans, although actually, in some ways, they are closer.

Do you sit between the Americans and the Germans?

No, they are very different too. The British/American cultural differences are written about a lot. I remember reading an article, years ago now, by Gerald Ronson about Heron's experiences in the US, famously saying—I think he was one of the first people to say it—that Americans and Brits, they speak the same language and use the same words, but they mean entirely different things. There is a lot of truth in that!

Divided by a common language, as is said?

Yes. And you know, you play tennis and golf and do all those things with them, but actually the drivers of behaviour are very different. Clearly there are differences between the law firm cultures too because there are very few lock-step firms in the US.

Perhaps you could explain the concept of the lock-step.

I'll come back to that.[2] But the Americans are driven by different things, and they have a different approach. They have different drivers of behaviour than we have, and it is quite difficult creating a common culture. If you work at it of course you can do it. It takes two or three years. We still haven't done it fully yet, but certainly you can see real progress. But when you do create it, I think you create something quite strong.

It is two years on now since the merger. How has it gone, looking back on it from a business point of view, in terms of, for example, clients' indication as to whether or not they are satisfied?

From a business point of view, I think it has gone very well. I think it is difficult to think that it could really have gone any better, and certainly the client feedback that we get is very positive. How can I demonstrate that? Well, if you look at the rate of growth of our fees—take the States, for example, during the last calendar year—the year on year growth in the combined revenues of the merged firm for that calendar

---

[2] In the event, the conversation did not return to lock-step. Broadly speaking, under a lock-step model of remunerating partners, the income of partners is determined exclusively by length of service as a partner, independently of performance—the longer a person has been a partner, the more he or she will get paid. For a full discussion of the pros and cons of this model, see David Maister, *Managing the Professional Service Firm* (1993, The Free Press, New York).

year compared to the aggregate of the revenues of Rogers & Wells plus Clifford Chance in the US, the rate of increase is something like 32 or 33 per cent in the US, whereas the average rate of growth of the top 15 law firms in the US was about 14 per cent. That is merger synergies coming through.

Then when you drill down beneath that and you look at particular clients, I think we've been quite successful—I would say very successful—in penetrating in the US, much more deeply, some of the key clients of the combined firms. And then again, when you look at specific deals and the profile of transactions and so forth, you can see the quality of the business is rising as well. So all of that is very positive, and the merger has helped—the stature of the firm has grown.

Do you still have different names in the jurisdictions?

We do at the moment. We still use the Pünder name in Germany and parts of Central/Eastern European, and we use Rogers & Wells in the US. I suspect that will go, fairly soon. We haven't really—although the brand has, if you like—benefited hugely from the merger. What I mean is the stature of the firm has increased, but we have not actually focused on the brand building yet because there have been too many other things to do in just integrating the firms. But now the integration issues are behind us, we are focusing very much more outwardly and the brand is impor-tant. I think as part of the brand building, we will go for the single name.

But if, internally, partners in Germany and US felt comfortable about trading under one name—let's say the Clifford Chance—then that may be one sign of full cultural integration.

Yes, I think so. It's quite interesting, because we had a discussion about this at our Board last week. I think it's not seen as a cultural issue at all. When it makes busi-ness sense to do it, we will do it, and I think people are comfortable that we are more or less there.

I think you hinted earlier that maybe, culturally, it's not quite where you want it.

Well, I think we are making a lot of progress culturally. We are learning huge amounts. The problem with any merger is that, when you are bringing together different firms from different cultures and people—and law is a people profession—you have got to face up to the issues and there are things that need to change. You have to drive through some of those things fairly early on because you have a window of opportunity. There is the euphoria of getting the merger done, and there is the market thrust that comes from it. But then you actually have to make it work, so people have got to work together and you have to drive some changes through. If you do it too fast, then you suffer; but if you don't do it fast enough, then you lose the opportunity.

Of course that involves issues which affect the way people run their daily lives, and most people will tell you that change is great, we should have as much of it as we can, but don't touch me! So there are bound to be, during the early stages of any merger, huge people issues, and you just have to face them. But those I think we got through probably about the summer of last year, and quite successfully I think.

When you merge law firms, it's different from merging, say, investment banks. You are not trying to cut people, or cut costs. You have merged because you want more lawyers. It's a question of getting people to work together in effective teams, effectively round their clients, and getting them to change the way they work and understanding what it means to work in cross-border scenes, so it's that sort of change. There are some people who will go and who won't make the grade in a merger, but it is not so much about people losing their jobs.

If you had your time again, is there anything that you might do differently?

Oh yes, I think so. What would I do differently? I don't think we got communication right. I don't think we spent enough time thinking about how to communicate effectively.

Internally, within the firm?

Internally. And I think that it is a very, very difficult issue. I don't know what the answer to it is yet, but I'm sure we should have had more time thinking about that earlier on. I think that some issues we possibly didn't hit quickly enough, but by and large I think we got most of that right. I think communication is the biggest issue that I would say we didn't quite get right.

Let's move on to something different. For non-lawyers certainly, but actually for many lawyers as well, the world of a banking lawyer is a mysterious one. Can you give us a flavour of this arcane activity into which most people have little insight? You have been a banking lawyer for many years, working on huge deals. Talk us through what you do as a banking lawyer in the City.

Well, in a sense, it was more interesting when it started back in the 70s than it is now. The banking markets grew up in the 70s, as I said, when the petro-dollars came flooding in to London. Something like 200 banks established themselves in London in the space of three or four years. They were there principally to recycle petro-dollars, so it was very much a question of lending those monies to foreign Governments and major corporates.

Those were quite exciting days because it was very much a question of just flying all over the world to negotiate transactions. For a young lawyer, it is really an amazing way of building one's negotiating skills. I can remember, for example, getting on a plane to fly to Saudi Arabia to negotiate huge loans that the banks were making to joint ventures between Saudi Arabian basic industries and the major oil companies. These were all joint ventures to develop petrochemical plants in Saudi Arabia. That was just an amazing experience.

You were acting for the banks?

I would act for the banks and would be negotiating with a company that was effecting a joint venture. This was back in the 80s, much less sophisticated than now.

It would be a joint venture between, say, the Saudis and a major US oil company. There would be two Chief Executive Officers and two Chief Financial Officers. You knew, when you were negotiating, that there were likely to be more disagreements between the joint venture partners as to how they wanted to go about this than there would be normally between the banks and the borrower. So that is a great way to learn about cultural differences and how to empathise with different cultures and how to negotiate.

Those were pioneering days. Life of course has become much more complicated now. I think the most interesting experience I had in those days was acting for all the banks who rescheduled the debt for Rupert Murdoch's News Corp. You may remember, he got himself into terrible difficulties in 1989—cash flow difficulties in the last recession—because of the high interest rates. Restructuring this was a huge complex task because there were so many lenders involved and different kinds of debt to be managed.

Explain a little more about the restructuring of debt?

The problem, when you have a large company like News Corp, is that it will have entered into any number of lending agreements with different consortiums—the banks, insurance companies, anybody who will fund. Some will generally fund the company; others will fund specific projects.

And this includes all the subsidiaries?

All the subsidiaries, the whole thing. If you had put a map of News Corp's organisation on the wall of Gresham College, it would fill it. There were hundreds of subsidiaries, and they were all interrelated. And of course, many of them would be cross-guaranteed, though not all of them. But if there is a default under one of these loans that could arise because a payment of interest is missed or because a repayment of principal is missed or just because a financial covenant is breached, then the domino effect of that is to trigger defaults under every one of these other agreements.

A borrower can quickly find itself facing the abyss, because if all of those loans have defaulted you are suddenly in a position where all your bankers are able to say they want their money back, and that basically leaves you insolvent. In that particular case, of course, we never got that far because the bankers recognised that the business underneath it was a very good, sound, solid business. It was a cash flow issue. But it then becomes a huge logistical nightmare to negotiate with different groups of banks who have different interests, lending to different parts of the group, to try and get everybody to buy in to a consensual restructuring.

So you have to understand the entire structure of the company. You have to understand all the debts that each of the elements have, and the interrelationships between all the debts and all the companies. In some sense, you have to reconfigure the whole lot?

Yes—you have to understand the business. You have to understand where the risks are, absolutely. For something like that I would say Clifford Chance would have had a team of probably around 50 or 60 lawyers working on different aspects around the globe.

And you were working for the lenders all the time?

We were working effectively for the lenders, yes.

And how long would that take?

Four or five months, in that case, because there is obviously a need to get it done quickly to get rid of the uncertainty that the company is faced with.

You mentioned another similar case.

There was another one—a similar thing really. Many of you might have heard of Guinness Peat Aviation, which was a very successful aircraft leasing company in the 90s. It had a huge fleet of aircraft and was the biggest leasing company. It got itself into difficulties where, again, it was faced with having to negotiate, or renegotiate, huge amounts of loans with large numbers of lenders. They are interesting situations for the very reason you mentioned: in order to do it, you have really got to understand the business—the risks and the whole situation—in order to be able to persuade people.

Does any single person have his or her head around the whole thing or is it real teamwork?

It's teamwork. It *has* to be teamwork—that's the only way. That's where I first learnt what working in a team, *really* working in a team, means; when the team is very much more than the sum of the individual people. Because the task that you are facing is so enormous and the time in which you have got to get it done is so short that it is only via real teamwork and team leadership that that can happen.

70

So how hard do lawyers work on these major matters?

When you are doing it, you can be working anything between 18 and 20 hours a day, week after week, until it gets done. You just have to keep at it.

One of the issues that is often raised in relation to City lawyers is the amount that they earn. How do you feel about that? To some extent, you have answered that by mentioning how hard they work.

I've never felt guilty about that. I think we are privileged. We have a very interesting profession, an interesting job, and we earn significant amounts of money. But remember that partners in a firm also own the firm. It is combining equity and salary as well. A law firm is a business and it is owned by the partners so, in a sense, what they are taking out of it is their equity interest and their salary. It is a significant amount of money, but at the same time I think people, partners and associates in law firms actually work very hard.

What about the liability side? Your exposure: I'm not sure that's well understood. How do you manage that? Clifford Chance now has "LLP" after it. It might be useful to explain what that means and the extent to which you can actually limit your liability.

Traditionally, and certainly under English law (and this has changed just recently because of the introduction of the Limited Liability Partnerships Act 2000) partnerships like ours could only operate as general partnerships. That means that partners are fully liable—individually and jointly and severally—for all the liabilities of the firm, and that has always been the position under English law until recently. So that one has always been faced with the position that partners in law firms, as with accounting firms, have everything—all their assets—on the line for the claims against the firm. I think this is an issue that has concerned partners in accounting firms and law firms for some considerable time.

Obviously we carry very significant professional indemnity insurance to cover ourselves against claims, at very significant cost. But these days, we have seen situations like Enron. Everybody is worried about the possibility of a wipe-out claim.

America introduced the concept of Limited Liability Partnerships some time ago now. Clifford Chance took advantage of the merger to revert into what was effectively the structure of Rogers & Wells. We set up an umbrella US limited liability partnership, and so we do operate as a Limited Liability Partnership. That raises questions and complications. For example, what does it mean and how is it recognised in different parts of the world?

Certainly the concept is to limit the liability of partners to the assets of the firm, bolstered of course by the very substantial levels of PI cover that we carry. I suppose that gives partners some reassurance in a sense: they feel that their assets are not entirely on the line, although, of course, the reputation of the firm certainly is.

I suppose that if you feel as a partner you are investing in the business, and you have your capital within the business (and that will be an extensive amount for many equity partners), then there must always be a sense that there is more than the business at stake. Your exposure can extend to your house and your car and your entire family's livelihood. And you might be exposed not by your own activities but by those of one of your partners, a person you may have never met.

It worries a lot of partners, and not others. People react in different ways. Some people really worry, I think very much, about the uncertainty that that it creates in their lives, and therefore to some partners it's really a concern. To others, less so. I don't think I have ever, in my whole time practising as a partner, lost a moment's sleep worrying about full liability. But a lot of partners seem to. To me, it's not right—they should not have to worry about that. We are a business and, yes, we are a profession. But, you know, the firm itself has very significant assets and it has huge amounts of PI cover. So I think in today's world, where we have got globalisation to the point that very, very significant wipe-out claims can theoretically arise, I think it is a legitimate concern.

How do you select your partners? Clearly it is vital that people who are partners are of the right quality. Partners make all sorts of decisions and sign off advice in the name of the firm and together you share liability for the service you dispense. Clearly in a small firm, where lawyers are all in one office, they all know one another and are well placed to judge how good an up and coming young person is, and whether he or she is doing good work. How does one do that across 23 offices? Bear in mind, for example, the cultural differences you mentioned. How is it, for example, that in London you can evaluate the performance of an assistant lawyer in Hungary?

First of all, I think there is a general recognition that the most important decision partners take in the firm in any year is the appointment of new partners. We have invested huge amounts of money in the system that we set up to do that. I would hate to have to go through the process today, I tell you!

We have what we call a New Partner Selection Group, which is a group of around six partners who are responsible for overseeing and vetting the new partner selection process. That is chaired by a very senior partner within the firm. It has been Leon Boshoff, and it is just changing to John East, who is a senior partner who is respected throughout the firm. That group is responsible for vetting and passing on the new partners.

The actual process to become a new partner takes almost a year; there are eight months from the date the nominations go in until the people are elected. Nominations for partners come through the global practice areas and have to be approved by the global practice area leaders (and, as I said, there are six global practice areas). There is a process within each practice area for putting forward only the very, very best people. When they are nominated they then have to go through an interview process with the New Partner Selection Group, and they have to sit a pretty tough course as well, so their skills are tested in that way.

And of course in order to get to be nominated in the first place, they will have to perform to a very high level during the six years they were associates in the firm. In addition, they should have experienced a combination of mentoring, regular appraisals within their groups and participation in firm training schemes. So we have quite a sophisticated internal training system.

Everybody gets a "passport", or profile, when they come into the firm, which tracks their progress and development throughout and sets various goals and training that they have to go through. It is a combination of classroom training, legal and non-legal skills training, things like leadership training, self-awareness, business awareness and project management skills as well. They have to go through all of that, and they have to go through appraisals within their groups.

The system has a way of throwing up the very best people, who then get put into the process I described for selecting, ultimately, the partners. It is a pretty tough process to get through.

Massively competitive?

Yes, very competitive, and I think the quality is getting better; the bar on the hurdle is being raised all the time.

Is it "up or out"? Alternatively, in some organisations, if you don't make partner, there is another level, to which career executive managers or principals are assigned. But many law firms seem to lay out an "up or out" career path.

No, we are more flexible than that. It is not a strict up or out. Partners are selected no earlier than after they have been qualified associates for six to seven years. But quite a lot of people are promoted after that: eight or nine, even 10 years.

So what is the average age of a new partner?

Well, it would be about 35.

And retirement age?

Well, it is very interesting; it's cultural. The retirement age now in the firm has gone up to 65, but partners have to go through a gateway process at 60, or some date after their 60th birthday.

This is to check what they are doing, what their role is, what their contribution is—and how these things should be—and on what basis they should stay after 60: whether as a full partner, whether on some sort of reduced equity interest, or whatever, and what the role is. Now, the average age for retirement in London is 52, which may surprise some people. It's not unusual though for City law firms—people get burnt out very quickly. And I would say that at Clifford Chance in London there is only a handful of partners who are over the age of 55. I could probably count them on one hand.

And what about in the US?

I think it will change a bit in the UK. It's true in all City law firms that having a bit more grey hair around and keeping some people a little bit longer would be good for the firms, but that's where it is today. In the US, people work much longer; they want to go on until they are 70 if they can. And, of course, some of them do. Litigation, for example, is so important in the States. Our practice in the States is about 50 per cent litigation, which is not unusual—all of the top firms have that, because it's such a litigious society.

Litigators get better as they get older, and so you see people coming into the best part of their career in the States as a big case litigator when they are 60, and they are still growing when they're 65. So these guys don't want to leave until they are around 70. The same is true in Continental Europe. If you look at Italy, Germany and France, people want to carry on for much longer.

Why is it so different in London? I think there are three or four reasons. One is that people do get burned out. The City is driven by transactions. It is a very, very transactional driven practice; it is deals, deals, deals. People become partners at the age of 32, they are doing deals; at the age of 40, they are a partner, they are doing deals; at the age of 50, they will still be doing deals. The deals may get bigger and have a higher profile, but they are doing deals. Eventually they are going to fall off the ladder for one reason or another. So it's getting burnt out. I think, somehow, in England there is a cultural difference.

In England we are able to divide our business life and our personal life much more successfully than in some countries. So your position in the community, your own community, does not necessarily depend on what role you have, what business position you are holding, and therefore you can say, "Okay, well I'm 50—forget the law, forget banking", whatever, and go and do something completely different. In the States, and on the Continent in Europe, it's very difficult to do that—your business life and your personal life are so closely tied up, it's much more difficult for people to make that break.

I would like to touch now on something entirely different, something that you hinted at earlier when you were talking about training. I know that you have personally been very interested in the notion of having your own Academy, which is quite a novel development for a law firm.

I am fairly evangelical on this. At Clifford Chance, our vision, or our promise, is to deliver to our clients something that is differentiated from what they can get from other law firms. It's an integrated global product where they will get the benefit of the team which is working across jurisdictions and across different legal systems, which will be solution oriented, commercially minded, filter the law, and deliver to the client ultimately a product which is what the client wants, something which is going to really help them; a solution oriented work product.

To do that, I think we need a revolution, almost, in terms of some of the training we do. Obviously we need legal skills training, so people have to be trained to be the very best lawyers. We get very, very high quality people. They are very good lawyers—that's taken as a given. In a sense, it's a lot of the non-legal skills that need to be taught, because I don't think law firms are really good in providing new challenges for people. If you work in a bank or a company or a firm of consultants, they are good at moving people around, giving them new career challenges every few years, and that helps to develop people—to bring the people out of themselves, develop them, and develop their skills.

In law firms we are not really able to do that in the same way. We are very transactionally driven and, as I said, people do deals, they do deals, they do deals. So we need to find ways of really developing their other skills—things like leadership skills, project management skills, self-awareness, business awareness, all of those things. And we ought to be able to do it, because the one thing that comes from a big firm and the mergers is scale and the resources to invest. If you were to compare what law firms invest in training, say compared to the big accounting firms or the big consultancy firms, it's pretty small. But, being a big firm, we do have the ability to invest in that, and that is what we are doing. So we have set up what we call the Academy. It's physical and virtual—most of it is located in Amsterdam, but it is virtual as well, in the sense that a lot of it is delivered through technology; and it's coupled to what I call the profile, which is something like a passport, that everybody gets when they come into the firm and which is intended to track their personal development as they go through the firm. We need to continue to invest very heavily in it, and bring in the very best people to teach in it, using, to some extent, partners as well to teach, retired partners and so on. We can do much more in terms of putting a good faculty in place.

You weren't tempted by the country chateau or castle? I've spoken at conferences of a couple of banks who have phenomenal buildings of that sort tucked away in Continental European hilltops.

I think my partners wouldn't let me spend the money! We do have a building in Amsterdam. It was a school. It's a big, impressive building, right in the centre of Amsterdam. There's a lot of classroom space there that we've taken on, and we use that for the Academy.

This is really quite different. You are differentiating yourself, not just from the point of view of clients, but actually trying to attract the best staff. Do you find that potential recruits are impressed and interested?

Yes, definitely. It's difficult to track. We ask and we get feedback. Undoubtedly one of the benefits from the merger in 2000 has been that we see the quality of the young people coming into the firm has gone up exponentially. They are attracted by the Academy and they are attracted by the firm: the firm's ambition and its pioneering spirit. There are all sorts of reasons that they come. But the quality of the people coming is definitely very, very high.

Final big question: in London, you are moving to Canary Wharf. This is a huge move because your current building is massive and dramatic. What is the thinking behind Canary Wharf? Are clients pulling you there?

We need a very big building. We moved into our current building, 200 Aldersgate, in 1992. It's too small for us now. Indeed, we already have other space in the City. So we needed urgently last year to find new premises. There are very few options in the City for buildings that are big enough to house us. We did look at all the City options. Canary Wharf we thought was attractive because the quality of the build is very, very high. A lot of our clients are there of course. It seemed a very good thing to do. I suppose, in a sense, it's in keeping with our pioneering character to be the first of the City firms to move outside the City. We thought we were going to have quite a difficult task on the communication side of persuading people of the benefits of going there, but actually it wasn't so difficult.

People being clients or staff?

Staff. It means increasing the average journey time for lawyers, and all staff within the firm, quite a bit. People are concerned about the level of infrastructure out there, the travel infrastructure at the moment, and how difficult it is to get there. But actually it wasn't difficult. We gave a series of presentations, and people have been down there to look at it. I think there's quite a high level of excitement now about getting down there.

So when are you moving in?

August next year.

How do you allocate rooms? I ask this because I had a crowd of friends in a major New York firm who were moving into a dramatic new building and apparently the most controversial issue was the allocation of the rooms, and in particular who were given the corner offices! How do you do it?

It's culturally different here in the UK. In any New York law firm, the room that you occupy is very, very important.

76

It's like in John Grisham's novels then!

It is exactly like that! And then when you become a partner, you want a corner room; and then as you become a more senior partner, you want a bigger corner. It doesn't exist in London at all, that feeling.

Do you think the feeling doesn't exist, or that the feeling is not expressed?

I think both.

You think people really don't mind?

No, I think not, because partners, culturally, have always been used to sharing their rooms with young lawyers, because we see it very much, and have always seen it, as a way of how you really teach and bring people on. People learn by just sitting and watching what other people do, so having young lawyers in your room is, I think, absolutely critical to actually bringing them on. And Clifford Chance, certainly ever since I've been a partner, has always done that. I think the other City law firms have done that. Whereas it's completely the opposite in the States. Even when you're a young associate, what you want, and what you dream of, is to have your own room.

You come in initially in a New York firm and you're usually sitting with another associate, two in a room, senior and a junior, and you just can't wait for the day when you get out of that and get into your own room, and then you never want to share again in life with anybody. So it is different. We are trying to change that in the States. Actually, we will have to move our offices in the States in the not too distant future because we will out-grow where we are at the moment. We're in the Met Life Building, the old Pan Am building, but we're going to have to move at some point. When we do, we will try to change that culture, but it will be difficult.

Are you going for cubicles and open plan, or are you still running with separate offices in Canary Wharf?

We're staying with offices, but they're all built to a very high quality. The offices are all good offices, and they're all very similar, so there will be no fighting over that at all. We'll have too much space initially when we move in and we will position the empty space fairly strategically down through all the floors. I just don't think it will be an issue. The practice areas in London will be allocated a certain amount of space each and then they will work out their plans within that, but I would be very surprised if it was a difficult or contentious issue. It wasn't when we moved into 200 Aldersgate.

Michael Bray, thank you.

CHAPTER SIX

The Rt Hon The Lord Irvine of Lairg
The Lord Chancellor of Great Britain

Wednesday April 10, 2002

Good evening. This is the final in this year's series of six interviews with senior lawyers and judges who, in my view, are shaping the future of the legal profession and the justice system in this country. I am extremely pleased to welcome to Gresham College, and to welcome on your behalf, the Lord Chancellor. Lord Irvine will be known to most of you in a variety of capacities but I should give some very quick biographical details nonetheless. He was educated in Glasgow and later in Cambridge, enjoyed an extremely successful career as a commercial barrister and, in parallel, was heavily involved with Labour politics. He was ennobled in 1987, in 1992 became the Shadow Lord Chancellor and then, in 1997, the Lord High Chancellor of Great Britain.

It is a pleasure to have you with us, Lord Irvine. I very much look forward to the next hour or so of discussion. I thought we might start on a fairly general basis. When I think of the Lord Chancellor's Department and the changes it underwent during the 1990s, in many ways I wonder if the phrase that best captures the approach you took was "the modernisation of justice". You and your department talked a lot about modernising justice and indeed that was the title of one of your White Papers. But let's look behind this surface use of language. What for you is the key purpose of your role as Lord Chancellor and of your department?

We are reforming the three major pillars of the justice system. The three main pillars are civil justice, criminal justice and administrative justice. The reform of civil justice is well under way and I believe that you could pronounce it, at least on an interim basis, a success.

With criminal justice, we are about to embark on a major programme of reform. I am not going to be able to be as communicative with you tonight as I would have liked to have been on that subject, although I dare say we can explore the parameters of the issues. That's because we will be producing a White Paper, based in part on Lord Justice Auld's report,[1] but across a much broader range in the criminal

---

[1] Lord Justice Auld, *Review of the Criminal Courts of England and Wales* (The Stationery Office, London, October 2001). Also available at *www.criminal-courts-review.org.uk*

justice system, and probably that won't be until July and final decisions have not been taken.

The other great pillar is administrative justice. There, there has been a report by Sir Andrew Leggatt,[2] which I think is potentially of very, very great significance to bringing together under one roof the administrative tribunals up and down the country that have so long been overlooked, not seen in the round, not looked at collectively since 1957 by that great public servant Oliver Franks. Interestingly, in that area there are more decisions taken by tribunals up and down the country every year, affecting people's lives, than in the whole of the civil courts system put together. So in our domestic agenda, that is the important area.

Also of course, I dare say you will want to touch with me on the constitutional responsibilities of the Lord Chancellor's Department; a broad range, particularly of course, human rights and freedom of information.

So, we have civil law, criminal law and administrative justice. I think it would be good if we dealt with each in turn. You mentioned affecting the lives of people themselves. This is one of your common themes, isn't it, and maybe this constitutes one of the key challenges you have set yourself in trying to reform the justice system?

Yes, you are to reform the justice system not for the benefit of the judges, not for the benefit of the court service, not for the benefit, dare I even say it, of the civil servants—we are all servants, the judges, the courts themselves—and the whole focus is on making access to justice for people more convenient, making the procedures swifter, more user friendly, less costly.

Let's deal with each in turn, if we might, starting with civil justice. In a sense, being appointed in 1997, because there was already so much activity in the civil justice arena, it must have been a little like walking in during the middle of a play. In 1995 and 1996, Lord Woolf had produced his Access to Justice Inquiry reports (and some months ago he sat in the very chair you are sitting in this evening and we talked about his proposed reforms). At the same time, there had been a fairly fundamental review of legal aid. I know you were conscious that these two initiatives should be aligned: on the one hand, Lord Woolf was anxious that there should be greater access to justice to far more people in society; on the other hand, the provision of funding for this access had to be practicable and sensible. So, you called in Sir Peter Middleton to undertake a review of these initiatives. Can you explain some of the thinking behind this, and the outcome?[3]

I personally was strongly sympathetic to Lord Woolf's views and his report and have given him the credit that he rightfully deserves for these. But also it has to be

---

[2] Sir Andrew Leggatt, *Tribunals for Users: One System, One Service, Report of the Review of Tribunals* (The Stationery Office, London, March 2001). Also available at *www.tribunals-review.org.uk*
[3] The civil reforms are also discussed by Lord Woolf (Ch.1).

remembered that Lord Woolf's report at that time was subject to a good deal of criticism from a range of quarters. I'm not saying majority criticism, but significant minority criticism, and we took the view, as an incoming Government, that in fairly short order we ought to conduct a review under a distinguished public servant. We asked Sir Peter Middleton, former Permanent Secretary, to review it for us. He did it very efficiently in a very short period of time, I think between May and October 1997 but you're straining my memory, and then we gave it the thumbs up.

We had a very, very difficult decision in fact to make in the early days, which was whether we were to implement new rules to simplify civil procedure, which would have profited hugely if we had had an advanced system of IT to back them up; and that I know is a subject, Richard, which is dear to your heart. We took a bit of a chance in going ahead. There were two really conflicting schools of thought in the Judiciary. I sided with Lord Woolf's that we give it a go and get on with it, with the old paper-based system. Others thought that it was too dangerous a venture without the IT. It would be a much superior venture with the IT, but we did take an informed chance and I believe it paid off. That was a critical decision.

I also think that was the right decision. I always say that if you delay a major initiative because you are waiting for IT, then you run the risk of waiting for a long time. But in due course, when the right technology is introduced, I think you will reap the benefits.

Just looking at the civil reforms themselves, what, for you, are the important underpinning principles? What's this all about? Leaving aside the associated catchphrases, because some of these are in danger of becoming clichés (such as "access to justice"), what in your heart is the civil reform process all about?

The civil reform process is obviously to bear down on delay, excessive legalism and excessive cost. That in three distinct points is ultimately what it is all about. As you know, as part of these reforms we took a decision that we were going to expand the small claims jurisdiction from £1,000 to £5,000; that the fast track jurisdiction was to go up to £15,000; the fast track jurisdiction was to have fixed time limits.

All in all, I would say that that has worked very well. The procedures have been enormously speeded up. In fact, I was at the District Judges' Annual Dinner very, very recently, and we have to remember, although we focus a great deal of attention on the more publicised big cases that take place in the High Court, 95 per cent of civil cases essentially begin and end in the district court. That is the court which makes most impact upon people's lives in relation to the overwhelming majority of disputes, and the President of the District Judges' Association, Judge Harrison, was telling me, without being complacent, that basically these reforms have succeeded very, very substantially and have transformed litigation in terms of speed and in terms of the promotion of settlements.

What about access, though? I think if there is an enduring concern, leaving aside the concerns that the legal profession might have, it is that people who are not eligible for some kind of financial support from the State simply cannot afford to assert their rights. I know you will argue against this, but it would be good to chat it through.

Well, I certainly agree that if we had a bottomless public purse, that would be a good thing. And I also agree that generally in the district court lawyers are not there. District judges though are trained to be hands-on and they see it as their duty to assist both parties. In the same way as, for example, in the employment tribunals, where there is no legal aid, which deals with a massive amount of work in the specialist spheres of employment—unfair dismissal, redundancy payments, areas that are very, very important—there is no legal aid, but the culture is that the legally qualified chairman is expected to assist the parties.

A related issue, it might be said, is the American experience. Some people assert that because, in various ways, it is easier there to engage lawyers and to go to law, then this apparently greater access to justice of itself gives rise to a more litigious society. What is your response to that?

Well, there is a tension between these two things and, as usual, it depends what initial standpoint you come from. I think most people who regard themselves as of liberal persuasion believe that the courts are part of the central fabric of the State; that people must be entitled to vindicate their rights in the courts, otherwise they're being denied a central attribute of their citizenship. That is the position from which I come.

On the other hand, there are those who think that people are too ready to bring their petty disputes to court, are too ready to sue and produce a litigious society. I am not in fact one of these. I know, for example in relation, say, to the National Health Service, that there is enormous concern in some quarters that clinical negligence cases are very, very costly and that the National Health Service can end up paying very large sums of money in damages or costs, and people question whether that money might be better spent on patient care.

On the other hand—and we could go on endlessly on this and I must not—we read all the time about disasters that happen to innocent people as a result of things that happen to them in hospital. Of course it isn't necessarily that the hospital has been at fault, but we know very, very well the cases, the tragedy of the brain damaged child, the tragedy of the quadriplegic and so on.

Also I think we have got to remember that the law is weighted. I think Lord Woolf developed this in a recent lecture, but it's something which I have said myself a number of times. The law is actually very weighted in favour of the medical profession in the sense that we do not want doctors who are too risk averse; we do not want doctors who are too concerned about avoiding claims at all costs and therefore not taking balanced medical risks in accordance with reasonable views as to appropriate medical procedure. I, on the whole, think that in relation to professional negligence we have got it about right; that is to say as to the law.

And from the district judges and others, are you getting any sense that people are overstepping the mark and vexatious litigants are coming out of the woodwork, or is there no perceptible change in attitude?

I think not. Of course vexatious claims are brought. There are means available to parties to apply to strike out absolutely hopeless claims, and that should always be available. But for those of us who have practised a lifetime in the law, we know only too often that although there are very many vexatious claims which ought to be struck out, we also know how many hopeless cases turn out to be won and turn out to be right in the end, and how many cases where one would have thought that a plaintiff would not succeed turn out after a thorough trial that that judgment is wrong and the plaintiff was entitled to succeed.

What about the Community Legal Service? Where does this fit into the landscape? I know one of your and your department's responses to the legal aid issue was to develop an entirely new infrastructure. Could you summarise your thinking behind the Community Legal Service and give us some kind of status report on how it's going?

Yes. The Community Legal Service is one of the achievements of my department since May 1997 of which I personally am most proud, and I think my department should be most proud. What we found was that the country was full of well-meaning organisations which did not co-operate together: the advice centres, the law centres, the whole Citizens Advice Bureau movement under the aegis of NCAB, the Law Centres' Federation. The whole range of these voluntary organisations that do superb good, but very often duplicate procedures, and very often people don't know what service is provided by these voluntary bodies which is relevant to their needs.

Also, when we looked at it in 1997, these services—not within the public sector, in the voluntary sector—were fractured and the pattern was of uneven geographical provision. These voluntary bodies of course very often are dependent for funding on local authorities. Some local authorities are excellent, and some vary in the level of support they feel they can give.

And then of course, primarily, there are the solicitors who provide legal services. The concept of the Community Legal Service was to bring together into Community Legal Services partnerships, the various bodies which previously did not work in formal co-operation. This I think has been a triumphant success. About 95 per cent of the country is now covered, ahead of the targets we set down for ourselves, by Community Legal Service partnerships. Something like 340 local authorities contribute to the work of these partnerships.

One point I want to make is that this is an initiative which is really heartening because the enthusiasm that I've seen around the country. As I visit various parts of the country, I always visit the partnerships and the law centres and the advice centres. There is an enormous enthusiasm for this initiative, and it translates through to bring pressure to bear on local authorities, with all the pressures that they're under, to give a significant high priority to the Community Legal Service partnerships.

How do you gauge success from the citizen's point of view? I appreciate it has gone well because I have been peripherally involved myself. I think many of us have been surprised by the extent to which these various organisations have cohered and collaborated, but from the citizen's perspective, how do you actually assess whether or not it's working?

I will be the first to acknowledge it is very, very difficult to provide measurements that would be statistically convincing. We have however got a Community Legal Service website. That website has won prizes and awards, it's highly successful—that's just a commercial plug. What does the website do? It enables an individual, either at the premises of one of these voluntary bodies or in a public library or wherever, to access that website and to get information through the website of where in the individual's own area they ought to go in order to get the help that they need. Now, previously what happened was that people with one problem or maybe a multiplicity of problems would go from pillar to post, not knowing what body would give them the help that they needed, and eventually they would just get fed up and not bother, and their troubles, sometimes quite overwhelming troubles in a family sense, would completely take over.

When I first heard about the Community Legal Service, I immediately recognised analogies with the world of medicine. For me, there were two aspirations that flowed from this line of thinking. On the one hand, while so much of law reform has been devoted to streamlining and improving dispute resolution, it seemed to me that from the citizen's point of view, what was as important, if not more so, was dispute avoidance (or dispute pre-emption). I often say that people want a fence at the top of the cliff rather than an ambulance at the bottom. I wonder if you share this aspiration for the Community Legal Service, that it will help people avoid getting into legal difficulties rather than resolving their disputes more readily?

And secondly, using the medical health promotion analogy, it seems to me that the function of law is not simply to resolve disputes or help avoid disputes, but actually to promote people's welfare. There are all manner of legal entitlements and benefits out there that people could benefit from if only they knew of the existence of the rules and regulations that govern their behaviour. Do you have ambitions in that direction as well? Because up until now the thrust of the Community Legal Service has been very much on helping people who have already got difficulties to resolve them more readily, more comfortably and in a less forbidding way. Do you think you can go further than that?

First of all, I agree with you about the parameters of the analysis. I think that you have to distinguish, as you do, between, dispute avoidance and dispute resolution. Dispute resolution is usually something that happens in a court, but I believe in methods of alternative dispute resolution short of court procedure. Dispute avoidance of course is absolutely critical, and that is one of the prime purposes really of the Community Legal Service. The Community Legal Service should furnish people with the information to enable them to keep out of trouble, and very often the Community Legal Service can, with people who have an incipient dispute. By providing the individual with a letter, by making a telephone call, by ringing up the Town Hall if it's a housing benefit issue, people can be given the assistance that provides the remedy without engaging dispute resolution.

The second broad point that you made was making people better informed. I think that too is hugely important because people have to know what their rights are. When I went to Cardiff—I can't remember how long ago it was now, but say about six or nine months—I visited a very, very good law centre that was absolutely a class act of its type. They had had brought to them recently a large number of problems about housing repossession claims being made by housing associations, which are supposed to be the good guys rather than the bad guys. They thought at first that this was a problem that showed that this housing association was, for some reason or other, sharpening up the criteria that it privately was applying to decide when to bring a possession action. It took them a little time to find out that that was not what the problem was about at all. The problem was about the history of delay in payment of housing benefit by the local authority, and they sorted it out. So the people who went complaining about being vulnerable to possession discovered that they had a right that was being infringed: prompt payment of housing benefit.

Can we turn to something rather different now? Criminal law. You mentioned this earlier as one of your three pillars. When Lord Justice Auld was with us at Gresham, we talked about his reforms. I think it's fair to say there has been a wide range of reaction to his, to Sir Robin's, very large report.[4]

That would be absolutely true!

But what was fascinating when we discussed various aspects of his review was the depth of the thinking behind the report. It was also revealing that on issues such as jury service, the media's rendition of Sir Robin's views did not adequately reflect his actual views. This evening, I wanted to touch on his report generally, your views on it, and what happens now from the Government's point of view. Secondly, if you are able to, I would like to explore the specific issue of juries, because I think that has caused the greatest amount of public concern.

If I can just summarise the position, it seems to me that Lord Justice Auld was saying when he was here at Gresham that (a) he was emphatically not suggesting any abolition of the jury system, (b) he was very concerned, however, that it was too easy for people to avoid their jury service and he was wanting to tighten up that weakness, and (c) he suggested that there were various categories of cases for which he felt a jury was simply not appropriate. To be clear—he was very keen to say that he wanted to preserve juries but he was anxious to change their emphasis and encourage their constitution to be genuinely more representative of society.[5]

Can we touch first of all on the broad context of this report? Later on, I want to speak about your views on such reports more generally but, for now, let's talk specifically about Sir Robin's. How was it conceived, who was responsible, what happens now in terms of Government process?

Well, it was obvious that there was a great deal of concern about criminal justice generally. The whole of the criminal justice system had not really been looked at in

---

[4] The criminal justice system is also discussed by Lord Woolf (Ch.1), Lord Justice Auld (Ch.4) and Lord Goldsmith (Ch.8).
[5] The jury system is also discussed by Lord Justice Auld (Ch.4), Lord Bingham (Ch.7), Lord Goldsmith (Ch.8) and David Lock (Ch.9).

the round for some time from a procedural standpoint. There had of course been the Runciman Royal Commission, which had not gained a vast amount of assent, and it was thought to be timely to have a progressive and highly experienced Lord Justice take a root and branch look at it.

You are quite right that the area of his report that has attracted most interest is juries, because there are huge philosophical differences about them. Let me just canvas some. It's extraordinary at one level, and this is not my view by the way, but it can be said that it's extraordinary that you have juries at all. Aren't they merely an intrusion into a professional function? Why don't we trust judges?

But then you could say equally about our magistrates' courts, where 97 per cent of criminal cases begin and end: this is an extraordinary concession by the legal system of a major European country to lay people. So we have got a tradition of either lay justice, magistrates' courts, or significant lay involvement in justice through the jury system. And then Lord Justice Auld—I mustn't go on too long philosophising . . .

No, please do!

. . . Lord Justice Auld really explored, I thought in a very, very interesting way, the very large claims that are sometimes made by people for juries. At the most, I would say, exorbitant level, it is that the juries are an aspect of popular democracy; that the jury is entitled to say "no" through its verdict to laws that it doesn't like. And of course we do know that juries did in the 19th century with capital charges, because of their view of the inappropriateness of the capital penalty for the offence charged, acquit. And we do know in modern times that it is sometimes said that juries acquit contrary to the evidence. One example that is quite often given in modern times is Clive Ponting and the Official Secrets Act. Other examples, nearer, more homely perhaps, is the MS sufferer who gets relief from his MS by smoking cannabis. Now, I thought in a very interesting section of his report, Lord Justice Auld took issue with that, and basically he came down on the side of a very strong view that nobody should applaud the jury for that, he would say. The jury swear an oath to return a true verdict according to the evidence and anything else is completely unacceptable.

Then Lord Justice Auld's proposition was that there should be a ground of appeal that the jury verdict was perverse. Now the argument on the other side is that there's no way that you could preserve the integrity of the jury verdict if you were going to allow an appeal to be based on the perversity of the jury's decision. So that is one very good example of a very difficult issue which Lord Justice Auld has fielded up to Government.

So how does the Government respond to this? You've highlighted the disagreement that there might be about juries. It's not a legal disagreement. It's an underlying social or philosophical disagreement about the nature of ordinary people's involvement in the judicial process, and indeed their involvement in the political process. How do you as a Government respond to a report like that? I don't mean, substantively, what will your answer be, because you have said we have to wait for the White

Paper on that. But how, as a matter of practical politics, are these difficult issues resolved?

We debate them, and we debate them pretty vigorously! The notion that there is some sort of faceless Whitehall machine that eventually spews out an answer is not the way it works, of course, as you know very well indeed. We have got, which is quite new under this Government, tri-lateral arrangements, tri-partite arrangements. There are three justice departments, essentially, which exist because of constitutional considerations. There is the Crown Prosecution Service, for which the Attorney General and his department are effectively responsible. Basically I'm responsible for the courts and the whole of civil justice, the criminal courts as well as the civil, and then of course there is the Home Office. So we have really to debate these things very, very, very thoroughly, and we do, and that's why we are in fact taking a little longer than we hoped that we would to come up with a White Paper which is responsive to Auld.

You touched on other highly controversial issues. For example, should we retain the jury in serious fraud cases? There is a very legitimate concern. On the one hand your stout defender of the jury system would say that it's a bedrock of our liberties. They apply the thin edge of the wedge argument: once you start interfering with jury trial as is, then where will it all end? On the other hand, we have got a very considerable scourge of serious fraud, and lawyers, without being patronising, are entitled to ask: is this of such complexity, is the accountancy of such complexity, is the complicated nature of the interlocking commercial transactions on the part of people who are supposed to have done all this because they practised to deceive—is this, with the best will in the world and without being patronising to the juries, beyond their competence? Does that mean that very serious criminals are going scot-free? Does that therefore mean that what we ought to have is judges alone trying these cases? Or judges with the requisite specialist experience in the commercial areas being addressed by these trials, perhaps assisted by lay assessors with expertise as well?

That is a problem that has been with us for a very, very long time. We all know, Richard, that Lord Roskill, many years ago now—I may get it wrong but I would have thought a quarter of a century ago—recommended that the jury should go in serious fraud cases. Well, Auld has resurrected that issue; it's a very, very difficult one for Government.

How do you feel about the Scottish "not proven" verdict? I ask this as a Scots lawyer. I asked Lord Justice Auld and he was rather dismissive, but I was hoping with your Scottish roots you might offer some kind of hope for it!

No, I'm not a devotee of the Scottish "not proven" verdict. I could of course rationalise it, but I think it's a bit of a cop out, isn't it? It's an invitation to put your hands up in the air and say, "Well, we can't really make up our minds". It's regarded in Scotland, I would have thought, as a very second class acquittal. And no—there is much which England imports which is good from Scotland, including the Scots, and a lot of Scots law of course in the criminal area—such as diminished responsibility.

We can all think of important areas where Scots criminal law has been ahead of English criminal law historically, but no, I'm not a devotee. I'm sorry to disappoint you.

No, no. I'll get over it. We can sit here discussing reform of the criminal justice system. And most people are concerned, of course, that the courts are streamlined and improved, and that once people are brought before the court system their cases are dealt with appropriately. But how does this relate to what might be regarded as more fundamental questions? Very sadly, we seem to be living in a society where there is an increase in crime. In London, for example, violent crime is on the increase, and drug dealing and abuse are on the increase; in the Hertfordshire village where I live, for instance, there are frightening and, it seems, growing levels of violent burglary. What is your role and your department's role in helping with this very grave problem?

Well, this really is a very timely question. One of the problems is that you could always concentrate resources on particular problems and it is often right to do so when the problem has become prevalent.

Now, I remember when we came into Government, there was a very considerable concern about persistent young offenders, and getting them to trial quickly was really not being achieved promptly enough. We developed what we called the Persistent Young Offender Pledge to reduce the time that it takes to bring the young offender from charge to disposal down from 142 days to 71 days, and we did achieve that just about a year ago. Now that of course is a very sensible thing to aim at because we all know that persistent young offenders can very often lapse into crime as a way of life, and therefore what they have to be is brought to confront the reality of their own criminality just as quickly as the system can cater for.

When, for example, I came into office in May 1997, we did perceive that there was a well-meaning but damaging culture of adjournments in the magistrates' courts. They felt, and I understand it, they felt that if they had a persistent young offender who is committing offences all over the place, then they ought to get all these cases in front of them at the one time, because that was more efficient in the name of resources, and there may even have been some court cases that would have suggested that too. At any rate, I wrote, as Head of the Judiciary and also as Chairman of the Magistrates' Association (which derives from being Head of the Judiciary), to the chairmen of all magistrates' courts saying there's a practical answer to what you say; we've really got to bear down on this culture of adjournments and we have got to halve the time that it takes and that way we are more likely to save young people from slipping into a life of crime.

Now, you say that crime is on the rise. In fact, the overall level of crime is on the way down, but there is no doubt that there is a deeply worrying increase in serious crime on the streets in particular areas of the country, including of course London—street robbery, offences with knives, car-jacking and so on. There are very, very serious offences. And one thing that Government can do, and it is thinking about doing but it involves translating resources, is concentrating resources into what we would call "hotspot", robbery hotspot areas. What that really requires is an integrated response from the various parts of the criminal justice system that have to co-operate effectively together to get results so that, for example, there could be

specialist robbery courts, fast tracking of these cases in the same way as the persistent young offender cases were fast tracked, having an improved and accelerated
quality of prosecution in these cases, just to prove to people—the people who practise these crimes and make people's lives a misery as a result—that the system is not
powerless but it can respond and very substantially increase the likelihood of detection, arrest, charge and conviction.

*We've talked about the civil and criminal systems. Can we turn now to administrative
justice and tribunals? You mentioned Sir Andrew Leggatt's review of tribunals. I was
involved to some extent with that review and, I have to say, was excited by the recommendations that were made. As you pointed out earlier—and this is not commonly
known—there are many hundreds of thousands of such disputes and cases . . .*

Maybe a million.

*Indeed. And these are settled in the tribunal system. There are around 90 tribunals,
about 60 of which are active, as it were. But, in many ways, there's not actually a
"tribunal system". We have a loosely related collection of tribunals. And these
tribunals tend, in my view, to be more closely related to their respective parent departments than to one another. In very broad terms, Sir Andrew's report suggested that it
would be more sensible to have a single, coherent tribunal system, and we should detach
the tribunals to some extent from their parent departments and, by analogy with the
court service, they should come together under one umbrella. Now, my impression—
although this is an impression gained not from the Lord Chancellor's Department or
indeed from any of the justice departments, but from across Government departments
more generally—is that Whitehall has not responded very favourably. That really dis-
appoints me because it seems to me that Sir Andrew's suggestion is compelling as a
matter of fairness. If someone has a dispute with a Government department, it does
surely seem strange if not inappropriate that the tribunal that exists to address the
dispute actually belongs in some sense to that department. Even if tribunal members
and chairmen do not feel in any sense prejudiced by this rather anomalous state of
affairs, as a matter of perception and practice, this did concern Sir Andrew's team.
I wonder, because I think it is a fine piece of work, what happens to a report like Sir
Andrew's and how optimistic one can be that it will be implemented?*

Well, I of course very strongly advocate acceptance of this report. I regard it as a
superb piece of work, but you are right that if you are putting forward a major piece
of reform of this kind that you are bound to tread on many toes.
    Let me dispel some misconceptions that there are. I know you don't entertain them,
but they are entertained around the place by those who are opposed. The proposition
is not that responsibility, for example, for employment law should be taken away from
the Department of Trade and Industry, which is responsible for policy in the employment tribunals, and magically go to the Lord Chancellor's Department. That way, we
would end up running the world, and I rather baulk at that. What we are really saying
is one point that you've made, Richard, and another slightly different point.

Our core business is running the courts, and one of the most successful agencies that I've got is the court service, which is responsible to me, my department; and just so you get the scale of it, about 10,000 people are employed in the court service in England and Wales; it's very, very big business. Now, we administer the courts; it's our core business, and we're vain enough to think that we make a good job of it.

What we want to do is to administer the tribunals without taking away policy responsibility from any of the sponsoring departments. We, however, would become the paymaster of these tribunals, and that brings me to your first point. I'm not in the least surprised that people who were engaged in assisting Leggatt would have found one of the most troubling things that the sponsoring departments, that is to say the departments with policy responsibility, were the departments who sponsored, in the sense both funded and ran, administered, these tribunals. Many, many people, including the Council on Tribunals, which is the body that oversees all tribunals, agreed with us that that was wrong, and they came out with evidence which was strongly supportive of Leggatt, and that has been particularly welcomed. The latter is more actively under discussion in Government at the moment than you may be aware, but I am hopeful of major progress.

I'll watch that space then! Can I turn now away from civil, criminal and administrative justice to the role of the Lord Chancellor?

Oh dear!

When I'm discussing this or speaking to you about it, can we depersonalise it? That is to say, we are talking about the role generally rather than you specifically.

I have no feelings!

In other words, I do not want to focus on you as an instantiation of the Lord Chancellor's role. I suspect you have never been called an instantiation before!

Something from Gilbert and Sullivan about it—embodiment of the law!

Senior Cabinet Minister, Speaker of the House of Lords, Head of the Judiciary—a walking refutation, it might be said, of the doctrine of the separation of powers. It's a difficult role for many reasons but not least because it does actually combine all manner of functions within the public sector that some argue, for constitutional reasons, should be kept separate. I know this particular issue has been debated recently, certainly in relation to the Lord Chancellor's role, and also for example in relation to Jersey and Guernsey as well, where similar debate has arisen.

90

The McDonnell case.

Yes. I suppose the biggest issue, or the issue that has attracted most attention amongst lawyers recently, is the extent to which the Lord Chancellor—not you, in particular, I stress again—should continue sitting as a judge. Are there tensions here? Are there incompatibilities here? Are there human rights issues here? Can you guide us through this minefield? It is clearly close to your heart, but it's also an issue, I think, that fascinates the entire legal world.[6]

Yes. First of all, what I want to say, not defensively but truthfully, is that the position that I'm about to express is the position that every one of my predecessors has expressed. In other words, those who have occupied this office since the challenges to it began, from Lord Hailsham through Lord Mackay and myself, have been convinced by experience that, although as you say it is apparently anomalous and is the product of history, what it does is work enormously effectively to uphold the rule of law and to uphold the independence of the Judiciary. The reason it does that is because the Lord Chancellor, historically, is a very senior Cabinet Minister.

All Lord Chancellors come to the office after a lifetime in the law imbued with legal values, the values of the rule of law, which we saw so severely under attack for example in Zimbabwe recently; the rule of law, the idea that the Government is subject to the law the same as ordinary citizens, an appreciation that the Judiciary are the weakest arm within the separation of the powers, and that they require a really strong upholder of judicial independence.

Lord Hailsham once said that the first duty of the Lord Chancellor is to uphold judicial independence and to ward off marauders from wherever, inside or outside Government. Interestingly, Lord Hailsham also once said that the reason that we ought to have a Lord Chancellor who sits in the chair in the House of Lords from time to time when his other duties permit him to do so, in that trenchant way of Lord Hailsham, he said, "That's the only guarantee that some Prime Minister won't appoint a no-good lawyer to this office". And the truth I think is that the office provides a much greater guarantee and protection for very basic legal values when they're under threat than could be provided by any minister of justice.

What we have to remember, of course, is that the Minister for Health doesn't have to be a doctor. No minister in any specialist area has to be a specialist in that area. Why does the Lord Chancellor have to be? Well, it is because the law is part of our system of government. It is because the powers are separated between the Legislature, the Executive and the Judiciary. The Judiciary is the weakest arm, needs to have a powerful advocate within Government, and an ordinary minister of justice, you know, would be a junior Cabinet Minister. I'm amazed when I visit many Continental countries how quickly the faces change, and you meet a new Minister of Justice. The Minister of Justice, generally, wants promotion out of the lowly job of Minister of Justice.

---

[6] The role and the future of the role of the Lord Chancellor are also discussed by Lord Irvine (Ch.13), Sir Hayden Phillips (Ch.15), Lord Mackay (Ch.17), Lord Falconer (Ch.18), Professor Bogdanor (Ch.19) and Lord Woolf (Ch.20).

Now the great truth about a Lord Chancellor is that he can't go up, he can't go down. Yes, he can go out, but it's very, very rare indeed, because Prime Ministers appoint strong Lord Chancellors in whom they have confidence.

One school of thought amongst the judges would respond, at least to part of what you say, by claiming: "We could stand up for ourselves as a body if, say, we had greater independence, with an independent Supreme Court; and we are more than able to articulate our grievances or express ourselves if we need to be listened to." What protections can you afford judges that you feel are otherwise not available to them?

Well, for example, machinery of Government changes that would take place adversely to the interests of the Judiciary before they had ever heard about them.

The point is that the Judiciary and everything associated with the concept of judicial independence, and a courts system which is not part of the ministry of the interior, the Home Office, but is firmly within a justice department, to my mind requires a strong internal advocate within Government to secure, because of the inherent weakness of the judicial arm within the separation of the powers. Now, I could give countless illustrations from experience of that proposition, but that will have to await until, if I ever write them, my memoirs!

Just one question—again not personalising the matter—but it is the case that sitting as a judge the Lord Chancellor will almost invariably be, or has been, less experienced than the other Law Lords. Is there an issue there?

Of course it is generally true, but I can't think of any Lord Chancellor post-war, or indeed any Lord Chancellor in the 20th century, who has not come to the office from a huge base of high quality legal practice. So no, I don't really think that that is a problem. Also, of course, the Lord Chancellor in this country, by statute, is the Head of the Judiciary; by statute, he is President of the Court of Appeal, President of the Chancery Division. It would be odd to occupy that office and not sit from time to time.

Do Lord Chancellors, as a matter of course, sit as Law Lords once they are no longer in office, because that is certainly permitted?

Yes, by invitation, and most—all, yes, I would say that all post-war Lord Chancellors have from time to time been invited, and their services are very welcome.

Just a couple of final issues to discuss. One thing that interests me is judicial inquiries and reviews by judges. It seems to me there are at least two broad sorts. On the one hand, there is the kind of inquiry by Lord Woolf, Lord Justice Auld and Sir Andrew

Leggatt, which were really reviews of parts of the justice system. On the other hand, there are judicial inquiries into matters of major social significance, such as those into BSE, child abuse in north Wales, and arms to Iraq. In both instances, senior judges are taken away from their judicial roles and undertake some kind of involved and usually quite lengthy review or inquiry. There is a view, however, that judges' energies and talents should be focused only on their strictly judicial work, and that it might be that independent reviews and inquiries could be undertaken by others. What is the thinking behind this? How do these initiatives come to be set up? Is it you who instructs the judges?[7]

That's not quite right. I would never instruct them, and I don't think any Lord Chancellor would instruct them, but you invite them. But I wouldn't invite them unless a decision had been taken within Government, collectively, that a judge, a senior judge always, is wanted to conduct this inquiry.

You mentioned very good examples. Another very good example recently is the Marchioness Inquiry about which there is a vast amount of public disquiet. Well, in a sense, I think that it is a huge compliment to the Judiciary that successive Governments turn to senior judges for this purpose, and the reason that they do is because the public have a well-founded confidence both in judicial independence and judicial impartiality.

At one level, judges are privileged, although it's right under the rule of law that they should be independent and free of Executive interference, and that they should have security of tenure of a much longer duration than is available to most other mortals. The other side of the bargain the State confers and guarantees independence, is that the judges guarantee impartiality, and I think that independence and impartiality are the two sides of one coin. Where you have areas of inquiry that cause huge public disquiet, then it is a tribute to the Judiciary that, for these really difficult inquiries, they are successive Governments' first port of call.

I can think of exceptions, both by you and by your predecessor. Sir Jefferey Bowman was invited to lead a review of the Civil Division of the Court of Appeal, and Professor Ian Kennedy was invited to conduct the Bristol Royal Infirmary Inquiry. So there are clearly instances where exceptions can be found or skills beyond the Judiciary are engaged.

Yes, but your two broad categories were absolutely correct. You have categories where judges are naturally used in particular areas of the justice system, like Auld, like Woolf; you have other inquiries where judges are used because of the colossal public sensitivity of the area of inquiry, and the feeling that the public will have a very considerable confidence in a report from a judge.

But you're quite right to cite Ian Kennedy's report; he of course is a professor, or was a professor in London, maybe he still is, with a tremendous experience in

---

[7] Judicial inquiries are also discussed by Lord Bingham (Ch.7), Dame Elizabeth Butler-Sloss (Ch.11), Lord Saville (Ch.14) and Lord Mackay (Ch.17).

medical ethics and medical negligence. I'm not for a single second suggesting that judges should be the exclusive port of call for specialist inquiries, but they tend to be, although you're right to point out the exception in that very important inquiry that Ian Kennedy conducted at Bristol.

Penultimately, can I ask about law reform? This has clearly been important to you and is part of the Lord Chancellor's Department's remit. I know, for example, that you have encouraged changes in the work of the Law Commission. Could you, in just a minute or so, summarise your thinking on how the Law Commission can become more mainstream?

Well, too often Law Commission reports have gathered dust in Whitehall. I'm pleased to say that recently there has been a major change. The Law Commission has got on to the Statute Book a major piece of legislation recently. My department picked it up and ran with it—it's land registration. That is what will introduce e-conveyancing in a very short space of time, and it will transform conveyancing, common hold and leasehold, trustee act—not the kind of thing that is talked about every night down at the Dog and Duck, but it really does hugely affect people's lives. So I am quite pleased with the recent record of getting Law Commission reports converted into legislation and on to the Statute Book.

But you're quite right, it has got to be more focused. Really what we are carrying forward is procedures that we put in place a few years ago to try to integrate responses from Government departments to this question, which my department asked them through a committee: "What focused help could you get from the Law Commission for the work of your department? But don't just tell us for the sake of telling us!" The other side of the bargain will be that if we, the Law Commission, come up with an answer that you really like, then you will run with it and promote it within Government as potential legislation. Because the pressures on Parliamentary time are colossal and you don't really get legislation, no matter how important the Law Commission may think it is, unless you get a Government department that's going to run with it and argue for it in the competition for scarce Parliamentary time.

And so to my final question. I have in mind the student or the pupil contemplating a career in law. What would you say to such a person—in a few words? It is a changing landscape so that youngsters should anticipate a very different legal world in the future. What would your advice to them be?

Go for it! If I had to choose again, and I had spent 19 years as a Queen's Counsel before 1997, I wouldn't make a different decision.

Lord Chancellor, many thanks indeed.

CHAPTER SEVEN

The Rt Hon The Lord Bingham of Cornhill
Senior Law Lord

Tuesday October 22, 2002

This evening's guest at Gresham College is Lord Bingham. I have had the good fortune to work with a number of very senior judges over the years and I can tell you with confidence that no judge in this country is held in greater esteem by fellow judges than Lord Bingham. He is currently the Senior Law Lord, but he is unique in English legal history in having also been the Lord Chief Justice of England as well as Master of the Rolls.

Lord Bingham, it's a great pleasure to have you with us this evening. Welcome to Gresham College. I would like to start by asking you about the work of the House of Lords. It might seem unusual to non-lawyers that there is a court in the House of Lords. How did this come about?[1]

It's one of these very many things that simply goes back several hundred years. Once upon a time the King exercised supreme authority as legislator, as judge and as Executive. Over the centuries, these functions have become distributed to Parliament, to the Cabinet and the Government and, broadly, to the Judiciary. But the old power in the administration of justice that the King used, in medieval times, to exercise devolved to the House of Lords, for reasons that I don't think are very plain, and the vestigial remnant of that is the jurisdiction now exercised by the Law Lords, who are members of the Upper House.

So that's the highest court in the land? Is there an issue, a difficulty, with such a court sitting in what might be perceived to be the middle of a Legislature?

Could I just make two points? You say the highest court in the land. I think it's a point just worth bearing in mind that it is the nearest thing that there is to a Supreme

---

[1] The judicial work of the House of Lords and the possibility of a new Supreme Court are also discussed by Lord Saville (Ch.14), Sir Hayden Phillips (Ch.15), Lord Mackay (Ch.17), Lord Falconer (Ch.18) and Lord Woolf (Ch.20).

Court of the United Kingdom, because it does hear civil and criminal appeals from England and Wales. It also hears civil and criminal appeals from Northern Ireland, and it hears civil but not criminal appeals from Scotland. Its membership at the moment includes a former Lord Chief Justice of Northern Ireland and has always traditionally included two Scots members, and so although it isn't a perfect court of the United Kingdom, so to speak, it is the nearest thing that we have.

In answer to your second question about whether it's really rather odd to have a whole lot of judges sitting in the House of Lords—yes, it is. There are those who say that there should be a complete separation of powers between the Judiciary on the one hand, and the Executive and the Legislature on the other, and we would all agree I think that there should. The defence for the present system, if one wants to advance one, is that functionally the separation is total, so that the fact that we are members of the House of Lords does not affect the discharge of our judicial duties, although it may sometimes affect the perception of them, which is not in itself necessarily unimportant.

But you do engage in debates in the House of Lords?

Less and less. I noticed last night on the television screen that one of my colleagues was contributing in a debate. There is another one of my colleagues who chairs a sub-committee of the House of Lords that deals with European Community legislation, and so when there is something on the floor of the House that relates to the work of his sub-committee, he will speak. But there are some of my colleagues who have never made a maiden speech. There are others who have made maiden speeches, but regret ever having done so! And there are others who have made maiden speeches and have made further speeches, but have now become virtually Trappist!

So the alternative would be a thoroughgoing Supreme Court? How might that look?

Yes, I have made it publicly very plain, I think, that my preference would be to have a Supreme Court of the United Kingdom, subject to the Scottish limitation that I have mentioned. I have no territorial ambitions in relation to Scotland at all.

I'm glad to hear it!

But I would wish to establish this in a different building and separated from the House of Lords. Whether people continue to be peers or not, I wouldn't regard as very significant.

It's hard for you to speak for all judges, but does that view enjoy sympathy across the Judiciary?

It certainly doesn't enjoy unanimity! I'm not absolutely sure, if you took a poll among the 11 serving Law Lords, how the vote would go. If you took a vote among former Law Lords, they would be against it. If you asked the Lord Chancellor, he would be more or less against it. I say more or less because I've heard him say different things. But on the whole, from the nation's point of view, it's extremely economical, costs very, very little, and it doesn't work that badly.

You say there are 11 of you. Retired Law Lords also sit, do they not? What's your full compliment?

Well, I say 11, but there is a complement of 12 serving Law Lords who are paid fulltime judges whose job it is to sit in the House of Lords and the Privy Council, which we'd better say a word about at some point. I referred to 11 because Lord Saville, as many of you will know, has been engaged for years now on the Bloody Sunday Inquiry so he simply hasn't been available to sit judicially at all.

Why don't we say a word or two about the Privy Council and we can jump back to judging and the Lords?

In addition to providing a panel of judges to sit in the House of Lords itself, or sometimes two panels by calling in people who have retired but are still under the age of 75, we do also provide a panel to sit in the Privy Council, which hears appeals from what we once used to call the Empire. Of course the big dominions, as they once were—Canada, Australia, India, South Africa—don't appeal to London anymore, but a lot of the smaller Caribbean territories do, partly because they are too small to maintain a comparable appellate structure of their own. So we do hear a lot of appeals from Barbados, the Bahamas, Jamaica, Trinidad, Antigua and so on, and they generate quite a lot of work, for two reasons. One, that their constitutions give them a right to appeal very frequently, even if the sum of money involved in local terms is trivial. For example, 500 Trinidad dollars or something entitles you to appeal, and that's much less than the American dollar. And secondly, it generates a lot of work because a lot of people get sentenced to death and don't want to die and so they appeal.

I know that in Scotland it has frequently been the case that House of Lords' decisions have been given by three English judges and two Scottish judges. How do the judges face the challenge of another jurisdiction?

If we're sitting hearing an appeal from, say, Jamaica, we sit as if we were Jamaican judges applying Jamaican law. So far as Scotland is concerned, it's absolutely true, as you say, that you can get an appeal on an erudite and esoteric point of Scots law decided by two Scotsmen and three Englishmen. I don't think there is any case on record where the view of the Scots judges has been outvoted by the English judges.

Last week, when we did have such a case of a very esoteric nature, we managed to arrange that there were three Scotsmen and two Englishmen!

This is something Scots lawyers dwell upon when you attend, as I did, a Scottish law school.

An interesting and entirely new jurisdiction arises out of devolution to Scotland and Wales. There was a great deal of public and Parliamentary discussion as to where problems arising out of the devolution of powers to Scotland should be decided. They didn't want these appeals to come the House of Lords Appellate Committee. It was ultimately decided they should go to the Privy Council. So it is now the Privy Council that decides whether something that the Scottish Executive or the Scottish Parliament has done exceeds the bounds of the power that has been devolved for them to exercise, and we have gone to great pains to make sure that there's a large Scottish representation among those who hear these appeals. But I read an article by a Scottish QC the other day in a magazine complaining bitterly that when they came to London to get decisions on these matters, what did they find but a lot of Scotsmen sitting there to decide them. So you can't please everybody!

What's the throughput of the Law Lords? How many cases do you hear?

It varies, obviously, from year to year, but we actually decide something in the order of about 60, 70, 80 full appeals a year, which is almost exactly the same as the Supreme Court of the United States. About the same number of cases are decided in the Privy Council and, in addition, decisions are taken on petitions for appeal because—certainly so far as the House of Lords is concerned—if you want to appeal you need permission to do so, and that means people looking into the case and deciding whether there's a point of public importance that deserves a further hearing. So in addition to the appeals that are fully heard, there is a body of petitions that have to be considered and ruled upon. And if one then pursues the analogy with the United States, they have vastly more petitions than we do. We have a few hundred whereas they have some 35,000, I think. How many of those the judges actually look at is another question.

I was recently looking through a book called The Law Lords, *written by a friend and colleague of mine at Strathclyde University, a man called Professor Alan Paterson.[2] In the 1970s, during Alan's research in Oxford as a doctoral student, he interviewed almost all the Law Lords of the time, and many of the Lord Justices of Appeal as well. This was bold! He was trying to find out how it was that judges came to their decisions. One of the questions he asked was whether or not the judges felt, in relation to the decisions coming before them in the House of Lords, that there could in some sense be a*

---

[2] Alan Paterson, *The Law Lords* (MacMillan, London, 1982).

right answer, or whether or not for most cases the arguments could be properly justified either way. What's your sense of this issue? Do you feel you're seeking a right answer or do you follow the arguments wherever they lead?[3]

I participated recently in a radio discussion of this very question[4] and I think Professor Dworkin is an adherent to the view that there is only one answer to every case, and there was a professor of jurisprudence among the panel on this radio thing who took the same view. There were two of us who were judges and one who was a professor of jurisprudence from Oxford and we all quite strongly took the view that this was simply not so, and when you're deciding a case you usually feel that there is a choice of answers, and one doesn't usually regard the answer that one ends up rejecting as being completely and utterly hopeless or untenable; you just regard it as the answer that you don't prefer.

I think there would be very, very highly technical questions about the construction of a will, the interpretation of a will or a conveyance, or something of that sort, where you could say: "This is a question of strict law and there's a right answer and there's a wrong answer". But the moment you move into a more value-laden area, such as whether Tony Bland's doctor should be entitled to stop feeding him because he had absolutely no prospect of recovery and his parents were going gently mad with the continuing distress over years of constant visiting; or an issue recently as to whether Mr Pretty should be able to assist his wife to commit suicide without any risk of prosecution by the Attorney General, these sort of questions, different minds take different views or are capable of doing so. To say that there is one right answer and one wrong answer is just not at all how it feels.

*Coincidentally, I heard that radio programme. The jurisprudence professor was Stephen Guest who is a major fan, indeed a biographer, of Ronald Dworkin. It seemed to me in that conversation there was a classical distinction. I think in many ways what Dworkin is saying is that there being one right answer is how it ought to be—it **ought** to be. I'd be interested to hear if you like this analogy—he likens the development of the Common Law to what he calls a chain novel.[5] The idea in a chain novel is that one person would write Chapter One and they hand it along to someone else to write the second chapter. And what would you do if you received that? You'd have to look at Chapter One, and you'd have to write a chapter that was coherent and consistent with, yet ran comfortably from, the previous chapter. You couldn't just dash off in any direction if you wanted to keep it coherent and consistent, and that's Dworkin's, frankly, prescriptive model of how judicial decision-making should develop. In many ways, in the interview, I don't think you as the practising judges were taking a view on how it ought to be—you were saying this is actually how it feels, and actually it doesn't feel as though there's some definitive answer out there if only you could see it. That's just not your personal experience, and it's actually not the personal experience of most judges that I speak to.*

---

[3] Judicial decision-making is also discussed by Lord Woolf (Ch.1), Dame Elizabeth Butler-Sloss (Ch.11), Cherie Booth (Ch.12) and Professor John Gardner (Ch.16).
[4] This radio programme is also discussed by Professor John Gardner (Ch.16).
[5] See Ronald Dworkin, *Law's Empire* (Fontana, London, 1986).

We don't disagree nearly as often as, for example, the Supreme Court of the United States or, I think, the High Court of Australia. They disagree with each other rather more frequently. But there is a significant minority of cases in which one or two members out of five will dissent. I don't think the other three would say, "Well, they're just wrong". They'd say, "We don't agree with them", and then the academics will write articles and say the two were right and the three were wrong, or more probably that all five were wrong!

That's interesting because also in Alan Paterson's book, The Law Lords, *one of the questions that was asked—and this is a generation ago—was the extent to which Law Lords were influenced by academic writings in their decision making and their analysis of the law. They were asked, as I recall, whether they regularly read journals like the* Law Quarterly Review *and the* Modern Law Review.

I think there are two different ways of approaching that. The first is whether as a routine matter like reading the newspaper in the morning you read the *Law Quarterly Review* or something, and I suppose the answer is some do, some don't. But by the time a case reaches the House of Lords it's probably generated some academic criticism already. If it raises a point of interest to academic lawyers, then one will certainly refer to what has been written about the decision that is being appealed from and one will assess the arguments advanced. One won't say, "Well, the Court of Appeal are clearly wrong because Professor so-and-so says so and he's a very, very reputable authority"! But one will read what Professor so-and-so says and make up one's own mind, but obviously attach weight to effective arguments. At least, one hopes so.

Could I go off on another tangent and into the Court of Appeal? Something you just mentioned leads me in this direction. When you sit in the Court of Appeal, what I've always found remarkable is that you can actually have two judges sitting. It interests me and I think it always interests lay people as well, because one would imagine that you should have an odd number. What's your feeling about that in practice?

I think everybody is conscious of there being a risk if you have a court of an even number. The rule is, if they disagree, there is no majority for reversing the judgment below. So if you win below and your opponent goes to the Court of Appeal and there are two judges and they're divided, then they open in the House of Lords, which is always regarded as an advantage. What one tries to do if one's organising the programme is make sure that in a case which looks as if it might give rise to a difference of opinion you've got at least three.

Can you tell me about the judicial relationship with the Home Office? As we've discussed, you are the highest court. One does get the sense—certainly in the way it's portrayed in the media—that over a number of issues the senior judges and the politicians at the Home Office can be at loggerheads. There are more general issues here about the extent to which, for example, the Home Secretary actually does and should get involved in what some perceive to be judicial decision making—in relation to mandatory life sentences, for example. Could you talk us through the overlaps and the relationships in the context of criminal law?[6]

The Home Office, by the nature of its portfolio, finds itself involved in a lot of highly contentious activities, including sometimes the police, the management of the prisons—including the running of the penal system—and of course, particularly in recent years, asylum, immigration and extradition. This has the inevitable result that the Home Office finds itself litigating a great deal, and if you look at the list of the administrative court that deals with judicial review at first instance, I think there are almost certainly more cases involving the Home Office as one party than any other single party.

The newspapers—we have some distinguished representatives here—sometimes give the impression, or have done in the past, that the Home Secretary always loses. Well, the truth is that when the Home Secretary loses it tends to get very fully reported, and when the Home Secretary wins it tends not to be news, and most of the time he does win. I don't know that anybody has ever done a count but he wins many, many more cases than he loses. As between ourselves and the Home Secretary, you could say we have no relationship. We hear cases involving the Home Office and we try and decide them.

Some judges, in particular the Lord Chief Justice, has a distinct relationship with the Home Secretary, and he goes to see him periodically, and the Home Secretary will usually discuss with him changes that he proposes to make and the Lord Chief Justice will express his views, which may be favourable or may not. I want, for reasons that will be understood, to keep a very long way away from the mandatory life sentence for murder because we are hearing an appeal on that subject at the moment, and I certainly don't want to say anything that could be thought to express a point of view.

You're exercising your right to silence, which is actually another topic I wanted to raise in a different context! In your book The Business of Judging[7] *(which is published by Oxford University Press, for those of you who want to buy a good read—and it is a very good read), you talk with passion about the right to silence. I wondered if we could now spend some time on this.*

The right to silence?

Yes, the right to silence both prior to appearing in court and also in court itself. I am keen to explore whether or not such a right should be afforded and whether or not it's prejudicial to the interests of the accused.

---

[6] The relationship between the Judiciary and the Home Office is also discussed by Oliver Letwin (Ch.10) and Lord Irvine (Ch.13).
[7] Oxford University Press, Oxford, 2000.

Well, this has been a very burning topic and it's quite a controversial topic. The law used to be that if anybody was found in very, very suspicious circumstances and a policeman said, "What are you doing? Why are you here? What's that hatchet you've got in your hand?" you were entitled to say, "No comment". Then when you were taken to the police station and they wanted to ask you some questions, you would say, "I don't wish to answer any questions". Then when you got to court and your opportunity came to go into the witness box and give your version of events, you were entitled just to stay put in the dock and not give your version of events.

Now, when it came to the summing up, the judge was required, as a matter of law, to say to the jury, "You must not draw any inference whatever adverse to this particular defendant from the fact that when he was asked why he'd got the hatchet, etc., he said 'No comment', and when he went to the police station, he declined to answer any questions, and when he came to court, he didn't go into the witness box to tell you all about it. You must put that out of your mind. He's got a perfect right as a citizen to behave exactly as he has done, and you must treat that as completely neutral, neither for him nor against him."

The average juror tended to think that was a lot of nonsense, and many jurors would say, "Well, if he'd got an innocent explanation for having the hatchet, why the devil didn't he tell the policeman when he was first asked, and then he wouldn't have found himself subject to this huge rigmarole", and so on. So the law was amended a little while ago to the effect that if in any of the situations I mentioned somebody had the opportunity to answer questions and didn't, or came to court and then gave an explanation different from what he'd given before, it would be open to the jury to draw an inference adverse to that defendant if they thought, in all the circumstances, it was fair to do so.

Of course it was always open to the defendant to give explanations as to why he hadn't chosen to answer the questions. He could say, "I was too drunk and I couldn't understand what was going on", or "I was under the influence of drugs and I wasn't myself", or "I wanted to wait for my solicitor and I thought it was very unwise to start answering questions before my solicitor arrived". So any explanation would be there for the jury, and the law was quite clear that you couldn't convict somebody just because he hadn't answered questions. The question was whether he had committed this particular crime with which he was charged, whatever it was, and whether it was fair in all the circumstances to treat it as a titbit of evidence against him that when he'd had an opportunity to give his version of it, he hadn't.

Many, many lawyers thought that this was a very oppressive and bad change of the law. I myself happen to think it was a sensible change to the law because it relieved judges of the need to tell jurors things that most of them thought were nonsense. But there we are—I'm not suggesting for a moment there's any sort of received view on this question. Some people still think the one, some people still think the other. The court in Strasbourg is pretty unhappy about anything which infringes what they regard as the right of a citizen simply to say, "Well, I'm not answering any question at all".

And on Strasbourg, on human rights generally—I recall somewhere in your book that you say everyone's a human rights lawyer now. How has the incorporation of the

Convention affected the work of the courts? There was, a couple of years ago, some anticipation that a floodgate would open. Is that yet to come, or was it misjudged?[8]

For many years I was a strong advocate of incorporating the European Convention into English law, and this was not actually because I thought it would revolutionise everything, but because I myself thought it was extremely damaging to the administration of justice in this country to encourage everybody to think that what was administered here was some sort of second class form of justice, and to get first class justice you had to go off to Strasbourg. And I also thought that the United Kingdom might fare rather better in judgments at Strasbourg if the court there had had the benefit of a judgment from a court here on the very point at issue, and one of the results of the Convention not being a part of our own law was that there were no judgments on these points being given by British courts.

As I say, I didn't actually think that the system would be turned upside down and that we would be found to be doing everything wrong, because we did after all invent a great deal of this jurisprudence in the first place. There was a fear, as Richard has quite rightly said, that the whole system would be swamped with a huge flood of claims based on human rights. In some other countries this did actually happen and they hadn't prepared very carefully and the courts were quite overwhelmed with the volume of cases. Here, I think we did prepare reasonably carefully: there was a two-year delay before the Act was actually brought into force. A lot of Government departments spent a lot of time trying to get things in order before the clock struck and, so far, the swamping effect has not really been seen, to the point where quite a lot of people just feel it's all a damp squib and wonder what all the fuss was about and why did we get excited in the first place. I don't agree with that criticism either, but you wouldn't expect me to.

I think it has had a beneficial effect on the way we see things, and undoubtedly the Convention has improved the rights of those who didn't appeal to any very strong vein of public or Parliamentary opinion in the past, like mental patients, prisoners, gypsies, homosexuals, transsexuals, people like that. So I remain an unrepentant incorporationist. But we mustn't assume that this thing solves all problems. I mean, nothing can; all we can hope is it's a force for good.

Can we move on to a different and difficult subject: the appointment of judges? That has been very much in the public domain as a controversial topic. What are your feelings on this?[9]

There is a great range of complaints on this subject. As I think most people know, the prime responsibility for the appointment of judges rests with the Lord Chancellor, and although he is a member of the Cabinet, and although he is

---

[8] Human rights are also discussed by Lord Woolf (Ch.1), David Pannick QC (Ch.3), David Lock (Ch.9), Oliver Letwin (Ch.10), Cherie Booth QC (Ch.12) and Professor Bogdanor (Ch.19).
[9] The appointment of judges is also discussed by Lord Irvine (Ch.13), Sir Hayden Phillips (Ch.15), Lord Mackay (Ch.17), Lord Falconer (Ch.18) and Professor Bogdanor (Ch.19).

appointed by the Prime Minister of the day, it is very, very clearly understood that for this particular function, as for other functions to do with the administration of justice, his duty is to be completely non-political.

I don't think anybody would suggest that any Lord Chancellor over the last 50 years at least, and certainly not recent Lord Chancellors, have been anything other than completely non-political. What they try to do is appoint the best people they can find. There are complaints that there are too few women appointed, and there are complaints that too few members of the ethnic minorities are appointed. I myself have been quite heavily engaged in appointing the higher ranks of the judges over the last decade, and all I can say is that the two Lord Chancellors with whom I have dealt have been very keen to appoint women and ethnic minority candidates when there were candidates who were better than anybody else. But what they have equally said they are not going to do is positively discriminate in favour either of women or ethnic minority candidates, which I think is the right approach because I very firmly believe that people belonging to both those groups will win all the recognition that they need on their merits. I don't think they need some sort of artificial hand-up. But these things take time and it can't happen overnight.

Now, there certainly are those who say the whole system is very opaque and it isn't exposed to the human eye and it would be much better to have an appointments commission, which is a point of view and that's the way that lots of other countries do it. I happen to think that it's a virtue to make one man or woman responsible. Lord Chancellors regard the appointment of judges as a very, very important part of their duties. Lord Hailsham said it was the most important function of any Lord Chancellor. I think it's a good thing to put one individual on the spot, because he or she knows that his or her reputation will stand or fall by the quality of the appointments made, so that the responsibility is very personal and very direct.

The problem, presumably, is not with any particular Lord Chancellor but with the perception that someone who can and does wear a political hat is involved in that form of decision-making. And people also perceive processes such as informal soundings as worrying. When you're close to the system and you have confidence in the individuals, one perhaps is less concerned because you see the reality—high quality judges are coming through. But if you're at a distance, it looks quite clubby.

Yes, I understand that. The Lord Chancellor has regular meetings with quite a large group of 10 or a dozen senior judges in addition to any soundings or consultations that he has outside that group, and I think he does his absolute best to try and inform himself as well as he can to make the best appointments. On the question of political slant, I could say with absolute total honesty, hand on heart, that over 10 years of being closely involved, I have never heard any reference to anybody's political position. Most judges actually don't have a political position anyway, or silks for that matter, QCs, I've just never heard reference to this.

Let's talk about wigs and other trappings—where do you fall in the debate as to the need to modernise?

The Law Lords don't dress up at all. I have spent the day sitting in court as I now am. Counsel do wear wigs and gowns. I would be perfectly happy to sweep them away. I don't think they are necessary to the dignity or whatever of the proceedings. I think the most difficult area is in the trial of crime, for two reasons. One, that that is where the public actually expect this particular form of dress to be found and people are very used to seeing criminal trials on television and so on. I think if one were going to make a change, it would be a good idea to do it in civil cases and appeals first, and come to crime later.

There is an argument which people sitting in country towns put forward that they can sit in court all morning dressed up in a wig and all that and then go out at lunch and find themselves next to somebody they're trying and they don't recognise the judge, and certainly it is the case that there is virtually no record of people ever being assaulted or attacked or anything of that kind. So that's really my position on that. It is an interesting thing.

Great efforts have been made in recent years with children. They're told they don't need to be overborne by everybody dressed up in wigs and gowns and so on, so they tend to get taken to the court the night before and the judge will show them round and say, "This is where I sit, and this is where you go" and so on. Then at the end they say to the child, "How would you like it tomorrow? Would you like people in ordinary suits or would you like them dressed up in wigs and gowns?", and the kids invariably say they'd like the full outfit please! So there we are. But basically, the answer to your question is, I'm against the wigs and the gowns, particularly in civil and appellate matters.

And presumably it's more comfortable sitting in a lounge suit than having a wig on your head?

Yes.

Jury trials have been much debated recently, not least because of Lord Justice Auld's review of the criminal courts. You have spoken out quite clearly on the issue of jury trials as well. I wonder if you could take us through your thinking?[10]

This again has been very controversial. My own position is a minority one on the subject. The present position is that there are certain offences of a minor kind which can only be tried by justices and magistrates, or district judges (magistrates) as they are now called, but essentially the magistrates' court, and no matter how much you mind being accused of speeding or something, you simply cannot have it tried any other way.

At the other end of the spectrum, there is a category of crime regarded as so serious that they cannot be tried otherwise than by a judge and jury, and that will

---

[10] The jury system is also discussed by Lord Justice Auld (Ch.4), Lord Irvine (Ch.6), Lord Goldsmith (Ch.8) and David Lock (Ch.9).

obviously include things like murder and rape and manslaughter and kidnapping—the whole panoply of serious crime.

The difficulty comes with the broad swathe of offences in the middle which can be tried by magistrates' courts and can be tried by a judge and jury, and the question which has given rise to controversy is who decides.

In Scotland the law is that the prosecution decides, so if the prosecutor says, "This is a case for the Sheriff Court" (which is the equivalent to the magistrates') or, "This is a case for a judge and jury", his word or her word goes. In England, it has always been the defendant who decides. What was proposed by Jack Straw, but he got defeated twice on the subject in the House of Lords by quite large majorities, was that it was the court, the magistrates' court, that should decide, with an appeal to the crown court judge if the defendant didn't like the magistrates' decision.

My position was that there was no injustice in the existing system, but that it was actually more sensible that the court should make a decision which seemed to me a very sensible decision for a court to make, and if anybody felt they were aggrieved or hard done by then they could go to the crown court judge, who would almost certainly be favourably inclined towards trial by jury. But what you have undoubtedly had in the past was some really quite trivial proceedings conducted, at considerable expense to the public, in front of a judge and jury.

As an example, when I was the Lord Chief Justice, I went up to Liverpool to meet the local judges and try a few small cases, and they lined up a list of 17 cases in order to make sure that if one of them wasn't effective another would be, and all 17 defendants immediately pleaded guilty. The only case they could find was a man, who was quite elderly and who had I think 66 previous convictions for shoplifting and who was accused of shoplifting on this occasion, taking a couple of things off a supermarket shelf. There was really no question of one sending him to prison, whether he was convicted or whether he wasn't, because it wouldn't have been a sensible thing to do.

I mention this as an example of the sort of case that one might think didn't really deserve that degree of elaboration in the trial. But Jack Straw was repeatedly defeated on the question and everybody said this was a very serious infringement of the rights of the subject, and that was the view that prevailed. I think there is now an alternative approach to the same problem by enlarging the jurisdiction of justices and having them sitting with a judge and so on, but we'll have to see the eventual shape of all this.

What about in serious fraud trials? Lord Justice Auld challenged the appropriateness of long, complex, technical trials being heard by juries.

Well, this has been around for a long time. There was a committee on fraud trials some years ago over which Lord Roskill presided. His committee recommended that there should be alternative means of trying very long fraud trials, and this is an idea that's been resurrected. Again, there are two schools of thought. One school of thought says no matter how much paper there is and how complicated the transaction and no matter how elaborate, ultimately the question is, was the man or woman honest or dishonest in doing this, that or the other, and that is a perfect jury question, and if it's sufficiently clearly and skilfully explained, the jury will have no difficulty in understanding it.

The contrary view is that matters of this kind, involving huge stacks of documents and tracing the complex financial transactions from here to there to the next place and on and on and on, are just not suitable for jury trial. The jury get inundated with paper, the thing is enormously complex, it goes on for months and months and months, and it's not usually being tried by the cross-section of the community who are meant to constitute the jury because the number of people who can take six or nine months out to sit in a jury is necessarily unrepresentative. I think a number of judges who have conducted these very heavy trials feel that that the whole process, without losing any of its fairness, would gain in a number of directions if it was a judge or a judge sitting with assessors. Whether the defendant would be worse off is quite a difficult question. I think if you look at the record, most people who are the subject of these long fraud trials get convicted. Whether because the jury feel having sat there for nine months . . .

But this is a continuing issue, and I think in the new Criminal Justice Bill there's likely to be a controversy about that suggestion. The Bar certainly, criminal defenders, are very much against it, and they espouse the first point of view that I've described. They say, when you get right down to it, the question at the heart of the case is always relatively simple—was the defendant honest or dishonest?

Most judges spend time judging but, increasingly over the years, it seems that some judges have been pulled out of judicial duty and have been involved with a range of judicial inquiries. This often takes some of the finest judges in the land out of judicial service. How do you feel about that, as someone who was managing a judicial team?[11]

Well, most of us have conducted inquiries in our time. "My inquiry" tends to be the sort of judicial equivalent of "my operation"—people tend to talk about it! In some countries, the United States for example and increasingly Australia, the view is taken that judges simply shouldn't conduct inquiries such as that into Bloody Sunday, or such as that of Lord Phillips into BSE, or Lord Scott into Arms to Iraq or any of the others. They say this isn't a judicial occupation and judges should stick to their mainline duties.

The other view is that it is a judicial occupation, albeit not a mainline judicial occupation, because it involves the assimilation and assessment of a lot of factual material and the making of judgments as to what happened and involves skills that a lawyer is deploying most of the time in his or her ordinary life. I think it's right to say that there is a growing adverse feeling to the appointment of judges for this kind of purpose, not because they're thought to do them other than well, but simply because it takes them away from the job they're appointed to do, and one certainly does regret the loss of judges for months or years on end for these other functions.

Lord Devlin once memorably remarked that the reputation of the judges being generally very high, every Government has attempted to plunder it in order to get judges to head inquiries. If ever there were a suggestion that a Government was wanting a judge simply to lend respectability to a conclusion that it wanted to be

---

[11] Judicial inquiries are also discussed by Lord Irvine (Ch.6), Dame Elizabeth Butler-Sloss (Ch.11), Lord Saville (Ch.14) and Lord Mackay (Ch.17).

reached, that would be highly objectionable. I don't think that has actually happened in recent years.

*That leads into the issue of judicial independence. It's hard for the public to know the
extent to which judges are actually independent of the Executive and the Government
of the day. There are suspicions perhaps that there are regular interactions, and so
again here there are suspicions that it may be all rather too clubby.*

I think we're very fortunate in this country because the conventions are very, very
clear, and one's independence as a judge is respected to an astonishing extent. I've
encountered people who would imagine that if one was hearing a case involving the
Government, one might get a telephone call from some official or other telling one
what they thought about it all. The answer is that is absolutely, completely unthink-
able, and in point of fact, officials and Government departments go to almost extraordinary lengths to avoid any suggestion of trying to put pressure in any situation
I have ever encountered.

*Can I ask you several more personal questions? You have held three remarkably senior
judicial roles—those of Senior Law Lord, Lord Chief Justice and Master of the Rolls.
How did they differ and how have you enjoyed each?*

Well, they differ very much because they are different functions. When I was the
Master of the Rolls, many members of the public thought of it as Lord Denning's
office and they would continue to write him letters, and one got really quite a
considerable postbag from interested, but concerned, members of the public
raising serious questions. Lord Denning would always write back to them and this
continued.

I remember getting a letter from a judge in New Zealand saying, "I have always
thought that the Master of the Rolls had the best judicial job in the Commonwealth".
I wrote back and said, "Well, I quite agree, I think so too", and it is in many ways a
very attractive but very busy and very demanding job. You are running the civil division of the Court of Appeal, you've got a great flood of work, a lot of it is very, very
interesting, and most of it of course doesn't go any further. So for 90 litigants out of
100, it is the final court. Tom Denning made it a very famous court and he was a marvellous exemplar of judicial style in very many ways.

The Lord Chief Justice's job is a different job because it has always had considerable criminal responsibility. The Master of the Rolls by statute is the President of
the Civil Division of the Court of Appeal; the Lord Chief Justice is the President of
the Criminal Division of the Court of Appeal. In the decade or so before I myself
was appointed it had become almost exclusively criminal, partly because of the
increased number of criminal appeals and challenges . . . well very largely I suppose
for that reason.

Also, because the Lord Chief Justice is the top of the legal hierarchy, he has a
representational function. He has a very enjoyable but quite demanding range of
representational things. He goes and talks to magistrates, he goes and talks all over

the country, he goes and talks to local Bars, he goes and visits prisons, places like Broadmoor—and so he does really have quite a busy life, in addition to coping with personal problems that arise. For example there was a case, not in London, where there was a dispute about adoption, and the mother of the child accused the judge of having made a sexual assault against her. This was investigated and proved to be absolutely, totally without foundation, but the Chief Justice gets drawn into this kind of problem. The judge, not surprisingly, was very deeply upset about this, and there was a question of what do you do then. So it's a very different job in many ways from that of the Master of the Rolls.

My present job is different again because there is very little administration. The Lord Chief Justice has a considerable burden of administration, the Master of the Rolls quite a lot, I have very little. But one does get a lot of very interesting cases to hear, and we pick the cases, as I have already explained, that we do hear, and they tend to go on longer than they do in some other courts.

You seem to speak with greater affection of the current role that you are in?

Well, I wouldn't have needed to do it if I hadn't wanted to.

One final question. We live in times of immense change in the legal system. What words of advice would you give to pupils in school or students at university who are contemplating a career in the law?

Well, I think the same advice one would always have given, which is yes, if you really want to. But I think the solicitors' profession and certainly the Bar are tough and they are competitive. You do well if you do well, but not everybody does well, and unless your heart is really in it, you had better do something else I think. There are, after all, too many lawyers rather than too few!

Thank you, Lord Bingham, on behalf of everyone here at Gresham College.

CHAPTER EIGHT

The Rt Hon The Lord Goldsmith QC
Attorney General

Monday November 11, 2002

Tonight my guest is the Attorney General, Lord Goldsmith. He had a distinguished career as a barrister, he was made a QC in 1987, and was the Chairman of the Bar in 1995. He founded the Bar Pro Bono Unit in 1996. He was made a life peer in 1999, and in 2001 became the Attorney General. He was appointed a Privy Counsellor in 2002.

Welcome, Lord Goldsmith; it's marvellous to have you with us. To begin, I will move straight on to the question of the role of the Attorney General. It's a role, I suspect, that most lay people have heard of, but I also suspect many would struggle to summarise the range and extent of your responsibilities. My understanding is that it has a history of well over 600 years. Could you walk us through what the role involves and the spectrum of your responsibilities?

It's actually over 700 years, because the first person who held the role which I have now was appointed in the middle of the 14th century. Essentially, it started as a role as advisor to the King, legal advisor to the Government as it then was, and a representative, going round the courts in the country looking after the King's business. But it changed over a period of time, and so the Attorney General now really has essentially three roles, or you can divide them into three parts.

First of all, I'm a minister. I have ministerial responsibility, like any other minister, for my departments. My departments are the Crown Prosecution Service, Treasury Solicitor's Department, Serious Fraud Office, Customs & Excise Prosecutions Office and the Director of Public Prosecutions in North Ireland. And as a minister I also share in collective responsibility for policy decisions, in particular—and this is a topic we might come back to—in relation to criminal justice. These days, criminal justice policy is a trilateral responsibility. It's the responsibility of the Home Secretary, the Lord Chancellor and the Attorney General. So that's the ministerial responsibility.

Secondly, I continue to have a responsibility as the legal advisor to Government. That means I'm the senior legal advisor to the Prime Minister, to Cabinet, and to my ministerial colleagues. It does not mean that I advise on all legal issues, by any means, but it means that I will advise on the most important legal issues that

111

will arise—the most difficult legal issues. Gone are the days when there were straightforward cases to come to me in chambers. And I will also represent the Government sometimes in court, which I do not infrequently.

The third area, which is the one that people probably find most difficult to understand, is my public interest function, because although I am a member of Government, I also sit apart from Government. I carry out public interest functions, particularly in prosecution, I make prosecution decisions—certain prosecutions can't take place without my specific consent—but the Director of Public Prosecutions, who reports to me, will also consult me on other cases.

I take those decisions independently of Government, not swayed by party political considerations, but purely and simply on the basis of the evidence and also the public interest, in a very general sense. In that public interest field, I also exercise functions in contempt of court, extradition, family law, appeals on sentences, unduly lenient sentences—again we may come back to that, it's a special area—in enforcing the law generally. Again, in those areas, I'm acting not as a Government minister but as the law officer of the Crown with responsibility for considering what the public interest is and deciding how to exercise the functions in that framework. It's a very long answer, but I'm afraid it's a slightly complicated role.

As legal advisor to the Government, a huge variety of legal topics must arise, so what size of team and what kind of individuals do you have working with you?

There are a large number of lawyers involved in Government overall, and most legal problems will be looked at first probably by a departmental lawyer. Then it will come through to my office. I have an immediate office which has 15 lawyers who will be providing assistance to me but, again, able to draw on the expertise of the departments. So if we're dealing with perhaps a European Community issue but which relates to agriculture, we'll be looking for specific background information from the legal advisors in agriculture. But the essential area covers a very wide area of law—human rights, European Union law, domestic law—and with the assistance of these lawyers, I try to provide the best advice I can.

When is it that a Government lawyer within a particular department decides to refer a case or a matter to you? And when do they resolve an issue themselves?

There are some ministerial conventions about this. They include if ever there is a difference between departments on a legal matter, and that does happen, and if it is an important area then it's required that before the Government is committed, Law Officers' advice should be obtained. Any minister can ask for my advice, and if anybody within Government has concerns about the constitutionality or the validity of, for example, a piece of subordinate legislation, a piece of delegated legislation, or even these days, and this is quite a lot of what I do, the lawfulness of primary legislation—does it comply with the Human Rights Act, does it comply with our obligations under European Union law?—then it will often come to me. And international law, that's another area I should add—I advise on international law too.

So that we all understand the structure—how does the Government Legal Service (the phrase that's often used) relate to the Treasury Solicitor's Department? Is Government Legal Service a term of art?

The Treasury Solicitor's Department is a solicitors' firm, as it were, within Government, which provides legal advice and litigation services to other departments who choose to follow this route. But there are many other lawyers within Government who provide legal services, who are not part of the Treasury Solicitor's Department.

For example, there are lawyers in fairly large teams who are legal advisers to Departments of State such as the DTI, Transport and the Home Office, and some in smaller teams who advise organisations such as the regulatory bodies. Together, these 40 or so organisations and around 1,900 lawyers, comprise the Government Legal Service, of which the Treasury Solicitor is the Head of Profession and for which I have ministerial oversight.

So, they all have a relationship with the Treasury Solicitor and, more or less directly, with me, and all lawyers in Government are entitled ultimately to come to me, for example, if they are concerned about the propriety of what they may be doing or asked to do. So I have an oversight over all of the lawyers in Government who are practising law. There are some lawyers who are not practising law, like the Prime Minister. I don't have oversight over him, but the others I do.

And disputes between Government and the outside world, as it were, they are all handled by the Treasury Solicitor, is that correct?

Many of them are, but not all of them. Civil litigation is also handled by the lawyers within some of the larger legal teams of particular departments. For example, the Departments of Work and Pensions/Health, the Revenue Departments and DEFRA have each got a body of lawyers who undertake litigation, often directly concerned with the prosecutions which they undertake. Or, on occasions, they make use of outside lawyers; they can do that too.

How is a decision made between keeping a matter inside as against instructing external lawyers?

This is a matter for the minister and permanent secretary of the particular department as to what model they want to use. I issue guidelines which identify the sort of areas that they should keep in-house. They're not rigid, they're not set in concrete, and they're really just intended to give a line.

For example, Government lawyers have enormous expertise in public law. They've got a great deal of experience in dealing with public law disputes, judicial review, claims that Government is acting unlawfully, and so really it wouldn't make a great deal of sense to go to an outside lawyer to handle that sort of litigation. On the other hand, if you want to do a PFI, if you want to do a commercial venture, if you want to enter into a partnership or set up an overseas subsidiary, you might well go to an outside firm of solicitors who have got that degree of expertise in order to do it.

Staying with the ministerial role, but leaving the Treasury Solicitor to one side, you also mentioned the Serious Fraud Office, the Director of Public Prosecutions (the DPP) in Ireland, and of course, our Crown Prosecution Service. Could you explain each of these for us, starting with the Crown Prosecution Service, because in its own right it is a massive organisation and absolutely essential to the criminal justice system? Later on, I want to chat about work across the criminal justice system; so this is, in part, by way of setting the scene.

Let's look first of all at the prosecutions within England and Wales. Most prosecutions are handled by the Crown Prosecution Service. They handle 1.4 million prosecutions a year. So the police will bring to the Crown Prosecution Service their cases and the Crown Prosecution Service will take them over. This wasn't the way it was done before 1986. Before 1986 the police did their own prosecutions, they had their own in-house solicitors or they went to outside people to do it, but since 1986 we've had this national service. So the Crown Prosecution Service is all round the country. We have 42 areas, which correspond to the areas that the police have, and they have area offices and branch offices connected with particular courts. They do the vast majority of the cases and they will bring the cases themselves in the magistrates' court, do them largely themselves, not exclusively. In the crown court, they will largely, but not exclusively, hire outside barristers to do the cases.

The Serious Fraud Office is much, much smaller. That handles perhaps 80, 85 cases a year. Those are the most serious and complex fraud trials. They are unique as prosecutors because they investigate as well as prosecute. So a case will actually come, the sort of cases that we've all heard of, to the Serious Fraud Office, they will decide to take them on, and they will then investigate the cases and then, if they think it's right, they will prosecute them. So that's lawyers and investigators working together.

There are other prosecutors. A number of the departments have their own prosecution systems—Department of Trade Prosecution, for example. I mentioned Department of Work and Pensions Prosecutions. Local authorities prosecute— I have no responsibility for local authority prosecutions. I have a tenuous responsibility for other prosecutions. Customs and Excise I should mention too, because they do a lot of prosecution as well, and I have had, since April, responsibility for them as well.

How is the decision made in a fraud case as to whether or not it should be handled by the Crown Prosecution Service or the Serious Fraud Office?

Somebody will approach the Serious Fraud Office and say, "Is this a case you want to take on?", and the Serious Fraud Office would look to see does it fit their criteria. Does it concern big enough sums of money? It has got to be at least a million pounds, but even that won't do it of itself. Is it a sufficiently serious and complex case that their sort of experience and resources will enable them to handle? So they will decide whether to take it on. If they decide not to, well then, it will be handled either not at all, or it will be handled by the Crown Prosecution Service.

And the DPP in Northern Ireland? Does it cover serious fraud cases?

No, the Serious Fraud Office actually operates in Northern Ireland too, but we've only had, I think, one case there in the last couple of years. The DPP in Northern Ireland is rather different, because in Northern Ireland at the moment most of the prosecutions are still done by the police, and the DPP, who has got a much smaller office, takes on particularly serious cases by agreement with the police. But we are changing that, and as a result of justice reforms in Northern Ireland, the Director of Public Prosecutions will build a system like the Crown Prosecution Service, a national system throughout the province of Northern Ireland, and he will take on all the prosecutions.

Will that reduce the role of police?

They won't be prosecuting. Their role in detection and investigation and evidence gathering will of course remain.

And just to clarify Scottish legal matters—as I always like to do—you are not responsible north of the border, are you?

No, the Lord Advocate, the Scots' Law Officer, is responsible for the Scottish criminal legal system.

Let's move on to the criminal justice system. You mentioned the unprecedented collaboration amongst the Lord Chancellor, the Attorney General (you), and the Home Secretary. There have been huge moves to try and integrate—or at least to bring more closely together—the operations of the criminal justice system. I would like you to speak about that, in the context of the growing alarm about increases in crime, especially violent crime. How is it that the measures that are being adopted and the various Government reforms that have been proposed are going to work out in practice? In particular, how will this collaboration between the various elements of the justice system impact on crime?[1]

---

[1] The criminal justice system is also discussed by Lord Woolf (Ch.1), Lord Justice Auld (Ch.4) and Lord Irvine (Ch.6).

This is also a big topic. It's probably worth just setting the context, because if you think about who are all the different agencies involved in the criminal justice system, once you start to count them up, you find a large number of bodies.

The Home Office has responsibility for the police, for prisons, for probation—so all of those bodies are involved in the criminal justice system. Then you've got the court system: magistrates', crown courts—which are separate at the moment—as well as the whole appellate court structure. On top of that, you have the prosecutors.

Until about 1999, we had a pretty clear division. The Home Office looked after the police, the probation, the prisons and criminal justice sentencing policy, and what sort of offices we should have. The Lord Chancellor's Department, headed by the Lord Chancellor, looked after the courts and the magistrates and the crown court judges, and my office dealt with the prosecutors.

But you can immediately see that if you've got three different departments, you already start to have the possibility of having conflicting aims and objectives. If the criminal justice system is going to work, it actually needs to be joined up much better than that. So in 1999, before I took office, the Labour Government decided to bring the three more closely together.

In my view, you can't put them simply into a single department because there are some very good constitutional reasons why you want to have them separate. You don't want to have judges answerable to the same person who is responsible for the police. You don't want to have prosecutors answerable to the same person who is responsible for the police. Each has got to have its independence, but you have also got to work together. We now have an overarching criminal justice system aim, so we all have the same ultimate target, we're all pointing in the same direction whilst maintaining our own independence.

That has also produced a structure in which ministers at the top are joined up. I've come this afternoon, for example, from a Cabinet committee meeting with the Home Secretary and the Lord Chancellor, in which we've been looking at the present situation and the year ahead, but also joining up on the ground. We've found that if you get the different bits of the criminal justice on the ground working closely together, you can actually make quite remarkable improvements. I don't mean you get a particular person banged up who shouldn't be; I mean that you can actually deal with the inefficiencies and the failures that people tend to read about in the newspapers.

We decided, for example, that we thought the time between arresting a persistent young offender and disposing of that young offender was excessive—it was over 140 days, 140 days for a young kid. Actually you've picked him up, you know he's a persistent young offender, you want to deal with him, and 140 days is a long time before you've actually reached a disposal. So we said, well, we're going to cut that, we're going to halve that, and we achieved that, so it's down to just under 70 days with the last figures. But the way of doing it was to get the three big agencies together: the Crown Prosecution Service, the police, the courts, and also the Probation Service, and go through the list of cases saying, "Well, what's happened to him, where's he gone, why isn't his case coming up yet, what's the problem?", so you can actually get them into courts.

You can do a great deal of working together. I want to build on all this—this is again, I'm sorry, quite a long answer—by producing a new system for a relationship between the Crown Prosecution Service and the police. At the moment, the police arrest somebody or summons them, depending on the basis, they look at the evidence, they decide to charge them, and once they've charged them they hand the papers over to the Crown Prosecution Service, who decide whether or not to continue with the case. That means a lot of cases are stopped. The Crown Prosecution Service looks at them and says "nope, wrong case, wrong charge, wrong evidence, drop it". 12 to 13 per cent of cases are discontinued. That's a huge number of cases where the Crown Prosecution Service are saying at the moment, "No, you've got the wrong charge", or "You've got the wrong person", whatever it may be.

What we want to do now, and I'm very strongly in favour of this, is to bring the Crown Prosecution Service in before that point, so they look at the evidence and they say, "Yes", and they then make the decision to charge, or they will say "No, we won't charge at all", or they may say, "We won't charge but if you've got this evidence or that evidence, we might charge". That's already showing quite significant results, because it's producing a co-operation between the police and Crown Prosecution Service, whilst maintaining their separate independence; that's important. I think it is going to be a very important part of the changes that we've got in mind.

Because that balance is different in different jurisdictions, isn't it? Indeed, in Northern Ireland, you mentioned that the police were themselves involved with prosecution. There is a different balance in many Continental jurisdictions . . .

And in Scotland.

So the shift that you are keen on is about ensuring cases flow more smoothly, so that continuity is ensured?

Better quality cases, the right charge, better prepared, so by the time they get to court, they're in a good state, and then the court can do its job, which is testing the evidence.

Some of the judges find it difficult to be regarded as part of the criminal justice system. They accept, of course, that they are a special kind of participant in the criminal process, but they view their role as that of independent arbiters, not officials or politicians who are pursuing broader policy objectives and certainly not as representatives of any particular Government. It has to be important that the courts remain independent?

Absolutely right. The independence of the Judiciary is one of the completely essential foundations of a democratic society—no compromise on that principle whatsoever. But the fact that a judge is independent when it comes to determining the case in front of him or her, doesn't mean that the judge should not be involved in saying, "Hold on a second, this case has now taken nine months and it hasn't got to trial—we should be doing something to get this case in front of us", or that the judge shouldn't be involved in saying, "Look, it's unsatisfactory that witnesses are being called to this court and kept hanging around for five or six hours, then called back the next day". There is no reason why the judge shouldn't be involved also in trying to make sure that the process of witnesses giving evidence is a satisfactory one, as satisfactory as it can ever be if you're coming along that sort of formal process. So there's lots of things that judges can be involved in very properly without in any way compromising their independence when it comes to the verdict.

And of course I can say in passing that many of the initiatives in relation to information technology are precisely to ensure that information flows from the beginning of the system to the end of the system in a seamless way.

Absolutely, and you've done a great deal to help on that.

But it is massively ambitious in technology terms because of the scale of the venture—given that you have eight or nine major legacy systems that are already in place. It's a long-term project, and obviously a sensitive one in some ways. Public perception, insofar as one can glean this from the media, suggests serious concern about rises in crime. What's the linkage, do you feel, between the reforms you have in mind and crime on the streets?

Actually a lot of crime has gone down. It isn't all a picture of crime having risen. It's quite interesting because people's perception is that crime has risen in areas where it hasn't, but an area where it did rise was in street crime. Interestingly, the people who are most at risk of street crime are not the people who think they are. It's actually young men who are most at risk from street crime. They're the ones walking the streets in the evening who have their mobile phones and their money taken.

But it's still very important, so we engaged, under the chairmanship of the Prime Minister, in an initiative to look at street crime, which has been brought under control over a period of six months. It has reduced quite significantly as a result of collaborative working, and really across the board; not just, although it included, police and prosecution service, dedicated teams able to give advice early, able to concentrate on key issues in street crime—one of the key issues is always identification, you've got to get the identification evidence very quickly—but also other departments too: Department of Education and Department of Health. The Department of Health in relation to drugs, which is a huge part of the problem on the streets. A lot of people who are committing street crime are committing it because they're getting money to fuel an addiction. The Department of Education because we've got a lot of kids who haven't got anything to do. And so you have to bring in those departments as well. There was a very successful what we called "splash programme" over the summer, where while school was out there were useful, interesting, innovative programmes which were being run really under the aegis of Department of Education and Department of Culture, which would provide lots of different activities for kids and was helping to keep them off the streets.

Do you look at other jurisdictions? Do you speak to other Attorneys General, if that's the plural of Attorney General?

I think it's Attorneys General, I think you're right, yes.

To what extent do you keep in touch and monitor progress in other jurisdictions? Do you meet? Are there conventions of Attorneys General?

There are not a lot, but there are some opportunities. I was in Paris over the weekend having meetings with French prosecutors and French judges, focusing upon the fight against terrorism, for example. Now, they've got a very different system from the one we have, but they're facing the same problems, so we do look all the time really to see what lessons we can learn from other systems, and I'm glad to say they look to see what lessons they can learn from us too. I even speak to the Scots about it as well!

And I'm sure you get eminent sense from these conversations.

All the time.

Sitting in the very chair in which you are sitting, we had Sir Robin Auld last year, who had conducted his very large review of the criminal courts. Of course his review went well beyond the criminal courts; indeed it looked across much of the criminal justice system in general. I am keen to have your general thoughts, first of all, on the review, and its impact on your White Paper.

Oh, it's an enormously impressive report: thorough, far-reaching, innovative, very sound analysis and research into the things that he was dealing with, and he looked at other countries, as I'm sure he said, in drawing together his conclusions. We have drawn very, very heavily from his report. We've got two major Bills coming: the Criminal Justice and Sentencing Bill, which draws on his report and also the report of John Halliday, which was into sentencing, and a Courts Bill, which also draws on what Sir Robin had to say about the way that the courts system should be structured.

But the White Paper also picks up things which don't require a legislative solution, but which Sir Robin Auld dealt with as well, such as case preparation and case management. Information technology is a big part of it, and that doesn't need legislation. It does need a lot of thought and resources.

Although we've drawn heavily on his report, we haven't picked up every single one of his recommendations, by any means. For example, he recommended that we should do away with the right to elect for trial by jury, and that's not one of the recommendations we've picked up, but his report has been enormously influential, and it will go down as one of the most important reports on the criminal justice system that there's ever been.

Let's focus on juries. This is something that I've discussed with other judges, including the Lord Chancellor, when he was sitting in the chair. Looking specifically at fraud trials, at serious fraud trials, and the role of juries, Sir Robin Auld questioned the appropriateness of the role of lay jurors in very long, very complex serious fraud trials. Where do you sit on that debate?[2]

This is not a new issue. This goes back to consideration by Lord Roskill, back in the 70s, so this is not a new idea. I've always been really concerned, I have to say, about having juries in the most serious fraud cases. I think: why? And first of all, because the burden on the jurors is intolerable. You're asking people to sit . . . we've had one that's finished today after 11 months—I mean, 11 months! People are called to do jury service for two weeks, and serious fraud cases now last, typically, six months, frequently longer. There was one that went on well into a second year. Now, first of all, how can you reasonably ask people that they should give up that part of their lives?

Secondly, the people who are in a position to do so, and I'm very appreciative that they do, necessarily have to be to quite a high degree self-selecting, because people who've got particular forms of employment, or jobs, or businesses to run, or professional people, couldn't give up that period of time. So you find that you call people to do jury service and the vast majority of them, for that sort of case, say that they can't do it. So it's quite hard to say that you end up with a random selection of the population, and that is one of the great things about the jury system. You're not ending up with a random selection of the population.

And what are you asking them to do? You are asking them to listen to months of evidence, and *listen* to it, because that's the way juries operate of course. We don't give them transcripts. They listen to months of evidence. In *Blue Arrow* the prosecution case took five months, in the course of which they heard detailed, complicated evidence about financial transactions, with constant cross-reference to documents. The story is not actually very interesting, and it's far less interesting if you hear it over five months. So I think we're asking—and this is what Roskill said, and research has demonstrated—you're asking people not only to spend a great deal of time, but to listen to and to try to understand extremely complex things in a very unsatisfactory form.

The third thing, to my mind—and I've seen a lot of these cases, particularly from the other side, from the civil cases—because you have to cut down on the issues as far as you can to make them intelligible and to make them manageable, so you end up not really presenting the criminality of these cases on some occasions. I think it's deeply unsatisfactory that if we have someone who's committed, if I can call it this way, a "blue collar fraud", a benefit fraud, someone who's been claiming social security when in fact they're co-habiting or they've got another job, we can deal with those people very readily, we can get them into court, we can put them into prison. But when you deal with "white collar" crime, it's so complex and so difficult that I really fear that we have a dual standard in relation to it. I think people would not have confidence if they thought that it's so difficult to get at these "white collar" criminals because of the complicated nature of the case, and finding people who are

---

[2] The jury system is also discussed by Lord Justice Auld (Ch.4), Lord Irvine (Ch.6), Lord Bingham (Ch.7) and David Lock (Ch.9).

prepared to sit for this length of time, that we can't prosecute. I wouldn't find that at all acceptable.

I believe, for those reasons, the fact that it really is entirely justified that we make an exception in that sort of category of case. Sorry, again it's a long answer!

Just to stress again, we are dealing with a tiny fraction of the number of cases going through the courts.

Very, very small, really small. The vast majority of cases will continue to be dealt with by juries if that's what the defendant wants.

So you are comfortable with and indeed supportive of trial by jury generally?

Yes.

Staying with criminal matters, can we turn now to unduly lenient sentences? Can you outline your role in relation to these?

Yes. We have a system under which, generally speaking, the prosecution can't appeal decisions by the courts with which it disagrees. The defence always can, usually can. You can appeal against conviction. You can appeal against your sentence if you think it's too long. But there is a limited power, which actually arose. You may remember the Ealing vicarage rape case that caused a great deal of consternation because of the sentence which was passed.

There is a limited power under which I can appeal against a sentence on the grounds that it is unduly lenient. I take it to the Court of Appeal. It's a limited number of cases because it's only the most serious cases that fall within the jurisdiction. I can only do that if the sentence is outside the range which a judge could have imposed, and the range can be quite wide because there's a lot of judicial discretion in these areas, and the Court of Appeal also has a discretion whether it wants to interfere with it.

Did you say it has to be outside the range?

It has to be outside the range. So, to give you one or two examples recently. Death by dangerous driving is something that really people, the public, feel very strongly about and I understand why. A few years ago, you probably wouldn't have found many people going to prison for causing death by dangerous driving, probably very few indeed. I've been, and my predecessors have been, pushing away at this, and on the whole it's exceptional not to have a custodial sentence for killing somebody, which is what it is even though it's not through dangerous but negligent driving. The Court of Appeal has to have the opportunity of setting guidelines which will then be applied up and down the country, and one of the ways that it does that is when I appeal against a sentence on the ground that it's unduly lenient.

But in that kind of case, you're saying there is a band within which a judge can rule, and it's only when it's beyond that range that you have an opportunity to appeal. But presumably, in terms of public opinion, the lower end of that band might, for many, be unacceptable, even though that band is within the realm of judicial discretion?

Yes, it might be, and sometimes I will take a case to the Court of Appeal to say, "Look, would you please review your guidelines". We did some cases in relation to domestic violence where it didn't appear that the courts, or some courts, were taking sufficiently seriously domestic violence, didn't see it as the crime that it is, perhaps because it was indoors and some judges would say, somehow, it was less serious. Well, sorry, people being beaten up, whether it's indoors or outdoors, is very serious, and as a quarter of murders—a quarter of deaths, homicides—are domestic, this is a very serious issue we have to deal with. So that was an example of taking something to the Court of Appeal to say, "Look, we want to send out a message this is serious". I did the same thing with street robbery earlier in the year, and the Court of Appeal gave a very clear statement about how serious that was and that the sentences should be tough, and that's had an impact too.

Sentencing policy and justifications for punishment are hugely complex matters and views about them shift over time. What's the process by which there can be a shift in policy in this area? Because it can potentially involve so many interested parties within Government, and within the Judiciary. Some judges might be leaning towards the view that the prisons are too full, and others might be inclined to think that the only way to send out an emphatic message to society about the unacceptability of certain behaviour is precisely to impose heavy custodial sentences. And criminologists and legal theorists debate this kind of topic and have done for many years. But how's Government policy formulated? How does it evolve?

Well, we've moved from a position of sentencing-anarchy to an attempt to be more consistent, and it was sentencing-anarchy in the days when there were no guidelines; nobody set any tariffs, judges decided up and down the country entirely in their own judgment. The only thing that would help you identify what the sentence would be was if the sentence was held to be too heavy by the Court of Appeal when there was an appeal.

Then the Court of Appeal started to lay down guidelines. It would take an area like drug trafficking or theft in breach of trust, and say, "This is a guideline case, this now tells you the sort of factors, judges, you should take into account, and the sort of sentencing you should impose". The death by dangerous driving included one of those: a case called *Boswell.*

We now have a further feature, which is the Sentencing Advisory Panel, which is an academic panel presided over by a professor—I mean, academic in the sense that these are not people who are actually sentencing, but they are expert in what they are doing. They will look, they will consult, and they will come out with a set of guidelines and say to the Court of Appeal, "Look, this is the sort of area we think you should be thinking about for this sort of level of sentence". They've done it recently with rape, and it has helped to add a degree of consistency.

At the end of the day, public opinion plays a very important part. If the public demonstrate that they believe that a particular form of criminal conduct is deserving of very tough punishment, eventually (I say eventually) that message will get through, sooner or later, sometimes sooner.

Let's leave the criminal world behind and jump to foreign affairs. In what kind of circumstances is your advice sought, for example in potential conflicts involving this country and other countries? What's your role in that context?

Okay. I'm going to be irritatingly taciturn about this particular aspect. When I give legal advice, I don't normally disclose the substance of that advice or indeed that I've given that advice. It's quite a longstanding ministerial convention that the Attorney General's advice, Law Officers' advice, is confidential. That enables there to be the sort of relationship that any lawyer and client would have of being able to talk openly without the fear that it's going to appear on the front page of the newspapers, and there's perhaps sometimes more of an interest in what I have to say appearing on the front page of the newspapers. I'm not going to talk about individual areas, but this is a Government which believes strongly in the rule of law, it believes strongly in complying with its international obligations, and these include international obligations which set out circumstances in which we might engage in the use of force.

And you're called upon to offer advice at what point?

I'm not going any further than that. I'm simply saying these are important areas. They are areas where, as I say, the Government rightly believes—it's a tenet of our belief—that we should comply with our international legal obligations.

I will probe no further! Moving swiftly on then, let's ask some personal questions.

Personal questions—oh!

Not that personal! You enjoyed a very successful career as a commercial silk, as a commercial barrister. Your current office is surely a huge change for you. How did you enjoy or sustain yourself through the transition? Has it been easy? Has it been harrowing?

It has been a very considerable change. In fact, in my early days I did quite a bit of crime. I sat as a recorder in the crown courts for 15 years, so I actually knew more about criminal law than some people sometimes appreciate. I did public law, and used to act for the Government when I was a junior barrister. But it's quite right that it has been an enormous change both in the way that one works and in the areas of law which I now cover.

How have I got through it? You rely as a minister very heavily upon the quality of the people who work with you, and I think we're very fortunate. I talked about the 15 people who work in my office as well as all the other lawyers. It's quite a plum job to work in my office. It's something that you want on your CV. People don't come for 15 or 20 years; they are seconded from other departments, and they come from the Foreign Office, or from the Home Office, or from the Department of Trade and Industry, or from the Crown Prosecution Service, or Serious Fraud Office, and they come and spend the time. So there's a very high level of expertise on which I'm able to draw.

Otherwise, I think the most striking thing about being in Government is it's just relentless, and I think that's what the modern world has done, and the media—the immediacy of Parliament, of people wanting to know what you're doing. It means that you don't have the luxury that sometimes you have in any form of activity in the private sector, of stopping and saying you're going to take a lot of time over this, not going to deal with this, going to take the day off, whatever it is. These issues have got to be dealt with now, and that provides an enormous excitement about it, but it does mean that the job is a relentless one.

At any one stage you must have tens, indeed hundreds, of balls in the air, as it were. Do you miss rolling up your sleeves and just devoting yourself to one complex matter or case, or are you quite happy to leave that behind?

It's an awfully long time since I've done that anyway really, I think even at the Bar. I do appear in cases, and then for a few hours when I'm actually in court that's all I'm thinking about, but it's a fair point.

As I mentioned in my introduction, you were the founder of the Bar Pro Bono Unit. It would be interesting to learn about the background to that and where you think the pro bono movement is going in the legal world in this country.

I think there's a very proud tradition among solicitors and barristers of doing work for free because they believe in justice. It sounds terribly pompous, but I believe it is right. Of course people want to get paid for the work that they do, they can't live otherwise, but I think a lot of people are prepared to put part of their time into helping people who need their help but can't pay for it.

And so I started this in 1996, after I'd been Chairman of the Bar, and I asked colleagues at the Bar, "Would you agree to give up three days a year? Would you commit to three days a year? We'll find cases which are appropriate for you to advise on or to do". I was tremendously encouraged by the reaction. I had 300 barristers who wrote back to me within about a day saying yes they would. The number has now grown to over 10 per cent of the practising Bar. That's a big proportion of people, and a lot of them do a lot more than three days as well.

They're prepared to do it because, as I say, they're happy to help, as long as there's a system in which we find the right cases for them. That's what the Unit does. The Unit is a clearing house. It is staffed, and receives cases in from all sorts of areas, then finds on the database who's an appropriate barrister to take it on, and then they're happy to do the work.

Where's it going to go in the future? There are lots of people involved in pro bono work. We had a pro bono week. The Law Society, the Bar Council, the other organisations, did this, and I went to different parts of the country, and it was enormously encouraging to see how many people were involved in it—specialist advice, people giving advice to particular groups of people, or running a general help session at a citizens' advice bureau. I think we will always need people who are prepared to give something of their time because however well funded the public legal system will be, there will always be gaps, and always be gaps for people to fill. It's not a substitute for having a properly funded legal aid system, but it does help as an adjunct.

Can I return to one of your other roles, the public interest function, because you touched on that at the beginning and gave a brief introduction to that, but you also mentioned that it was unlike your other ministerial responsibilities, because you had to assume an independent—I suppose a quasi-judicial—role?

Yes. Classic area for independence is the prosecution decision. There was a very famous case in the 1920s which actually caused the collapse of the first Labour Government. It was the Government of Ramsay Macdonald, and it was a man called Campbell who was the Deputy Editor of the *Workers' Weekly*. In the 1920s you'll all recall what the historical situation was. He wrote an article which was calling on soldiers not to break strikes in the event that there was a General Strike. It technically amounted into incitement to mutiny, and the Attorney General of the day, Sir Patrick Hastings, decided to prosecute. He then changed his mind, and it was believed he changed his mind after a Cabinet meeting, and he withdrew the prosecution. That produced a great controversy about why it was, and whether it was appropriate for a decision about a prosecution to be influenced by political considerations. Campbell, I should say, was a Communist but was a very decent man, good war record, and it was going to be deeply unpopular for a Labour Government to appear to have been prosecuting him. It resulted in a vote of no confidence in the Government, and the Government fell.

So that indicates how deeply ingrained the idea of independence of the Attorney General's role is. Other examples would be, for example, contempt of court. If a newspaper does something which is going to interfere with a fair trial, then I may prosecute it for contempt of court. I did that with the *Sunday Mirror* when it caused the collapse of the Leeds footballers' trials. I've done it with the BBC. I've done it in slightly different circumstances with a newspaper called the *Manchester Evening News* over providing information in breach of an injunction about the whereabouts of the two young men who had murdered poor little Jamie Bulger.

So those are all taken without consideration of what my political colleagues might think would be a good thing or a bad thing, and I pick on newspapers because that's an area where people would traditionally think, oh well, politicians don't want to have a go at newspapers because they depend upon newspapers. As far as I'm concerned, that is an irrelevant consideration. I don't actually think anyone's ever lost a General Election because the newspaper had been pursued by the Attorney General of that particular Government, but I think it's very, very important indeed that my only consideration is public interest. My concern is people should have a fair trial and newspapers shouldn't interfere with that, and if they do interfere with that, I will not hesitate to take them myself to court and prosecute them.

How do these cases come to your attention? Does this happen systematically?

Different ways. A defendant may complain to me; a judge may complain to me; occasionally I will pick something up myself and ask for it to be looked at.

And do you find it difficult to take off your ministerial hat?

Not at all, no, not at all. I'm not going to be another Attorney General to bring down a Labour Government, but I know what my role is, I know what considerations are legitimate and what are not, and I regard the integrity of the office of Attorney General as something that I must not tarnish.

One final question for you, and it is one that I ask all my guests at Gresham. How would you respond to a pupil or student who asked you about the merits and demerits of pursuing a career in the law?

I would say it's an enormously rewarding career. It's a difficult career, but go for it as long as you're prepared to be flexible. The way that we practised law when I started, well, it's not the way we practise law today, and it'll be different again in a generation's time.

And where would you see greatest changes arising? In the work of solicitors or barristers, or do you anticipate transformations throughout?

Well, it's going to sound awfully, awfully as if I'm sucking up when I say this, but I think information technology is going to make one of the biggest differences, Richard. You know, we do things much more now in writing rather than orally, we have to do much more outside court than in court, alternative dispute resolution is different. You know, when I started to practise, the idea was that you would get ready for the battle in court and that was all that mattered. I think people will move between being barristers and solicitors. Some people will continue to operate as referral lawyers; others will be seeing the clients and handling the mechanics of the case—lots of changes. But the essential job of trying to help people, and to help people to put their case, I think will remain, and that's what I have found the most satisfying as a lawyer—unscrambling the facts, understanding what really is at the heart of it, and then trying to put forward, on someone else's behalf, in the best possible way, what their case is. That's very satisfying.

Lord Goldsmith, thank you very much.

CHAPTER NINE

David Lock
Chairman of the National Criminal Intelligence Service
and the National Crime Squad

Thursday December 12, 2002

Welcome, in this inclement weather, to Gresham College. It's my great pleasure this evening to welcome David Lock. David has a variety of interesting things to discuss with us tonight. His background is fascinating. He was a barrister in practice for 12 years. In 1997, he became Labour MP for Wyre Forest. During his time as an MP, for a couple of years he was a Parliamentary Secretary at the Lord Chancellor's Department. He lost his seat in 2001 but earlier this year was appointed Chairman of the National Criminal Intelligence Service and the National Crime Squad.

David, I'd like to discuss a number of issues with you. Indeed your background gives us a whole host of fascinating topics to chat about. Can we start off with the circumstances of the loss of your seat, because I think it's an interesting story—a tragic tale in many ways—and it raises some fascinating questions of principle?

Well yes, let's start at the low point. It was very, very simple. In Wyre Forest, there was one big town, Kidderminster. Kidderminster had a hospital. The hospital had an Accident and Emergency (A&E) Department. The unanimous medical view was that the A&E could not continue, simply wasn't safe to continue, but that was not what the local public wanted. It wasn't what some of the local medical community wanted, but as they began to understand the medical issues, so they reverted from opposition to silence. The public were up in arms, and an independent candidate emerged who played on campaigning for what the public wanted, which was the restoration of their full A&E services. He was a retired consultant at the hospital and he won the election as an Independent.

What's happened now? Has the A&E service been retained?

No, the A&E closed as a full A&E and went down to a minor injuries unit, which served something like 75 to 80 per cent of people who previously went to A&E. This was about a year before the general election. In fact it was less than that, because it

129

closed because the consultants refused to take it through the winter because they said it just wasn't safe, and they were entirely right.

For you though, as an MP, this must have pulled you in a number of directions. Talk us through your thinking at that time and how you came to establish the position you eventually took.

If you're an MP, you are elected by the public. In one sense one's judgment is tempered by public opinion, and one is not an entirely free agent. The object of a Member of Parliament, to some extent, is to get re-elected. The re-election rate in the United States from sitting members of the House is something like 94 per cent, so you have to do something pretty spectacular there to lose your seat. It's the same in this country.

But the issue that I was facing, which was very interesting, was what do you do if the public wants something that cannot be delivered? The public wanted a full A&E service at their hospital. All the medics who understood these things, and all the independent reports from outside, said it's just not possible: you cannot have the range of backup services that you need to run a safe A&E; you can't accord with the National Service Frameworks; you can't train junior doctors, junior doctors' hours changing means that there are constraints; the growth of specialist services means there are constraints—a whole variety of medical reasons. You just can't do it. You need a population base of something like 400,000 to run an A&E, and this hospital was serving 100,000.

So what do you do if you're an MP and your public wants something that you cannot actually deliver? It seems to me there are two positions you can take. You can either say, "I'm elected by the public, I'm there to represent their views, I should go and campaign for the retention of the A&E, even though I know in my heart it's not possible", or you say, "No, I'm not, I'm a representative, a delegate, and my job is to engage in the process but actually say look, I'm terribly sorry, you know, I'll do you the best model available, I'll campaign for the best practical option". But it would be fraudulent to stand at the front of the queue to lead a delegation to go and see a minister saying "We want our A&E back" if in fact that's not an option which any minister could deliver and you knew in advance. Both options are arguable.

With a background as a lawyer, you always think, what's the best case, and there was no case here. This was a kind of summary judgment in favour of change, and I took the option that I should engage with the public and try and explain. It was politically the wrong option because I lost my seat. I know other MPs in other circumstances who were fighting the campaign to retain services that they knew were not in the best interests of their constituents to retain, but they needed to get re-elected, and they needed to get re-elected in order to carry on doing all the other good work they were doing as MPs. So it's a very interesting dilemma.

If you had your time again, would you do things differently?

I would do a lot of things very differently, but I don't think I would take a different position, because in the end you've got to wake up, look at yourself in the mirror, and actually think that what you're doing is worthwhile. I think some people can. I just don't think I could actually stand at the front of a delegation going to a minister and saying "We want our A&E back" if in my heart I knew that it was a complete non-starter. Nobody had ever produced a plan or a scheme to make it work. If they had, then of course that would be different, but the reality was that it just wasn't going to happen.

So you moved on. Before we move on to your new roles, looking back on your time in Parliament and indeed in Government, how do you feel? It was a good chunk of your life. How do you reflect on that period? Now, interestingly, you're partly in the private sector and partly in the public sector. Is it with nostalgia that you reflect on your purely public life?

Parliament is a beguiling existence. People fawn to you. There's a sort of superficial feel of importance. But, you know, in the public's estimation of the kind of veracity and the standing of people, estate agents and politicians are down the bottom, so it's not something you do for great public standing. There's a difference between how people think of politicians generally and how they react when they meet a Member of Parliament. It's a very interesting contradiction.

My main memory of it is working incredibly hard. I thought being counsel, running heavy commercial cases, was pressure. Well, it is nothing like being a Member of Parliament! And secondly, being deprived of sleep for four years. The recent changes to the hours in the House of Commons are well overdue. It is crazy to run your Parliamentary system on the basis that people will only be ground down to vote for things because they get deprived of sleep. And thirdly, I've got the weekends back, so I see more of the kids, because the treadmill of being a minister and being a constituency MP in a marginal seat with the single issue from hell is quite wearing!

What about work left undone? You were very active in the Lord Chancellor's Department in a number of areas of court and law reform. Of the projects with which you were involved that you weren't able to complete, are there any you hanker after?

Well, I always knew that if I was fortunate enough, which I didn't think I would be, to get re-elected—in fact, I was 99 per cent confident I wouldn't be re-elected—that I wouldn't stay in the Lord Chancellor's Department. The nature of politics is that you move on. So I was resigned to the fact that whatever happened in the election, that was the end of my time as a minister in the Lord Chancellor's Department. The Prime Minister might have put me somewhere else, might have said "thank you very much, you can go back to the backbenches", but it was always going to end. So in a sense, the time that you spend investing in the legal projects was always going to be a limited time and you know you're passing the ball on to somebody else. You know that from the beginning.

The establishment of the Community Legal Service, the beginnings of the Public Defender scheme, the reform of the CPR, reform of court funding, of funding in civil cases, conditional fees, all those things—there was a time when I was holding the ball, and maybe I managed to run a few steps forward, but there was always going to be a time to pass the ball to somebody else.

From the outside, that looks rather strange. Not so much strange in the sense of unusual; but from a management point of view, it seems—and this is true also of civil servants—that politicians and civil servants often invest huge amounts of time becoming expert and specialist and knowledgeable in a particular area, and just when they're reaching the peak of their powers in terms of that expertise, they move on somewhere else. Does that strike you as a sensible way to allocate human resources?

Well, the FCO always send Arabists to South America, because if you send them to the Middle East, they go native! It is a strange way, but the justification for politicians is in a sense that they're not specialists, that you come in having a whole general range of experience, and that cases are put to you and you learn the position.

You don't go into a department already with a wealth of experience in that department's problems. You go in with a wealth of experience of the wider Government generally. The Prime Minister used to tell us at regular intervals that we were ministers of the Government, not ministers in our department, and that you're actually there, in a sense, to stop the turf wars between departments.

It's about trying to govern for the best interests of the Government generally, Great Britain Plc and the political process. Whereas people who have been in Whitehall perhaps too long and too narrowly see things in terms of the budget development for their own department, or the advancement of the particular interest they've got in the competition within the department for resources. So in a way, shifting ministers round is a way of stopping them identifying too much with their department.

What kind of training does a minister get? How do you acquire the skills to become what we might call a generic minister, someone well versed in ministerial functions, whatever they may be, but presumably including human resource management, understanding a brief, dealing with lobbies? In short, ministers need a whole bundle of different, and I think quite diverse, skills. Is there formal training or are you thrown in at the deep end?

There's very little formal training. But the nature of the political process we have in this country is that, generally speaking, you start your politics in your local political party. You then work up to local council, which is like Government, with all those issues but on a small scale. Then you become a backbencher Member of Parliament, and as a result you lead the lobbies to the minister. That teaches you how a good minister works and a bad minister works because you're on the other side—you're a consumer of ministerial services.

And at all times you're involved in the political process, which is all about the great power structures, like tectonic plates, and the interest in politics is where the plates rub up against each other. So as a minister, or as a backbencher, one's been involved for a long time around the edge of the plates, and being a minister just moves you slightly nearer the edge, but at all times you're constrained by senior ministers.

There's always the illusion that if only I get one stage further up the ladder, I'll have real power free from constraints. It just never happens. So the difference between being a backbencher and being a PPS and being a junior minister is incremental in your sense of being able to control events. There's not a great seismic difference, and as a junior minister to the Lord Chancellor one still is very much subject to the whim of the Lord Chancellor, and then of course the Lord Chancellor is subject to the control of the Treasury and Number 10 and so on.

Could we leave politics behind and talk about the National Criminal Intelligence Service? NCIS is a vital organisation, and yet my suspicion is that public awareness of its roles and responsibilities, indeed of its very existence, is fairly low.

And we prefer to keep it that way! The National Criminal Intelligence Service is the intelligence side of the response—the UK response to serious and organised crime—and the National Crime Squad is the primary operational side.

So in a sense, you're the nearest thing that the UK's got to the FBI?

Yes, heavy with symbolism that, but the nearest, roughly. There is an enormous problem with serious and organised crime in this country. Class A drugs don't just happen in our streets, they come through very well organised criminal businesses. There are 10 per cent of people in Slough these days who are illegal immigrants. They don't happen by chance to come here. Most of them have paid large amounts of money to criminal gangs, who've moved them across frontiers.

So criminal business is big, big business. NCIS's job is to collect intelligence on the top few of the serious criminal players and to collect intelligence on serious and organised crime, and we do it through a whole variety of means, some of which we make public and some of which we don't. The National Crime Squad is the operational response against serious and organised crime groups and runs a large number of operations at any one time.

Two questions spring immediately to mind. First, how much crime falls under the rather vague heading of serious crime (including crimes within your province and other serious crimes such as violent crimes) and what proportion are more trivial crimes, those that clearly are a nuisance and unacceptable but aren't posing the scale of threat that you're talking about?

My second question is this: what's the relationship between what I would think of as everyday crime on the streets and serious organised crime? We know, or think we know, from fiction and the media, that organised crime in the United States and in Russia is on a massive scale. But I've just got no sense of whether we face a similar order of threats in the UK or how indeed one would quantify the threats.

It's very difficult to give you an answer, but in Bristol, which is a medium-sized city—there are many other similar examples—there are a number of problem drug users. Those problem Class A drug users probably commit about £150 million worth of crimes a year. The police in Bristol City probably spend about 70 to 80 per cent of their time dealing in one way or another with criminal responses to this small group of drug users—shoplifting, assaults, car thefts, dysfunctional domestic situations arising from problem drug users, the problems with the children of drug users and so on. It's the same for Social Services and other agencies of the State, and the same with the prisons. So of that £150 million of crime, that's feeding a drug habit, in that one city, which is all down to organised crime distribution groups.

Organised crime is importing those drugs, is storing them, is arranging for distribution networks, is turning the powder cocaine into crack, almost certainly in this country, and is then arranging for the networks to sell them, and they are very sophisticated businesses that pay no tax and will exploit any loophole in a relatively economically-free society. And that's just Bristol. Birmingham, Sheffield, Bradford, Liverpool, Manchester, Glasgow and so on—the scale of organised criminality is huge, but the effects are local, and the effects are mostly not created by the people that we target. They are the causes, but the effect is local.

How do you quantify, or indeed measure, your success? To what extent do you feel that you understand the scope of organised crime? Might it be that there is such superbly organised crime that one wouldn't even be able to detect it, or can you always recognise signs of its existence?

We have an assessment of the quantity of Class A drugs, in the heroin and cocaine that comes into this country each year. The best assessment we've got from our intelligence, from MI5 and from the other intelligence services is confidential, but you can assume that it's in the tons. There is a proportion of those drugs that we stop each year. There is another proportion that we have some intelligence about but we don't stop, either because the intelligence comes afterwards, because we're tracking it, because the intelligence is unspecific; but we know that an organised crime group is importing drugs, we're working on them, we'll get them eventually; but whilst we're working on them, they are in business.

If they weren't in business, we wouldn't be working on them. Ergo, if it takes us 12 months to get the intelligence and evidence, that's 12 months' trading. It is probable that there is another segment in these tons run by people we don't know about. So it is quite correct in Class A drugs that there is an element—I'm sorry, I can't tell you how much—of people who are what the Customs would call "clean skins", people who we simply don't know anything about. It's a cash business, particularly in cocaine. Heroin is slightly different, but in cocaine particularly it gets imported, it gets distributed, and much of it is purchased out of legitimately earned income, particularly in London, and the best route we have to getting at that is through following the case. But yes, there is a proportion that we know nothing about inevitably. It's a closed conspiracy of silence of criminality.

You mentioned drugs again and again. Are you saying that the main focal point of organised crime is drugs?

DAVID LOCK

It has been in the recent past. As the sentences went up, so organised immigration crime became a better risk:return ratio.

Explain a little bit more about what's involved.

Well, we don't know what drives organised criminals. Is it opportunism? How much do they assess the risks and the returns? Why do they choose to move into certain areas of crime? There are many answers. There are different organised criminal networks. But there's some evidence that as the dangers of being involved in an area rise, so criminals move over to make their profits in other areas.

The classic example is in the 60s and 70s organised criminals were involved in armed robbery, but then they realised that you could make much more money, with much lower risk, by importing drugs, so a lot of the people who were involved in armed robbery in the 60s and 70s moved into drugs in the 80s, because the returns are much better. Some of those may well be moving into organised immigration crime. Other people are coming into organised immigration crime through ethnic minority networks.

VAT fraud is a problem, where organised smuggling is a problem. There is an opportunity for organised smuggling because our duty rates have such great differentials and so we know, everybody knows, the scale of organised smuggling there. We do know that there are multi-commodity criminals, who will turn their hand to anything where the risk:reward ratio is right.

In NCIS, you focus on, and you used the phrase, the "top few" criminals. Is it the case that there's a finite and relatively small number of kingpins, as it were, whose elimination would make a vast difference? "Elimination", perhaps not being the best . . . !

Elimination might be a slightly extreme word, Richard!

"Exclusion", then—exclusion from the community in some way, perhaps by incarceration! How's that?

I think the simple answer to that is yes. There are individuals who are in control of criminal networks, where a sustained attack against them would undoubtedly be in the public good. They are people who are very, very distant from the scene of any criminality. They are the organising minds, the financiers, the arrangers, the putting together of people who trust each other, the high scale negotiators who work through a series of trusted lieutenants, against whom it is very, very difficult to get any evidence, because anyone who testifies against them is liable to be looking to cash in their life insurance policy. But yes, there is a limited number of these people, and then as you work down the scale of criminality, so the numbers increase.

135

And of the top few—and please don't answer this one if you're uncomfortable—is there a standard profile, do you think, a standard psychological profile, or even a predictable socio-economic background? Are they indeed from families that have a tradition through many generations of organised crime, or are these people sociopaths who appear from nowhere, opportunists who recognise that they have particular talents that they can bring to bear in a criminal way?

I think the answer to that is yes, there is an answer, but I don't think it's one that I can really share with you!

Well, let's move quickly on!

Sorry about that—I've got to draw the line somewhere.

Here's another one you might not feel able to answer, then. It's about the relationship between the kinds of criminal activities that are your responsibility and other threats to national security—terrorism and so forth. My intuition is that there must be some kind of link there. So to what extent do you work with MI5, MI6, and other branches of military intelligence—in sharing information systems, sharing processes and so forth? I would have thought you have criminals in common, as it were?

I think I can say firstly MI5 and MI6, Security Service and SAS, are primarily concerned with threats to national security, and we are a criminal intelligence agency. We work closely together. There are information flows between us, as you would expect. I can't say what, and I can't give you any details.

There is a terrorist finance team within NCIS, which looks at terrorist finance. It's a very, very difficult subject. The estimate of the finance needed to set up the September 11th attack—I can say this, this is in the public domain—is about half a million pounds. Well, in terms of criminal financing, that's nothing, absolutely nothing.

So it's needle and haystack stuff, and a lot of it's run through perfectly legitimate charitable trusts, which makes it even more difficult. There is increased working together between MI5, MI6 and criminal intelligence. Let me just give you one example. If you've got a criminal gang whose modus operandi is to facilitate the smuggling of illegals into this country, and you wanted to bring in some al-Qaida sleepers, you of course would just bring them in with everybody else in the same method, and they come in under the wire so to speak. Identifying who out of the many thousands are economic migrants, are legitimate refugees, and who are sleepers for future terrorist activity is a crossover between the agencies and is very, very difficult.

So there is a lot of interrelation between the two, and there are cross-secondments. There are secondments both ways. We have people working for us who have been at one or other of the intelligence agencies and vice versa. My experience is that the intelligence agencies are incredibly professional, very organised, and very disciplined, and the idea that they're a bunch of cowboys out of control might be a convenient fiction but doesn't actually bear analysis with the facts at all. They're doing a very, very difficult job, and they can't talk about it.

A huge amount of information processing, in both the conventional sense and technological sense, must be involved, I would imagine. Moving in another direction, you are a Left wing lawyer, a champion of human rights, a powerful advocate of civil liberties in a number of contexts, and now you find yourself in a role where the organisation that you chair is responsible, presumably, for all manner of buggings and surveillance activities. How do you reconcile on the one hand the liberties and freedoms of the individuals who, as innocent individuals until proven guilty, should not be subject to interference with their daily activities, with on the other hand the need, from the point of view of gathering evidence and detecting and investigating, to intrude? How is that balance drawn in practice and how do you come to terms with it in your own mind from a theoretical point of view? You can take theory and practice in whichever order you prefer![1]

In one sense we are the buggers and burglars for the State and we put bugs in people's cars, we put probes in ceilings, we monitor people's telephone conversations, we monitor their email. Why do we do this? How can you possibly justify doing this? I think there are two answers.

Before you answer that, I wonder if you might also be able to reflect the following in your answer as well. It seems to me that this dilemma is quite similar to a situation in relation to terrorists, where, certainly under recent legislation, we are not following the normal rule about presuming innocence but are actually detaining people with less evidence than would ordinarily be needed. I don't know if this analogy is sound, but it seems to me the impingements on liberty that you are discussing raise similar issues of principle.

Yes. The problem is, all investigatory work starts with intelligence; all work from the police, detective work, starts with intelligence. Intelligence is what you believe you know but you can't prove, and evidence is what you can prove. If we are serious about having a strategy against organised crime, then we have to recognise that there are no non-complicit witnesses, virtually all the time. Everybody is involved in the business, and either through fear or coercion or being part of the conspiracy, there simply are no witnesses. So if you don't use technical attack, if you don't use undercover officers, then you will not prosecute these people, and so the top few will simply act with impunity.

It's a question of proportionality. It would not be appropriate to use technical attack and these serious intrusions into people's privacy if the worst that these people were doing were a series of cat burglaries. It is against the law, it is an

---

[1] Human rights are also discussed by Lord Woolf (Ch.1), David Pannick QC (Ch.3), Lord Bingham (Ch.7), Oliver Letwin (Ch.10), Cherie Booth QC (Ch.12) and Professor Bogdanor (Ch.19).

infringement of the civil liberties of the victim, but it's not sufficiently serious in societal terms to justify a very serious intrusion into an individual's privacy and civil liberties. If on the other hand what you're dealing with is somebody who is arranging a large scale importation of guns to be used by criminals to further their business, or a large scale importation of heroin which is going to create a whole new generation of addicts with all the societal problems around it, the degree of intrusion into the civil rights of an individual in those circumstances is justified to a much greater extent.

And of course from our angle what we do almost always ends up in a court, being defended. All our procedures are governed by the Regulation of Investigatory Powers Act. If we want a telephone tap, we have to go to the Home Secretary personally to sign the warrant. If we want a technical attack, we have to go to a very, very senior police officer who has to sign the warrant. We are regulated by the Interception Commissioners, who come in and review every single technical attack warrant that we generate. So the level of societal oversight may be secret but there is very tough scrutiny.

But in the end, society has got a choice, put bluntly. Either we do it in this way and we have a chance and we take out the Mr Bigs or we don't have a society run by the Mafia as has nearly happened in some countries following the collapse of Communism, or we say, "No, the civil rights of individuals are much more important than the common good, and the techniques that we have to employ to go against these people are so intrusive that we prefer to have the chaos of organised crime being in charge". But there's no middle ground, because these are the only techniques that are going to create an intelligence and an evidential case against these people at the very height of criminality. So you either do this or you give them free rein, and tough as it may be, those are the choices as I see it from where I sit.

The interesting question, in one sense, is not should do we do these things. I'm absolutely convinced we should. It's: what's the right sort of regime so that there's public interest scrutiny over these very intrusive powers when they are exercised? And my experience is that we have a very tough regime at the moment. If John Wadham, the Director of Liberty, was here instead of me, he would say it's not tough enough, but interestingly John wouldn't say that the response is not to ever bug somebody, not to ever intercept anyone's telephone, because he would say—*even* he would say, I think, I've chatted to him long and hard about this—that the degree of the threat makes that type of invasion of privacy response proportionate.

Many conclusions might follow from what you have just said. One is that the rights of the individual are not overriding. I say this just as an observation—not as a criticism or endorsement of your position. It's a classic utilitarian argument, is it not, that the methods are justified by the overall greater good to which they give rise? And, of course, one objection that can be levelled at this version of utilitarianism is that, in individual cases, a given approach can perhaps contribute handsomely to the greater good but, at the same time, worryingly, can give rise not just to breaches of rights but also to clear injustices.

On a slightly different tack, I wonder if a distinction can be drawn between detaining someone, incarcerating them, with less evidence than is normally required, as opposed to observing or intruding upon people but not necessarily reducing their freedom of movement or their freedom of action. Can you see a distinction there?

Yes. I'll deal with the first point. I don't think this is a new problem, because when we remand somebody in custody who has been charged but not been convicted and who is subsequently acquitted, that individual may well have spent eight or 10 months, or a year, in custody for a crime which the State failed to prove that individual committed, and that's a gross intrusion in their rights as well. But on balance we say that it is better to have it that way than to have the general body of people who are charged out there, many of whom are guilty, committing further crimes.

So it's another utilitarian argument, but the argument that I've put in regard to intrusion is exactly the same. What's the degree of interference with individuals' privacy, individuals' liberty, which is justified by retaining the common good? The argument on terrorists is much, much more difficult, and here the problem is essentially this: what happens if we know from intelligence that somebody is an active terrorist but we don't have evidence that you can put before a court?

It's relevant here that what we get on telephone taps in this country, unlike virtually the whole of the rest of the world, is not evidence, and can only be used for intelligence. So we know from telephone taps, perfectly legitimately granted, that we have an al-Qaida cell setting up, we know they're active, but we don't know what they're doing. It's not specific enough to charge anyone even if you could use this in evidence, but we know they're active.

Also, there may be a foreign national who is here in this country, maybe illegally, but because where they have come from is not a state to whom we would deport people, because it would interfere with their civil liberties and human rights, we can't actually deport them. So we can't say, "This individual is not conducive to the public good in this county, we're going to deport you". It can't be done because we can't deport them back if, for example, they're from Sri Lanka and they're a Tamil; if we suspect them of being a Tamil Tiger, we simply cannot deport them back. We cannot deport people back to Sudan. We cannot deport people back to Iraq. What do we do in those circumstances?

There are two views, roughly speaking. One view is we maintain massive surveillance on them until we get to the point where we've got enough to charge them criminally, but we allow them freedom of movement up till that time, and we arrest them at the point when they are about to commit the terrorist outrage. The other view is that if you've got enough of an intelligence case, it is a utilitarian balance of rights, you can justify locking them up, but if they can find another third country where they will go to, they can be deported there for the public good.

The latter is the route the Government has taken because policing is an inexact science, and how would the public feel if we said in the aftermath of a terrorist outrage, "yes, we knew they were planning this, or we knew they were planning something, we didn't know what, and we were shadowing them, but we didn't quite get there in time and therefore a lot of people lost their lives"? There are no easy answers here.

It is interesting because much of this is constrained by law, in the sense that the admissibility or inadmissibility of telephone taps is clearly an issue, and of course the standard of proof is clearly an issue. If, for example, in terrorist cases, at least in the first instance, the issue of detention was determined on grounds less than on the "balance of probabilities" and certainly not "beyond reasonable doubt", this would enable a considerably different approach to investigation and arrest. It's perhaps unimaginable because the criminal system embodies the higher standard of proof and it has certain rules of inadmissibility, but inherent in these is a whole view of political morality, a whole view of what's acceptable in terms of people's freedoms and our impinging on their freedoms.

It does seem to me that some of these bigger issues should be up for discussion; the admissibility issue particularly. I think it's fascinating when you have a look at a book by Harvard law professor, Alan Dershowitz, entitled Reasonable Doubts.[2] *This is a slightly different issue but I think it's relevant: why it is that in the OJ Simpson case it appeared to many lay people that many of the police officers were lying. He called this "testilying" rather than testifying. And the issue is that these officers are so convinced of the guilt of an individual, but at the same time are so concerned that the evidence they have would be successfully challenged by clever lawyers in court, that they think it is morally justifiable to plant evidence.*

Now, on any view of the legal system, no lawyer would defend the planting of evidence, but there are some fascinating issues around admissibility and inadmissibility. It's one area where non-lawyers get tremendously frustrated, because often when people, in the jargon, "get off on a technicality", it's precisely because the evidence hasn't actually been gathered in an appropriate way. It's not clear to me why, for example, phone tapping is not admissible?

Well, that's a whole debate we're having at the moment. It's very interesting. I can give you three answers to that. The first is very pertinent in this country at the moment. The Bishop of Birmingham's report into the Damilola Taylor murder was very interesting, because everyone was expecting the CPS and the police to get slammed, and whilst they didn't come out with three ticks in the box, they came out with at least one-and-a-half, and the thing that really got slammed was the criminal justice system. But they didn't criticise the trial judge, what they criticised was the rules of evidence, which the trial judge applied, which restricted the evidence that was available to the jury.[3]

Now, it does seem to me—and I've thought this for some time—that we have a bit of a schizophrenic view about juries. If we believe the jury is the best way to be a fact finder, we have to trust that the jury has the ability to weigh evidence and give it appropriate weight and determine where the truth is. Fine, but at the same time we say, "Well, we can't let the jury have any evidence about which there may be any concern because they might take it the wrong way", so evidence of previous bad character doesn't go in, and evidence of dubious provenance doesn't go in. Now, one would think logically that if you believe that the jury is an appropriate way of judging a criminal case and reaching a view, giving appropriate weight to the different bits of evidence, you would say, "Put the whole lot before the jury because we trust the jury to be able to sort out the wheat from the chaff", and I think that, essentially, was what the Bishop of Birmingham was saying.

I have for long thought, and indeed argued many moons ago in my doctorate, that the notion of pure fact finding is fictional because fact finding in the courts, whether by jury

---

[2] Alan Dershowitz, *Reasonable Doubts* (Simon & Schuster, New York, 1996).
[3] The jury system is also discussed by Lord Justice Auld (Ch.4), Lord Irvine (Ch.6), Lord Bingham (Ch.7) and Lord Goldsmith (Ch.8).

or by judge, is so heavily rule-governed and rule-constrained that it isn't pure fact finding in the ordinary language sense of it. It's a highly structured and systematic and limited process.

I agree with you. I defend the jury, I believe in juries, but I'm not blind to the logic-alities in the way we approach them. I remember being in Sweden. The Swedish Lord Chief Justice, who's a delightful lady and like everyone's granny, said to me, "Ah, you have juries in England", and I said, "Yes, we have juries and we're proud of them", and she said, "Ah yes, sometimes your juries, they convict people who are not guilty". I said, "Well, that's true sometimes, but we have the Court of Appeal for that", and she said, "Ah yes, but I believe that sometimes it takes a very long time, I've heard of the Birmingham Six and the Guildford Four". I said, "Well, it doesn't work perfectly, and we now have the Criminal Cases Review Commission". And she said, "And I think also in England you have juries and they acquit people who are guilty", and I said, "Well of course, you know, in a sense if they're acquitted, you don't know, but a lot of police think that far too many people do get acquitted, and yes, it is true that the acquittal rate in Liverpool Crown Court is something like 78 per cent". And she said, "And it's true also, and this bit we don't understand, they don't give reasons in either case. How can you have a system where you're found guilty or innocent but you never know why?".

I think she has a point. Part of Lord Justice Auld's report said that juries should be given questions to answer to structure their fact finding and I'm disappointed that it's been dropped. I suspect part of the reason it was dropped is that there's actually a fear that juries come to the right decision by some mystical process, and if we ask them too many difficult questions they'll never come to the right decisions!

There is an irony here because many of the objectors are saying they want juries to be free to think in an unconstrained way and shouldn't be given a too structured and limit-ing framework. But that's actually inconsistent with the rules of evidence, as I was men-tioning, that govern what it is they're allowed to take notice of and what's admissible and so forth.

Juries take an oath to do two things, as I understand it, which is take the law from the judge and to try the case according to the evidence. Some of their staunchest defenders defend them on the basis that they make up the law as they go along and they don't take a blind bit of notice of the evidence, and that produces sort of palm tree justice. Now, sometimes this is undoubtedly true. One thinks of cases like Clive Ponting, where it was an overriding public interest that caused the jury to acquit. But is that really what we want to defend juries on? I think it's very, very difficult and very interesting.

And that has happened in a number of notable criminal trials, where on any view, or certainly in psychiatrists' views, the accused were not capable at the time, incapable of understanding the nature of the event, and yet they've been convicted criminally.

Certainly, and then six months down the line they get taken to a secure hospital because, having been convicted, the prison psychiatrist then says, "no, this chap's away with the fairies", and so they're in the same position as they would have been had they not been through the process. But no system is perfect. All systems have anomalies, so pointing out the anomalies of the system doesn't necessarily mean the system is bad.

What's striking is that many of the novel situations seem to cause us moral dilemmas, whereas the status quo, for most of us, does not. That is to say, many of the rules on admissibility and inadmissibility are just taken for granted, but the kind of debate we were having about the justification of your bugging or launching surveillance raises issues that are no different. These are the kinds of discussions one could have in actually evaluating the jury system as it is. It is so firmly embedded in our own minds that juries work in a particular way and they are contained by the rules of evidence and they are directed by judges, but one could equally have debates about the nature and the acceptability of all of that.

I have asked many of my guests here at Gresham, certainly most of the judges who have sat in your chair, about the role of juries in serious fraud trials. Where do you sit on that one? Lord Justice Auld was certainly doubtful about whether or not this was appropriate or productive.

I think the best justification for a jury is that the events that they are being asked to judge are within their experience and they bring their every day experience, their understanding of events, a framework within which they can make decisions, and that they bring a bit of common sense into the jury box. They are akin to a mini-Parliament, and so they judge on the evidence. But they understand what it's like to be in a pub on a Friday night at 11 o'clock when the music is loud and people have had a bit too much to drink and they're all argy-bargy and there's a bit of pushing. When that's described to them, they can smell the sawdust, they know what it's like.

To ask a jury of people who are prepared to take six or nine months out of their working life, which then constrains the type of people that you're going to choose, to judge a serious fraud case in a business environment where they're likely to have virtually no experience—where they can't smell the sawdust because they've never been in a boardroom taking difficult decisions, they've not been on the stock exchange, they've not been doing high finance in a city environment—to say that as a society they are the best people to make judgments of honesty and dishonesty and understand the framework in that environment I think is virtually indefensible, because all the justifications for a jury simply don't add up in those circumstances.

In the old days, we had special juries. I was reading *Bell v Lever Brothers*, the famous employment case from the 1930s, which was decided with a special jury. In those circumstances, you could have a special jury. In fact, I don't think in practice you could get one these days, but the traditional jury, drawn from the ranks of people who can give up nine months of their life to sit on a jury, almost by definition means that they are people who don't have the framework within which to take the decisions, and therefore I'm with Lord Justice Roskill, and all the other reports that have looked into it.

Actually you're with most of the people I've interviewed and certainly with the Attorney General, who spoke here in almost identical words a number of weeks ago.

Two more questions; indeed two final questions. One: wigs, gowns, and the trappings generally—how important do you feel they are to the credibility and the authority of the courtroom? Would you abolish them or do you feel they're worth sustaining?

I don't think the majesty of the law is dependent on 17th century dress.

Well, that's a swift disposal of that one! Let me turn, then, to my final question and it is one that I ask of everyone sitting in your seat who's had a career in law. What would you say to a young student, to a pupil in school for example, who has it in mind to pursue a career in law? Is this something you'd recommend or warn against?

The law has been a fascinating backdrop for me to have a career so far, and I hope it continues. The traditional idea of a legal career was where you trained as a barrister or solicitor immediately after university, you then went into a firm, you worked your way up, you became a partner, you got a secretary, you got a company car, you served out your 20 years and then, aged 57, you went on to the golf course; or as a barrister, you did pupillage, you went into chambers, you stayed in those chambers until you became a judge. I think both of us sitting here are forerunners of slightly different types of legal career.

I would say yes, become a lawyer, but law is a series of skills that you learn, and how you apply them is going to become more different than we can imagine, because already the traditional career paths are becoming fewer and fewer. But frankly, the new ways of being a lawyer are actually much more challenging and much more interesting, and it's a great career.

Why don't we finish on that note, then? David Lock, many thanks.

CHAPTER TEN

The Rt Hon Dr Oliver Letwin MP
Shadow Home Secretary

Monday January 27, 2003

Tonight I'm delighted to welcome a guest who is our first non-lawyer in this series at Gresham College. Nonetheless, he is someone who's clearly very involved with law and order. He is the Rt Hon Dr Oliver Letwin MP.

Just a little bit of biographical detail. Oliver Letwin was educated at Eton and then at Cambridge, where he attained his doctorate. He went on to spend a short time in the academic world. He then enjoyed a spell in public service, most notably in the Prime Minister's Policy Unit in the mid-1980s. In 1986, he moved to Rothschild, where he became a director in 1991. He continues to work there, but in 1997 he was elected MP for West Dorset. In 2001 he became Shadow Home Secretary and last year was appointed to the Privy Council.

It is a great pleasure to have you with us. This evening, I want to explore a variety of issues concerned with law and order. But by way of background, it would be fascinating to learn something about the role of the Shadow Home Secretary and, in that context, the role of the Home Secretary and the Home Office generally.

I wish I knew the answer to that question! Well, the role of the Home Secretary is fairly—no that's exaggeration—I was going to say it's fairly clear, or some parts of it are fairly clear. He is there to administer the prison system and the police. He's not there to administer the Judiciary or the court system. He is there to administer the Probation Service and the Crown Prosecution Service. He is also there to try to ensure that the law of the land in relation to criminal justice is appropriate, except that in almost every dimension his activities cut across those of the Lord Chancellor and a large part of the activity which you might have thought the Home Secretary conducted, he doesn't, because the Judiciary actually conduct it. This is something that we may wish to discuss.

Most people think that Parliament under the inspiration of the Home Secretary of the day passes laws which, for example, allocate sentences to crimes, but it is not so. Parliament allocates definitions to crimes and maximum sentences to crimes and occasionally mandatory sentences for crimes, although those aren't really effective, but it doesn't actually allocate the norm, which is done by the judges. So the Home

Secretary does many things but not most of the things or not all of the things which most people think the Home Secretary does.

The Shadow Home Secretary is a shadow, and is a shadowy figure. Part of the job is certainly to bring out more clearly for the public, in our adversarial system of politics, what the Home Secretary and his Government are really doing, as opposed to what Government might claim that it's doing. Part of it is to formulate an alternative set of policies which can be put before an electorate at a General Election in relation to the things I've been describing—criminal justice, crime prevention, policing, prisons and so forth. And the third bit is very mysterious, which is to be part, I suppose, of the British State where it's joined together and where the whole public is joined together in an effort to combat common enemies.

One mustn't suppose that in the end those of us who are engaged in democratic politics are engaged in warfare, although sometimes the papers try to make it look as if it's warfare and sometimes politicians conspire in making it sound as if it's warfare. In the end we're all on the same side of the barricades in defence of our democracy and our liberties against certain kinds of incursion, and the Shadow Home Secretary is certainly part of the apparatus of making sure that the whole British political establishment protects the interests of the public where they are threatened. For example, I receive briefings on things that are going on in order that I don't engage in irresponsible actions in politics, which isn't true in some of the other departments of State, where they're more nakedly political and there's less common ground then there needs to be in the Home Office for the safety of the public.

You have raised a huge number of topics there. Let's dive into one in some detail: the interaction between the Home Secretary and the Home Office on the one hand and senior judges and the Judiciary on the other.[1] To make this more concrete, I thought we might usefully chat about the recent controversy arising from the Lord Chief Justice's judgment in mid-December which gave rise to sentencing guidelines, which in turn were discussed and, to some extent I think, misrepresented in the press.

Incidentally, Lord Woolf sat in your very chair some months ago and we had an interesting discussion about human rights and terrorism, which I'd like to turn to shortly. But if we can focus first on the sentencing issue. I know you came out fairly strongly against, I think you put it, "the wishy-washy approach" to sentencing. Why don't you expand upon that?

Well, first a structural point. I am, at the level of personality, a tremendous admirer of Lord Woolf. You must have, and anybody here who was present when he was sitting in this chair must have, sensed his charm and his humanity and his intelligence, and I think on the whole, as a judge, he's been a very remarkable and a very good judge. As Lord Chief Justice, he's called upon to do a job that I think is structurally bizarre. He's asked to give sentencing guidelines, which actually means that he's asked to set the sentences, not of course of particular persons for particular

---

[1] The relationship between the Judiciary and the Home Office is also discussed by Lord Bingham (Ch.7) and Lord Irvine (Ch.13).

crimes, which is done by the particular judge in the particular case, but in the sense of setting the norms.

Most people in the country, as I mentioned earlier, think what I thought before I started doing this job: that they elect a Parliament and a Government partly in order to determine what should be the norms of sentences and which things should be regarded as crimes and which not. Part of the effect of this disjunction between the way in which most people see the matter and the way in which it actually is, is that it takes one hugely by surprise.

I'll give you a very personal and immediate example of that. I didn't know that Lord Woolf was setting new guidelines for the sentencing of burglars, and indeed there was no reason, constitutionally speaking, why I should have known that he was setting new guidelines until somebody rang me up from the Today programme to ask me what I thought of them. As I didn't know what they were at the time I was being asked this question, it was difficult to answer immediately—not that that always impedes, incidentally, either politicians or the press! So I found myself in the ludicrous position of being called upon to make a comment after 20 minutes of having found some digest of what Lord Woolf had originally said, and so at first I was extremely cautious. I then set to work later in the day actually to read the full text of the guidelines, which incidentally I got hold of with some slight difficulty.

Most Members of Parliament will not, as of today, have the slightest idea of what was in these guidelines. I find this entirely a bizarre feature of the scene and I therefore proposed amendments in the Criminal Justice Bill which had the effect that the setting of the guidelines and norms would be subject to sustained democratic debate. I can't think of anything more appropriate to be discussed in Parliament than that, and indeed I think there ought to be a process in Parliament which means that the nation as a whole has an opportunity to debate these things so that the sense of public opinion can emerge and politicians can decide how far they wish to pay attention to that, how far they want to lead it and so on.

I think the Judiciary have a role, the Judiciary need to be consulted in this process, and I certainly think that it needs to be a very careful process. Hence, we suggested that the Home Affairs Select Committee, for example, and indeed the parallel of it in the Lords, should be asked to consider the thing and produce a report rather than merely launching into some debate across the floor of the House. But I wanted to see a structure in which there is Parliamentary and democratic debate about sentencing policy.

Just before we go on to the substance, there is a Sentencing Advisory Panel.

There is.

To which the judges pay considerable attention. I clarify this to highlight that the involvement that judges have in sentencing policy is not entirely self-sufficient. They do take soundings and they are offered guidance. However, it seems that there's an issue here—that of the level at which judges should be involved. Most people would agree that judges must be allowed room for manoeuvre—broadly, their discretion—to decide particular cases according to the facts and so forth, so a framework is provided within which they have to operate. You are suggesting that this framework needs to be rather more restrictive, for several reasons: one is democratic, namely, that other people should have input; but, secondly, in terms of promulgation, you are pointing out that the way in which people are currently made aware of fundamental sentencing policy is not the same way as people are made aware of other legislation or regulations. You concede, of course, that judges must be allowed some discretion, but I think you're saying that, because what is at stake is so fundamental, judges should have less discretion when it comes to sentencing. And I suppose you might want to generalise that and apply the argument in other areas of life beyond sentencing.

Why don't we now delve into the issue of burglary, because I think this raises some important questions about public perception of the role and function of prison, public perception of the nature of the Judiciary, and indeed public perception of politicians who are involved with debates about punishment.[2]

Yes. Let me just say, to clarify absolutely, I'm not suggesting that there should be less discretion for the trial judge in a particular trial than there is at present. I wish to maintain that. I'm saying that Parliament as opposed to the Judiciary should set the guidelines which constitute the norm, the reference point.

So, in the specific case of burglars, you would want to say that it should be for Parliament to determine policy in respect of first time burglars. It should be for Parliament to say that such a person should, say, not expect go to prison. Is this what you have in mind?

That kind of statement, or on the contrary, that a burglar should expect on the whole, normally, to go to jail and for a given period on the first offence. That sort of thing I think is something that Parliament ought to be setting, yes. Then of course the trial judge may say, "This is a particular burglar in the case of whom there is a huge mitigating circumstance or a huge aggravating circumstance" and vary around that.

So far as the substance of the burglary case is concerned, I should say that I don't start with the proposition that the more people in jail the better. I've been preaching on the contrary for the last year or more that it is extremely distressing to discover that the recidivism rates from prison are appallingly high, particularly high in the case of young people, and I've become more and more passionate about the need to do much more than merely put people in prison.

For example, I've argued that we should not regard persistent young offenders as having been properly dealt with if they're chucked in a youth offender institution, dumped back on the streets after three or six months or a year, and put back into the hands of the same gangs and the same drug dealers and the same lack of housing and jobs and so on that they started with. I've argued that on the contrary we should have much longer term rehabilitative sentencing where there's a much shorter period of custody and a period of open custody, based on some of the best examples around where voluntary bodies have gone back to the idea of reforming

---

[2] Punishment and sentencing are also discussed by Lord Woolf (Ch.20).

the character of the person concerned and teaching skills and changing the way in which they view themselves and life, and have then provided a prolonged period of fairly intensive supervision and support.

Again, one can see this in the best examples already available. C-FAR, for example, in Devon, operates such a programme. Many people leave young offender institutions without knowing where they'll spend the first night. I argue that for persistent young offenders we should have a programme where they are found housing and either employment or education, that there is somebody who is their tutor, mentor, supervisor, however you put it, who's there on tap to try and set things right when they go wrong, as they inevitably will, with landlords, with employers and so on; that there's a support mechanism, in other words, and a supervision mechanism which means that we actually try and lead people off the conveyor belt to crime.

I've also, for the same reason, been advocating policies to lift people off the conveyor belt to crime at a series of earlier stages. The policy is to offer parents who are having difficulty with children, children who at school, very young, are already showing signs of being alienated from the rest of the class, not obviously committing any criminal activities at that stage, but clearly in need of some help. I have argued that we should offer help to parents of such children in bringing them up because there's plenty of sociological evidence that they can then do better. I've also argued for special measures to try and get a huge increase in the number of intensively rehabilitative places for drug treatment, for those young people on cocaine and heroin and crack, to help to get them off drugs and off the conveyor belt to crime. So I want to sketch the background, which is that I very strongly believe in rehabilitation and not merely in punishment. I don't think punishment is, by any means, a successful method if left on its own, in many cases.

But when it comes to burglary, there is a remarkable set of facts that seem to me to resist being dismissed, and which are indeed admitted by the Home Office in its own research. The pattern in the UK has been that burglary, in common with many other crimes, was rising fairly remorselessly, whether you look at the British Crime Survey or at the reported crime statistics, up till about 1992 when Michael Howard became the Home Secretary and pressurised the Judiciary—it had to be done that way because of the structural defect that I was describing—into intensifying sentencing for burglars. Since 1992, whilst many other crimes continued their upward course, burglary responded. Burglary figures, again whether you look at the BCS or the recorded crimes statistics, started falling downwards very sharply and remorselessly year by year. The Home Office research indicates—somewhat to the surprise of the researchers I think, if you read it it has all the tone of voice of people who didn't expect to find this result—that sentencing for burglars, in terms of custodial sentences, appears to have a non-negligible effect on levels of burglary.

Now, against the background of believing that there's much else besides that needs to be done, I believe that there will be severe problems for society if burglars have a very unclear message, which is I fear what they've been left with now. If on the whole burglars know that they are unlikely to be apprehended because our policing is woefully deficient—very slow to catch-up with burglary, slow to be there, burglars don't tend to wait for police officers to arrive—and if the burglar also knows that if caught it's quite likely that they won't be convicted because there are very severe difficulties about case preparation and cases that go awry and so forth; and if they also know that at the end, when they are convicted, they are very unlikely, if it's the first offence, to go to jail, then I think the signal that we are effectively sending to many people

149

who are contemplating committing burglary is broadly: "don't worry too much, why don't you go ahead". I think we will see, as a result of the moves that have been made, that burglary begins pretty remorselessly to rise again, and I think that would be very unfortunate, so I did come out quite strongly against this proposition.

I'd just add one codicil, which is that, if community punishment is to be an alternative—and I think for some things it is an entirely appropriate alternative—but if it's to be an alternative, then it has to be serious, and I'm afraid what's happened is that community punishment, or punishment in the community, however you describe it, has in very many cases that I've seen with my own eyes turned into a joke, and that is very regrettable. I don't say all of it; some may be perfectly serious. But now something like 30 per cent of cases of community punishment of young offenders literally consist exclusively of the young offender writing a letter of apology. A letter is a fine thing. I'm all in favour of people writing letters of apology. But it is not an adequate response to a serious crime. When that's the case, when we have community punishments which are simply inadequate, the idea that they are a suitable alternative for a burglary, which is a serious offence against the person who is being burgled, seems to me inept.

Underlying all of this is an issue of perception, relevant both to those who are contemplating crimes as well as to the public generally; a perception of what prison is like and a perception of what community service is like. It does seem that large numbers of people are dissatisfied with prison, above all else because it seems a breeding ground for further crime, and dissatisfied with community service because it does seem rather feeble in many circumstances. Indeed, I suppose the Devon experiment, of which I've read, in some ways sits conceptually between the two. It's not an issue of semantics, but the labels of "prison" and "community service" are often unhelpful because they can send out very clear but misleading images in people's minds.

There is also, for those who hanker after some kind of retribution, a sense in which prison is an appropriate response, whether or not it deters; that people who commit crimes should suffer a serious loss of liberty that those who have to engage in community service simply don't suffer. So there's that whole set of issues, some of which are about packaging. But there's also, from a legal point of view, the issue that if you are, say, a first time burglar, perhaps sentenced to a year in prison, then you're entitled after six months to get out—in fact, you may be out after 90 days and you'll be on home curfew. The amount of time in prison may be relatively small. Now, it may well be, from your point of view, that spending some time in prison is the important issue and the length of time is less so, but I think the public's general understanding—and this is not meant to be insulting or patronising—of the legal realities is such that people expect a seriously lengthy custodial sentence and are amazed when, in practice, what results is just a few months off the streets.

Well, factually, you're clearly right. The last part about the early release scheme is one that I have criticised, and indeed the disjunction between what happens and what appears to happen, I criticise. I think there is strong reason for moving towards honesty in sentencing, where the sentence is the sentence. I accept that if that were to be the case then we would also need some different system of incentives for people to engage in good behaviour in jail, and so one might reverse the thing, and that's something we need to think about. In other words, you would set a six month sentence instead of a year if you meant a six month sentence instead of a year, and you would have your sentence increased if you behaved badly. I think that it's a problem if society is presented with facts which are not facts. It's one of the things that undermines people's confidence in the criminal justice system, if they believe that the reality is not what they're presented with.

Having said all that, I do think that the shock of going to prison can very often be the most effective part, unless there is a serious programme of rehabilitation. Now, nobody ought to be under any illusion that even in well-organised circumstances 90 days in prison is going to lead to any serious amount of rehabilitation, but even 10 days in prison, or indeed for some people 24 hours in prison, may have a significant deterrent effect. It depends on the case, the person, and so on. So I don't think that one should argue that simply because prison sentences may not be very long, prison is necessarily an inappropriate response.

On the point about retribution, I don't think there's anybody who can rationally argue that there is not an element of retribution in sentencing, and I say that because if the sole purpose of sentencing were deterrence, it would clearly be a rational policy to hang people for every parking offence. There would be very little illegal parking if everyone who parked illegally were hanged. It would be an extremely effective deterrent. But I suspect that most people in this room, I hope everyone in this room, would share my view that it would be a disproportionate response to a parking offence. I personally would be dead!

In other words, we think there has to be an element of retribution in sentencing. There is a proportionality, there is a relationship between the seriousness of the offence and what is an appropriate response, and that is an idea of retribution. So you have to admit that there is an element of retribution in sentencing, but I personally don't think that we ought to set our sentencing policy on the basis of seeking society's retribution. I think we ought to set our sentencing policy admitting the importance of some degree of proportionality, but we ought to base our sentencing policy on what works.

The overriding aim of sentencing policy, within the constraint of some degree of proportionality, ought to be to try to minimise the number of us that are murdered, burgled, raped, robbed and so forth; that seems to me a desirable social end. So I think we ought to worry about whether people commit burglaries more frequently if we give them the signal that we're going to have community sentences and they don't mean anything. I agree with you that the sort of experiment that I'm talking about with long-term rehabilitative sentencing as well as the shock of custody might offer something serious and tough that people would buy into, because they would see that it's likely to have the effect of actually getting people off the conveyor belt to crime.

It's clearly a complex mix of retribution, eliminating the person from the community if there's a likelihood of repetition, deterrence, rehabilitation and so forth, but just to swing back to our earlier discussion, you're suggesting, aren't you, that this precise debate is one that should be had within the democratic forum of Parliament rather than within the Judiciary?

Yes.

We could talk about that very subject at great length but I think, regrettably, we should move on. Why don't we talk now about asylum, because I know you've taken a great deal of interest in this. And this is a topic that is very much in the news just now. There are many angles of approach, but why don't we start by offering an outline of the scale and scope of the problem?[3]

That I can do. Let me warn you in advance that I can't tonight—because I'm going to be announcing tomorrow—tell you what our response to the scale of the problem is. Had I known that you were going to ask me about this, I would have begged tomorrow as the right day to be having this conversation!

It just shows how spontaneous we are in Gresham College! Hopefully, you'll be indiscreet.

No, I won't—I've got into enough trouble being indiscreet in my political past! The scale of the problem is very serious, but it comes in two parts, and I think it's extremely important to distinguish the two parts. There is a current national emergency, and then quite separately, there is a long running structural problem. The current national emergency is that there are in Britain today, and there are entering Britain today, significant numbers of people who have it in mind to blow us up or poison us. I have a strong objection to being blown up or poisoned, and I think it's reasonable, indeed absolutely necessary, that the State should seek to protect the public against that kind of activity. Now, there have been threats . . .

Can I just jump in there? I'm sure you would agree with this, and this in no sense takes away from the severity of the issue, but surely the terrorists to whom you refer are surely a very small fraction of potential asylum seekers?

Absolutely miniscule—I'll come on to that—absolutely miniscule, 99 point something per cent of all asylum seekers are utterly harmless and innocent individuals. I'll come on to the connection between this threat and asylum in just a second. But there are people trying to enter this country and people who have entered this country who do have it in mind to blow us up or poison us. Now, there have always been, or anyway for a very long time have been, people who had it in mind to blow some of us up. I was in the Grand Hotel in Brighton with Mrs Thatcher on the night when we were blown up; I have some personal experience of being blown up. And that was a serious matter. But the fact is that the scale of the danger at that time to people on the mainland of Britain, and even to people in Northern Ireland, was very much smaller than we currently face.

I think it's extremely important to recognise what the Prime Minister has been at pains, quite rightly, to emphasise: that we are dealing here with people who are more

---

[3] Asylum and immigration are also discussed by Lord Mackay (Ch.17).

numerous, more clued-up, richer, more connected with other people outside the country, more prepared to sacrifice their own lives, and with ambitions to kill many more people than the IRA ever deemed it sensible in their own interests to do. The IRA broadly wanted to blow up politicians and innocent bystanders got caught when politicians or army officers or judges or somebody was being blown up, but by and large, they didn't aim to kill off very large numbers of citizens.

This is not true of some of the people we are now facing. We saw that on September 11th. I hope that will turn out to be the worst of the outrages; I doubt it will. Under those circumstances, the security services have been engaging in an enormously arduous and, to a degree, successful campaign to identify the relevant people and to root them out. We saw an example of that in recent weeks in Manchester, having preceded it by one in London and one in Birmingham and one in Bournemouth.

But they are playing a game of catch-up, because as they identify those who are in this condition, more enter. Why? Well, first because our borders are porous; there are no adequate facilities at our borders to identify people entering the country who may have such activities in mind, and it's quite easy to enter the country improperly at present. Second, because even if people are apprehended improperly entering the country, once they claim asylum they enter a system which is in a state of chaos, and because it's in a state of chaos—including for many people, for example, having two or three different sets of files for the same person in different names; for many people having files which take literally months to circulate the country—because it's in a state of chaos, it's almost impossible to imagine the security services effectively vetting those who have entered it. As a result, as we saw in Manchester—although you're absolutely right, almost every asylum seeker is not a terrorist—all three of the people who were apprehended in Manchester after the killing of a policeman were asylum seekers. They had used the system and its chaos as a means of disappearing into the woodwork.

Now, if we were facing the possibility that there would be one small bomb some-where sometime, I don't know that this would be something that could adequately be described as a national emergency, but that's not the possibility we're facing. The possibility we're facing is of very serious and wide-scale destruction of life, and under those circumstances I think we desperately need to address the character of the emergency in some appropriate fashion that re-establishes some degree of ability for the security services not simply to be playing catch-up, and as I say, we'll announce what I mean by that tomorrow.

Can I just interrupt again for a second? This is not to be pessimistic and this is not a reason for not tightening asylum policy and practice and law, but is it not the case that even if asylum and the way in which it is administered are tightened up, that imagina-tive, determined terrorists will find some other way to move in? To what extent is asylum the key issue when it comes to terrorists managing to gain entry to this country, or is this just one potential leakage to be plugged?

Well, the control of our borders, in the sense of proper mechanisms to prevent people getting undetected, and the tightening up of asylum will not provide a foolproof mechanism, of course you're right. Providing an enormously strong strong-room in a bank is not a foolproof mechanism against a well-organised team of bank robbers. But if every bank had its strong-room open and a large passageway from the banking hall down to the storeroom where all the money is and a sign pointing "This Way", one imagines that there would be a larger amount of bank robbery than at present, and that's the problem. It's not that we get a foolproof solution, nor can ever expect to, but that at the moment we're providing something so far from the foolproof solution that Britain must be an easier target than it need be, and that's a real problem.

But in many ways it's an investment decision, that is to say, a decision about where you should put your (or our) resources. One could put a good deal of resource in border control, one could put greater resource into intelligence gathering, or one could put a great deal of resource into tightening the asylum system. I'm trying to get a sense of balance in this.

Well, wait until tomorrow and you'll see what balance we strike! I agree, of course, there are issues of where you direct resources.

You may not wish to answer this, but tomorrow, is it a rounded package?

Yes. And talking of rounded packages, it is a current national emergency that involves asylum only as part, as you rightly say, of the jigsaw. But alongside that— separate from it but connected with it, because it's the genesis of the chaos—is the longer range question of how to operate a fair, rational, humane, sensible system of Britain contributing to dealing with the problems of the refugees of the world.

Is your main criticism of the current asylum system to do with process or to do with substance? That is to say, is it the way it's administered, the delays, the cost, the inefficiencies, on the one hand, or the substantive law that allows, for example, a former Taliban soldier to be allowed entry to this country under asylum law? With what are you more uncomfortable—is it the process or the bigger picture?

I think there are deficiencies on both sides. I had thought for a period that because the current method of administration is so weak, so ineffective, so ill-conceived and structured, we could hope to solve the problems by making that administration more effective. For example, I've been recommending for the last year that processing of applications for asylum seekers should go on in small one-stop shop centres, where all the people involved are dealing with people who are applying from one country or region. Then they could know something about the people about whom they are making decisions, have translators who speak the relevant language on the site, have all the people who are going to be involved in the application on the site, and therefore not be shovelling paper round the United Kingdom, having lawyers 200 miles from their clients, having files being lost and replicated, and not making decisions about someone from Kazakhstan at 9, from Afghanistan at 9.15, from Poland at 9.30, and so forth.

I had hoped that by those means and by re-instatement of the original bilateral agreement with France and a few other measures, one could hope to restore order to the chaos. Perhaps one could, but I have to say that I have become increasingly sceptical, both about whether there is the political will to engage in that kind of restructuring of the administration, and secondly, whether as a matter of fact, even if one were to restructure the administration in that way, one would sufficiently address the general scope of the problem. I'm not now talking about terrorism but about the general scope of the system in chaos.

I think there's no doubt that the root of the difficulty is that the world which was pictured by the international system that we now have was a world very substantially different from that which we now live in. In 1951 when the Geneva Convention was signed, and even in 1967 when the New York Protocol was signed which extends the effects of the Geneva Convention to those who are refugees after 1951, and even actually when people were beginning the negotiation of the Dublin Convention which locks in both of the previous ones so far as we're concerned, the world was really substantially different.

To take us back to 1951, the '51 Convention was meant to deal with the effects of the Holocaust and refuges from Stalin, and it applied exclusively to those who were refugees from before 1951. There were very, very tiny numbers. Even as recently as 15 years ago, I believe that there were approximately 3,000 applications for asylum to the UK; now, including dependents, there are around tens of thousands. The number of refugees in refugee camps 15 or 20 years ago was very tiny. Sporadically it grew, but then it declined again as a particular situation somewhere in the world got better. There are now, by the UNHCR calculations, something like 15 million people in refugee camps around the world, which is an appalling fact.

Incidentally, interestingly, our total contribution to the UNHCR effort to look after them is £34 million, whereas we spend billions on looking after the asylum system, much of which goes on people who are judged eventually not to be refugees, or on lawyers, or on contractors, or parties other than refugees. If all 15 million people currently resident in the refugee camps were to apply to enter Britain tomorrow, I doubt that democracy would sustain the effects of the Conventions to which we are signatories. So what we actually do—I know that most people don't like facing up to this, but it's the case—what we actually do is to apply a wealth test. I can't imagine how we've got ourselves in this position, but it's what we do. If people are rich enough either to be able to get themselves here or to pay a people trafficker to get them to our borders or the border of some other relatively safe country, then they can be processed for asylum, but if they're not, then they languish in the refugee camps.

Now, this is something very far from a rational system, and it has the further effect, not just in Britain but in other peaceful countries, that there are very large numbers of people who are now able to use the asylum system as a means of evading immigration controls. This causes all sorts of trouble for Governments that are trying to maintain rational immigration policies of a kind that will prevent friction, recognise the legitimate aspirations of individuals and accommodate the need in the economy for key workers. When, in addition, the fact that people are able to use the asylum system as a way round the immigration controls compromises the ability of genuine refugees to receive fast and efficient admission, then it sounds like there's a structural defect. There's something wrong and I'm no longer convinced that sheer administrative responses are likely to solve it in the near future. That's as much as I want to say about that until tomorrow.

A few minutes ago, you were talking about a national emergency. Last year, here at Gresham, I was discussing with Lord Woolf and David Pannick QC emergency legislation in terrorist times and the extent to which human rights could actually be impinged upon or cautiously put to one side. Much seemed to turn, as a matter of law and as a matter of practicality, on whether or not it was viewed that the circumstances in which we find ourselves do indeed constitute a state of war, or a state of national emergency. Because in either event, many of the liberties that one would normally take for granted, or a terrorist or suspected terrorist might take for granted, would be suspended. If you were Home Secretary, how would you address this issue? While there are elements of the current climate that suggest a national emergency, it seems to me unlikely that any Government would currently declare a national emergency, and if that's the case, are we actually setting the bar too high in terms of human rights?[4]

Well, the definition of a national emergency is a significant issue. It's not the whole of the question about the balance that's being struck by the jurisprudence surrounding the European Convention on Human Rights. I rather suspect that you're right, notwithstanding the Prime Minister's recent remark that a terrorist attack is now inevitable. This is a remarkable remark. I'm critical of that remark. I think the idea that Government should regard as inevitable the elimination of some of its citizens is a bad attitude. I think it would have been better had he said, and had he thought, that it was very likely and that we were going to try by every possible means to prevent it. But the remark indicates at least, and that's to his credit, that the Prime Minister takes the current terrorist threat very seriously.

Now, I go back to the question, how big? How possible is it that at some time in the next couple of years something will happen which is so big that it threatens the normal conduct of our society? I don't know. But that in itself is extraordinary. All the way through the period when we lived with the IRA making significant attacks, there was never the slightest question of something happening that would threaten the whole foundation of what we take for granted. And I think therefore we've moved on to a new plane, and I think the Prime Minister thinks we've moved on to a new plane. Yet it's clear that there's a reluctance to declare an emergency, and I suspect that the sad truth is that an emergency will not be declared unless and until some very major event has actually occurred. Now, it can't be a rational basis for policy to expect—or even class as inevitable—a very significant attack on the lives of perhaps many people, and yet not to be willing to take steps to avert it until after it's occurred.

Yes, we can only protect ourselves after it happens.

After the event—that can't be rational.

---

[4] Human rights are also discussed by Lord Woolf (Ch.1), David Pannick QC (Ch.3), Lord Bingham (Ch.7), David Lock (Ch.9), Cherie Booth QC (Ch.12) and Professor Bogdanor (Ch.19).

But then again, many of the facilities, the tools and the protections that the police and the security services would want to invoke are not fully available other than in times of national emergency. It may be that there is an interim state in which one can find oneself, one that does not currently have recognised status between times of reasonable peace on the one hand, and out-and-out war on the other.

Yes, maybe we need more categories.

You were talking earlier about the treaty definitions—for example, those of the European Convention on Human Rights and the 1951 Geneva Convention—not really contemplating the refugee and asylum position we find ourselves in today. It's similarly true when people have debated and legislated in relation to national emergencies; I think people have had in mind major warfare between nation states, rather than the kind of threat we face today. Where do you sit on human rights in relation to terrorism? Under legislation from last year, we are now able to detain people in circumstances that would not normally be consistent with our criminal process, our standards of criminal proof and our presumption of innocence. Are you comfortable with this?

Well, I supported it, and I led my party into voting for it—with some reluctance, because I don't think that it was the best solution available. But as it was the best solution that we were offered by the Government, I supported it. I am convinced that it would have been preferable and would still be preferable, which is why I've continued to argue for it, that we should go through a process in order to be able to enter a reservation against Article III of the European Convention on Human Rights in order to be able to deport the people who are currently being detained indefinitely.

The process one would need to go through is one of denunciation under one of the Articles, and re-accession with a reservation against Article III. This is the somewhat inelegant process which is required because you can't, as you will know, derogate against Article III.

The purpose of entering the reservation, which incidentally will be parallel to the French reservation, is that the jurisprudence is very clear. I've never been sure whether this is something that is really justified by the text but let that be. In the case of *Singh and Singh*, where Jack Straw when he was Home Secretary wished to deport two people to India because he regarded them as a threat to national security, he was prevented from doing so by the judges because the judges ruled that they would be subject in India to inhuman and degrading treatment. As a result of that case, it's become clear that in any country where there is some delay before the death penalty is exacted, deportation is impossible under Article III. I think that the right attitude to that would have been to enter a reservation against it, by means of this rather inelegant process, in order to get to the stage where we could provide for people who are presently being indefinitely detained instead to be deported. Part of my reason for that is that indefinite detention is now, regrettably, on the British statute book—admittedly for foreign nationals, admittedly for people who constitute a threat to the State, admittedly with my support—but it's there, and I fear for the day when somebody will look at this and say, well, if it can be done for foreign nationals, it can be done for domestic residents, British citizens, and that's a slope down which I don't want to go.

I'm afraid that was my next question. It seems to me that many people would want to cast the net wider because they could see that some people who are perhaps British citizens pose as great if not a greater threat than those foreign nationals who are being indefinitely detained. Are you entirely uncomfortable with indefinitely detaining British citizens?

I am very uncomfortable with it. You asked at the very beginning of this what is the job of the Home Secretary and what's the job of the Shadow Home Secretary. The most difficult single job of either is of course this very balancing act, the balancing act of public safety against individual liberties. There is never a right answer for all times. During conditions of war, we have traditionally suspended habeas corpus. That is a pretty draconian measure, but we did it because when we were fighting the Second World War, we were trying to defend the very system which incorporated it, knowing that if we didn't take draconian steps we might end up with Adolph Hitler running Britain, who certainly would not have been much concerned with habeas corpus or much else besides.

So this balancing act is a balancing act which has to be conducted against the background of the shifting scene of reality, and because it's human beings doing it and we're fallible, it's very difficult to make the judgments about which way to shift the balance at a given moment. I can foresee that there might be some time when things were so bad that one would contemplate indefinite detention of British citizens. I don't think, bad as things are, that we've got to that stage yet. I hope we never will, outside conditions of, for example, a repetition of the Second World War. I am worried therefore about institutionalising things which might lead us to opt for that without as much hesitation as we ought to have about it. But I accept this is a very, very delicate balance.

One of my fears is that if we don't take sufficiently adept and effective steps to protect the public, and if something goes very wrong, the calls for more draconian action than is actually required may lead to the very outcome that the terrorists wish to achieve—the crumbling of Western liberal democracy. The ultimate aim of the terrorists is of course not merely to kill people but to undo what they regard as a decadent Western liberal democracy. What I want to do is to preserve Western liberal democracy. Judging whether, at any given moment, it is more at risk from terrorists or more at risk from the measures we take to defeat terrorism is a pretty delicate balancing act.

That's a fine note to end on. I did, incidentally, have about 10 possible topics in mind for this evening and I think we've covered about two and a half of these. So if you had another four hours, we could finish our chat! I do want, however, to ask you one final question. I always ask people sitting in your seat about the advisability of pursuing a career in law. Instead, tonight I will ask the same of a career in politics. If you were speaking to a pupil at school, or a student at university, who was contemplating a career in politics, what would you say to them?

158

Well, I would say that if you are a megalomaniac, and if you love the sound of your own voice, and if you are willing to engage in an enormously arduous profession with no thanks and a great deal of ridicule, and if you don't mind being regarded by your fellow citizens as little better than a murderer or a rapist, then you should opt for this!

Dr Letwin, many thanks.

CHAPTER ELEVEN

Dame Elizabeth Butler-Sloss
President of The Family Division

Tuesday February 11, 2003

I'm particularly pleased to have with us tonight Dame Elizabeth Butler-Sloss. She is, as many of you will know, one of the country's top judges, best known perhaps in family law as well as a number of other areas relating to medicine that we'll be discussing today. Dame Elizabeth is also our country's most senior female judge. She became a High Court judge in 1979, a Court of Appeal Judge in 1988, and in 1999 the President of the Family Division of the High Court.

There are many things I could say by way of introduction, but time allows me just to pick a couple. You have innumerable honorary degrees, but particularly and unusually from the medical world, which shows just how highly regarded you are in the area of medicine as well as in law. I was going to say above all else—and perhaps it is—but you are also a very staunch supporter of Gresham College, so it's particularly nice to have you back with us tonight. I thought we might start by talking about the Family Division itself, of which you're President, because the scope of the work of the Family Division is rather larger than might be supposed?

Yes. We do, obviously, all ordinary family cases: we deal with parents and children; we deal with divorce, but usually at a lower level; we deal with money or what's sometimes called "the big money cases" when the millionaires are in dispute, or generally the husband who's the millionaire is in dispute with a wife who wants some of the millions. But the other field that has become increasingly important is in dealing with those who are adult but not able to make their own decisions, and we make decisions about life and death; about whether there should be sterilisation; we had one case, for instance, a circumcision. We have a number of extraordinary cases all coming through the medical field, and I suppose the one that hit the headlines was Miss B.

To which I'd like to turn shortly. Tell us a little bit about your role as President. What does that mean for you in terms of the balance of your work?

Well, I sit as a judge for three days a week, generally, sometimes up to five. I sit in the Court of Appeal for a third of my time, and I sit as a trial judge for two-thirds

161

of my time, but I think my more important job is literally managing the High Court Family Division, 18 judges plus myself. I have a considerable management role now in dealing with the county court at two levels, and I have, I hope, some influence on the magistrates' court. I discuss proposed legislation when the Government wants me to be consulted, and I sit on innumerable committees!

We've had many judges sitting in your chair, as it were, but one difference in you're your work, I suppose, is that non-lawyers may have stronger views on, or greater insight into, the many issues that you decide. I can see a contrast here with people who come before commercial judges who may be looking at phenomena such as bills of lading or collateral warranties. So it may be that your own work attracts greater public attention precisely because there's an inherent interest in family matters or issues of medical law. Do you find that the work of your court is discussed more than that of other courts?

Well, everybody who is married or unmarried, with or without children or grandchildren, has a view on family matters, particularly if they have been the victim, as they would see it, of court proceedings or indeed have friends or relatives who have; yes, of course.

Why don't we discuss what in many ways is the most challenging and, I think, interesting aspect of your work: issues relating to medicine and consent. I have in mind some of the very, very difficult decisions that you've been called upon to make. You mentioned Miss B. Perhaps we can chat through that as a case study, and then discuss some of the issues that flow from that case and, in particular, how it is that you as a judge wrestle with these very difficult moral and legal matters.

I think the first thing is that I worry very much while I'm doing it, and I've managed to train myself not to worry at all when it's over. I mean, if I'm wrong, it's too late, so I do sleep reasonably well at night.

Could you take one case and talk through the issues, insofar as you're able to?

Well, Miss B was very interesting. She was 43. She was from the Caribbean. She'd had an unhappy childhood, and she had fought her way up to the top in her particular post in a leading hospital. She was struck down quite unexpectedly by a broken blood vessel in, I think, the back of the neck that paralysed her from the neck down, and she suddenly discovered, from having managed everybody, she was being treated effectively as incompetent. She was in Intensive Care for 12 months and she eventually took proceedings herself from her hospital bed that she should be able to have the artificial ventilator, without which she could not breathe, turned off. I mean, she couldn't move a finger.

And the issue that came before you?

It was an issue of competence, because she has the right not to have treatment she chooses not to have if she is competent to make that decision. What the doctors couldn't bring themselves to do was do it, because they became very fond of her. She was still in the Intensive Care Unit, and they of course are trained to keep people alive. If she'd been in a hospice, I expect there would have been a different situation, as one of the consultant psychiatrists giving evidence pointed out.

Is that kind of case different from others? For example where a party has wanted someone else actively to bring about his or her death? Because you've been involved with decisions of that sort as well, haven't you?

The only types of case that come at the moment to the court relating literally to whether someone should be allowed to die rather than to live are the permanent vegetative state cases, where people have had these appalling anoxic injuries to the brain, as a result of which they have no cognitive ability at all, none. I think the most extreme example is they could have operations without anaesthetic. Those people have no future. In the Tony Bland case, the 17-year-old Hillsborough boy who had the misfortune not to die because he lived for three-and-a-half years in this twilight world, the House of Lords called his life futile, and there is no duty on the medical profession to prolong life which is futile. Their business is to try and heal people.

When you come to make these decisions—and in different contexts I've asked different judges this same question—how do you go about your decision-making? The related, more specific question here is: to what extent are you constrained and guided by existing law or are you drawing on other non-legal sources? We find embodied in the law I think, if one's taking two broad principles, this balance between on the one hand the right to self-determination and to make one's own decisions, and on the other hand the sanctity of life principle. It seems to me that the law favours the former rather than the latter, if I can crudely summarise the position. Is that a fair summary of the law as it is? Or is it left for you to decide in individual cases? And how do you make these terribly difficult decisions?[1]

Six questions I think!

At least! But feel free to answer them in any order!

---

[1] Judicial decision-making is also discussed by Lord Woolf (Ch.1), Lord Bingham (Ch.7), Cherie Booth (Ch.12) and Professor John Gardner (Ch.16).

Well, since you happen to have as your speciality IT, you'll be relieved to hear that I write all my judgments on a computer provided by the Government on your advice! So that's the starting point.

I must jump in and say that you have been using a machine longer than I have.

I'm older than you! But you're a good deal more expert at it than I am. I've listened to your expertise on this before now. But my view is that every decision I make must be made within the ambit and within the guidelines that exist in law. Every now and again, if there is no actual example, the judge is going to have to take the existing situation, look at the previous cases, and perhaps move out into the unknown. I personally do that as little as possible. I don't think I'm a reforming judge but I've been in situations where I have to do it, and so far as these life and death cases, that is in a sense simple for me, because the House of Lords—I sat in the Court of Appeal in *Bland*, and the House of Lords had laid down the rules. Then I had, post the Human Rights Act, to look to see whether the Human Rights Act made a difference to the House of Lords. I have to say I rather enjoyed that—the only time I've been able to review whether the House of Lords was right! And I'll never again be allowed to do that. But I came to the conclusion that the House of Lords' decision in *Bland* was compatible with the Human Rights Act.

I don't accept that we don't put the sanctity of life very high. We do, but we recognise that the medical profession—and it's always in a medical case you're looking at, in my experience—the medical profession should not be keeping people alive for whom such effort is futile, and therefore there is a limit to keeping people alive. You only have to look at the medical profession itself with brain stem death. They turn off the machines. They don't come to the courts for that. The permanent vegetative state cases are more difficult because they are being kept alive by artificial nutrition and hydration, usually through a peg in the stomach, which is a tube into the stomach, and so that is more difficult; but I'm happy to say, in these very sad cases, I follow the House of Lords.

You must work a lot, therefore, with expert medical witnesses. Could we explore this area a little, because I suppose, to a large extent, since Lord Woolf's reforms and his recommendations on expert witnesses, that this aspect of the legal landscape has changed significantly. Could you provide us with a little bit of context and background here?

I've just done whether or not two young people with Variant CJD in the terminal stages should have totally new treatment, never tried on people, based on very erudite research done by a leading forensic neurologist in Tokyo. He gave evidence in the case in the video-link court in the Royal Courts of Justice, and I gave a judgment, which is public though I'm not sure it's been publicised, which set out what should be done. But I had a very large number of people there. I say large number: five or six doctors with particular expertise in CJD, but there's very little expertise on Variant CJD. Since then I've had to deal with a metabolic disorder, and I had I think all the leading people on metabolic disorder in the court.

I've been looking at the law on a number of occasions under the Human Fertility and Embryology Act 1990. I've dealt with a renal issue, whether a young man should have a renal transplant, who can't make the choice himself, and I had I suppose all the renal experts in court—well, not all of them, but certainly four or five of them. I'm not alone in this. The other Family Division judges, particularly in children's cases, are getting these experts. I think the largest number that I've had is eight, but Mrs Justice Bracewell had nine.

Generally, do you find that experts before you tend to agree or disagree? And has this changed since Lord Woolf's reforms? Because one does hear that, historically at least, the word "gladiatorial" well described the interaction between experts.

Not in the Family Division. We had these rules long before the CPR, the Civil Procedure Rules, and the Civil Procedure Rules to some extent took from us. We have always tried to get the experts to agree. We think it's crucial to have an experts' meeting, at least by telephone conferencing, preferably to meet. The best way with experts is to ask them to address, firstly, what are the issues, secondly, where do they agree, and find out the areas of disagreement. You usually cut it down so that you don't get more than two or three of these very eminent men or women in court.

Is it the case that when they actually come together, they tend to be more agreeable?

Yes, very much so. They each of course are asked questions, and give answers, but the point comes when they are faced with a particular case and the views of others, and they usually will have very well defined areas of disagreement, but a great many areas where they actually agree, and then in court you find that they are moving much closer, sometimes to settlement point.

Are the experts from different sub-disciplines or are they all experts in the same broad disciplines?

Well, in one case about a baby with very severe sub-dural haematomas, retinal haemorrhaging, aged about two months, who clearly had been shaken, by the end of the case there were two forensic pathologists, two or three paediatricians, two at least neurologists, somebody who could understand the MRI and CAT imaging, and, of course, an ophthalmologist. I find it actually riveting but terribly difficult. I got a marvellous skeleton argument from one of the counsel, and the first sentence was: "I'm sorry to say that the medical evidence in this case is dense"! Nobody disagreed!

Are many of the experts before you people who, while falling short of being career medical experts, do nonetheless do a lot of expert witness work? Or is the kind of case that appears before you so specialist that it's likely to be a fairly rare occurrence for the doctor to have previously appeared in court?

I think some are rare, but almost all the senior doctors become medical experts, if we can possibly persuade them into court. One of the worries that I have, and I publicly announced particularly to the medical profession, is about the doctors who were very eminent as clinicians but who have ceased to have actual hands-on experience of patients. I'm not sure how helpful they are in giving their views. The point comes like a judge who is not sitting very much or at all: certainly doctors who don't have patients, the value of their evidence diminishes substantially.

The same happens in the IT field as well, because many people retire from technology and yet the whole discipline moves on so very quickly.

It doesn't always stop them expressing their views!

No. I can well imagine that. And of course medical science can move on such that received wisdom at some stage can, many years later, be seen to be misguided. Perhaps you're unable to comment on this, but I recall there was recently an issue over a family where there were two cot deaths in the one family. And while at one time this had been considered to be highly unlikely, indeed statistically almost impossible, later research had suggested it was not nearly as improbable as initially believed by experts.

Yes, that was Sally Clark. No, I'm not in a position to comment on that.

No, but I can see in any event that . . .

I think another area there, if I might just take you on, is the very interesting area of the very young child, usually the baby of six months or under, sometimes up to 18 months, who receives some sort of injury to the head, sometimes within the brain, sometimes within the sub-dural area, and it was thought that you needed, to get that sort of injury, a Road Traffic Act type of impact, such as if you were a very wicked man you would throw the child against something like a wall. I mean, that happens sometimes. I think one or two or more children die every week. I mean, the figures of death of children in families is quite alarming. But the better received wisdom is that because a young baby has a very, very floppy neck, that under three to six months, particularly with neonates, who are a month or under, quite limited damage to the neck can create appalling injuries within the brain and sub-dural area. But the argument at the moment is whether that sort of injury can be the result of children playing with a baby or just casual careless handling, or whether it is something that remains unusual which shows a degree of culpability as opposed just to accident, and there's quite a difference of opinion between groups of the medical profession on this issue. I very much hope, and I have suggested, that this urgently needs research, peer-vetted research on the effect on very, very young babies.

Presumably you can draw on research from all around the world. It's not just UK expertise and research that influence you?

Not only do I look to the decisions right round the world, particularly in the Commonwealth, clearly the common law Commonwealth, Australia, New Zealand, Canada, to some extent the United States, occasionally South Africa, but also the medical profession, of course, and they bring that research from across the world to court.

You mentioned other jurisdictions. Is there a community of senior judges working in your areas who meet regularly or communicate freely with one another?

Not much. We have absolutely excellent arrangements and meetings between judges of different countries, for instance Anglo-American, very successful Anglo-Indian, but none of those include Family. But I've just completed a bilateral conference between Pakistan and the United Kingdom, in England, in London, at the beginning of January, where the Chief Justice of Pakistan came with a number of other judges, and we have agreed a protocol for the return of children from any of our respective countries, including Azad Jammu and Kashmir, which is more or less under Pakistani control, that children who are basically British children of Pakistani origin should come back here, and children who are living in Pakistan who are moved by a parent without the consent of the other parent to the UK will be sent back to Azad Jammu and Kashmir or to Pakistan. They have a federal jurisdiction so it would be to Lahore or Karachi or somewhere. I mean, it's the most marvellous breakthrough. And the enthusiasm of the Chief Justice of Pakistan and the judges with him was wonderful, very exciting.

What's the legal nature of such a protocol? What is it, in law?

Well, in the United Kingdom, we were supported by the Foreign Office and by the Lord Chancellor's Department, and someone from the Home Office turned up to find out what we were discussing. The Ministry of Justice in Islamabad, the minister then in position, not now, gave me lunch and said, "Don't let the politicians touch this. You, the judges, go and do it". And we, the judges, did. None of it contravenes our existing law, but it is an indication that we would basically follow the principles of the Hague Convention on child abduction. We also discussed, in great detail, the situation of forced marriages, which are wrong, compared with arranged marriages, which are perfectly acceptable.

And what was the outcome of that discussion?

Well, that they are very anxious that young people . . . do you know there are a thousand or so young people from the United Kingdom going either to Pakistan or to Azad Jammu or Kashmir from the UK, ostensibly for holidays, but in fact to be married against their will to people they have never met, very often don't speak the language of the particular area they are going to? The Foreign Office is working very strongly to get these young people back if they can, and the forced marriages are as much anathema to the Pakistani Government and the Pakistani judges as they are to us, because it's contrary to the Koran, where consent of the woman is an essential part of the Koran, and also they know it happens. This happens a lot in Kashmir, the Pakistan Kashmir, and the Chief Justice there is very insistent that something must be done to stop it.

Could we turn now to family law more generally? I suppose one of the most controversial areas, where really very strong views are held, is in relation to fathers' rights. I think it is fair to say that there's a view that the courts do not favour fathers in custody cases.

Untrue.

I want you to clarify this. Can you take us through the issues and the difficulties you face?

Well, I suppose the starting point, I mean, I don't want to make this too long an answer, but the starting point is that when a couple break up, and it's irrelevant whether they're married or unmarried, the usual situation is that the woman keeps the children. It's not because she is better than the man, but it's how it usually happens, and the most important thing for children is continuity and stability, and so to a large extent, the parent who has the children, unless there's something wrong with that parent, will probably keep the children. In a minority of cases, that's the father. In the majority of cases, it happens to be the mother. But the law is that the rights of each parent are equal with the rights of the other parent; the welfare of the child is paramount under section 1 of the Children Act, and that is our ruling mantra if you like, and very important too, because it's statutory. Section 1 says, "welfare of children is paramount", and we observe it. Clearly, with the Human Rights Act reminding us the mother has rights, the father has rights, the child has rights, but overriding all that, as Strasbourg, European Court of Human Rights, says, the overriding concern is the child.

Well, now if the child stays with the mother, which is the more usual situation—but not intended to be so by the Judiciary I hasten to say—the difficulty then becomes that the stress of the parting, which is usually agonising for people—a failed relationship, corrosive very often, continuing to fight the battles during the latter part of the breakdown of the relationship, using the children sometimes even without meaning as pawns to get at the other parent, each parent is doing it sometimes—interferes with sensible arrangements between the parents and the children in a small minority of cases. Most parents are perfectly sensible, but there is a very small, but very vocal, minority. And because more fathers than mothers don't have children to live with them, it's inevitable that they are the group who say most, but of some of these organisations, like the Equal Parenting Council, mothers are members.

Now, there are two groups of fathers, in my view, those who deserve to see their children and those who don't. The ones who are most vocal are those who don't, but they carry with them a number of very decent people who are for one reason or another disadvantaged in not seeing their children. One of the reasons is, some-times, that the mother is unreasonable, and the weapons, if you like, in the locker of the judge for making a mother see sense to let her child see his father are very limited. We can put the mother in prison, but if you put the mother in prison and the child loves the mother and doesn't love the father very much because he hasn't seen him, it's not actually going to help contact. If the mother says, "Look what your father did. I told you he was a dreadful man, and I'm going to prison", it doesn't help good relationships. So it's not a very usual thing to put a parent into prison. The alterna-tives really are mediation, which is excellent and works in a lot of cases but needs more resources, and just the judges trying to get the parents to see sense.

Now, some mothers have good reason for not letting their children see the father because they were treated with violence or intimidation during the marriage or during the relationship, but that's a different group of people, and those you can see why they don't want the child to see the father. But the ones that we're talking about, with Families Need Fathers and Equal Parenting Council, they've got some good points, but I don't believe that they should be battering the judges. I don't think there's much more we can do except try to make the parties see sense. What we need is information to couples who part, at the point of parting, when they've got to deal with the children; and mediation where possible to persuade them all to see sense.

Can I leap in? At what stage is mediation?

Well, information tells them what the odds are, what they're doing. It might tell them that the children are entitled to know what's happening—children very often aren't told—that the children ought to be allowed to say to mother "I love Daddy", because the mother assumes that the children can't stand daddy because she can't—these sort of very basic things. And the mediation is to try and bring the parents closer together because they are going to be tied to each other, or ought to be, for the rest of the childhood of the child, in order to make the life of the child easy to move from one parent to another, and when it doesn't work it's tragic. It's tragic for the grownups, but it's much worse for the children. Now I'm a great believer in both parents. I think fathers are very important, and I think fathers should be seeing their children, but there are very real problems in relation to the parent looking after the child and how you manage it. Actually I think the third thing that might be done is what was suggested by Mr Justice Wall in a Children Act Advisory Committee Report on having greater powers of enforcement so that you could in fact require the parent being unreasonable to have to go to counselling, to have to go to some sort of community service, to have to go to all sorts of things; for the father who perhaps has been unreasonable and has been pretty angry to go to anger counselling. But we haven't got the powers under the family legislation to do this, nor at the moment are there resources there; particularly not resources for fathers who bitterly regret their misbehaviour in the past, would like to have anger counselling, like to go off on courses, and there's no money for it, or very little.

I think in one of your papers you point out how many fathers only see their children once or twice a year after divorce. I found this (a) surprising and (b) a depressing statistic.

I think it's appalling but some fathers walk away. I can see in a sense why they do. I think some fathers just leave and do not concern themselves with their children. Other fathers try and do not try hard enough. I would not wish to shut the door on a father until I was absolutely forced to it but, at the end of the day, if the child is suffering because of the unsuitable way in which the contact is going on between the absent parent and child, and if this is having an adverse effect on the mother, which is upsetting the child, then contact may have to be stopped. But before you get to that situation you can use Contact Centres, which are the most marvellous resource, run by volunteers, growing up all over the country, who provide, you know, tea, coffee, orange juice, and a clean, decent place staffed by volunteers, with lots and lots of toys. The father and child may be able to go there and have contact in a neutral and non-threatening environment. I helped to open one in Swansea quite recently, and all the local community sent in their toys. They were brilliant toys, and on the opening all the people who had helped brought their children in to play with the toys, which were then going to be used by children coming in on contact with parents whom they weren't otherwise seeing. And you've only got to be a boarding school parent on a wet Sunday afternoon wondering where to take your child to know how marvellous it is for young parents sometimes, without much money, having somewhere to play with the children for two hours, you know, sit on the floor and play with the jigsaws and the rest of it, and this is the sort of thing provided.

Who's driving that initiative?

Well, there is now a National Association of Child Contact Centres, of which I'm a patron. There are two sorts of these Contact Centres, each managed locally, but affiliated to the National Association. Two sorts, one which are volunteers for ordinary families, and one which are supervised either for parents where the father has been violent and therefore it's not quite safe for volunteers to deal with him in case he loses his cool, and also in local authority cases where children are in care but want to see their parents and the parents want to see them. They also use these supervised Contact Centres. Very few of them, inadequate resources, and an absolutely marvellous way of dealing with families.

What kind of cases would come before your court, then, in the family arena? Actually, it would be very useful if you could explain, particularly for non-lawyers, the structure of the courts system insofar as family disputes are concerned. Where do the cases go, and how do they eventually reach you?

How many hours do you want?! A very brief resume . . . The family jurisdiction under the Children Act is in four separate courts: the magistrates' court, which is called the Family Proceedings Court, the county court at two levels, and the High Court. What is intended is that the magistrates' court deals with the least complicated cases and the High Court deals with the most complicated. Divorces generally come into the county court and all that goes with divorce—which includes children and particularly what happens to the matrimonial home and what money is there and how should it be divided—generally is heard in the county court. The really difficult cases in divorce and money and children are heard in the High Court.

Can I break in? Uncontested divorces: what happens to them?

District judges deal with those. That's largely done on paper, with, I think, they go into court just to pronounce the decree nisi.

Okay, but there is no involved evidential process or courtroom trauma?

Well, an affidavit is sworn, and an acknowledgement of service, but it goes through on the nod. It takes three months from day one to the end, which is why Part IV of the Family Law Act with its elaborate arrangements for giving everybody time to think, which was going to take 15 months, was not I think going to be popular—when anybody realised you had children, you couldn't get a divorce in 15 months whereas now you can get one in three.

Which is quite quick.

Which is very quick.

Do both parties have to appear in the district courts?

No, nobody has to appear. It's all done on paper if it's uncontested. You have to admit, if you are the respondent, that you've behaved unreasonably or committed adultery, or two years' consent, but you've got to be party to the two years to have that, or five years if one of the spouses won't agree to it.

171

So it's similar to Scotland.

Yes, very similar. But the important areas that we do in the High Court are declarations as to legitimacy, declarations, which isn't very important nowadays, on parenthood really; declarations as to whether foreign divorces or foreign marriages are valid; and particularly the Hague Convention on child abduction, which in England and Scotland and Northern Ireland, unlike much of the rest of the world—I think there are 80 odd members of the Hague Convention—I think we're one of the very few parts of the world where all cases are heard exclusively in the High Court and by High Court judges.

How common is child abduction?

I think there are half a dozen a week coming through the High Court, certainly three or four a week. Some of them settle. Some of them—they've changed a bit. There used to be, in 1980 the Hague Convention was passed, with I think 20 or 30 countries. It's been implemented in various countries; in England in 1985 I think—the 1985 Child Abduction and Custody Act, which incorporates the Hague Convention and similarly the European Convention. But the importance is that if the country which is a signatory, as we are, sends an application for the return of a child, it is the duty of the English court to return that child to whichever country makes the application, so long as you can show the child is habitually resident in the other country, that the parent seeking the return of the child has a right of custody, and that the parent who has abducted the child has actually done that, has actually refused to return the child or has actually removed the child without consent of the other parent, and there are a number of defences which are quite difficult to prove. We have a very good record in this country on sending children back, usually to Australia, New Zealand, Canada, or the United States, which presents great problems if the other parent, the abducting parent, wants to live in England.

And this all happens through the Family Division of the High Court?

Yes, it's operated through the Lord Chancellor and there's what's called a Central Authority, and each country has a Central Authority that receives the application from the other country or makes the application to the other country for the return of the child.

What about appeals? What's the appeal process and how does your court, and how do you personally, get involved in appeals within the family area?

From the High Court, the appeals are to the Court of Appeal, so I have to be very careful that when I'm sitting in the Court of Appeal I don't sit on a case which has come before me at any time. The appeals from the circuit judges go to the High Court.

Forgive me, is that the Civil Division of the Court of Appeal?

Yes. The Family Division, some judges in the Family Division sit in Crime but most judges don't. The circuit judges go to the Court of Appeal. District judges go to the circuit judges. Magistrates go to the High Court, unless released by me to a circuit judge who's a Deputy High Court judge. That's the current position.

What's the throughput? I've no sense of how many divorces give rise to legal disputes and therefore . . . ?

I don't know statistics, but divorces, contested divorces, are probably one or two a year. So far as money disputes, you more or less have to go to court if there's a matrimonial home or there's any money. It's much better to have an order in what we call ancillary relief, which is money cases. So they come through the courts even if they're not really in dispute. Children, they have to come under the divorce law for a certificate to tell the court, usually the district judge, what the arrangements are, but that can be quite a short process.

What of mediation? When is that used most often—in relation to the financial disputes or the custody disputes?

Both. The mediation in financial disputes is probably limited to where there's something to have a dispute over, but you'd be surprised where the disputes lie. For instance, you have a tenancy, a local authority tenancy—who is going to get the tenancy after they part? So it matters as much to people with very little money as it does to people with a great deal of money; in fact more, because it's very difficult to get a roof over your head.

And to what extent is legal aid available for these kinds of disputes?

I'm not able to say what the figure is but it is at a fairly low level. There are a very large number of people coming before the courts who qualify because they're at a very low level of income, and I gather that the overspend on the Legal Services Commission Legal Aid Bill is considerable. Family work, I'm afraid, is very expensive.

You mentioned many other committees and responsibilities and the list is formidable. But can you give us a flavour of other activities with which you are involved, especially those that are in and around your judicial duties?

173

What, separate from or in and around?

Well, indeed, both! But let's look, first of all, at activities in and around your judicial role and then, if we have time, we can perhaps move to activities that are very largely separate from your work as a judge.

Well, I'm in regular discussion with the Lord Chancellor's Department. I'm currently very involved in delay in child care cases, and the delays are unacceptable and the Lord Chancellor recognises it, and I'm on a number of committees . . .

Just to stop you there: what's the nature of this challenge? I've no sense of the scale of the problem.

Well, the ambition is—I mean the ambition is not terribly high—that we should get a case which has started in the lowest court. All care cases, when the local authority take children away or threaten to take children away, have to start in the magistrates' court. That's a statutory requirement, that they all start in the magistrates' court, and they float up if they're sufficiently difficult. Those cases, if they do float up, we hope to contain within 40 weeks, but right round the country, we are taking far longer.

What's the source of the delay?

Got another two hours?!

This is an interesting one, so it is worth dwelling upon.

The social workers are very overstretched and understaffed. They don't necessarily bring the cases quick enough. The courts are overburdened. The guardians under CAFCAS are having a considerable problem in providing guardians quickly enough. Social workers have a problem providing reports quickly enough. We're having great difficulties in the more difficult cases with experts, medical experts or psychological experts, in getting their reports in a reasonable time. One thing after another is adding to the delay. I've written a paper to the Lord Chancellor that sets out each delay in detail, but it's very worrying.

And is it a managed process, in the sense of involving judicial case management as is being attempted in civil justice? If not, who is actually responsible for progressing a case from beginning to end? Or is it like a baton that's handed from one person to another?

rampaging up and down the Middlesborough General Hospital, totally fit, and being kept there and then placed with a rapidly diminishing number of foster parents. That was not my business. That was going through the courts at the same time as I was chairing, with three very distinguished assessors examining what went wrong on the management side. I had a consultant paediatrician, who became President of the Royal College of Paediatrics and Child Health, I had a Director of Social Services, and I had a recently retired Chief Constable, and with them we looked at every single case and saw what went wrong, and there was a very alarming pattern of failure of communication and the refusal of different agencies to talk to each other, which got literally to a point when they wouldn't talk to each other, and the kids were all being picked up and taken off to hospital, identified as having been sexually abused, and taken off to foster parents. I mean, some were, some weren't, and there was a grey area, and we don't know with that grey area.

Who instigated the inquiry? How does such an inquiry get set up?

I think it was my brother actually, as Lord Chancellor. He had the difficulty that the Prime Minister said this has really got out of hand, MPs, questions in the House of Commons and so on, 125 children, what was going on? And it was the sheer number I think that got the headlines, together with the MP up there who, quite rightly, made a great fuss. So the Prime Minister wanted somebody to chair it, and my brother said it probably would be politic because there was some Marxist-Leninist feminism views around. The social worker had some strong views, and there was a certain element of women against men, and so I think my brother said, well, I think you better have a woman judge, and there were only three women judges, and by a process, I have to tell you, of elimination, because the other two were not available, I found myself doing it.

Did you have to go there physically?

Of course.

You were based there, were you?

Oh absolutely, I spent seven or eight months there.

And that was the fact-finding and interviewing. Then there was the writing?

No, it wasn't interviewing. They all came and gave evidence to the inquiry, and of course part of the evidence was what had happened, but a great deal of the evidence was medical evidence, evidence about how the courts were working, evidence about

177

how Social Services were working, evidence particularly about how the police and police surgeons were working. I went through each of these, well, we went through each of these areas.

And how did the inquiry proceed evidentially?

They didn't have to be on oath but they were obliged to come to court, to come to the inquiry, and obliged to give evidence.

And who examined them?

I had Lord Justice Thorpe as counsel to the inquiry, and as counsel to the inquiry he asked the questions, and I think we had 38 lawyers eventually. They didn't all ask questions, not quite all!

And your findings?

Well, like *Victoria Climbie*, we gave a considerable number of recommendations— I kept the report relatively short by modern standards. I think it was 200 pages, which is far too long, but half of it was what had happened. The recommendations were fairly voluminous. Some have been implemented. A very large number seem to me to be re-emerging in a number of inquiries ever since.

Because it is a frustration for a number of judges who have been involved in inquiries that considerable effort goes into the process, many recommendations are made but, frankly, not all of them are then implemented.

I'm Chairman of the Security Commission, which is a wholly different thing, which a judge always chairs.

Pardon me, the Security Commission?

Security Commission, looking into what went wrong when people gave secrets to someone, not necessarily spies, sometimes people selling information. Anyway, I'm current Chairman, but when I was the alternate Chairman, Lord Lloyd held an inquiry, at that time he was the Chairman, and basically the recommendations we gave on that occasion were exactly what Lord Lloyd had given in two previous reports and had been going back for 10 or 15 years, and in exactly the same way on these sort of inquiries prior to what I said. In the Cleveland Report, I was perhaps more comprehensive, you might say unkindly, voluminous than the others, but they were very similar, and they've been similar since. I mean, some things have been learnt. The problem now is not what the advice is, because the advice nowadays is good, the problem is implementing the advice.

And that requires . . . ?

It requires effort. It actually requires communication, and I think the most important thing that you need to say to the agencies is: "Talk to each other, get to know each other, pick up the phone and talk to each other, get onto first name terms if you can, have a cup of coffee, have a cup of tea". Have I time just to give you one example?

Please do.

When I was doing Cleveland, and the doctors weren't talking, the paediatricians weren't talking to the police surgeons, the social workers weren't talking to the police, and so on.

When you say not talking, was there acrimony?

Oh, serious acrimony, yes. I mean, they just weren't helping each other. There was a total breakdown in communication, everywhere, except Hartlepool. And because I was Chairman of the inquiry, I went to every part of Cleveland to meet people, to find out what was going on. Unlike being a judge where that would be absolutely wrong, as Chairman, it was what I should do. So I went to the police station, the centre of Hartlepool, where the police gave me and my Assessors a cup of tea and said, "We've asked the social workers in". I said, "You've done what?". He said, "We've asked the social workers in. They're always coming in to have coffee with us". There was nowhere else in Cleveland where they were on speaking terms, but in Hartlepool, the social workers came in, "Hello, John", "Hello, Jack", you know, "Okay, Liz?". They all stood around, had a coffee, we had a chat, and I said, "Why is it working here?". "Oh, we get on," they said. Fantastic!

And that was the difference?

Yes.

One final question of you that I ask of everyone who sits in your chair here at Gresham, and that is this: if a pupil or student contemplating a career in the law asked you what you thought of the idea, what would you say to them?

Well, I think I'd say you've got to have enthusiasm, stamina, be bright enough without being brilliant—I mean, there are brilliant people like Lord Bingham that have sat in the chair, but you don't have to brilliant, but you've got to be bright enough. But don't do it unless there is nothing else in the world you really want to do!

Dame Elizabeth, many thanks.

CHAPTER TWELVE

Cherie Booth QC
Barrister, Matrix Chambers

Wednesday March 26, 2003

My guest tonight is Cherie Booth QC, one of the country's best known barristers. She studied law at the London School of Economics, was called to the Bar in 1976, became a QC in 1995, and specialises now in employment law, discrimination law, the law relating to human rights, and in local Government law, all of which are areas I'd like to discuss this evening.

Can we start off, however, by clarifying the role of the barrister, because I think for many, and for non-lawyers especially, the world of the barrister looks rather arcane and unusual. Could you therefore chat us through what it's like to be a barrister and perhaps what a typical case, if there is such a beast, involves for you?

Well, people always ask me this, about what my typical day is, and the one thing about being a barrister is you don't have many typical days. The TV governs a lot of people's idea of a barrister's life and that tends to be, of course, about criminal law. Many barristers are criminal lawyers but I'm not one of them. The sort of work I do does not involve addressing juries or dealing with questions of whether people are guilty or not guilty, but is much more about people's civil obligations to each other, and particularly in relation to human rights, the relationship between individuals or groups of individuals and the State. Those sort of questions come before mainly our High Court, and involve arguing not so much about facts but about legal principles. That's not to say that I don't do cases which involve trials; in fact, I love witness actions because it is like a drama. You can never be quite sure what your witness might say, and you can have this marvellously constructed legal argument which goes from A to B to C and will guarantee you'll win the case, and then your client goes into the witness box and instead of saying A says D and your whole case just unravels before you, so that is always very challenging!

So how do you come to be instructed? What's the process?

Well, members of the public can't come directly at the moment to barristers, although that has been relaxed somewhat recently. I get a lot of people who do write

181

to me directly, but all of them are told the same thing: that if you want to instruct me, you have to first of all go and see solicitors, and they then choose the appropriate barrister on the basis of their expertise. How a solicitor gets to decide to use you is something of a mystery sometimes I think to members of the Bar, particularly when you're starting out, because when you're a beginner at the Bar nobody knows who you are or what you can do and you rely very much on the contacts that your chambers have and the contacts that your clerk has, and by doing the cases you hope that if you do them well the solicitor might try and use you again. Obviously, as you get on in practice, you can develop a reputation, and in my case solicitors can look up, say, employment or human rights cases in the Law Reports and see my name as being involved in the case and then they may think that you're the person to do another case in a similar area. But when you're starting, you very much rely on the reputation of the chambers that you're in.

Could you say a little bit more about that, because I think most people are familiar with solicitors being organised in firms that are owned by partners, but that's not the model, of course, in the world of the barrister.

No, all barristers are self-employed, so from the very beginning your profits are your own but you have to meet your own expenses, travelling, books, office expenses etc. Certainly when you start that can be difficult because you have to pay all your expenses in advance and you do not get paid for the work you do on a case until the end of the case. It can also cause problems when you take maternity leave, as I did recently, because you don't get maternity pay and if you don't work you don't get an income. Most barristers practice in chambers and share our expenses but not our profits. We share the cost of our accommodation, the cost of our library, which is obviously an important cost, our IT costs, and our staff costs. In Matrix we now call our clerks by a more modern term, practice managers. They manage your practice; they're rather like the actor's agent. They're the ones who say to the solicitors, "This is the good person". A solicitor might often know a clerk and ring them up and say, "I've got this little case, have you got any up and coming youngsters who will do it cheaply?", and the clerk will then say, "Well, I recommend so-and-so or somebody else", and then gives the barrister an opportunity to make an impression on the solicitor.

There are over 70,000 solicitors in private practice. What's the scale of the Bar in comparison?

I brought the latest statistics here. There are at the moment approximately 13,000 members of the practising Bar, which includes both those who are self employed and those who work for companies of some kind; 10,747 actually working like I do as a self-employed barrister, of whom 73 per cent are men and 28 per cent are women.[1]

---

[1] Women in the law are also discussed by Dame Elizabeth Butler-Sloss (Ch.11).

Let's reflect on that for a while. How's that changed over time?

That has changed massively over time. You said I was called in 1976, and I didn't realise it at the time—in fact if I had realised it at the time, I'm sure I would never have thought that I could possibly make a career at the Bar—but the year I was called was the first time that the number of women called to the Bar went into double figures, and it went from 9 per cent of people being called to the Bar being women to 16 per cent. In the years prior to that it was much, much less. Now in fact, if you look at who are called to the Bar this year, it was actually 49 per cent of the people called to the Bar were women, and the year before it was actually 50 per cent, so it's much more evenly balanced. But in my day there were very few women, and if you look at the women called to the Bar in the 1960s, even fewer. What was interesting is that a few months ago, because I'm a bencher at Lincoln's Inn now . . .

You should explain what that involves.

All barristers have to belong to one of the four Inns of Court, and I'm sure the people in the City are all familiar with that—Middle Temple, Inner Temple, Lincoln's Inn, Gray's Inn—and they were essentially training organisations for barristers, that barristers used to come down together and learn their trade by grouping together round the Inns of Court. In fact, nowadays training is done by professional bodies, and by the Inns of Court, who have some educational programmes. But part of the whole way of qualifying to be a barrister is you have to eat your dinners, which means you have to take so many evening meals with other student barristers in the Inns of Court halls, and the idea of that is that you meet with your contemporaries and you meet with more experienced barristers and you learn by talking to them about the ethics and the ethos of the Bar.

All the Inns of Court own quite a lot of property. They own the property that's here, Lincoln's Inn over here and Gray's Inn, are all actually owned by the various Inns.

The governing body of the Inn is made up of the benchers, and the benchers are elected from senior members of the Bar. So you join the Inn as a student member; you have to pay to join the Inn—I was lucky because I got a scholarship so that was paid for me. Then when you are called to the Bar, you're called to the Bar at one of the individual Inns, and then you become an ordinary barrister member of that Inn. After years go by, you may or may not—particularly if you become a Queen's Counsel, you probably will—be invited at some time to become a bencher. I became a Queen's Counsel in 1995, and in 1999 I was invited to become a bencher. Then you are part of the governing body of the Inn, and there are various committees who are responsible for the running of the Inn. I forgot why I was mentioning that . . . ! Because I was a bencher of the Inn, and my husband was an honorary bencher. Because actually Tony and I met when we were both students at Lincoln's Inn, so Lincoln's Inn brought us together, and when he was made Prime Minister he was made not a proper bencher but an honorary bencher. In fact, Lincoln's Inn I think has seven former Prime Ministers plus Tony as members of the Inn—Mrs Thatcher of course being also a member of Lincoln's Inn, and Spencer Percival the only PM to be assassinated was also a member of Lincoln's Inn. There's a long list of them; they have their coats of arms on the Inn.

The Inn gave a dinner where they invited Tony and I to go, and that was just this summer, and they presented Tony with a picture of the students who were called— 81 students were called to the Inn when Tony and I were called in 1976, and they had a picture of us all lined up on the steps with some of the benchers, including Lord Denning, who was a bencher of the Inn and a very famous one and very good to the students. The thing that strikes you, looking at it now, is in the middle, the front row, there's a group of basically 12 women, and the rest of the 81 were all men. Afterwards I said to the Librarian who had found the picture in the Inn's archives, "do you know what's happened to the women now?", and he said he could only trace one woman who was still practising and that was me.

That's remarkable. Please go on.

Of the 12 women, however, about half of them were from the Commonwealth countries and so were anyway not going to practise in our country, but the rest of them, as far as the Librarian can tell, and we can't be 100 per cent sure because they may have changed their names when they got married, I'm the only woman left in practice from that intake. On the other hand there were 69 men, of whom just under 30 are still practising, and that's because some of the people who are called to the Bar never practise at all, and the others leave as the years go by, including Tony of course! Of the men, five have become Queen's Counsel.

How do you feel about equality of opportunity at the Bar now, not least for young female graduates who are seeking placement in chambers?

As far as equality of opportunity for women goes, I think that there's not so much of a problem these days for young women getting taken on as pupils, or even getting taken on in chambers. I think the difficulty that women find in practising at the Bar is when, and I've said this often, is when they come to have families and how they can balance work/life and how that fits in with self-employed practice at the Bar. That appears to be when the crunch time comes. Now, that wasn't the case in the 70s—when I was taken on, it was perfectly common for chambers to say, "Well, we don't want a woman in chambers, we've got one woman". In the 60s, chambers would say, "We don't want a woman at all". In fact, I attended a conference in Dublin about women in the law, and Mary McAleese, who's the President of Ireland, a barrister and an academic lawyer, addressed the conference. She pointed out in her speech that when she did her law degree in the 1960s the book that every aspiring law student was given to read was *Learning the Law* by Glanville Williams.[2]

---

[2] Glanville Williams and A.T.H. Smith, *Learning the Law* (12th ed., Sweet & Maxwell, London, 2002).

I sensed you were going to mention that book. Yes, every law student is encouraged to read it.

Learning the Law—it's the classic text about what it is to be a lawyer. Glanville Williams, in the edition when Mary McAleese was a student which was in the late 1960s, in that edition he actually says categorically that women are not suitable for the Bar. They may be able to be solicitors, but not barristers, because their voices wouldn't carry and they would be distracted by their family commitments, and because they wouldn't have the authority to convince a jury. She actually read out a whole passage from this book, which was a classic example of prejudice.

That's interesting, because the reverse might be the case now—in some ways, the flexibility of being self-employed better suits the working mother, as against the demands of being a solicitor in a City law firm.

I'm inclined to agree, I think it's a great career for a woman actually, and for me, especially now, the fact that I am not answerable to anybody, means that I have a great deal of flexibility. So when Leo came along unexpectedly, I didn't earn when I took up my maternity leave, but that was my choice. No one was agitating for me to come back and look after my clients. Many women solicitors I know who are ambitious to be taken on as a partner can sometimes find it a little difficult, particularly when their partnership decisions may be taken at a time in their late 20s and early 30s when they might also be thinking of having children, and they worry that if they have children they'll be thought of as not having the commitment to the firm and the clients. Of course the solicitors share their profits, which barristers don't do, so it does enable me to have much more flexibility. On the other hand, like anyone else who's self-employed, I think you spend most of your time worrying that no one's ever going to send you another brief, and so you are always in fact pushing yourself harder than perhaps your partners ever would.

That's the paranoia of the self-employed person. Looking ahead a bit though, to the challenges facing the Bar—what do you think they are? Do you see an ongoing role, in perpetuity, for a split profession? Do you welcome that? Do you think that barristers will decline in numbers, or that they'll become increasingly more specialist? How do you see it unpacking?

I think myself that there is a very good argument for a split profession because of the special expertise that the Bar can bring. We said before about the 70,000 odd solicitors all over the country. Now, some of those are concentrated here in the City in London, in huge firms where they have over a thousand people dealing with very specialist work, but many others are scattered up and down the country in cities like Liverpool or in small towns like Chester or in rural areas, providing a much more broadly based general service to a local community. Most of those solicitors wouldn't necessarily have the access to particular expertise in areas in their own firm and would therefore need to look somewhere else to get that expertise. The advantage of the Bar for them is that the Bar is not competing with them in their local area or for their clients. The Bar works with them, the barrister works with the solicitor. For example, in my areas of work, such as education law, I do a lot of work for the local education authorities, but you know, one day I might be doing a case in Northumberland and the next day it might be in Hampshire, and I get my expertise by the fact that people all around the country can send me that work. So I benefit from that, but they also benefit because they don't have to have it, my expertise, in-house, they can sub-contract that out to me.

The analogy's not great, but in a sense it's a bit like in the medical world, with the GP and the consultant specialist. That said, there's now the shifting field of advocacy, in which we've seen the advent of solicitor advocates. Has that made a difference, and do you think it will?

I think the opening up of the rights of advocacy has made a difference, and it may lead, I think—the Bar Council thinks—it may lead to the numbers at the Bar shrinking to some extent, but then the Bar was much smaller 20 or 30 years ago. The fact that it's expanded so far is a fairly recent phenomenon.

I have never actually appeared in a High Court case with a solicitor advocate. I have, because of my employment law, sometimes appeared in an employment tribunal where a solicitor might be on the other side, but not recently, because I'm a Queen's Counsel. They wouldn't send me to an employment tribunal if it was a simple case, because if it was a simple case, why on earth would you be paying for me. It would have to be a complicated case, and so you tend to be against other Queen's Counsels.

There seem to be two kinds of solicitor advocates. There is the solicitor advocate who's almost like a barrister and who may also be self-employed and might actually do small work in the local county courts or in the crown court, the magistrates' court, and then you have the solicitor advocate departments that the big City firms have, which is a completely different sort of animal, probably in a more narrow field.

I think the problem for the Bar is that solicitor advocates could lead to us losing our recruits. Some of the young people wanting to come to the Bar may say, "Well, if what I really want to do is advocacy . . .", and most barristers want to do advocacy, though not all—a chancery barrister might not do any advocacy or very little, a tax barrister doesn't do that much advocacy, they're doing advice work the whole time—". . . but if I want to do advocacy and I'm a young woman trying to decide what to do now, a law undergraduate, do I take the risk of supporting myself, seeing whether I may or may not be taken on as a tenant in a set of chambers, running up the overdraft, or do I in fact join a big City firm where they have generous salaries and a career structure and I might be able to do the advocacy as well?". On the other hand, if you do that, you lose one of the big advantages of the Bar, which is the flexibility that being self-employed gives you and the ability to some extent to control your own destiny; whereas if you go into one of the big City firms, then you become a part of a much larger machine and they will decide where you actually specialise.

I think one of the difficulties facing many young aspiring lawyers in that position is they don't really know at that stage what area of law they would like to specialise in, and

I often hear young lawyers suggest that if they go to a firm of solicitors, they'll be exposed to a wide range of legal specialities, whereas they don't seem to think the same will be the case if they go to the Bar. This is perception but not reality perhaps?

I actually don't think that's really true—it depends. If you go to be a solicitor in a local firm in, as I say, Chester, or even some of the firms in Liverpool, though they also have big firms, then you will see a broad category of work, won't you? You'll see some sort of conveyancing, you'll see some crime, you'll see some matrimonial, and you'll see some general civil. If you go to one of the big City firms here, then you will probably do, what, four rotations in departments which themselves are very, very specialised. So you might know a huge amount about . . .

Capital Markets, for example?

Yes, some large City transactions in Capital Markets, banking, a certain area of the insurance market, but you won't actually have that wide an experience of people or other kinds of legal work. You go into barristers' chambers, and although barristers' chambers tend to specialise much more today, among the individual barristers there's still a wide spread of practice, and particularly so for the younger members starting out. And, you know, the key is to get your advocacy experience.

Let's talk about chambers themselves, because you're a member of Matrix Chambers, and I wanted you to speak about that. Many non-lawyers, when they hear of Inns of Court and being called to the Bar and being a member of a set of chambers, they feel the whole thing sounds rather detached and old-fashioned. Now, my understanding is that the establishment of Matrix was, at least in part, an attempt to demystify and to be more forward-looking. Can you talk us through the thinking behind Matrix; and indeed the name Matrix itself—where did that come from?

I suppose talking about Inns and everything else is a little arcane, but you get really quite fond of the traditions of the legal profession, so I certainly wouldn't say that. What we were more interested in Matrix is breaking down some barriers with our clients, mainly our solicitors, and trying to make ourselves more accessible and being prepared to use new ideas, using new technology, making more links with academic lawyers, and trying to put into practice perhaps a little bit more modern management techniques. As for the name, Matrix, the group of us who started out were sitting round a table trying to think of a name. We didn't want to call ourselves . . .

An address (as is the case with many sets of chambers).

An address, well, for a start, we didn't have an address, so that was a slight technical problem because at that time we hadn't got a building so we couldn't do that.

We decided that we didn't want to call ourselves, as many chambers do, after famous ancient lawyers, and somebody—I don't know why—came up with the idea of Matrix because the definition of that in the dictionary is about a matrix of ideas, an interchange of different ideas. One of the things about Matrix was that in the Bar recently the idea has been that we should specialise, and so chambers are getting bigger, but they're also specialising in fewer areas. We were a group of practitioners in various chambers, all from different practices but had in common an interest in human rights, and we felt that was a much broader, that was an overarching, broader thing that we had in common; and so the idea of the matrix of all the different ideas coming and intersecting like that, in there is where you find human rights. Then we discovered that another meaning of matrix was fertility and motherhood almost, and as it happened at that time a number of us were expecting children, including me. In the first year of Matrix, I think we had eight or nine babies, including my own, and so that was also quite appealing, this subsidiary idea of fertility.

Has it worked? (I don't mean the fertility thing!)

We've had more babies since, yes!

Cancel that.

The interchange of ideas? Yes, I think it has, absolutely, it has worked.

That's not what I meant actually. I was not referring to the exchange of idea, although that is interesting. No, I was actually meaning in commercial terms: has being a differently branded, more distinctive legal business attracted more work? Has it attracted recruits? Does it feel different?

It has certainly attracted recruits. I think we started off with 25 and we're now up to 41; and indeed, one of the things we thought we were doing was setting up a small, specialist set, but 41 is not terrifically small, though nowadays you can get chambers with 70 or 80 so we're still certainly not large in those terms. But that's partly because the way modern practice is, certain areas of practice need certain numbers just to carry the caseload. Interestingly, in that 41, we started off with four academic members and we now have eight, which is one of the things we were very interested in: building links with academic lawyers. A number of chambers do have academic lawyers involved, but they tend to be what are traditionally called door-tenants, which means they have their name on the door, basically don't really interchange with chambers at all, and we wanted very much to have a new relationship with academic members, which we have done, and use them by bringing them into our cases. We try and build teams to deal with cases and actually say to solicitors, "We can offer you a team of expertise", and within that we might—particularly for cases in the appeal courts and the House of Lords—we might say, "We actually have an academic specialist in this which will bring a depth to the team", and that's worked very well.

When you're managing law firms, once you get over 25 or 30 lawyers in the business, you've got a big management challenge. Having lots of lawyers working together under the one roof is often likened to herding cats. Similarly, who manages Matrix? How does it actually tick over?

We actually have a management committee with five members of chambers. They meet weekly and of course we have a fantastic Chief Executive, Nick Martin, who is employed by us and runs chambers and oversees the administrative team of 15. One of the other things we wanted to do actually in Matrix, was to break down the barriers often found in traditional barrister chambers between the administrative staff and the barristers, and we wanted to integrate our staff much more in the running of chambers. We had our Annual General Meeting just last Saturday, and all the members of staff attended all the sessions and contributed to the discussion about where we were going and what our priorities were and everything else, which is quite unusual in barristers' chambers.

Do all barristers at all levels come together for that?

Our General Meeting is everybody, and on our Management Committee—I can't remember the current composition—I think may only have one silk, we might have two, and then junior members at different stages, including Alison McDonald, who was taken on last year or the year before, so one of our most junior tenants is actually on the Management Committee giving an input.

You mentioned human rights. I'd like to talk further about that. The likely impact of the Human Rights Act generated an enormous amount of literature and interest and speculation. It has also been at the core of your own practice as well, I believe. Can you talk us through the human rights regime and what it's meant to you?[3]

Human rights in two minutes!

I was thinking of two minutes and 30 seconds, but if you wanted to speak swiftly, that's fine by me!

---

[3] Human rights are also discussed by Lord Woolf (Ch.1), David Pannick QC (Ch.3), Lord Bingham (Ch.7), David Lock (Ch.9), Oliver Letwin (Ch.10) and Professor Bogdanor (Ch.19).

Certainly one of the impetuses for the setting up of Matrix was the coming into force of the Human Rights Act 1998 on 2nd October 2000. That Act incorporated the European Convention on Human Rights into our domestic law. People probably don't realise that though the European Convention on Human Rights was signed 50 years ago and was actually drafted by some British politicians and lawyers, it was not something that was directly enforceable in our own courts. The UK was one of the first signatories of the Convention but it wasn't until the first Wilson Government in the 60s that individual members of the public in Britain could actually bring a case to Strasbourg. Between that time and 2000, when the 1998 Act came into force, if you thought that your European Convention rights had been infringed, you couldn't enforce those rights directly in our courts, you had to go to Strasbourg. That was a long and arduous journey, and one of the ideas about the Human Rights Act was to bring the rights home, to enable this international treaty that we'd signed to be enforced by our courts, not just so that people could have a remedy here but also so that our judges could contribute perhaps in a more positive way to the growing jurisprudence internationally about what human rights mean.

A number of us in Matrix met because there the Government undertook a huge training programme for the judges and many people who were the core group for Matrix were training the judges, and at the same time were talking about the impact, and the idea of having a chambers to respond specifically to this arose.

The other important point to note about human rights is this: there is a danger that the public think human rights is just about protecting the criminal, protecting asylum seekers and it is of course about protecting minorities who may not be very popular; but actually the whole ethos behind the Human Rights Act is about balancing the rights of individuals with the rights of the wider community. That was one of the things we were very keen to try and foster within Matrix. This idea that human rights is actually about everybody and it's not just about individual rights, it's about having a conversation within society about how we balance individual rights and protections of minorities with the desire of the community to protect itself. So, for example, it is important that we treat genuine asylum seekers properly, but it is also important that society protects itself from people who want to come into our society for the purposes of terrorism. How do you get the balance right in such cases? And in a completely different area, which people don't always associate with human rights, although it is an area I do quite a bit, human rights is about making sure that the State recognises the dignity of people in old people's homes. It was reported recently that in one home it suited the people who ran the home to feed the residents their breakfast while they had them on the commodes, because that was just easier for the staff routine, and no one had thought that that was actually a matter of human rights. It's about their individual dignity. You know, human rights is a lot more than just about prisoners or criminals; it's actually about recognising the dignity of everybody, and in particular the way the State treats people who are vulnerable.

What do you think its impact has been? I don't mean on the legal world, but on your clients and society generally? Is it too early to tell, because the regime has not been operating for long? What's your sense of its effects?

There's been a large number of cases, and members of Matrix have been in quite a few, often on both sides of the argument. In a number of cases, the courts decided that existing practices were in fact consistent with human rights. In some cases though there have been changes. On the whole I think the Act has done two things. One, it has broadened the debate; it has certainly forced the courts much more overtly and openly into talking about policy issues. In administrative law when we are talking about the acts of the Executive, local authorities for example, there has been a change in the way the courts will assess what a public body is doing to the individuals in its care. Previously we had the Wednesbury Test. When you wanted to challenge a decision that a local authority or a Government body had taken about you, the courts would only intervene if no reasonable public body could have reached that conclusion. As a result of the Human Rights Act, they now apply a more flexible test, that of proportionality, which allows the court to probe a lot more deeply into the reasons why a public body acts as it does. So if a local authority wants to close an old people's home then they may have to justify to the court why that is the case. They can't just say, "Well, other local authorities could reasonably come to this view and therefore you, the court, must accept that", which is what Wednesbury would have done. Now they have to justify why their need to close the home overrides the desire of the old people to stay in a familiar place. I think it's made quite a considerable impact on our judges and on the way we argue our cases in court, and it has affected law generally. I think where it's not done as much as I might have hoped is in changing the culture, not the legal culture, but the wider society. We need to get everybody thinking more about human rights and what it means, not just lawyers but the people who work in local Government, the people who work in central Government, everybody, about what it really means to respect the human rights of each other.

While that cultural shift won't happen overnight, I do think that the language of rights, often the rhetoric of rights, is expressed and used far more frequently than in the past—not always in a complimentary way, but rights are talked about, and so to some extent are entering people's consciousness. Whether by business people or policy-makers or people in education, it seems to me people are aware there are a new set of criteria against which their actions are now being judged. They might not welcome it, they might not fully appreciate it, but the rights movement is an undeniable phenomenon.

But what we have to ensure is that everyone understands that human rights is not a one-sided thing. It's not just about rights, actually, most of these rights are not absolute; what it's actually about is balancing rights with responsibilities. It's balancing the interests of the individual with the legitimate interests of the community, and it's about using the courts almost as a way of mediating that and making sure that the balance is proportionate. So often, I think, there's a distinction perhaps between civil liberties and the civil libertarian argument, which is: "I can do this and as an individual that's my right", and a more human rights view, which is not just about what I can do, not wholly individualistic, it's also about how what I do balances with the impact that makes on the wider community, and how far the wider community is entitled to say to me, "You can't do all that for the good of the others", and how we maintain that balance. I think we're still working on that. I think sometimes politicians who talk about human rights forget that balancing, and in their rhetoric ignore the fact that human rights does acknowledge the role of the community as well.

You were mentioning the judges earlier, and you were expressing the hope that our judges might contribute to European jurisprudence, as it were. Has that yet come about or is it too early?

I think it has in many ways. Actually, it's not just European jurisprudence I was thinking about. I think one of the exciting things about being a lawyer at the moment is that international law and international norms, legal norms, are being more and more discussed as globalisation takes place, and as the world comes together. There is more of a dialogue going on about, what do we mean by fundamental rights? Are there things that we can all agree on, whatever our religion or no religion, whatever part of the political spectrum we're on? Are there some fundamental things that we can accept that as human beings we're entitled to expect to be protected and we're entitled to demand from the State? Now since we have had the Human Rights Act, you do find that you will quote a judgment from South Africa where they have a constitution, or from Australia where they don't have a constitution though they're thinking of implementing a Human Rights Act along our lines, or from New Zealand where they do, and Canada. There is a dialogue certainly among the common law countries of the world. Sadly, America is not participating in that anymore, and the American judges have in recent years, they've taken a more narrow view about using foreign cases. They seem to think that the US constitution is the first and last word and some of them resist the idea that they have anything to learn from the rest of the world. That's not something that our judges do, they are prepared to have a much broader look at what is going on in the world and try and see where we can get legitimacy that isn't just culturally specific.

I think that wasn't true either of American judges, say, 50 years ago.

No, it wasn't. One can think of some examples of American judges in the past who were very interested in developing the common law, but they have become more isolated in recent years, unfortunately.

In England, do you think this changes the nature of judicial reasoning, of judicial decision-making in the upper courts? Does it make it harder for you, in a sense, to predict the way the judges are going to come to their decisions? Do they have a wider range of criteria upon which to draw? As you know, sitting in your seat we've had all manner of top judges and I have asked some of them some standard jurisprudential questions: how do you come to your decisions and how much discretion do you feel you have? They generally seem to say that they do feel contained and constrained by a fixed body of rules. However, it does seem to me that in introducing human rights, the sorts of arguments that one is now seeing in judgments draw more generally on broader principles and broader issues of policy.[4]

I think I would make two points about that. One is that judges should be constrained by the nature of their role, not to just go off on frolics of their own and impose their own prejudices, that is true, but then it's also always been true that judges have developed the common law and there have always been policy reasons behind that.

One only has to think of *Donoghue v Stevenson*, the classic case, where the tort of negligence was established. There was a policy behind that which wasn't always overtly articulated. It is being articulated a little more openly now. But I had a classic case of that, *Re S*, a case about the Children Act 1989. Essentially, it was a family law case, which I only got involved in when we went to the House of Lords.

The Children Act had been instituted in 1989 in response to decisions in Strasbourg which said that the way we took children into care wasn't acknowledging the rights of parents and their rights to have their family life recognised, and in 1989 a new system had come in for taking children into care, which had been operated ever since. One of the fundamental principles of that was that once a child—before you took a child into care, you had to go to court, you had to get a court order, but in the end the court would make an order transferring care of this child to the local authority, and once that happened the court would do no more. That would be the end of the court's role; responsibility then passes on to the local authority, who get on with the job.

By 2000, it had become clear that for various reasons—not all of them bad ones, some of them because of very understandable pressures of resources and everything else—children who were going into care weren't always getting the best care from the local authorities. In particular, when judges were making care orders, the local authority would come along and say to them, "We have a plan for this child, it's going to go to a foster family, or they're going to be placed for adoption, or we're going to try and put this child back", and then two or three weeks after that, or two or three months down the line, none of that plan was being implemented and the child was left, well, in limbo in some ways, something wasn't happening. And in fact during the 1990s, the judges expressed concern to the Government about this problem, because they felt that there should be a way that the judge could intervene if the plan that the judge had told was going to happen to the child wasn't implemented. They felt there should be a way that someone should be able to bring that matter back to the court if it wasn't working, or it hadn't been implemented.

And then in 2000 a case came before the Court of Appeal where precisely this had happened. In two different cases in fact, where care orders had been made on one basis and either, in one case, absolutely nothing had been done because the council had no money to implement the plan, and in another case, the situation changed. The case came before the Court of Appeal who suddenly decided that the child's family life wasn't being protected and instituted something called the "starred care order" which allowed the case to go back to the judge. At that point there was consternation among local authorities, because they had no resources to implement this starred care order; there was worry in the courts about getting bogged down with

---

[4] Judicial decision-making is also discussed by Lord Woolf (Ch.1), Lord Bingham (Ch.7), Dame Elizabeth Butler-Sloss (Ch.11) and Professor John Gardner (Ch.16).

all sorts of cases; and so the matter went to the House of Lords. When we argued the case, we actually had to put before the House of Lords a lot of evidence that hadn't been before the Court of Appeal because the Court of Appeal had come up with this idea very much at the end of the judgment. We pointed out to the judges the difficulties over resources. It will mean that these children with a starred care order will uniquely in the care system have special rights which other children won't have, and therefore will distort priorities within the department. We pointed out the strain on the court and the danger of even longer delays. We argued that this was a policy decision which should be debated in Parliament and decided in Parliament and not by the judges overnight deciding to change the law. The House of Lords agreed with that, and said that the Court of Appeal had gone too far in using the Human Rights Act in that way. That was a fascinating discussion, because at one time the court wouldn't have even attempted to get involved in those issues.

Returning to an earlier theme, that of what's it like to be a barrister: how does appearing before the Court of Appeal differ from doing so in the House of Lords? What's more daunting, and which do you relish more?

There are two differences. The Court of Appeal is three judges. They sit in far more cases and their cases tend to move much more quickly. You can only go to the House of Lords if either the Court of Appeal gives you leave—and in 99 per cent of the cases the Court of Appeal won't give you leave because traditionally they say it's up to their Lordships to decide which court cases they have—or if the House of Lords gives you leave because they think it's a point of law of public importance that's going to set the tone for the rest. In the Lords there are five judges. They don't wear robes. They sit as a committee. They have a lot more time to consider the issue. You have far fuller written briefs to the House of Lords, who will ask you a wide range of questions, some of which won't necessarily be completely about your case but about the implications of your case for the development of the law. That is very challenging and interesting. The Court of Appeal is equally challenging, but the Court of Appeal has much more of a day-to-day workload.

Can you focus on the instant case?

Focusing on the instant case, you know, what is the issue here, let's deal with the issue here, the House of Lords has a more leisurely . . . they're certainly not leisurely in their minds, but they have the ability to perhaps see the wider picture, so in the House of Lords when you bring a case, you will often refer them to a lot more academic articles about the area or around the area, which the Court of Appeal I think quite often might like to do, but they don't really have the time to do it.

Fascinating. Let's look now at a different topic: discrimination. You work in that field of law a good deal. What would be of particular interest is to hear about an actual case with which you have been involved. Does one spring to mind?

I'm waiting for a decision in the House of Lords at the moment, which is a case called *Pearce v the Governing Body of Mayfield School.*

Let me jump in and ask you, when you're waiting for a decision, is that an anxious moment for you? Is it tense?

No.

Are you resigned, or . . . ?

(Laughing) No, I've done what I can by then. We argued this case at the end of February and we're waiting; the Lords, it will probably take three to six months before they'll pronounce, so if you were anxious about it, it would be a bit of a torture! Once you've argued your case, it's over, isn't it, and there's another case, which is one of the joys of being a barrister really. You're only as good as your last case.

Sorry, I interrupted your flow. Tell us about the case.

That's about a teacher in a comprehensive school in Hampshire who eventually resigned from the school, took early retirement she says because of the way the pupils over years had tormented her because she was a lesbian. She then claimed that the school had discriminated against her on the grounds of her sex, because the children had called her all sorts of names, which frankly in my innocence . . . One of the things they called her was a lemon. Now, I can remember my Grandma from Liverpool saying to me, "Don't be a lemon", and she meant don't be stupid, but apparently it is a term that means you're a lesbian.

This is an education!

It is an education! I'm sure it's not what my Grandma thought it meant, in fact I know she did not! But the argument was using words such as "lemon" or "lessie" which describe females, that turned what was clearly discrimination of the grounds of sexual orientation into sex discrimination as well. I was actually for the school, and I said, "no this is absolutely wrong, what we're actually talking here about is discrimination on the grounds of someone's sexual orientation", which is not covered by the Sex Discrimination Act—it is going to be covered soon because of a European Directive—and that the court shouldn't make the word "sex" in the Sex Discrimination Act mean something that it doesn't mean. That argument had succeeded in the Courts below.

195

So you're saying that discrimination on sexual tendency grounds isn't the same as discrimination on gender grounds.

And therefore that the courts shouldn't construe the Act as if it was. We won in the employment tribunal, we won in the employment appeal tribunal. By the time we came to the Court of Appeal the Human Rights Act had come in, and because the Human Rights Act, Article VIII, means you need to respect someone's private and family life which can include their sexual orientation, the argument was, well, whatever the position before, now you should extend that definition to sexual orientation. We won in the Court of Appeal, and we went up to the House of Lords, and we'll wait and see whether we win again.

But for me it was quite an interesting case because a few years previously I'd done another case before the European Court of Human Rights, called *Grant v South-West Trains*, and in that case I was actually arguing for a lesbian that she was discriminated against on the grounds of her sex because South-West Trains offered unmarried different sex couples concessionary fares on their train, but they wouldn't offer that concession to same sex couples. So I'd had this argument and I'd made all the arguments that were being used against me.

In the earlier case the employment tribunal referred the matter to the European Court of Justice in Luxembourg. In that court there are two stages: you first of all have a preliminary opinion by the Advocate-General, who'd actually found in our favour; but then the whole court makes a decision, and we'd lost in the whole court. I was faced with this prospect that I might have argued in front of the European Court in Luxembourg that Sex Discrimination did cover sexual orientation and lost, and then later the House of Lords, when I was arguing the opposite, you know, might decide against me . . . !

So it's just as well you lost first time round!

I think that we will probably win, but who knows?!

Well, we'll wish you luck with that. Sadly, we're coming to the end of our discussion. One final question, and this is a question I ask of everyone in your chair, as it were. If a school pupil, for example, came to you and said he or she was thinking about a career in the law, would you wholeheartedly recommend it? What would you say to such a pupil? What wise words of counsel would you offer?

I've always said to anyone who asked me, I think it's a fantastic career. I have loved every minute of it. I don't regret any minute of it. I'm so pleased. I didn't know what to expect when I went into the law, because no one in my family had been to university, let alone had any dealings with anyone in the law, and it wasn't the sort of thing that people like us would do, and so it was very much a sort of leap into the dark, and somehow or other I landed on my feet and I've enjoyed it ever since, and I still enjoy it, and I anticipate enjoying it for a number of years yet. So any young person who comes and asks me that, I always encourage them to do so, but I say, "You have to be prepared to work hard, and you really have to want to do it". On the other hand, with my children I've been much more holding back, but that's I think just because as a mother I don't want to say, "Oh great, you want to do what I want to do", you know, I want them to be able to make their own decisions as to what they want to do and not to do it because our family now has a number of lawyers—not just me, but my husband, and of course his uncle, two uncles in fact. So there are lots of lawyers in our family now.

So they should study law but not because their parents ask them to.

Absolutely!

Cherie Booth, thank you so much for joining us at Gresham College.

CHAPTER THIRTEEN

The Rt Hon The Lord Irvine of Lairg
The Lord Chancellor of Great Britain

Tuesday April 29, 2003

This evening I am holding my 13th discussion here at Gresham College and, I am very pleased to say, it is the second time that we have had the Lord Chancellor with us. The Lord Chancellor will be known to all of you. He was called to the Bar in 1967, became a QC in 1978, a life peer in 1987, Shadow Lord Chancellor in 1992 and the Lord Chancellor in 1997.

A very warm welcome to you once again, Lord Chancellor.

Much has happened in the year since we last spoke, so we have a good deal of ground to cover today. I thought I would delve straight in on quite a tricky issue, that relating to the notion of a Ministry of Justice. I think it is fair to say that the Lord Chancellor's Department is currently the subject of quite a bit of scrutiny and discussion, and many people who are in opposition to the department in one way or another would suggest that the country would be better served by a Ministry of Justice. Now, in one sense you are not the best man to describe and defend that proposition, but could you introduce us to the arguments surrounding the debate that has ensued?

Certainly, yes. First of all when people talk about a Ministry of Justice, they have got to define what they mean by a Ministry of Justice. Now, normally a Ministry of Justice would be a department of state which dealt with the whole of the law—civil and criminal, and probably the courts, tribunals and judges besides. That, for example, would probably be more or less the French model. Now we have a distribution of responsibilities in this country which does not correspond to that, particularly because the Home Office is responsible for the criminal law and criminal procedure, as well as many other areas of responsibility besides. The Home Office essentially, and a true Ministry of the Interior, would be responsible for our external borders—that is to say things like immigration, asylum, visas, passports, travel—and security within our borders—the police, the security services and prisons. But also in our country the Home Office traditionally has been responsible for the criminal law and criminal procedure. I myself wouldn't argue against that at all, in fact I rather think that that is a good balance of responsibilities for us, because in our country the need to maintain law and order—which is the responsibility of the Home Office—is thought to include the whole concept of keeping the peace, is thought to include

199

defining the principles, the rules, the conditions under which people go to prison, and that is the function of the Home Office in this country. Now you could argue that it should be the function of a Ministry of Justice, with the Home Office reduced purely to a Ministry of the Interior, but I certainly don't support that. I think the balance of responsibilities are about right in our present system, but that tells against a Ministry of Justice in the strict sense.

In a sense, there are, I suppose, two views that could be expressed when people are saying they want a Ministry of Justice. On the one hand, they could be saying that they think within our country that the administration of justice—whether it be criminal, civil or administrative justice—should be the province of one department of state. That is the model that you have rejected. On the other hand, and I suppose this is a cruder theory or suggestion, it can be said that the Lord Chancellor's Department, as currently constituted and administered and without extending or diminishing its roles, should be changed so that the department is headed by a Government minister, rather than by a Lord Chancellor who is President of the Supreme Court.

What I have been trying to point out is that by rebranding the Lord Chancellor's Department as a Ministry of Justice, you don't make it a Ministry of Justice for the very reason that you gave, because as you suggested the paradigm of the Ministry of Justice—and as you say people might argue for this, but I have made it plain that I don't—the paradigm is where you have a single department which is responsible, as you say, for the whole of the law—the criminal law, the civil law and all the courts and all the tribunals. But we don't have that in this country because we regard criminal law and criminal procedure as a responsibility of the Home Office—the Ministry of the Interior if you like—which is responsible for maintaining law and order, keeping the peace and determining the conditions under which people go to jail.

Now it can be argued of course both ways round. Many countries vary in the distribution of these responsibilities; but as I say, you don't create a Ministry of Justice by rebranding the Lord Chancellor's Department as a Ministry of Justice, nor by changing the name of the Lord Chancellor's Department do you alter in any way the quality of services that are delivered to people.

I do want to focus on this issue of the specific role of the Lord Chancellor, as against the role of Minister of Justice. But, before we do so, can you clarify the extent to which your department looks after the administration of the criminal courts?

Yes, forgive me, of course, we look after the administration of the courts—both civil and criminal—that is to say the whole of the court system; the magistrates' court system is going to be integrated into the rest of the criminal court system; we are going to become responsible for the whole of the tribunal system, all that is correct; but responsibility for policy in relation to the civil law is for the Lord Chancellor's Department, for the criminal law it is the Home Office.

So let's look at the Lord Chancellor's role and, of course, in all of the discussion, I am inquiring not so much about you personally as the role itself. There are so many ways of tackling the subject. I wonder if we might join the debate by talking about the separation of powers doctrine and judicial independence. First of all, though, it would be helpful for us if you could you start off by describing for us the range of the responsibilities of the office of Lord Chancellor?[1]

Yes, I will try and do it in a word or two. There are about 3,000 judges in this country, full and part-time, they are serviced by about 10,000 staff; tribunals, there are about 240 hearing centres in the country, there are about 3,000 people who work in tribunals. The Lord Chancellor is responsible, as you have said, for the Judiciary and the administration of all these courts, and of course the Lord Chancellor's Department is responsible for the civil law. Also the department has become responsible, since the last election and since a further redistribution of responsibilities in Government by the Prime Minister, has become responsible for human rights, for freedom of information, for data protection, for House of Lords reform, for electoral matters, for matters royal and ecclesiastical, even for referenda.

You fill your days.

Absolutely. It gives me something to look forward to every day.

One of the key issues that arises for constitutional theorists is that of the separation of powers. You clearly have an Executive responsibility, being a senior member of the Cabinet. You clearly have a judicial responsibility as the most senior judge in the land. And, as the Speaker of the House of Lords, you clearly have a legislative responsibility as well. I would like to take a step sideways into the separation of powers argument, because I have read speeches you have given on this and I believe they raise fundamental questions.

You have probably read speeches other people have given.

Indeed. But there is, I think, a strong intuition amongst many that if a separation of power does not subsist then that is a cause for concern. But if I understand your arguments correctly, you are keen to point out that in this country we don't in any event strictly observe the separation of powers doctrine.

---

[1] The role and the future of the role of the Lord Chancellor are also discussed by Lord Irvine (Ch.6), Sir Hayden Phillips (Ch.15), Lord Mackay (Ch.17), Lord Falconer (Ch.18), Professor Bogdanor (Ch.19) and Lord Woolf (Ch.20).

That is absolutely correct. This country has never adopted a rigid view of the separation of the powers, we are pragmatists, we are not theorists, we don't apply theory to situations that work and make changes that cannot be proved to confer benefits. The most significant constitutional development probably in the 18th century was the development of the Cabinet system, and of course the Cabinet system itself violates the separation of the powers because in this country—when I say violates the separation of the powers, I mean violates a strict doctrine of the separation of the powers in this country—you may not be a member of the Cabinet—that is the chief Executive body of Government—you can't be a member of the Cabinet unless you are a member either of the House of Commons or of the House of Lords. In the United States of America you may not, if you are a member of the Senate or the Congress—both Houses if you like of the United States Parliament—if you are a member of either of these you can't be a member of the Cabinet. Therefore America applies a strict doctrine of the separation of the powers, Britain does not.

My recollection is that it was Montesquieu, a French theorist, who, in the mid-18th century, actually derived the doctrine of the separation of powers from what he thought he saw in England. We shouldn't want to dispose of over 200 years of theorising too easily, but to some extent is the whole separation of powers argument something of a red herring?

I do think that a broad separation of the powers is certainly required, but you mustn't introduce it in an over-rigid way that makes things worse, as distinct from making things better. Now one of the central features of the office of Lord Chancellor, which we can talk about, is that the Lord Chancellor is the head of the Judiciary. The office of head of the Judiciary, and office of Lord Chancellor, is one and indivisible. The central organising principle of the administration of justice in this country—I am not suggesting it couldn't be done in other ways—but the central organising principle is that the Lord Chancellor is the head of the Judiciary, and as head of the Judiciary he or she is responsible for providing administrative support which is really the judicial administration of judicial activities, and the whole co-operative framework between the Executive and the Judiciary, through the Lord Chancellor, derives from the fact that the Lord Chancellor is the head of the Judiciary. This can be illustrated in many, many different ways. There is a vast amount of management today by judges, or involvement by judges, in the management of the justice system, and that extends from the bottom to the top. It extends from resident judges who are responsible for the administration of crown courts, crown court centres; designated judges who are responsible for the management of civil courts; resident family judges of family court centres; all under a system of presiding judges. And then the Senior Presiding Judge goes around the country, circuit by circuit, and sends to me, in my capacity as head of the Judiciary, the very fullest reports and frank candid reports on what is going well and what is going badly, in every part of the country, both administratively and judicially. And he is full and frank in a way which I believe derives from the fact that the Lord Chancellor is head of the Judiciary.

I could multiply examples and put you all to sleep, but one of the best examples is complaints against the Judiciary. As you know, one of the problems about litigation is that usually there has got to be a winner and there has got to be a loser.

Sometimes of course both sides claim victory, but generally there is a winner or a loser, and losers very often feel aggrieved. And I have a huge mail bag of complaints against the Judiciary, many of them—many of them—are complaints about the judicial decision itself, which can't be entertained because of judicial independence. It is not for the Executive to interfere in the decisions that judges give; if you are aggrieved with the decision that the judges give, then what you have to do is to appeal. But there are also complaints about misconduct, that is when judges are supposed to have said things, or behaved in ways that a judge would not be expected to behave. Now I want to tell you that that is an infinitesimal number of cases every year, but of course every judge is an ambassador for the legal system and if the media, rightly, fasten on to one of these cases where a judge says what he shouldn't say in open court, then it is my responsibility to deal with it.

Now if I was, if I can put it this way, if the Lord Chancellor was a mere Cabinet Minister and not the head of the Judiciary, then I don't think that function would exist, it would have to be dealt with in some other way. But when for example a judge expressed himself—and I can't emphasise too often how rare this kind of occurrence is—when a judge expressed himself, let's say disparagingly, of the Vietnamese community in this country, attributing, say, as people can do, to a whole community the sins of one, or expressed them, or as another judge said something similar about the Nigerian community, then that is something where I would rebuke, or warn, or reprimand, or in an appropriate case say that a judge should go for racial awareness training on occasion run by the Judicial Studies Board. Now judges accept rebukes and reprimands from the Lord Chancellor, they accept advice as to how to improve judicial conduct. I can't say often enough, for the record, how very, very rare this is, but this, if you like, jurisdiction of the Lord Chancellor is accepted because he is the head of the Judiciary and that is an integral part of the office.

It was interesting in your response that you said in respect of substantive decision-making by judges, that your office, as part of the Executive, could not interfere. In other parts of your response, however, you talked about being head of the Judiciary. Is it meaningful to ask when you are, in a sense, managing the Judiciary, whether you are doing so as the most senior judge, or as part of your Executive function?

I would say that the two blend in to one, they are actually one and indivisible, that is the unique nature of the office of Lord Chancellor. But the way in which you can participate in the administrative support and management of the Judiciary is hugely enhanced by the fact that one is the head of the Judiciary. So when the presiding judges have their annual conference and have a day's conference and talk about all manner of things that affect the administration of justice up and down the country, I am invited to address them, and address them on what I think are the current pressing issues where improvement is needed, where change is needed, where we can do better, and so on. Well plainly I am invited to that in my capacity as head of the Judiciary.

We have looked a little at the separation of powers and, I think, we have noted that it is not strictly applied in this country in any event. When criticism is levelled at the role of Lord Chancellor, it is rarely focussed on the dual responsibilities for legislative and Executive functions. This duality you share, frankly, with many other Secretaries of State. Rather, the issue that people focus on—the crux of the matter, I believe—is the acceptability of having both judicial and Executive roles.

I entirely agree with that.

A related issue, I suppose, is the overlap of judicial and legislative responsibilities enjoyed by judges in the House of Lords.

The Law Lords, you could make the same points in relation to the Law Lords.

So, it seems to me that at the heart of people's dissatisfaction, or concern, or anguish, or misunderstanding, about your role is this overlap between the judicial and the Executive roles. And you have said to me that in a sense they are indivisible and that is the very nature of the office. You had said before, although I am not sure if this was a great choice of words, but you have said that you were in a sense a buffer between the Executive and judicial roles.

I had better not say anything about that.

What I want to explore further are the roles, for example, of monitoring judicial performance and reviewing complaints on the one hand and reviewing reports of courts' activities on the other. You argue that these need to be undertaken by a judicial figure and I accept that because, by and large, and this is something the audience may or may not appreciate, the reality is that judges do strongly prefer to be managed by other judges.

I think that is a very important truth.

I don't want to challenge that. But I think the challenge one could make is that the Lord Chancellor's role does not need to extend beyond that of being the most senior judge, and that the Lord Chancellor need not also be a member of the Executive. Leaving aside any debate about ministers and ministries of justice, why do you need the senior judge also to sit in Cabinet?

This is the unique nature of the office, and it is through the medium of the office that there is highly effective co-operation between the Executive, who must provide the administration for the judges, and the judges themselves. And as you say, the judges prefer being managed by judges, and the judges are always very jealous, and understandably so, to protect their judicial independence. But the fact that, if you like, the senior judge, the head of the Judiciary, is also the person who from his position in the Executive is duty bound to provide administrative support which the judges require in order to function, means that in this country, through the medium of the office of Lord Chancellor, we have the judicial administration of judicial functions. And what I think is very, very revealing is the degree to which this is accepted by the judges. Of course if a single judge, eminent judge, expresses a different view, that gets a lot of attention, but what has to be appreciated is that the overwhelming majority of the higher Judiciary want the Lord Chancellor to continue to be head of the Judiciary; and in fact when the Council of Judges, who represent the whole of the higher Judiciary in this country, gave evidence to the Wakeham Royal Commission on House of Lords Reform, they were at pains to say that if the link between the Law Lords and the House of Lords—because the Law Lords, who are our supreme court, sit also in the House of Lords, but also the House of Lords is our supreme court in its judicial capacity, the 12 Law Lords who sit there—they were at pains, the Council of Judges, to say in their evidence that if there should become a supreme court, and the Law Lords if you like should become detached from the building called the House of Lords, and there should be an attractive supreme court building in the heart of London, that should not make any difference, they said, to the office of Lord Chancellor. The Lord Chancellor should be President of that supreme court. So people who criticise this, perhaps on rather un-British purist grounds, should bear in mind that those who operate the system see its merit.

The cynic would say that many or even an overwhelming number of judges are bound to prefer to be managed by other judges because it is all part of one judicial club. Of course they would prefer to report into a judge who is one of their own kind and sees the world in the same way as they do. Of course they would be hesitant about being measured using parameters that might ordinarily by applied by a regular politician.

I think there is a lot of truth in all of that and it is basically the cause of the position of the Judiciary. As you know, if we are talking about the separation of the powers, whether it is the Legislature, the Executive, and the Judiciary, and the Judiciary are in a sense the weakest part of the separation of the powers, nominally the strongest part of the separation of the powers is Parliament, but if Parliament is dominated by a very strong Executive, that is to say a very strong Government, then that is where real power resides, and of course the Executive comes into collision with the Judiciary because in a democracy, under the rule of law, it is the job of the Judiciary, if the Executive breaks the law, to say so and to hold it to account. And therefore it is I think unsurprising in that context that the Judiciary see the merit of having a representative of the Judiciary in Cabinet and having a member of the Cabinet in the Judiciary who is recognised; one of whose recognised constitutional duties is to uphold the independence of the Judiciary. In some countries, as we know, the independence of the Judiciary is a very frail flower indeed.

But there is a tension between the independence of the Judiciary on the one hand and the accountability of judges on the other, and there are a couple of issues I would like

CHAPTER THIRTEEN

to dwell upon that flow precisely from this. First of all, what is your role in terms of judicial accountability?

Well it is the judge's function to make decisions in accordance with the rule of law. In that sense, judges—for their decisions are accountable, if you like, to the higher courts through the appellate system—but ultimately the judicial decision making process is accountable to Parliament, because Parliament is the senior partner; and whenever the judges give a decision that Parliament, or the Executive puts it to Parliament that this decision is wrong and not in the public interest, then it can be changed.

In what sense am I accountable? Well I am not obviously accountable for judicial decisions, these are for an independent Judiciary. I am, I think, accountable for the overall quality of the judges in this country because of my role in appointing them, and the Lord Chancellor is certainly accountable for the overall quality of the administration of justice.

How does that accountability manifest itself? Well now there is a new Lord Chancellor's Select Committee that is a Select Committee of the House of Commons, that is a new thing, but before that there was the Home Affairs Select Committee, and there still is, but I used to give evidence—the Lord Chancellors give evidence—to them; Lord Chancellors give evidence to the Public Administration Select Committee; Lord Chancellors give evidence to a joint committee of both Houses of Parliament—the Human Rights Committee. I am accountable, as a member of the House of Lords, to questions from members on the floor of the House. I have got a minister in the House of Lords, I have two ministers in the House of Commons, and they are accountable, so accountability is clear. But perhaps the strongest new vehicle of accountability will be this new Select Committee which I very strongly welcome.

I have recently suggested that judges themselves, individually, should be more account-able for their performance, and I have argued that just as, for example, in major pro-fessional firms senior partners are now subject to performance appraisal, and the same is true of many public servants in local and central Government, then judges too should be subject to performance appraisal. I hasten to add I am not advocating this in rela-tion to the substance of their decisions. To some extent, but not entirely, the appeal system does that job. But I am recommending performance appraisal in respect of the way judges behave in court, how quickly they turn around their judgments, whether or not they speak clearly and politely to court users and so forth. What is your initial reac-tion to the notion that judges should have their performance appraised in the same way as other public officials, and indeed as professional lawyers in private practice?

In practice of course there is a vast amount of appraisal, but by other means.

I have in mind a more structured and systematic . . .

I know that, but for example the appeal system is a system of appraisal. No judge obvi-ously likes being reversed on appeal, no judge likes being told that he has got it wrong.

206

Although some of the finest judges have regularly had their decisions overturned . . .

And some of the finest judges of course deliver the most controversial judgments, and Lord Denning delivered in the course of his long judicial life many judgments which did not prevail at the time, but prevailed later, either in the House of Lords of 20 years later or indeed in Parliament itself. I am thinking of the married woman's equity, as I am sure you know.

It could be, however, in the case of less able judges—and clearly there is a spread of ability in the Judiciary—that some may actually opt for non-controversial play-safe decisions precisely to avoid appeal.

What the Judicial Studies Board says to judges when they are being trained, and don't forget there is a vast amount of training through the Judicial Studies Board which is designed to ensure that judges are sensitive, they are aware of social issues, they are advised how they should conduct themselves in particularly sensitive situations, for example classically ones involving race issues or ones involving sexual offences or rape, there is an extensive amount of training in these areas. Also I mentioned the complaints that come to me. We have in this country people who rightly are not shy of complaining. I pay an enormous amount of attention personally to the complaints that come in. I think I deal with about 1,000 a year myself, and probably about 200 of them are mediated through Members of Parliament, and I deal with all of these personally, I hope with care, and as I say give advice to judges accordingly. And no judge obviously is going to welcome a complaint about him being upheld by the Lord Chancellor. Also of course the community itself judges whether there is a judge whose standard of conduct could be better. As I told you, the senior presiding judge goes around the country gathering all manner of information about performance of judges and the performance of the system locally. So there is a vast amount that goes on. Strictly, what you are talking about of course is disciplined performance appraisal which would be by judges, of judges, on some kind of regular basis.

In the same way, perhaps, as officials within your own department when they have annual reviews of their performance and their career development. This will include discussion of their aspirations, agreement as to areas where there is scope for improvement and identifying also where the individual has done especially well. For judges, this is not conceived as a critique of performance but as a genuine opportunity, in a systematic, sustained way, to review what a judge has been up to and to see where they would like to go.

We do have that at present for some part time judges, we have that for deputy district judges. The difference of course is that they are not full time judges, deputy district judges, and we are about to introduce it for recorders. Recorders are part-time criminal judges, people who exercise the whole jurisdiction of the crown court, which is a very senior criminal jurisdiction; and they are part-time judges who may be regarded as on the first rung of the judicial ladder; and we are about to introduce a form of appraisal for them, and that of course is very sensible because it allows you to form a view as to their qualities in terms of the possibility of promotion. It is very resource intensive, let me tell you. The cost of doing it across the board will be vast.

One person who does not seem shy of appraising the performance of judges is the current Home Secretary. I speak slightly disparagingly of Mr Blunkett because he had the audacity to turn down an invitation to come and speak with me here at Gresham College.

I will bring all my influence to bear on the Home Secretary to encourage him to accept, and I can assure you that you would have a very, very entertaining evening if he could be persuaded to.

I will hold you accountable then. But what is your view, if you are able to say, on his reactions to various judicial decisions when they seem contrary to his own policies or inclinations?[2]

What I would say is that the Home Office is really enormously successful in the courts. When you read in the media—and I am very conscious that there is a lady and at least two gentlemen of the press here, and many others besides—it is as if the Home Office never goes into court but gets a drubbing from the judges. Well it is completely untrue. The fact is that the Home Office wins nearly all of its cases and loses only a few. In fact if I can give a plug for our Attorney General, Lord Goldsmith, his record of success in the courts is of a very, very high order. But in a Government in a country governed under the rule of law, the Executive does lose sometimes; but the Executive always has the whip hand because if it doesn't like the law it can change it.

But there is an extent to which the distinction between the responsibilities of judges and those of the Home Secretary may not be entirely clear. After all, as we discussed earlier, the Home Secretary has responsibility for a significant chunk of the justice system. So, it must be confusing for many lay people when they hear of a decision by the judges and then hear criticism of that decision by a person who is responsible for a slab of the justice system.

Well it is true that in a country governed by the rule of law, each part of the separation of the powers, the Executive, the Judiciary and Parliament, has to accept each other's separate roles. I think that broadly speaking most people do understand these distinctions and they want them to be maintained.

---

[2] The relationship between the Judiciary and the Home Office is also discussed by Lord Bingham (Ch.7) and Oliver Letwin (Ch.10).

Today has been a busy day for you. This morning you were appointing new QCs and spoke at the ceremony for that, and of course this evening you are at Gresham College. Two huge commitments in the one day!

There has been a bit more besides.

I am sure. I don't know what the filling was but I do consider us to be one serious piece of bread! But in your speech this morning I suspect you may have unsettled some of the new silks by suggesting the whole QC system is up for discussion and consultation.[3]

Which it is.

Can you talk us through your thinking behind this?

Well I would just be repeating the speech that I gave, as you say, this morning at about 11.15.

Can you give us a 30 second précis?

A 30 second précis. Well the principal issue has become whether it, today, should be regarded as a natural function of the State to be responsible for appointing lawyers to a promotional rank within their profession. The State doesn't do it for any other profession. The State of course does it, for example, for the Army let's say, the armed services, but in the sense that appointments in the armed services are a matter for the State but our soldiers, and our sailors, and our airmen, are employees of the State. What is remarkable about the QC system is that the State is appointing people who are in the private sector, and who are self-employed, to a promotional rank. And the primary issue is whether in this day and time that is an appropriate function for the State. Now I hasten to say, as I said this morning in my speech to all these new silks, that I retain an open mind on the subject, but I think the time has come to go out and get firm views from right across the board.

There are clearly many arguments for and against, I am sure. But I can see a distinction between barristers and other professionals beyond the law. It seems to me there is no analogy in medicine, or chartered surveying, or accountancy, or audit, for example, to the barrister being, in effect, an officer of the court. Am I right?

---

[3] The future of QCs is also discussed by Sir Hayden Phillips (Ch.15), Lord Falconer (Ch.18) and Lord Woolf (Ch.20).

They have duties to the court, that is absolutely correct.

I think therefore there is a closer linkage between barristers and Government than between other professionals and the State.

Certainly you could argue that the State has an interest in the integrity of barristers, and has an interest in their quality because of the contribution that they make to the efficient administration of the courts. I look forward to seeing whether that is an argument that is put by some consultee.

Just to follow through, some of my clients are auditors and tax specialists and their overriding duty is clearly to their clients. So long as they are complying with relevant law and regulation, they have no further duty to the State. In contrast, a barrister has this twin set of duties—to his or her client and to the court. It seems to me, therefore, that if you wanted to sustain an argument that barristers are different from other professionals, then there is here a line of reasoning that one could exploit.

There is.

Good. Let's turn now to the appointment of judges and QCs, another area of huge controversy. We haven't got too much time left but I would like to focus on this for a few minutes. However, given we have given some air time to QCs, let's focus now on judges. As a backdrop to the question of judicial appointments, we have already spoken about the independence of judges and how vital it is that they are impartial, not swayed by external factors in their decision making. When it comes to appointments, there is some discomfort in some people's minds about the way in which judges are chosen, about the extent to which advancement seems to be promotion from some kind of internal club, and about the lack of transparency generally. Now, I know you have done much work in trying to overcome these misgivings. Could you summarise the various precautionary measures you have put in place during your time in office and then reflect on the extent to which you think you have gone far enough.[4]

Well I have always maintained, and said in public, that I retained an open mind about the possibility of a Judicial Appointments Commission, and I have now intimated that we are going to go out to consultation on that, and we do it at a point in time when I myself believe that the system for the appointment, actually both of Queen's Counsel and of judges, has been made about as good as it can be made. And I think therefore that the time is right to go out to consultation.

---

[4] The appointment of judges is also discussed by Lord Bingham (Ch.7), Sir Hayden Phillips (Ch.15), Lord Mackay (Ch.17), Lord Falconer (Ch.18) and Professor Bogdanor (Ch.19).

People know basically what product is produced. I think the judicial product in this country is enormously high, I think people have to think very carefully about it. This is not merely a sort of British national vanity, I think it is generally accepted that we have a higher Judiciary of very, very considerable quality, internationally regarded, and also—and you can't say this about every country—incorruptible, that there is no example of a judge in the last 100 years who has taken a bribe, and we have a very fine judicial system. Now that is not to say that the current methods of appointment are written in stone, but what we have to bear in mind also I think is that of course it could be outsourced to an extent to a quango. I am accountable to Parliament for the overall quality of the Judiciary, and an unaccountable quango wouldn't be, and there is always a risk with a quango that there will be quotas and compromises which will stand in the way of the merit principle.

The system that we have got now for the appointment of judges, say at circuit bench level, is that there is an interview by a panel of three—a judge, with one of my impartial civil servants actually in the chair, and a lay person—and then recommendations come to me. So far as the High Court goes, there is the most extensive discussion between me and meetings of the Heads of Division, that is the senior judges, where we canvas the merits of prospective appointees to the High Court bench; and we have now got a Judicial Appointments Commission, not one that makes the appointments, but one which is very high powered as eight Commissioners, and they have the right to sit in on every interview of a prospective judge, on every discussion that I have with the Heads of Division about the comparative qualities of the people who are considered to be appointed. All the material about these people comes to me from impartial civil servants who have no axe to grind one way or another. And then there is often discussion in the presence of an independent Appointments Commissioner who is there to see that everything is being done properly, that nothing is being said or done which is inconsistent with the published criteria for the job; so there is an enormous amount of actual continuous surveillance. The independent Commissioner is entitled to see every piece of paper, every record, nothing is kept from the Commissioners. So it is actually as transparent a system as could be devised.

Now of course we might have a Judicial Appointments Commission. It would be a bit bizarre to have a Judicial Appointments Commission continuously supervised by some other commission, but you would probably have the rules of the quango, which is what it would be, you would have an inspectorate which would go in and do some kind of audit check and produce a report, but it is totally different in quality from what is happening at present. But that is something that people will have to think about. And there are two questions really: one, is this objectively an honest and fair system; secondly, do the public have confidence in it? And it may be that it could be said that the public would for some reason have confidence in what might be an inferior article, we don't know, we will have to see.

What do you think is the strongest argument against the current system? Imagine perhaps you were instructed, in your days as a barrister, to argue against the system. What would you have focussed upon? What, if anything, worries you most about the system?

I think that what worries me most is that ill informed criticism diminishes public confidence.

I have to ask you a question with a Scottish flavour every time we meet. It's just in my bones. So here's the Scottish one. When you were asked at a Select Committee about the Scottish system of judicial appointments, it seemed that you didn't seem to want to dwell on the approach north of the border. But it is true, is it not, that in Scotland they have changed the system.

It is true, but you could point to any other country in the world which has a different system and you could say, "Well if they do it that way there, can't we do it the same way here?". Well that is always true. We have to, however, find what is the best system for ourselves, and very often in all the things that we have been talking about this evening, what is the principal determinant of the way a particular country goes is its traditions, its cultures, its history and so on. But none of these are frozen in aspic, they can all be changed, and I have put these issues out, or will be before the summer putting these issues out for consultation so that we can see if they can be settled once and for all.

If I can try and summarise your views, as I have heard them: you are completely comfortable, as a matter of fact, with the transparency, the rigour and the quality of the judicial appointments' process. The concern, therefore, is whether or not your comfort is shared by people who may not be familiar with the system?

Yes. For example, there is a lot of talk, and it is repeated constantly in the media, about how the whole system is based upon secret soundings, and there is such an affection for the expression "secret soundings", and I agree it has got quite a ring to it—secret soundings—that those who know that the soundings are not secret, still can't banish the expression from their very considerable lexicons.

Pleasingly alliterative!

It is, well I acknowledge that, but is it true? Well the soundings of course are not secret. Those people who are the consultees are publicly known, so there is nothing secret about that. What consultees say about anybody about whom they are consulted is confidential, and that this system has in common with every appointment system that you can think of. And therefore to stigmatise this as secret soundings is completely unfair, but I have no doubt at all that what I have said this evening will not make a whit of difference, and those who have an affection for this expression will continue to use it.

I will stop using the expression, I think. Sadly, we are now short of time and yet there are three things I still want to ask you. The first is about tribunals. I was flicking back through my notes from last year's discussion and we talked then about the review of tribunals by Sir Andrew Leggatt.[5] At that stage, it was uncertain what would be happening with Sir Andrew's, in my view, outstanding report on the future of tribunals. We said then that we would "watch this space". So what has happened in the interim?

We are in business—there has been a decision taken within Government now to give effect to Andrew Leggatt's report, and I agree with you it was absolutely excellent. There was a good measure of resistance to it, which is completely understandable because when you are setting up a new unified system, people whose own parts of what will be a future single system are being run very well, are naturally apprehensive if the new tribunal service will be as effective for the interests that they serve. Basically what I think you will be interested to know is that if you take the tribunals, employment tribunals, benefit tribunals, criminal injury tribunals, disability tribunals, you name them . . .

Almost a million decisions a year.

Yes, they decide more cases every year in fact than the civil courts do, so it is hugely important to people. And the way in which it is worked up to now is that the individual departments of state which are responsible for let us say benefits, which is the Department of Work and Pensions, the Department of Trade and Industry which is responsible for the employment tribunals, well they administer and fund their own tribunals and they are also responsible, in the two examples I gave, for benefit law and employment law. What the Leggatt report means is that all these tribunals will be administered by the Lord Chancellor's Department. Over a period of years it will take to give effect to this it will mean, if you take the hearing centres that there are up and down the country for tribunals—about 240—one will be able to collocate, bring together jurisdictions in a single place; in the great urban centres one will have centralised tribunal centres, there will be the opportunity for chairmen of individual tribunals to enhance their job interests by sitting in more than one tribunal; that will provide a more efficient spread of work. And let us not forget the workers—the 3,000 or so people who work in these tribunals will have the advantage of working within a new and unified structure with better career opportunities.

So reason has triumphed over what to some extent were tough words?

I would say natural scepticism.

The second in my final set of questions is this: what would you like to have achieved by the end of this Parliamentary term?

---

[5] Sir Andrew Leggatt, *Tribunals for Users: One System, One Service, Report of the Review of Tribunals* (The Stationery Office, London, March 2001). Also at *www.tribunals-review.org.uk*

There are basically three great pillars of the justice system. The first is civil—I think that has been substantially reformed and improved from 1997 onwards. We are embarking through the Courts Act, the Courts Bill as it now is, to unify the administration of the criminal courts, which involves really merging the court estate with the magistrates' court estate which essentially belonged to the local authorities. Again that will be productive in efficiencies and career opportunities for those who work in the new system. The tribunal system will not be reformed in that way, nor even will the unification of the criminal courts be completed by the end of this Parliament, but the building blocks will have been laid down; and also I think we will have decisions by then on these issues that you were asking me about the structure of the legal profession itself. I can think of lots more.

Finally, although it might seem uncharitable to ask this, but what do you think about retirement, your own retirement?

What? I get up every morning, looking forward to the day ahead so much that I think I can say with complete confidence that I am not the retiring type.

And on that double truth, on behalf of tonight's audience, let me thank you, Lord Chancellor, for joining us at Gresham College.

Postscript

On 12th June 2003, just six weeks after the above interview, the Prime Minister announced the abolition of the role of the Lord Chancellor. This development had not been the subject of consultation with the Judiciary. The manner and substance of the announcement have been the subject of widespread criticism. This issue is the subject of intense discussion in later chapters of this book.

CHAPTER FOURTEEN

The Rt Hon The Lord Saville of Newdigate
Lord of Appeal in Ordinary; Chairman of The Bloody Sunday Inquiry

Thursday September 30, 2003

It is my very great pleasure tonight to welcome Lord Saville to Gresham College. I welcome him not just as a guest but also as a friend and a collaborator. He was called to the Bar in 1962, was made a QC in 1975, 10 years later became a High Court judge at the Queen's Bench, in 1994 became a Court of Appeal Judge, and three years after that was elevated to the House of Lords. Not so long after his elevation to the Lords he was appointed Chairman of the Bloody Sunday Inquiry, a full-time role that he still occupies today, and something we're going to discuss at length this evening. He is also President of the Society for Computers in Law, and Chairman of an organisation known as ITAC—the Information Technology and the Courts committee—set up in the mid-1980s by the Lord Chancellor to try and co-ordinate all the various activities of computerisation across the court system in this country.

So, a very warm welcome to you, Lord Saville. Can we start our discussion by focussing on your career? Can you tell us a little about what kind of work you did at the Bar, and we'll move from there?

Well, I started in at the Bar in about 1962 and joined a commercial set of chambers, that is to say chambers that concentrate on big, commercial disputes between insurance companies, shipping, banking and that sort of international affair, and stayed in those chambers until I became a judge in 1985. So virtually all my career as a barrister was concerned with commercial matters.

And how did you find the transition from barrister to judge?

Interesting, because although I went into the Commercial Court, in those days— and I think it still obtains today—you do a session in the Commercial Court and then you go out and you try crime on circuit. So I got thrown into the deep end because the first case I did was a murder trial in Birmingham, so that I had to learn very quickly because I'd really done very little criminal law before, although I had of course been on the judges' training courses.

215

What was the difference, in terms of your workload and indeed the nature of the work, when you moved from the Queen's Bench to the Court of Appeal?

Well, there is a difference in both regards. Most of my time was spent in the Commercial Court. The major event of those years was of course the Lloyds litigation, which broke upon us in the early 90s, and at that stage looked fair to overwhelm the courts with actions between The Names and their agents, between insurance companies, re-insurers, and so on, and that was my first experience of large scale management of cases; because unless we successfully managed that litigation, the Commercial Court offering a world service for the resolution of commercial disputes would have been sunk under the weight of the Lloyds litigation. We did succeed in making our way through it with quite a lot of management, extremely ably carried on by my successor when I went to the Court of Appeal.

The workload in the Court of Appeal, it is very interesting, but your feet do not touch the ground. You do every type of work. They're always very careful of course to put a specialist in the team of three that listen to cases. In particular, I had never done any family work at all, and of course sat with people like Elizabeth Butler-Sloss, who is pre-eminent in her field, an extremely nice person to work with, and from whom I learnt a very great deal. It's very exciting in the Court of Appeal. You really are at the leading edge of what is happening in litigation today and in this evening's newspapers and so on, but it is mighty hard work. You put down one case, you pick up another. You have very little time to write judgments and you are very glad indeed, or at least I was, when the end of term comes. But it was quite fascinating and you did see every type of legal work and legal case coming up to you in that Court. It was in fact a marvellous experience, but it was quite nice when it stopped.

There are around 35 Court of Appeal judges at any given time. One of the things that has always intrigued me is that, whilst you often sit as a group of three judges, there are also many circumstances in which you sit as two judges. Could you say just a little about your experience of that, because I think it's fascinating, the notion that there is not the possibility, other than if you both agree, of a majority of 2:1 or the like?

Well, it never happened to me, and I do know it is extremely rare. Most cases in the Court of Appeal, you sit there, you listen to the submissions and so on, and you come out and it's quite extraordinary how your colleagues and yourself have all formed the same views even though you haven't discussed the case at any length at all. And so dissention, dissent, is actually very rare indeed. If in fact there was a case with two judges and they disagree with each other, well then there is a mechanism I think for it either going before a three-judge court or otherwise, but I never actually had the experience myself. We always agreed without any difficulty on what we thought the answer was.

That I think is the common experience. You were a relatively short time in the Court of Appeal and then elevated to the House of Lords in 1997. Can you explain the timing of that in relation to your appointment to the Bloody Sunday Inquiry?

Well, I was appointed to the House of Lords in July 1997. The vacation then came along, so I started in as a House of Lords judge in October, and I was asked to do the Bloody Sunday Inquiry at the end of January the following year, so hadn't had a great deal of experience of judging in the House of Lords. In the early stages of the Bloody Sunday Inquiry, when we were collecting material and so on, I did have time to go back and do a few cases, including sitting on the second time round of the General Pinochet case. But as the Inquiry progressed, it became busier and busier, and for the last three or four years it has actually been a full-time job.

Just before we go on to the Inquiry—as most guests this evening will know the ongoing role of the Law Lords is very much a matter of debate. Certainly it is the subject of a consultation exercise. And a new Supreme Court to replace the Law Lords as the final court of appeal is anticipated. What are your feelings about that?[1]

I've always thought that we should comply with the separation of powers in the sense of getting the judges away from the Legislature and indeed the Executive, so I've always been in favour of a division along those lines. So the proposition that we should disappear from the House of Lords and be the top court of a Supreme Court system is one which I support. It's interesting, however, it has worked in the past, but it does lead to difficulties, particularly with the role of what used to be called the Lord Chancellor, because in recent years that has become, in my view at least, a much more politicised position and raises great difficulties as to whether or not he should sit on given cases, or indeed any case at all. My own view is that since we want to have this separation and keep the Judiciary separate and independent, a person in the position of the Lord Chancellor shouldn't sit on any case at all, whether it's got a political bent to it or anything else. So I'm in favour of the general proposition. I'm worried, however, because it seems to have been announced in circumstances where nobody gave any or much thought to where we would actually go.

Physically?

Physically go, and this is quite important, because in this day and age we need and expect backup; we are starting to employ judicial assistants along the sort of lines that have been used for many years in the United States Supreme Court. There of course they are called "law clerks". We're very pressed for room indeed at the moment in the House of Lords, but if you're going to make this change, which I'm in favour of in principle, then we really ought to make it properly and to give the top court proper facilities and proper backup systems so that we can be proud of what we have provided to the top court. Now, whether or not the Treasury has been consulted on that, I don't know, but it's likely to cost a lot of money. So I am slightly

---

[1] The judicial work of the House of Lords and the possibility of a new Supreme Court are also discussed by Lord Bingham (Ch.7), Sir Hayden Phillips (Ch.15), Lord Mackay (Ch.17), Lord Falconer (Ch.18) and Lord Woolf (Ch.20).

concerned that proper thought will be given to providing us with proper premises. Some years ago, because there's such pressure on rooms in the House of Lords, it was actually seriously suggested—this was before I was a Law Lord—that the Law Lords might like to decamp off to Millbank Tower and have two levels of that tower somewhere up near the top. Well, Robert Goff, who was then the Senior Law Lord— this is all I've heard from others—who was the politest, gentlest person that one could possibly come across, gave a very short answer indeed to that sort of suggestion. We have to be properly housed. We'd be a laughing stock otherwise. And if you go and look at the Supreme Court facilities in Canada, the United States, Australia, then we really ought, as the birthplace of the common law, to have proper facilities ourselves. So I do hope that very important aspect of hiving us off is properly considered and properly dealt with.

And by facilities, are you meaning physical premises, research resources, information technology, assistants, secretarial and administrative support and so forth?

Yes, and decent rooms in which the hearings can be held.

The Law Lords just now sit in lounge suits, do you not?

Yes, we do.

I wonder if that would change with a Supreme Court, because when one imagines a Supreme Court, you can quite naturally imagine being robed up.

I don't know. We're about to have a discussion between all the Law Lords—I hope it's going to take place in the next week or two—as to our responses to the two papers that have been produced on the subject. I don't think we've yet considered whether or not robes or gowns would be a good idea. It's not the top of our list of priorities.

I can imagine that. Would there not be a loss to the House of Lords generally in not having judicial input, the judicial minds as it were, offering thoughts and guidance, observations, recommendations on legislation as it flows through the system?

I think in one sense there would, but I'm uneasy with full-time professional judges entering into the legislative process because I'm a believer in the separation of powers. I personally think there is a solution to that. There are a large number of retired Law Lords who are still fit and able, and it seems to me that there is something to be said for the case of making them life peers, and so they, who of course will have had a lifetime's experience in the law and will of course know the people who follow them, would I think be well able, if they gave up a judicial career altogether, to appear in the House of Lords and to provide the sort of assistance that you've mentioned. I am against, myself, existing full-time professional judges, even people as important as the Lord Chief Justice or the Senior Law Lord, sitting as part of the Legislature. I just don't like that. I think we ought to be entirely separate and independent, and be seen to be entirely separate and independent. Others I know hold a different view, but that's the view I would express.

I don't normally take questions from the floor, but I have been handed one this evening that I think is a good one. It is addressed to "Monsieur Le Professeur" and is from "Jim". He asks in respect of Lords of Appeal in Ordinary: "Can you explain the 'in Ordinary' bit?". Law Lords, as we call you, are indeed formally known as Lords of Appeal in Ordinary. Can you clarify this one?

I'm very sorry you asked me that question because I don't know the answer! Historically, in theory at least, the House of Lords has been the final court of appeal, and it's only in the last 140 years that they have actually used only professional judges, and I think that was the name given to them when they finally decided it would be a good idea if the top court of appeal was only staffed by professional judges who'd had a long career in the law. But who actually chose that title, I don't know. It does remind me of a story though. We were making some claim on some insurance, and my wife was called by the assessor and she took a few details down for us, and the lady asked my wife what her husband did for a living and she said, "Well, he's a Law Lord", and there was a bit of a pause and then the lady went on with the questioning. Right at the end of the telephone conversation, this lady said to my wife, "I'm sorry to ask this, but can you tell me exactly what a war lord does?"!

Excellent!
Can we move now to Bloody Sunday? First of all, can you give us an indication of how you came to be appointed as Chair of the Inquiry, how you set it up, and what the rough chronology of events has been and will be? I should say to everyone present that there are clearly many matters that Lord Saville won't be able to address in the course of our discussion because the Inquiry is still being conducted. But I'm hoping that our guest can talk about the process, talk about the technology, and talk about the experience, and so give us a flavour of what has been a remarkable public judicial inquiry.[2]

Yes, I can certainly do that, but I can't of course offer any view as to the subject matter of the Inquiry. We're still continuing on it. I was working on it until half past five this afternoon, and indeed listening to a witness until five o'clock this afternoon.
    Derry Irvine, when he was Lord Chancellor, he asked me to do the job. I wasn't quick enough to think of a suitable excuse! I don't have an Irish grandmother or

---

[2] Judicial inquiries are also discussed by Lord Irvine (Ch.6), Lord Bingham (Ch.7), Dame Elizabeth Butler-Sloss (Ch.11) and Lord Mackay (Ch.17).

anything like that, and anyway, it seemed to me to be a challenge. At that stage—
we're talking now in January/February of 1998—none of us, nobody, had any idea
of the sort of size of the Inquiry. So we set out really not knowing what we faced.
There was an immediate difficulty. Most inquiries are staffed and run by people from
the Treasury Solicitor's Department, who have got a wealth of knowledge about
public inquiries, and they were the people who had to run Brian Hutton's Inquiry
in the last few weeks. We couldn't use them because they were seriously criticised
with regard to the role that they'd played in the previous Inquiry, held by Lord
Widgery way back in 1972. So I had to search around various departments to find
people who were completely independent of anything concerned with Bloody
Sunday, and came up with a series of extraordinarily able senior civil servants.

Anne Stephenson was the first secretary to the Inquiry. A secretary to the Inquiry
is a very senior civil servant who runs the administration of the Inquiry, which is a
very big job and is a very important role. Also, at that stage, the legal secretary to
the Inquiry, was Philip Ridd, a solicitor who came from the Inland Revenue. So the
three of us sat down. I had then to go and see two possible colleagues, and Bill Hoyt
and Ted Somers, one from Canada and one from New Zealand, they kindly agreed
to come and help out so we'd have a tribunal of three. Ted Somers had to retire in
the course of the Inquiry from ill-health, so now we have an Australian, who used
to be in the Federal Court there, called John Toohey. Bill Hoyt and I have been in
there from virtually the start. And then we set about trying to retrieve everything we
could from the Public Record Offices for Northern Ireland and this country, from
the Ministry of Defence, from half a dozen other departments that were concerned
with the events of that day. I also had an enormous advantage in managing to persuade Christopher Clarke QC, who I regard as one of the very best barristers around
today, to come and be our lead counsel for the Inquiry.

Over the next two years, we all spent our time collecting, analysing and collating
material, taking statements from thousands of people, including a large number of
people who were on the march in that city on the day, and of course a large number
of soldiers. We couldn't, in my view at least, confine ourselves to the events of that
afternoon. We had to look at the background, background events in Northern
Ireland, the Government of Northern Ireland as it was in those days and what they
were doing. So there was an enormous amount of research, and that culminated two
years ago in Christopher making his opening to the Inquiry.

*Can I step in? Can you, very briefly, summarise the facts, as it were, the background to
the Inquiry?*

Well I can't really say what actually happened because the whole thing is in violent
dispute between various parties, but the whole incident: there was a civil rights
march in the city to protest against, amongst other things, internment without trial
which had been introduced six months earlier. The authorities decided that it
was too dangerous to allow the march into the centre of the city because of the risk
of the centre of the city being further bombed and destroyed and of confrontation
with opposing groups. A large part of Londonderry had already been destroyed
in the preceding weeks and months, so they put up barriers to stop the march, and
the march indeed was stopped and turned away; but there was an element of the

crowd, mostly young people, who rioted at these barriers, and the idea was that some troops—the Paratroop Regiment—would go in and arrest them. After that, it becomes a matter of the most lively dispute, but some 20 minutes after that had happened, 13 people had been shot dead and some 14 injured. Our Inquiry is about the circumstances in which those deaths and injuries occurred.

And the earlier Inquiry that you mention? Can you offer us a snapshot of that?

The earlier Inquiry was conducted by Lord Widgery, and although he's been most bitterly criticised by some people, one has to admire him and his staff for the speed with which they did it. That itself has been an item of criticism, but it's a bit hard on Lord Widgery, since Parliament itself asked him to do it as quickly as he possibly could. He was to report in 10 weeks. But it was bitterly criticised as being a whitewash, as being an insufficient investigation into the facts. We're not sitting on appeal from Lord Widgery, but the fact of that criticism is undeniable.

Can I just take us off on a tangent, because something that's often asked is—very current—is that Lord Hutton's Inquiry proceeded, certainly in the first stage, proceeded extremely quickly, and yours is taking many, many years. There are significant differences, and I think it's important that you clarify them.

Yes, I think the comparison is a bit unfair. Lord Hutton I think had 75 witnesses altogether and 10,000 or so documents. We have 20 or 30 times as many witnesses and probably the same factor of documents. We are also looking not at something that took place a few weeks ago concerning a few Government departments and the BBC, but a violent, on any view, confrontation involving hundreds of soldiers on the one side, thousands of civilians on the other, with the IRA present in the city. So I think it's a little difficult to compare the two things. The one comparison that I would make is that we both used the same IT, and no doubt we'll be talking about this shortly, but it's certainly a demonstration that the IT we are using is suitable for smaller scale inquiries as well as a large scale one like the one I'm trying to conduct.

And we will turn to technology in a few minutes. But I stopped your flow. You were describing the setup . . .

I can't remember where the flow got to!

I know where we were—you were discussing the opening speech of counsel.

Oh yes, Christopher's Clarke's, about 50 days, and it was a masterly analysis of the material that we had at that stage; and it did demonstrate—more than I think anything else—that we really were making a real stab at conducting a full, thorough and totally impartial inquiry. It's all there if anyone wanted to read it. It's on our website.[3] At the end of the Inquiry, which we hope is not going to be too many months away, Christopher will be making his final summation.

I might explain—people probably know this—but the purpose of having counsel to the Inquiry is that he, and in our case they—because we've got a number of them but Christopher is the leader—is so that they can prepare the case, ask the questions, and it allows the tribunal to be one removed and means that there have been no suggestions that the tribunal was sort of descending into the arena or being partisan or anything else. Of course we work very carefully indeed with our counsel, and it's our decision in the end, not his or theirs, but we really couldn't do it without them. There just aren't enough hours in the day.

Christopher's got a team of four juniors assisting him, and I've never seen people work so hard as those people have worked since 1998. It's a huge exercise. If you take, for example, the witnesses we've been having this week, who are some of the soldier witnesses, anything that anyone else has said in relation to what these particular people might have done or themselves say has got to be cross-checked and analysed and any questions framed so that we can be sure that we've asked the individuals in question everything of relevance. If you can imagine, with coming up to 800 witnesses, that's a massive task, and I'm just full of admiration at the way they've done it, as I believe are all the interested parties—both the soldiers' counsel on the one side and counsel for the families of those who died or were wounded on the other. It is a most amazing effort.

Can you take us through the progress of the Inquiry, including your relocation to London and so forth? It would be useful to get a sense of the timing of events and activities.

Well, we started by having a beauty contest to get professional lawyers in to take statements from witnesses. We didn't have the staff or indeed the experts that we could employ directly, so we had a beauty contest, which Eversheds won. They then sent out a very large team, initially to Northern Ireland, to take statements from those who were there on the day or who knew something about the events of the day. That was a very long task because there were between eight and 12,000 people on the march, and there were a lot of people who said that they knew things that we ought to know about. On the days immediately following Bloody Sunday, the civil rights organisations took a large number of statements from individuals who had been on the march, so we did have some contemporary statements as well. In that regard, an interesting thing happened. We discovered and finally tracked down a lady who'd been in the city on the day, and she was a civil rights worker from the United States, and she'd made tape recordings the day afterwards, two or three days afterwards, of various people who came and told her into a tape machine what they'd seen and heard and done. We finally tracked this tape down after about two years and we brought it back from the United States, and as witnesses came in to

---

[3] *www.bloody-sunday-inquiry.org*

give their evidence, we took them downstairs to what we call our Witness Liaison Suite, asked them to put the headphones on and said, "Is this your voice?". They were astonished, most of them. They'd forgotten they'd done it, and suddenly, there was their voice speaking to them from 30 years ago. We got a lot of reports that a lot of people said, "Yes, it is and I'd forgotten entirely I'd done it". So that's the sort of material we were chasing down.

As well as Eversheds getting statements, of course we were chasing the Ministry of Defence for all their documents, we were chasing the archives of what was then the Northern Ireland Government for all the documents relating to the planning for the day, all the documents that related to how the troops were deployed, what sort of tactics they were using, and so on. As I say, this all took a very long time to prepare, and to a degree it's still ongoing, although we're now beginning to wind down the collection of evidence as opposed to its preparation.

And after the initial Eversheds' task, when did you actually start sitting? It would be interesting if you could describe the hearing room—we'll go onto the technology in a second—to give a flavour of the layout so people can visualise.

Well, I've always been rather interested in information technology in the courts; and indeed Richard and I have—long before the Bloody Sunday Inquiry—been friends and colleagues trying to persuade the courts, the court service, and those who have got the purse strings of course, that the proper use of information technology would very much improve our court system and would in the end prove beneficial in terms of money. So, being made Chairman of this Inquiry seemed to me a golden opportunity to try and put into effect what I believed was the case, and so we have a large amount of information technology, which was, again, put out to tender, and I can, if you like Richard, describe some of it now?

Yes, let's do that.

Well, in no particular order, we scanned all the documents, many thousands of photographs that were taken on the day, several hours of what we call "actuality footage"—because there were a large number of TV companies, both from this country and the United States, who were actually filming the day as it unfolded—and we in effect scanned all those into our servers. So all the documents, photographs and films, and indeed the statements as they come in, and indeed the transcript of the evidence as they give it, is all stored electronically. Now, that has a number of huge advantages. The first I think to mention is that this is a public inquiry, set up under an Act of 1921. If you go into an inquiry that doesn't use these facilities, although it's called a public inquiry as a member of the public you would find it very difficult, if not completely impossible, to understand what's going on, because you won't see the documents, you won't see the photographs, you won't see the actuality footage. But as you've seen from Brian Hutton's Inquiry, if you scan all these in, you can then display them on screens to the public, you can put them on your website on the internet, and so if the public come in to an Inquiry—like this afternoon when a soldier was being questioned about his statement, about bits of the actuality footage, about still photographs and so on—the public can understand what is going on, because they're seeing what we're seeing. So really, by the use of this technology, for the very first time, you can make inquiries like these truly public. So that's what we did with the documents, and any of you who care to come down to the Inquiry—we shall be down at the Methodist Central Hall until the end of October—will see, you can sit there and you can see what we're seeing.

Can I ask you a question about that technology? This is further to a discussion I was having today with our friend and colleague Sir Brian Neill, who was another pioneer in judicial technology. He was speaking about the amount of time judges used to spend finding the relevant documents, particularly when there were three judges on the bench . . .

I was just about to come onto that! This is a very practical point. It sounds silly, but it in fact means that the information technology we are using can save a huge amount of money. If you have any big case, be it an inquiry or any other form of case where there are multiple parties, as we've got, and if you like, three judges, and we've got three judges on the tribunal, and you're doing it on paper, and a barrister is asking witnesses questions on the documents, you will say, "Would you go to bundle 306, page 410". Those of you who are professional lawyers will know what I'm about to say. Everybody then turns to get that bundle out of the shelves, find that page. Somebody has to make sure the witness has got the right bundle. Somebody has to make sure that the three doddery judges sitting on the bench have actually got the right bundle. The question is then asked, some 30 to 40 seconds have gone by, the answer is given to the question, and you move to the next bundle, and the next wasted 30 to 40 seconds happens. Now, if you add that up over a day, it is a very substantial period of time. If you come down to the Inquiry you will see one of the barristers saying, "Now, Mr X, I'd like to look at what you said in 1972 when you made a statement to the military police. Could we have ABC123 please?". One, two, and that is on the screen for everybody to see. So you are saving an immense amount of time because you've scanned the document in and you can get it up on the screens straightaway.

The other thing we can do that makes life much easier is, with regard to every witness, we keep a dossier of that witness's evidence. That witness may have said something in 1972. If it's a soldier, he may have made a statement to the Royal Military Police, he may indeed have given evidence to the Widgery Inquiry, made a statement to the solicitors of that Inquiry, he may have talked to the press, he's made a statement to us, and then you've got the transcript of when he's asked questions, and he may have made marks on certain documents in the course of giving his evidence. Electronically, we can assemble that into one dossier for that witness. Electronically, we can have an index that will cross-reference that to other matters of relevance in relation to what he has said. So you've saved an immense amount of time doing that, and you've made it immensely easier to assemble and analyse the material at the end of the day.

We have Livenote. I expect most of you know about Livenote. This is real-time transcription. Heather, who is our Livenote writer, sits beside the witness and plays around with this machine as the witness speaks, and she is about a second-and-a-half behind the witness, so that as you watch your Livenote screen, what that witness says comes up in type.

It's a conversion from stenography to digital text.

Yes. On that screen, each individual lawyer and each member of the tribunal can make notes on the evidence as it goes on, can colour up a section and attribute it to any issue or issues and so on, and that's the same for all the lawyers as well; and indeed Livenote has got its own indexing system that you can use. So there you have the facility of seeing in print immediately what the witness has said.

We also have an audio recording of everything that takes place either in the Central Hall here or in the Guildhall in Northern Ireland, and that's quite a clever machine too, because if you typed in, for example, "11.35am 3rd of June 2002", the machine would think for a bit, and then you can hear the voice that was speaking at that moment. So that is a useful tool. It certainly will be an interesting historical record.

In terms of the Guildhall and the Central Hall, they are mirror images of one another in terms of the technology in place. Is that right?

They are. We originally thought, and indeed we ruled, that the entire Inquiry should take place at the Guildhall on the grounds that the Guildhall was at the centre of the city where these people were shot and wounded, and it seemed the obvious, correct place to hold an Inquiry of this kind. But the Court of Appeal told us we were wrong about that on the basis that to do that would interfere with the Article II Human Rights Act right of the soldiers, because the Court of Appeal perceived that there was a real risk that they would be attacked if they went over there. So, on the basis of that decision, we had to move lock, stock and barrel to London to hear the soldiers' evidence. We looked at the costings of this and in the end it was cheaper to set up a complete, separate IT system in London, rather than trying to bring the Guildhall equipment back over here, so that's what we've done. It is in fact a mirror image. Although the two halls look different, all the facilities, electronic facilities, are exactly the same.

How many screens are there in the rooms?

Quite a few. For various reasons the soldiers don't have one set of counsel, they have a number of different sets of counsel, because some things the soldiers say conflict with some things that other soldiers say, so they can hardly have the same lawyers. To a degree, it's the same with the families, so there are probably about 20 separate sets of lawyers. Each will have a screen. There are then the screens for the public. So it's quite a number of screens, and each of my colleagues and I also have a screen each. Well, we have two screens each in fact, on one of which you can see the documents as they're put up, and on the other you see the Livenote transcription as it appears.

And that's the same set-up as in Lord Hutton's Inquiry?

Exactly, yes.

The question, I suspect, on many people's lips, is how much did the technology cost?

The cost of the technology, it's not cheap. It costs about £15,000 a day to run. That actually is only a small proportion of the daily costs of the Inquiry as a whole, most of which is, if I may use the expression, eaten up by the lawyers' fees. There's not a lot we can do about that. People are I think entitled to have lawyers. Certainly, it would be difficult to suggest that the soldiers who are accused of murder or conspiracy to murder should appear at an inquiry like this without legal advice; and equally, the families of those who died or were wounded, who want to know the truth, it seems to us equally the case that they should have lawyers to make sure that what they believe happened is properly presented to the tribunal. But it costs. It costs a great deal of money. As far as the cost of the IT is concerned, we are all convinced that this is far outweighed by the benefits. It's very difficult to draw an exact comparison, but the sort of figures that we and others have come up with is that we save about a third of the time that would otherwise be taken. Now, if you work that back at a cost to the Inquiry of about £60,000 a day, you are talking about a great deal of money indeed, bearing in mind that we've been going for six years.

Tell us about the virtual reality system, which is probably the most advanced system that you have in place.

The virtual reality system is something we use because the city of Londonderry, or Derry as a lot of people call it, has changed greatly in the years that have gone by. In particular, in 1972 there were three very large high rise flats called the Rossville Flats, around which a lot of the action took place, and they were swept away, oh, 20, 25 years ago. So we recreated a virtual reality city using computer graphics and also photographs of the city where it remained the same today. You can get this up on the screen, and we've got a number of hotspots on a map, about 60 altogether, and if you click on the hotspot you will get a view from that particular position. You can then expand the view as though you were walking towards the object you are looking at, but you can also swing that view around 360 degrees on the screen. This has proved very useful indeed to a number of witnesses, who can then be shown this and say, "Oh yes, I was standing there and I saw this taking place over here", against a context of a virtual reconstruction of the city as it was, and can mark on the screen, which is recorded, the places to which they are referring.

What we do with the witnesses is, when they come in to give their evidence, they go downstairs to our little Witness Liaison Suite, we give them a cup of coffee or whatever they'd like, and then we tell them how to work the virtual reality. A large number of witnesses have come up, obviously keen to give evidence, even keener to show that they know how to work the virtual reality! One or two, well more than one or two, quite a few of them have said, "Well, can I show you on the virtual reality?" and it has been a very useful tool. It's . . . rudimentary is the wrong word, but it was worked up five years ago, and today, if you did the same thing, with the extra power of computers, you could make it very much more sophisticated. You could probably put figures into it and all the rest. But it's worked very well as a tool to assist us and the witnesses in understanding what happened.

What's the main lesson that emerges, do you feel, about the use of technology for the courts more generally? I think you and I have shared for many years a frustration that most of the technology you've been talking about, other than the virtual reality technology, has in fact been around for 10 or 15 years and yet has been under-exploited in our courts. What are your thoughts on the more general applicability and potential of these technologies in the court system?

Well, I'm very much in favour of using them. There are of course small scale cases where it isn't worth the investment, but any case of any size, and I'm thinking of criminal cases as well as civil, it seems to me that it would enable justice to be done quicker and better, and in the end at less cost, because time equals cost in the law and if you can reduce the time you're going to reduce the cost. We've made actually quite substantial strides in the court system over the last 10 years. If you go back to the early 90s, to a large degree, it really was like wading in treacle. You couldn't persuade the powers that be that this really was the way to go. Well, I think that battle has been won. The perennial battle remains, which is to persuade the Treasury they ought to put money in. But I think we've come a long way, Richard—I think you'd probably say the same.

I would. I strongly share your sense that, overall, this would bring significant savings and greater efficiencies. I think it's true to say today that the criminal justice system is attracting a great deal of IT investment, whereas the civil justice system is, in technological terms, the poorer cousin.

Well, it is, and the Government decision is to the effect that the civil justice system should finance itself. I'm not at all sure I agree with that. It seems to me that part of a democratic Government's function is to run and indeed to finance a system of justice, both civil and criminal, and I therefore disagree with the proposition that the civil justice system should be financed from the people that use it, but that's my own personal view. But we continue to try. I mean I haven't had much time recently because of the Inquiry, but we have made strides. It's very slow, but I think people now at the top are beginning to realise that this is the way to go. There are of course all sorts of offshoots, as Richard has put in his books. You're not talking necessarily just about better ways of doing things, you're talking about entirely new ways of doing things—like online dispute resolution, or in the court system the small claims systems, which you can work by computer. This I am convinced is the way we shall go and the way we ought to go.

Returning to the Inquiry, one feature of it has been the involvement of judicial review. Could you explain what this is and in what context it has been invoked?[4]

Yes. Tribunals of inquiry, like my tribunal, which is set up under a 1921 Act—but there are plenty of other tribunals set up under other Acts—all come under the court's jurisdiction, which has jurisdiction to review the decisions of bodies like tribunals, and which will correct them if it perceives them to be wrong. That is what's happened twice with us. We came to the conclusion that with limited exceptions the soldiers should not be anonymous, because in our view, the risk to them was not sufficiently great to allow that inroad on the openness of the Inquiry. The Court of Appeal said we were wrong about that, so the soldiers are anonymous. Similarly, as I've said, the Court of Appeal said we were wrong when we said we thought the soldiers should go to Northern Ireland to give their evidence. The Court of Appeal considered that the risk to them was too great.

I don't for one moment think that the interference by the courts in wrong. In fact, I think it's essential that there is this independent body in the form of the courts who can listen to and, if necessary in their view, correct the rulings of tribunals like mine. I didn't agree with them of course, because I'd already thought the opposite, but it's right that that should exist, because—especially in an Inquiry like mine, which is concerned to a very large degree with human rights—if three members of the Court of Appeal think that we would be likely to infringe the soldiers' human rights if we required them to go to Northern Ireland or if they weren't anonymous, well then we would of course faithfully, and have faithfully, obeyed that view. So I'm not saying it's wrong. What I am saying of course though is that it is likely to cause very substantial delay and considerable additional expense. Well, that's the sort of price you have to pay if you're going to have a reviewing system like we've got in this country. The cost of moving us to London was many, many millions of pounds, and the cost of going through tens of thousands of documents to make sure that every soldier's name was removed and a cipher put in its place was desperately time-consuming and also enormously expensive. But this is the trouble. If you have an inquiry into an event like Bloody Sunday, which involves these human rights considerations, involves a large number of people, and indeed in the case of Bloody Sunday, involves going back 30 years, it is going to take a great deal of time and cost a huge amount of money. We accept that we have spent a very large sum of money indeed.

We have to justify all the money we spend to the Northern Ireland Office audit people, but it is inevitable that in an inquiry of this size, if you are going to do it properly, a great deal of money has to be spent. Whether this is the best way of dealing with an event like this, I don't know, but I have to conduct an inquiry under the 1921 Act, and I and my colleagues have taken the view that we must take the

---

[4] Judicial review is also discussed by David Pannick (Ch.3).

steps that we have taken, and the Court of Appeal has taken the view that we must anonymise the soldiers and bring their evidence to London, and that, as I repeat, has cost a lot of money. Whether there's a better way, I don't know, but I'm having to do it this way and we're doing it as best we can.

You mentioned the human rights dimension a couple of times. There's an Article II issue?

Yes. I don't think anyone in the Government realised when they set this Inquiry up that it is in fact what one could describe as an Article II Human Rights Act inquiry. Article II of the Human Rights Act protects the right to life. It is, the European Court of Human Rights has said, a corollary of that that if the State takes human life through its agencies, then in order for the Article to work properly there has to be a proper investigation into that taking of life; so that it is now incumbent on this country, since we've incorporated the Human Rights Act, the Human Rights Convention in our law, that in the case of the State agencies taking the life of individuals there has to be an inquiry under Article II of the Human Rights Convention. In this case, State agencies in the form of soldiers shot civilians. So, this is possibly the first Human Rights Act inquiry that has taken place, although I don't think it really dawned on the Government when they asked me to do it that they were doing it for Article II reasons.

When I speak to judges and we're talking about you, many say they feel sorry for you because you've been away from the House of Lords for so long. It's clearly an Inquiry of immense gravity and significance, but is it fulfilling? What kind of professional experience has this been for you?

Yes, it is fulfilling. It is quite fascinating. It's very hard work, and it's going to be very, very difficult to decide what happened because of, firstly, the passage of time—people's memories obviously become suspect, although we do have a great deal of contemporary material—but secondly, because of the violent difference of opinion between the Nationalists who were on the march that day and the accounts given by the soldiers as to what happened. The extreme view that's been expressed is that this was all a plot by the British Government to shoot a few of the Nationalists in the city of Londonderry in order to teach them not to have no-go areas, and therefore the shooting was authorised at the highest level, by which I mean the British Cabinet, and duly carried out. That's an extreme theory on the one side. The extreme theory on the other side is that the soldiers went in to make a few arrests of people who'd been throwing stones and met a hail of machine gun bullets, nail bombs, petrol bombs and the rest, coming from the IRA who'd planned to ambush them. Well, those are two extreme theories, so there's quite a difference at the extremes on the views as to what happened. We will have eventually to sit down and assess all the material and try and decide where we think the truth lies. There may be instances where we are unable to reach a conclusion simply because the evidence doesn't allow us to do so.

But it's fascinating. It continues to be fascinating. It's ... I'd been judging for about 15 years before I went to the House of Lords. I was looking forward to judging there, I've done a bit of judging there, but I've been on this now for six years, and in a way it's satisfying to try and do something really carefully and thoroughly. Whether we succeed or not you people are going to tell me at the end of the day, but I've enjoyed the management part of it. I've enjoyed working with our counsel. We have constant sort of management meetings. We get problems arising every day, in a whole variety of cases—how are we going to get this witness to come, can we fit this witness in, one witness in before the other, what shall we do with this witness who's refusing to turn up, is it right to subpoena him, shall we allow this witness to be screened from view, does he have a proper case for screening from view? So, these are all ongoing problems, as well as sitting every day listening to and making a note of the evidence that we're hearing.

A lot of people have said, "Oh, how dreadfully sorry we are for you stuck in this", and they're wrong to feel sorry. It's a big job. Whether we do it properly or not, we'll have to wait and see, but if I asked myself back in 1998, knowing what I know now, would I have said "no" to Derry Irvine, I think the answer is "no, I would still have said yes".

Would you like to plug the chapter in the book?

Yes, I would, very much! I brought it in for the purpose of plugging it.

Back in the summer, Brian Neill, who is a retired Court of Appeal judge, celebrated his 80th birthday. I've done a lot of work with Brian Neill, and so has Richard. Brian Neill was one of the very first people, donkey's years before me—I'm now talking about the early 80s—who saw that the use of information technology in the courts was the way to go. If I thought I was wading in treacle in the early 1990s, it's nothing to what he experienced, which to a large degree was almost derision, but he battled away. He worked through ITAC, which I now chair, the Society of Computers and Law, and almost alone was giving the message that now everybody has accepted 20 years on. He was also a remarkably fine judge, and his speciality was defamation.

So, Richard and I, having one of our curry suppers, thought three years ago that it might be a good idea—and I think this was really Richard's idea rather than mine—to celebrate Brian's 80th birthday by getting together a number of people to write chapters on defamation and on information technology, put them together in a book, and then have a dinner to celebrate Brian's 80th birthday, and to present him with the book, he not knowing that that is what we had done. Well, this is what we did do in July. This is the book. It's called *Essays in Honour of Sir Brian Neill: The Quintessential Judge.*[5] It has an introduction and foreword by the Lord Chief Justice and the Senior Law Lord. It has chapters on defamation and on IT. It has a chapter from Richard, and it has a chapter from me on the use of IT in the Bloody Sunday Inquiry.

---

[5] Mark Saville and Richard Susskind (eds.), *Essays in Honour of Sir Brian Neill: The Quintessential Judge* (LexisNexis, London, 2003).

So, that's my plug for this book. The profits from it, if there are any, will go to an outfit called BAILII, that's British and Irish Legal Information Institute, in which Richard and I and others, including Henry Brooke—Lord Justice Brooke who has written a chapter in this book—have been working on for the last five years. BAILII, as we call it, is the idea that legal materials in a democracy should be available free to the public; and through the internet we would hope to be able to do that, to provide a site where you can go to any statute, you can go to any statutory regulation, you can go to any case, you have a search engine, so that anyone who wishes to do so in our democracy can, free of charge, find the law. Now, we followed Australia on this, because they've got AUSTLII, which is the Australasian Legal Information Institute. But ours is now up and running. We need funds. People have been very generous. But any profits from this book will go to what I regard as a highly worthy cause. So, I think that's the end of the plug for the book!

Marvellous! Can I ask you, by way of final question, and I ask this of all my guests sitting in your chair: if a young person said to you that he or she was considering a career in the law, what would you say? What advice would you offer? Would you be encouraging or discouraging?

Well, perhaps I've been lucky, but I've had what I regard as a marvellous career. I would not change one minute of it. And whether the younger people here are thinking of being solicitors or barristers I don't think really matters, it is a marvellous career. It has moments of languor, like any career does, but it's intellectually highly satisfying. Of course I look at it from the point of view of a barrister. Advocacy is exceptionally hard work, but extraordinarily rewarding. The one lesson in advocacy is not that you are a marvellous speaker, but that you are able to get the case up and do the work that is necessary. But if you do that, you have a most satisfactory, satisfying career, whatever part of the law you go into. My career at the Bar, as I said, spans commercial work, I travelled abroad a lot, I did cases abroad a lot, and I repeat I would not change a minute of it. I'm very, very lucky to be, at the age I am—I'm now getting very doddery indeed—to be able to look back and not regret a minute of my career choices or my career. So my point of view is, go for it! I think you would have a most satisfactory, rewarding career, whatever branch of the profession you went into.

Lord Saville, thank you very much.

Chapter Fifteen

Sir Hayden Phillips GCB
Permanent Secretary, Department for Constitutional Affairs

Tuesday November 25, 2003

My guest tonight is Sir Hayden Phillips, and he can claim, or I'll claim on his behalf, to be the most experienced Permanent Secretary, the most experienced civil servant, working in the land today. The role of Permanent Secretary is itself the most senior in a Government department. And Sir Hayden's department is the Department for Constitutional Affairs. He also has the title of Clerk of the Crown in Chancery, which we may discuss. He has held senior offices in the Treasury and the Home Office and in the Cabinet Office as well, and was Permanent Secretary of another department, the Department of Culture, Media and Heritage, to which he was appointed Permanent Secretary in 1992. It was in 1998 that he was appointed to what was then the Lord Chancellor's Department as Permanent Secretary, and since then, as many of you will know and indeed we will discuss tonight, that department has mutated into the Department for Constitutional Affairs.

Sir Hayden—a very warm welcome.
   I thought we might begin by talking about the civil service in general and I feel bound to suggest, perhaps because I watch too much television, that most people's perception of civil servants is much influenced by the television series Yes Minister. *If you will forgive me, are you indeed Sir Humphrey?*

I was always going to say, Richard, it was almost as if you felt you had to be absolutely in tune with peoples' perceptions. It's one of these things. There are wonderful elements of truth in the series, and it's all done in such a carica-tured way that in fact it's not really like that at all. Although very occasionally, you'll be in a meeting—I remember the time the first series was at its height—and you'd be in a meeting with your Secretary of State or whoever it was, and suddenly both of you would realise that you were behaving exactly as you would in a television programme, and that led you bursting into giggles. Can I just do one bit of marketing, which is that I did actually appear as Sir Humphrey on the stage last January in something called the Parliamentary Palace of Varieties, which is where members of the House of Lords and the House of Commons perform for charity. Little did I realise at the time that I'd end up working with Charlie Falconer as my Secretary of State, because he played Jim Hacker and I played Sir

233

Humphrey in this sketch, and now we are, almost a year later, actually working together.

Reality imitating art! When I tell friends that I work a good deal with civil servants, a number of questions commonly follow. They relate to the relationship between the civil service and ministers, about the role and impact of senior civil servants, about how policies are actually made, about who actually drives the affairs of state. I wonder if you could start us off by talking in general terms about the range and scope of the civil service and then say a little more about the role of the Permanent Secretary and his or her interaction with ministers.

Well, the civil service is still very large; we're talking of some hundreds of thousands of employees. Now, the vast majority of those people are, one way or another, delivering services direct to the public up and down the country, in my case, through courts and tribunals all over England and Wales; through benefits agencies, and all sorts of operational activities. Most of the policy development work, although this is changing to some extent, has been done traditionally, and is still to some extent done so, by a much smaller number of people mostly working in Whitehall. But one of the great changes that's occurred during my 36 years in the public service has been the way in which people in senior positions are expected now to have had both experience of really running things as well as sitting and thinking and advising; and if people want to have a successful career nowadays in the Government service, I think I would say to all the young people who join, "Make sure that you collect a portfolio of experience of actually being out there in the real world, running things, dealing directly with the public, as well as sitting in Whitehall, meeting ministers and writing them clever bits of advice".

During the Thatcher era, towards the end, the distinction arose between an Executive Agency and a central department, and my understanding is that at that stage it was thought that policy-making and service delivery could be divided and the notion was to set up these so-called Executive Agencies that would, in a more business-like way, be charged with the task of delivering service, while back at HQ, in the central departments, the policy would be made. How has that evolved in the 15 years or so since the idea was revealed?

Well indeed, when I went to the Treasury in 1988, I was very much involved in what was then called the Next Steps Programme, which was the beginning of the creation of all these agencies, and it was very understandable why that was done at the time. A lot of people criticised Whitehall for running, if you like, a command and control mechanism from the centre, so that everything was done by the rulebook, there was too little risk taking, and the whole process of trying to improve services did not have enough of a sharp focus. I think some great improvements were made as a result of that development through the 90s. I think now we've reached the point at which, while we don't want to throw that focus on service delivery away, what people are much more conscious of is if you make too sharp a break between policy development and actually running things out in the real world, you will get the policies wrong, and when you lob your policy over the wall to your Executive Agency, it will say this is not deliverable. So, what we're certainly engaged on very much in my department now is trying to make sure that the connection between those, for example, running the courts and those thinking up wonderful new policies to implement in respect of that are really joined up together.

In your department, the court service was conceived as a traditional Executive Agency, to some extent apart from the central policy-making body, namely, the Lord Chancellor's Department. You're suggesting they're coming together so that policy-making is more informed and inspired by experience out in the field, as it were?

Yes. If I was to bore you and everyone else with the organisation chart of what is now the Department for Constitutional Affairs, I think you would see a very different structure now from what you would have seen when I joined five years ago, with what is more fashionably, or used to be fashionably called, matrix management working, so that you do get a much greater intermingling of the policy thinkers and the deliverers than you would have had before.

Turning to policy-making itself, can you give us some sense of how that proceeds— social, economic, criminal policy? The Government of the day must either carry on with some line of policy thinking or develop and enhance new bodies of thinking. How does that happen, and as regards the civil servant's role and the senior policy-maker in the civil service, do they drive the policy, do they implement the policy, are they a catalyst for policy-making?

I think two comments on that. First of all, there is a moment in a political cycle when Governments change, and at that moment, the party that comes into power when there is a change has brought with it a manifesto of policy objectives which the civil service have not been involved in helping to formulate. That's a sort of, that's a defining moment. It happened in 1997. It happened in 1979. And in those circumstances there's a very important role for the civil service in providing the operational continuity but also demonstrating their ability to adapt to what may be a whole set of new ideas.

Once a Government is in place, and has got some maturity, the process of policy development, to my mind, is a result simply of a continuing dialogue between ministers and officials. You are always looking to see where you can make improvements, and that's part of the policy formation process. Some people would say too many initiatives are taken, but equally, you are listening to others outside, you are reacting to events. Out of all those ways, you can get new policy development formed.

What I think has happened, particularly over the last two or three years, is a much clearer determination to have policy worked out in a much more planned way, through projects and programme teams, so just as—and you and I have worked

235

together on these things—we might have some big information technology development project and programme. Say for example, if we are having a policy task of trying to look at the criminal justice system, you go through a process of very careful analysis—in this case, we invited Lord Justice Auld to give us some external view of what might be done. Then you set up a good and high quality team of people to think through how to carry that into action, and then you produce another team, as it were, to create the real events on the ground. So it is a much more, I think looking back over 30 years, it's now a rather more formalised process in many ways than it was when I first joined the civil service.

And who encouraged that more structured and systematic approach to project structure and programme management? Was that driven from civil servants or was that something many of the new ministers hankered after?

I think ministers, new ministers, under the present Government hankered after a more structured approach. A lot of the policy advisors who had worked with them looked for that. I think the civil service had recognised that we had to do this in a more deliberate way, particular in getting the connection between thinking up new ways of doing things, i.e. policy developments, and making sure they really happened. So they'd come back to that the connection between policy thinking and actually delivering improvements on the ground needed to be strengthened.

So the trickiest time therefore must be, I suppose, when a new Government comes into power. I would imagine it transpires that some of their policy objectives are unworkable, or perhaps too ambitious to be introduced all at once. There presumably follows a process of negotiation and discussion that leads to a manageable number of practicable initiatives. Is it indeed a tense and difficult period?

I can only speak for myself. I've not found it so. In my experience, that's actually rather an exciting period. If you're taking a professional view of what your job is, it's a good challenge to be confronted by a whole set of new policies. You've got to be grown up and realistic with ministers, new ministers who come in, about the cost of things, how long they might take, but what I think you have to avoid saying to them—this is a real *Yes Minister* remark—is to say to them, "Oh we thought of that 10 years ago and it didn't work"! This does not induce confidence and trust between new ministers and civil servants. So yes, there is a process of negotiation and dialogue and hammering things out, and not everything can be done overnight. But you will remember very clearly the speed with which the Government in '97 implemented the independence of the Bank of England. It was remarkably quickly done, I think within something like eight to 10 days of the election all that work was done. Now, of course there had been some thinking done by the Labour Party in opposition, and there clearly had been thinking in the Treasury against this eventuality, but it was done remarkably quickly. So, very occasionally, and I would say more often than not probably, the civil service can move with remarkable speed.

Is it very different working under Governments of different political complexions or is it the individual personalities that make one's life different as a civil servant?

I think, in professional terms, it's more personality in my view, in my experience, than party politically. I think that it's the personal relationship, particularly between Permanent Secretaries and ministers and other senior civil servants and ministers that matters. It's like a series if you like of arranged marriages. Your task is to make it work rather than not make it work. Given the way in which sometimes some ministers move around with great speed, you get through quite a number of marriages in quite a short period of time, and I managed to get through five in six years at the Department for Culture, Media and Sport. But each one of those worked differently, and out of each relationship you can get quite a lot of strength.

Let's focus on your own work in the Department for Constitutional Affairs. Can you, first of all, give us a sense of the scope of that department's activities, and then we can move on and talk about your specific role as Permanent Secretary. Thereafter we can talk about some substantive issues that have arisen recently that I think it would be useful for us all to reflect upon.

The traditional core activities, which we still continue—we can comment on further changes later on in the conversation—are essentially the running and management of the courts—most of the courts, not all of them—the appointment of the Judiciary and relations with the Judiciary, and the provision of legal aid—now about two billion pounds of public money in support of those people in the courts who require it or need it. There are lots of aspects of that which are more complicated, but they're the core central functions.

Can I interject on behalf of the audience? Can you clarify the division between civil and criminal work, and relate that to the respective responsibilities of the Home Office and your department?

There are three criminal justice departments, just to complicate life, in this country: the Home Office, ourselves, and the Crown Prosecution Service under the Attorney General. We deal with the criminal courts and their management and the appointment of the judges who sit there. The Home Office is responsible for criminal justice policy and criminal procedure, but some people will have observed the fact that we are now working much more closely with the Home Office and the Crown Prosecution Service in trying to get the whole criminal justice system to work more together. My department is certainly responsible both for civil justice policy and for the civil courts, although pretty well every department of Government, in one way or another, has policies which result in changes in the law, which will lead to new civil offences or new criminal offences. So that's basically how that works.

In relation to the management of courts, we are on the threshold of a major change in bringing together responsibility for the magistrates' courts and the court service-run courts, so that in 18 months time, the number of staff working in the courts will have doubled, well almost doubled, from 10,000 to 18,000, when we create this new unified court administration as an agency of the department. Beyond that, I expect that we will have a new unified tribunal service, again run by my department, which will add in another five thousand staff. So we're becoming quite a big service delivery organisation. Now, just to finish off, in addition to that, from the General Election of 2001 and then more functions in 2002 and then more functions in 2003, we have taken on a whole range of constitutional responsibilities in addition to our core justice functions from the Home Office, from the Cabinet Office, and most recently, from the Office of the Deputy Prime Minister. So we now have responsibility for the overall devolution settlement, for example, and I'm also responsible for the Scotland Office and the Wales Office. So we have substantially added to our portfolio, it's enriched the work of the department, and it now looks rather different than what it did five years ago.

Can we just jump back to tie a couple of strands together? Take the development of the policy thinking that led to the unification of the criminal courts and also of the reform to the tribunal system. These initiatives came under the umbrella of your department. But how did they evolve? I am keen that our audience can see in practice how long it takes to mount such programmes and how quickly you have in fact moved.

There have been three major moves to reform three parts, let's call them the three pillars of the justice system: civil, criminal and administrative. The civil reforms began with Lord Woolf's report, now quite some time ago; I think we're looking at 1996.

His interim report appeared in 1995 and the final report was published in 1996.[1]

You were involved in these. I was then dealing with arts and sport. When I arrived in the LCD in 1998, those reforms were beginning to come on-stream. They still took some time fully to come on-stream. A lot of that, as you know, was about better case management, more hands-on management of civil cases, and that had begun to have quite a remarkable effect. What then happened was the then Lord Chancellor, Lord Irvine, and I talked about the impact of that change, and we looked at the criminal courts and we thought, "well wait a minute, surely we ought to be trying to apply some of these principles in the criminal area", and there were other problems that we faced. So just as we had asked Harry Woolf to help us solve the problem of the civil courts, so we asked Robin Auld to go away with his team and think about what we should do in the criminal courts; a very deliberate process of saying, now we've addressed civil, let's address crime. And then similarly, we felt exactly the same needed to be done in relation to the scattering of administrative

---

[1] See Lord Woolf, *Access to Justice—Interim Report* (Woolf Inquiry Team, June 1995) and *Access to Justice—Final Report* (HMSO, July 1996). Also available at *www.dca.gov.uk*

tribunals all across Government. I think more people go through the tribunals in this country than go through all the civil courts, by a long margin, and they are dealing very directly with conflicts between the State and the citizen, and with employment disputes, and things that really matter to people. This has not been looked at for 50 years. I think the Franks Commission was the last time that anyone had looked seriously at administrative justice. So this was very deliberate, and as I say, the then Lord Chancellor and I decided we were going to have this sequence of reports, reviews and policy developments to deal with what I call the three pillars: civil, criminal and administrative justice. So it was a very planned programme. Of course, you can have these ideas; but you then have to persuade the rest of your colleagues in Government to agree with you, that sometimes takes a bit of time, but we've got there in each case in the end.

So, the process for each was, first of all, a judicial investigation or review or report, then, as I recall on every occasion, a fair period of consultation with all affected parties, moving thereafter towards legislation and change. The cycle consumed four or five years from cradle to grave. I think this is rather swifter than most people would imagine when they think of fundamental changes to the justice system.

They have taken a while, but not as long as I think they might have taken say two decades earlier. One of the most critical things in this area is getting the slot in the legislative programme for your Bill. Once you've secured that, then you know it is really going to happen, and then you can get on with planning the work.

I think you misunderstood me. I was actually suggesting that the reviews and their implementation were conducted quicker than people would have expected, rather than slower. But, talking of speed, can we move on to more controversial matters, because in mid-June of this year, it was announced, and it was out of the blue for many people, I think, that the role of the Lord Chancellor would be abolished. That has given rise to a whole bundle of activities and discussions and debates; and I thought we might track our way through these. I suppose there are two sets of issues here: there are the substantive issues in and around the abolition of the role of the Lord Chancellor, not to forget the matter of judicial appointments and the establishment of a new Supreme Court. But there's also, I think, a process issue, and I think it's as well we address it: many people were critical at the time that the announcements of constitutional reform were made that the new landscape had been sketched with the benefit of very little consultation, and, in particular, with virtually no consultation with the judges. You were at the heart of this. What's your response to these misgivings over process?[2]

I read very carefully the transcript of Harry Woolf and Igor Judge's press conference the other day and I very much approved on one thing which the Deputy Chief

---

[2] The role and the future of the role of the Lord Chancellor are also discussed by Lord Irvine (Chs 6 and 13), Lord Mackay (Ch.17), Lord Falconer (Ch.18), Professor Bogdanor (Ch.19) and Lord Woolf (Ch.20).

Justice, Lord Justice Judge, said in answer to a question, which was: "It's no good harping on about what happened in June. What we've now got to do is to get on and make sure that what happens, actually happens now, is done well".

Can I just say that I suspect the reason he made that point then was because he was anxious that the media should focus on the substantive views of the judges on the proposed reforms and should not let the debate be dominated by the question of who was consulted and how. Similarly, this evening, I do not wish the debate over process—over how the Government consulted and how the reforms were announced—to dominate, but I thought it might be useful to spend a few minutes on it.

Don't forget that the previous Lord Chancellor had announced before then that we were going to go ahead and consult on the creation of a Judicial Appointments Commission, that we were going to go ahead and consult on the future of Queen's Counsel.

Indeed, sitting in this very chair on the 29th of April 2003 . . .

I think he may have announced it.

He announced it then, because he had spoken to the newly appointed QCs on that very morning.

Absolutely. And so, we were clearly in a position before the announcement to review and look at what I call the old heartland of the Lord Chancellor's Department. So that change, those changes were in the pipeline, and I think when you reflect on that and see what the readiness was to think radically in these area, I would say—but then I would wouldn't I?—it's not necessarily surprising that the Prime Minister came to the view that it was no longer sustainable to have someone who was both the most senior judge in the country and also one of the most senior Cabinet ministers in the country. I know people were, in a sense, taken by surprise, but I think if people reflect on the arguments that have been going on for some time, they might come to the view that that sort of change was inevitable and the question wasn't therefore whether it occurred, but when it occurred. And obviously, if you make an announcement that you're going abolish something which has existed for a thousand years, there is a slight intake of breath—understatement of the year for some! But you also have to decide whether you proceed that way, or whether you say—and this is a legitimate discussion to have—whether you say, "Well I'm thinking that we might do this, you know, I'd quite like to know what people think". I think that's fine where you have a defined issue of public policy, but if you raise a question mark in that way, or the Government does, over a particular role of such sensitivity, I think there is a case that it could be damaging, because you get in for a long period of debilitating argument about whether a particular office or role should continue to exist. So there are other ways of looking at this development from just simply the "shock, horror, goodness gracious, look what they've done" approach. I think that people have quite quickly settled down to concentrate on the real issues that now arise, and through the consultation process we're having at the moment.

I think there were two issues. One was that people were saying, "We should have been consulted". We won't discuss that again this evening. Others were saying, "We wonder if the full set of ramifications of the abolition of that office had been thought through". Presumably you are now teasing out the strands of that second area. Let's focus on some issues of substance then. The Supreme Court is an interesting topic, and one on which people sitting in the very chair you're in tonight have expressed a view. Lord Bingham, for example, said quite clearly that he approved of a Supreme Court, and others who've been guests of mine at Gresham College have agreed with him. However, if one looks at the response of the Law Lords themselves to the proposal to set up a Supreme Court in place of the House of Lords as the final court of appeal in the country, they are divided on that very issue. I thought, to ease our audience in gently, we could perhaps give a little bit of background to the work of the House of Lords in its judicial capacity and the broad recommendations that there should be a new Supreme Court.[3]

The creation of a Supreme Court, in the sense that we're now discussing it, I think was meant to take place—there may be people in this audience who know the right date—but it was meant to happen I think in 1876, or possibly even earlier, but we take a little time sometimes, despite the suddenness of the June announcement, it sometimes takes a little time for people to get round to major constitutional change.

What is actually technically known as the Appellate Committee of the House of Lords is of course the final court for difficult issues of the law in the United Kingdom as a whole, and it links up with work that's done by the Judicial Committee of the Privy Council in relation to some overseas territories that bring their cases here. They, if I may say so without sounding sycophantic, are a very distinguished bunch of very senior and very good lawyers indeed, and I think the general view internationally is that the quality of the judgments they come to in this country is very, very high.

The problem I think was both an issue of substance and an issue of perception. The substance is, is it right in the modern world that the highest court of the land should actually be a part of the Parliament and that judgments are given in the chamber of the House of Lords? That is an issue. The Senior Law Lord has made his views perfectly clear; he thinks that is no longer the right way to do things. But there is also an issue of perception—I'm sure if you asked most people what the Law Lords were they thought they were a group of Parliamentarians first and foremost rather than the highest court in the land, and again, I think you've also got to deal with the issue of perception, which of course came up in the Pinochet case. I think

---

[3] The judicial work of the House of Lords and the possibility of a new Supreme Court are also discussed by Lord Bingham (Ch.7), Lord Saville (Ch.14), Lord Mackay (Ch.17), Lord Falconer (Ch.18) and Lord Woolf (Ch.20).

by creating a new Supreme Court, it's going to have the same responsibilities as the Appellate Committee of the House of Lords, but separate from Parliament and in its own right. In my view, it's one of those things whose time has come.

I just read today, and I hadn't read it before, Lord Hobhouse's additional set of observations, written by him as a supplement to the Law Lords' response to the consultation paper on the new Supreme Court. Basically, it seems to me he is saying two things: first, he is saying he doesn't believe a business case has been made out in support of the establishment of a Supreme Court. Secondly, and constitutionally, he is saying something rather different, namely that a lot of the arguments in favour of setting up a Supreme Court are based on what he claims is a misunderstanding of the doctrine of Separation of Powers, which has traditionally been expressed as the proposition that the Legislature, the Executive and the Judiciary should be kept entirely separate. Lord Hobhouse suggests what is more important, and always has been more important, is the doctrine of judicial independence, which he claims—and I'm not supporting this, I'm just offering a rendition of his argument—that judicial independence means independence from the Executive but not necessarily independence from the Legislature. He does not accept that judges engaging as legislators necessarily prejudice the independence of the Judiciary; but he does argue that there has to be a very clear independence between judicial activities and Executive activities. I've never seen that rendering before. It amounts, it seems to me, to a watered down version of the Separation of Powers doctrine.

In any event, I wonder how relevant discussions of constitutional theory might be, because the pragmatist in me wants to know this—is it definitely going to happen? Will we certainly have a new Supreme Court, such that there is little point in debating its merits and demerits, justifications and criticisms? I know that the establishment of this new court has been set as an objective, but could it yet be that the business case is not sufficiently strong or that other, better safeguards might be put in place to keep the judges independent? Or, in political terms, is this a dead certainty and now the only question is one of how best to implement it?

Well, I can't predict that Parliament will pass the legislation. When you listen to the Queen's Speech tomorrow, I think this will be one of the measures that will be included in the Queen's Speech. I think what you said, and I haven't read what John Hobhouse has written, shows that there is scope for differing views on the subject. I'm in the happy position of being able to explain the Government's policy rather than enter into the debate. The only practical point I'd make, which I'm sure is not necessarily the sort of point that some Law Lords would make, is that when you look around the world, on the whole, you see advanced democratic countries making a distinction between the Legislature and the Executive and the Judiciary, and not just between two parties of the State. Look at the United States, Australia and New Zealand and Canada; in practice, what most of, what all of these countries have done is to make distinctions between the membership of the three branches and not keep a coalescence or conflation of two in one.

Yes. I think it is hard for many people to understand that judges may enjoy a legislative as well as a judicial function. One of the counter-arguments is that the Legislature,

242

and in our case that is to say the House of Lords, has benefited enormously from the insight of judges when new legislation was being introduced, or new policies and principles were being discussed. But, of course, the consultation paper itself suggests that it may be possible to have retired Supreme Court Justices as Lords and, I think it's true to say that on this issue the Law Lords are again divided. Some feel that a select few senior judges should still be allowed in the Legislature and others don't. It's a fascinating phenomenon, is it not, that the Law Lords' response is, in five or six places, divided. (You can see from the footnotes in the document who is for and against the contentious issues.[4])

And that reflects the way in which they of course give judgments.

Absolutely.

They have behaved absolutely in their normal mode.

This does rather help politicians and policy-makers, however, because for almost every proposition, you have at least some distinguished Law Lords in support. Quite unlike that, however, I think is the response of the Judges' Council, which I think speaks more in one voice. Also, as you mentioned, there's also a fascinating transcript available online of the accompanying media conference held by the Lord Chief Justice, Lord Woolf, and the Deputy Chief Justice, Lord Justice Judge. You can read all the questions and the responses, which I think in many ways is more revealing and interesting than the 110 page or so document.[5]
*   A related issue that I would like to explore is the public purse. I think Lord Woolf powerfully makes the point that there are many courts up and down the land, or at least some, that have leaking roofs. If you were to re-accommodate the Law Lords in a suitable building, which would need, I would have thought, to be a grand building, that's clearly going to be a very expensive exercise, when such funds could perhaps be put to better use, perhaps even repairing roofs. This goes to the heart of Lord Hobhouse's suggestion, that the business case has not yet been made. Are we at the stage of investigating buildings or is that premature?*

No, no, we're investigating buildings; we've got to get on with it. We would hope we'd have somewhere for them to live when the legislation has gone through, and you've clearly got to look at something which is wholly suitable for a Supreme Court of the United Kingdom. I think though that it's easy to exaggerate the resource tension here. We, for example, have been . . . We have plans for a whole range of court buildings across the country, which I won't bore you or the audience with the detail of, and for example, in Manchester, the civil justice courts in Manchester are

---

[4] *www.dca.gov.uk*
[5] *www.dca.gov.uk*

appalling, in appalling condition, and we are taking action to deal with that. We're going to build a new civil justice centre in Manchester, the result of an architectural competition, an absolutely splendid modern building. So I don't think that simply as a result of having to find a new Supreme Court we will do serious damage to our responsibilities to the rest of the country and to the ordinary courts through which ordinary people go.

Let's put the Supreme Court to one side; I think we've have explored that enough. What about the question of QCs and the appointment of QCs, and whether or not indeed QCs should be called such? Could you give the audience some sense of the issues here?[6]

Yes, I shall be very careful on this subject, because unlike the Supreme Court or a Judicial Appointments Commission, the Government has not said which way it is going to move on this. I think there have been criticisms of the Queen's Counsel system for some time. These rather crystallised in a report from the Office of Fair Trading, which said when it looked at the arrangement it thought that basically it was anti-competitive, and that what was being done here was to select a relatively few well-qualified, on the whole barristers, to be given this status, as a result of which, it was alleged, they increased their salaries vastly, not necessarily to the general benefit of the population at large. That was the criticism. This was hotly countered of course by a lot of people in the legal profession and others, and this debate has been going on. We put out a consultation document ourselves some time ago, which started to ask some questions about whether it was any longer sustainable to have this system, and that included also the issue of whether it was right—and this is the other issue—whether it was right that the Government should intervene in the private sector market in order to give promotions to a group of lawyers. Where else, people said, does that happen in the United Kingdom? After all, as far as I know, the Secretary of State for Health doesn't promote people to be consultants, and nor does the Government appoint professors, and so why did the Government intervene in the legal services market to do this? Now, we've asked those questions quite openly. We've asked what public benefit there is in the system. Do we need this, in the modern words, quality kite mark, or do all the solicitors' firms have enough intelligence and information about who's good or bad as an advocate to provide a service to their clients? Consultation closed on the 7th of November. We've got all the information in that we're going to get in. We now have to sit down and make a judgment as to what we're going to do, and on that, my lips are sealed.

One question—clearly, if you can't answer it, please don't—on timing: when do you think the Government's likely to formulate its policy?

---

[6] The future of QCs is also discussed by Lord Irvine (Ch.13), Lord Falconer (Ch.18) and Lord Woolf (Ch.20).

Oh, I think that we're going to have to come to a view and make an announcement I expect at some point in the early New Year, but I don't think it will be before then.

Appointment of judges—that's another hotly contested issue. Again, if you can give us, by way of context, an overview of the debate, we can then perhaps dip into a few of the issues in more detail.[7]

For a long time now, despite all the improvements I think we've made in the system, there has been criticism from some quarters that the appointments of the Judiciary were largely in the hands of a single minister, the Lord Chancellor, who was both judge and Cabinet minister—we are back to the issue of abolition. There have been criticisms that it was skewed towards people choosing new judges in their own image, that we weren't open enough to the diversity of the population of lawyers who were around to be appointed, particularly criticisms in relation to black and ethnic minority lawyers coming through as judges, and also to a degree gender issues, about the lack of female judges. So there have been a number of criticisms around, to some extent growing. Over the last, what, six or seven years, starting under James Mackay, the whole process of making these appointments has been substantially tightened up. Up to, but not yet including the High Court, it's done on the basis of an application only. There's an interview process, a senior civil servant, a judge and a lay member interviewing the candidate.

Is that up to and including the High Court?

No, up to but not including the High Court. There has been, and this is both criticised and applauded, depending on your point of view, a very systematic process of consultation with the community, the peer group community, and judges who are seeing people to get their comments on individuals. So a great deal of information is in fact available about this, but I think the heart of the issue had become whether or not this was a sustainable position for the longer term, that so much power and influence appeared to be concentrated in the hands of one minister, whatever constraints he had voluntarily placed upon himself. About two-and-a-half years ago, the then Lord Chancellor and I decided that what we ought to do in any event to try to improve the sense of what is now called transparency, i.e. openness, and have an audit trail, was to appoint a body, known as the Judicial Appointments Commission, with an inspecting, auditing function. We got that going; that seemed to those who live in the world of the Judiciary and the law in itself quite a major step. I think that has proved really very effective in opening up the subject to greater debate, and I think the present Commission has played quite a considerable part in moving that debate forward.

---

[7] The appointment of judges is also discussed by Lord Bingham (Ch.7), Lord Irvine (Ch.13), Lord Mackay (Ch.17), Lord Falconer (Ch.18) and Professor Bogdanor (Ch.19).

As I said earlier, Richard, we'd got to the stage earlier this year, before the changes of the 12th of June, of coming to a clear conclusion that we had to open up the issue about whether there should be an independent Judicial Appointments Commission, so that the power and influence of the Executive, of Ministers in this area, was much more constrained than had been the case in the past. That is where we are going. That is the direction in which we are moving.

I'll make one comment on the concerns of the Judges' Council, which is very much about the independence of the Judiciary being sustained. The object of all the measures we've so far announced is to enhance that independence rather than undermine it, but we had got ourselves into a frame of mind in this country, because of the central position of the Lord Chancellor, that somehow that office was the protector of judicial independence, of independence of the appointments system. Looked at logically, and through the experience of other countries and other jurisdictions, that actually is a rather difficult argument to sustain for the future, which is why we would argue that the proposals the Government is now making are designed actually to enhance judicial independence rather than to undermine it.

Concerns over judicial independence are really at the heart of the Judges' Council's response to the consultation paper on constitutional reform. The most extreme challenge, or line of argument, is that if you have a Government that can take so radical a step in relation to the Judiciary as to remove the office of Lord Chancellor, then how can we ensure that the newly articulated independence of the Judiciary is safeguarded with appropriate checks and balances in place? What mechanisms might achieve that? A phrase that has been used is a "constitutional settlement" enacted through statute, based on some kind of concordat between the judges and the Lord Chancellor.[8] I think the consequence of the swiftness of the announcement and the lack of consultation have given rise to a climate in which the issue of judicial independence has become a key sensitivity, and I wondered what your response is to that? You said that in many ways a number of the changes are designed to enhance judicial independence. How can we offer judges the comfort they need that they will function independently in the future? Is the notion of a constitutional settlement appropriate?

Well yes, I think it is. I would say that we want to respond absolutely positively to that concern. As I say, the object of the announcements was clearly to separate the Executive from the Judiciary, not to have muddied waters and muddled thinking. One of the key objects of that is to make sure the independence of the Judiciary is ensured, through legislation, which the Government will bring forward. We have got to find, it may not be too grand actually to call it a new constitutional settlement, about the relationship between the Executive and the Judiciary in a whole range of areas that affect the Judiciary, which we will have to put through. The best mechanism to give assurance and comfort to those who are concerned is to show them what safeguards and checks and balances we intend to put in place for the future, lay that out in legislation where legislation is required, have that debated thoroughly

---

[8] The constitutional settlement and the concordat are also discussed by Lord Falconer (Ch.18), Professor Bogdanor (Ch.19) and Lord Woolf (Ch.20).

through Parliament, and try to persuade people during that whole process—which will take place over the next month through the next year—that we have thought this through and we are very concerned to make sure that judicial independence is at the heart of the new constitutional settlement that emerges after the abolition of the office of Lord Chancellor.

Is this going to be one big bang or will be it be, in timing terms, phased? That is to say, will the abolition of the office of the Lord Chancellor, of the role of the Lord Chancellor, coincide with the establishment of the Supreme Court and a new judicial appointments structure, or are we too early yet to know what the critical path might look like?

I would like to feel that we were capable of it all happening on one day, because that would be the cleanest and smoothest way to proceed, but I think it's a bit too early to tell. A lot depends on the Parliamentary passage, a lot depends, in relation to the Supreme Court, whether we have a building ready or not. I think in relation to creating a Judicial Appointments Commission, you have probably got to build up its workload over a bit of a period of time to avoid a hiatus. For example, it might not be sensible on day one when it is set up for them to take on the appointment of all of the 30,000 lay magistrates in this country. It might be more sensible for the department, with suitable arrangements, to hang on to that responsibility for a while. But no, I think basically, what we want to try to do is to reach a point at which, having abolished the office of Lord Chancellor, these other organisations can be ready to function, and that enables me to say one other thing about the change that was made. There is another strand in all of this, other than constitutional change, which is to enable the department and its Secretary of State to focus much more on the delivery of services to the public. When you think, as I was saying earlier, that the department is, what, now 12,000 strong, it will be 20,000 strong in 18 months' time; it will be 25,000 thousand strong in three years' time; you are talking about a pretty large department of Government, and a turnover, if I can put it that way, of three billion pounds a year. So that is in itself comparatively a very large job indeed, and it's quite difficult to provide all the political focus you need on that work, which is in the public interest, if you have a major pre-occupation with being also the head of the Judiciary at the same time. That's part of the rationale of what we're doing. And also, frankly, for the Lord Chancellor and I to live in the House of Lords, and all of our staff to live in a series of buildings in Victoria Street and elsewhere is not, I have to say, a very efficient way of doing business in the modern world, and I think there can be advantages for the whole department in that change being made, which would of course be facilitated when the Lord Chancellor is no longer Speaker of the House of Lords and does not have to sit on the woolsack every day.

You are migrating as it were?

At the moment, we're nomads. We travel backwards and forwards up and down Victoria Street. In the mornings, we're in our modern offices in Victoria Street, and in the afternoons you can find us in our Pugin splendour in the House of Lords.

I suppose when historians look back on this period, from say 1995 to 2005, it may be seen as having endured more change in the legal system, in the justice system, than any decade in history—when you think of the changes in the civil, criminal, and tribunal systems, in the structure of the Judiciary. An exciting time to work? Have you enjoyed your time as a Permanent Secretary?

I have—you're doing my lines for me now, this is very good. When I decided to try to become Permanent Secretary in the Lord Chancellor's Department, I did it both because I felt I had done six years in the previous job and that was enough and I thought it was time to move on, but also because I had seen what was going on. I'd worked in the Home Office for quite a while, I knew a bit about the justice system, and it seemed to me that the Prime Minister and the then Lord Chancellor had a pretty radical agenda in mind for the justice system and for the Lord Chancellor's Department, so I was willing to put my name forward and fortunate enough to get the job. Some people said to me, "Why on earth would you want to go there? It's a very strange place!". They said, "You ask the Lord Chancellor's Department what it thinks and it tells you what the judges think. Then you ask them can they do something and the answer is no". They conveyed this wholly negative impression. I don't think that if someone was looking at the department now that caricature would hold at all, and so it has been a very exciting period. I mean I, like you, I try to explain to people who don't know about this world in which I now live, how radical and rapid have been a whole series of changes that have been going on, and how even the department that I joined in 1998 is much less recognisable now for those of us inside it and involved in Whitehall and much different from what it was. So it has been a very exciting thing to do.

More generally, finally in fact, just as I always ask my legal guests how they would advise a student who was contemplating a career in law, then, similarly, can I ask of you—if speaking to a student contemplating a career in the civil service, what would you say to them?

I wouldn't necessarily say to them, first of all, "you should contemplate a career in law rather than the civil service", although for my own part, my 15-year-old son has made it quite clear that that is what he wants to do and he does not wish to be a civil servant. However I have one daughter who does. I would say to them two things. Personally, I've had a fantastically varied and rewarding career, in a whole range of departments and also working in the European Commission in Brussels. From 1974 onwards, every single job I've had has been intrinsically interesting and increasingly, as I've moved through the system, closer and closer to doing really important things and being engaged in really important public issues. If that's what you like, and it can be enormously motivating, then that reward is still there, so I would encourage people to join. I was tremendously encouraged to read the other day in the newspapers that the fast stream of the civil service, the top graduate entry bit, had been reckoned to be the first choice last year for people's careers and had come back again to what it was like in the late 1960s when I joined. Over the last year, 14,500 people applied to join the fast stream for 411 places. Now,

I hope that tells you something about people's level of interest in public service in the modern world, which was not always fashionable, frankly, through the 80s and 90s, but I hope it is becoming fashionable again. I would be very encouraging about it.

Sir Hayden, it has been a pleasure having you with us. Thank you.

CHAPTER SIXTEEN

John Gardner
Professor of Jurisprudence, University of Oxford

Wednesday February 25, 2004

Until now in my Gresham interviews I have spoken largely to judges and to legal practitioners, but our insight into law has surely been incomplete so far because we have had no exposure to the academic legal world. In pondering who might actually fill that gap, I thought immediately of tonight's guest, John Gardner, who is Professor of Jurisprudence at Oxford. Now, we'll be talking in greater detail about what jurisprudence is but, at this stage, I simply want to say it is one of the more academic and theoretical aspects of legal study, and so is an ideal topic, I think, for Gresham College. Indeed, it is ironic, as a college, that we haven't had an academic here sooner.

John, as I say, is the Professor of Jurisprudence at Oxford and he took up that prestigious chair at the remarkably young age of 35. He was educated at school in Glasgow and then studied at Oxford. He's held a variety of positions, at King's College, London and at Oxford, but his academic life has been focused on legal theory. He has, therefore, been thinking deeply about a variety of legal issues, and I want to give some insight tonight into the kinds of matters that occupy a jurisprudent.

John, welcome, it's great to have you with us.

Thanks very much.

Can we start off with what I know, because I used to teach jurisprudence myself, is a vexed question—what is jurisprudence?

In Oxford, we advertise our undergraduate law course under the grand title of "the Honour School of Jurisprudence", and we mean that to be taken seriously. Literally translated, "jurisprudence" means wisdom about law. When we teach law, we don't mainly have in mind that we'll teach people to be lawyers, although many of them do become lawyers. We have in mind that we'll teach them some legal wisdom. To acquire this legal wisdom, the students take the law of contract, and criminal law, and all those predictable things. But they also do a course called "jurisprudence" and this is jurisprudence in a more specific sense. It means the theory or philosophy of law. What an undergraduate student would study under this heading would be big timeless problems about law. What is law? Why do we have it? When is it legitimate? What are judges for? How should we understand what judges do? Those questions arise not just in the English legal system, not just in the common law world, but everywhere where there's a legal system, and one of the things we investigate with the students is to what extent the answers are the same everywhere, and to what extent they vary from one legal system to another.

When I was involved in jurisprudence, largely in the late 1970s until the mid 1980s, it was marvellously alive: very exciting; innumerable conflicting schools of thought; everything that one would want in philosophical debate. To some extent, I have left that world now. Has much happened in the past decade or so? Is jurisprudence still thriving? Has it peaked? Where are we?

Maybe I'm not the person to ask. Obviously I think it's at its very peak now! Seriously, the subject has moved in the last 50 years from the hands of lawyers, straight legal academics, into the hands of philosophers. Most of the people who teach and study in my area now did their doctoral research in philosophy more than in law, and that's made the whole thing in a way more technical and less accessible. But there are more people doing it nevertheless; it's a much bigger operation. In Oxford at the moment, in a law faculty of about 70, there are 10 or 12 people who are philosophers by training rather than, or as well as, lawyers.

And you're certainly not the person to ask my next question. In my day, as it were, Oxford was the global home of jurisprudence. Is that still the case?

In the late 1980s, when I was a graduate student in Oxford, the intellectual scene was buzzing. Then in the early 90s, when I had my first teaching job there, Oxford went rather quiet as a place to study the philosophy of law. At that point, things seemed to be most alive in New York. But now we're at another point in the cycle, and Oxford is arguably the liveliest place to be again. We're certainly attracting an extraordinary number of excellent postgraduate students. These fluctuations are not mainly because of changes in personnel. In fact, some of the most important personnel have been constant for many years. Mostly the changes have been in other places, in the external environment. At the moment, we're the beneficiaries of a new enthusiasm for anglophone philosophy of law among Continental Europeans, as well as what seems to be a new intellectualism among Commonwealth law students.

Let's try now to create the flavour of jurisprudence. I propose we do this in two stages. First of all, we might focus on some classical jurisprudential issues, and then we can follow up with some insight into your own current research interests. One way to start is with your two immediate predecessors, both extremely eminent figures: Ronald Dworkin, and before him, Herbert Hart. There was in the world of jurisprudence, indeed there still is, something known as the Hart-Dworkin debate.[1] *Here we have two intellectual titans at cerebral war with one another for many years, and the conflict actually became quite lively. I wondered if we could chat about this.*

Yes, the conflict strikes me as lively too, but then again, I'm a philosopher, and I find strange things lively. One interesting feature is that it wasn't ever clear what Hart and Dworkin were fighting about. Or at least it wasn't clear over time, because the debate moved on, and a reply would be met by a rejoinder that somewhat changed the topic. So part of the excitement was not knowing what was going to happen. It wasn't just always more of the same.

It all started with what seemed like a very simple and unostentatious claim that H.L.A. Hart made in a famous book called *The Concept of Law*, which was the claim that in any legal system—this is true, he said, everywhere where you find law— you'll find there's a rule which tells you what are the ultimate sources of law in that system. In English law, for instance, there is the rule that what the Queen in Parliament enacts is law. Hart admitted that this was a simplified version of the rule that applies in England, but he gave it as an example of the kind of rule he had in mind. He called it a "rule of recognition". He said anywhere you find law, you'll find such a rule; every legal system has to have one. The way that it would identify law would be by identifying people, officials, who had the right to make law, and in the case of English law, it was Parliament, or "the Queen in Parliament", which is the technical term.

Dworkin—amazingly inspired, especially as a young scholar—made an attack on that idea in his very first article. He said that legal systems have another basis: it's not this rule of recognition, it's a domain of legal principle which nobody ever created, which isn't the work of any officials. If you want to know what the domain of principle contains, it contains an idealised version of what's going on in the courts. If you look at the courts, you'll see officials doing their mundane, humdrum things, sometimes getting it right, sometimes getting it wrong, but if you abstract from the humdrum things they are doing, you'll discover a set of guiding principles, an ideal that they're all aspiring to live up to. This ideal can't be made directly by any officials, so it can't be included in what Hart called a rule of recognition. And so Dworkin offered an alternative way of understanding the basis of a legal system.

You can see straight away why it is a rival approach, not a complementary one. Hart had said that all law is made by officials. Dworkin answered: "Here's some law that isn't. Every legal system has principles that are related to what the officials say, but are not themselves made by officials". Well, so far so good. But as time went on, Dworkin's work became more ambitious and it became harder and harder to understand whether there was a difference between him and Hart, and if so, what it was. By the 1980s Dworkin was contemplating not just the nature of judging, not just the nature of law, but the nature of concepts and the nature of philosophy. The earlier criticisms of Hart became somewhat lost in the process. Personally, I found Dworkin's earlier criticisms more fruitful.

---

[1] See, for example, H.L.A. Hart, *The Concept of Law* (2nd ed., Clarendon Press, Oxford, 1994) and Ronald Dworkin, *Taking Rights Seriously* (Duckworth, London, 1977).

But there was, literally, a postscript on all of this, wasn't there, because Hart's book, The Concept of Law, *was first published in 1961. However it was after his death, wasn't it, in 1994, that a postscript to the book emerged.[2] Can you take over the story?*

Well, it was biographically very interesting, because as time went on Hart became more and more pained by the intellectual distance between him and Dworkin. He felt it was his duty to respond to Dworkin's later work. It was never going to be the last word, because it was quite clear that Dworkin would continue the debate after Hart's death, as indeed he did. But Hart felt that he should nevertheless offer an authoritative restatement of his position that joined issue with Dworkin's more ambitious 1980s work. You can tell when you read the result that Hart was not enjoying the task. It doesn't hang together very nicely, and he gets some of his own earlier positions into a bit of a muddle. In fact, this was reflected in the way the writing was done. Hart died in 1992, but he wrote the postscript in the 1980s. He kept several drafts on the go, and he amended one and then forgot that he had done it and amended another one, so when the editors came to put it all together after Hart's death, they had a tricky job. There were often rival suggestions in the rival drafts and it wasn't clear which, if any, was Hart's final view. The editors did a fantastic job in the circumstances but they were editors, not authors, and they couldn't just write their own improved version to hide the obvious problems Hart had experienced in formulating his replies.

You've mentioned Hart's rule of recognition. More generally, a popular characterisation of Hart's position is that his is a rule-based theory of law. He talks about there being two forms of rules in a society, those that confer powers and those that impose duties, and then he talks about the necessity for rules of change, which allow rules to be changed, and then he talks about rules of adjudication that allow judges to settle disagreements. So people often say that Hart's is very much a rule-based model of the law, and then along comes Dworkin, who says that to understand the law purely in terms of rules is to miss something far more fundamental.

You've already hit on a point at which Hart and Dworkin were at cross purposes. Dworkin thought his job was to be a kind of abstract legal practitioner, to give philosophical advice to judges and lawyers about how they ought to proceed. In fact he thought it was the job of all jurisprudence, including Hart's jurisprudence, to provide that kind of advice. Hart, by contrast, had no such ambition for himself. He didn't have any views, at least none that he disclosed in his work, about how judges should decide cases or lawyers should argue them. So far as we know, he wasn't in favour of judges doing what Dworkin said judges should do, but he also said nothing against it. He just didn't discuss it. He was discussing what had to be there before we got to the question of what judges should do. When people claim that Hart's thinking was very rule-based, they often build into that claim the thought that, according to Hart, judges should spend their lives looking up rules. That's

---

[2] In H.L.A. Hart, *The Concept of Law* (2nd ed., Clarendon Press, Oxford, 1994).

just not something that Hart ever said, or suggested, or even discussed. So far as we know from his work, he would have been as happy with a world in which there were very few rules, and judges therefore had to do a lot of creative thought, as with a world where there were many rules and therefore judges had to do very little creative thought. All he said was there have to be some rules, including a rule of recognition, and that's where it all begins.

But he makes it very clear, doesn't he, in his introduction to The Concept of Law *that his is a work of description whereas, as you say, Dworkin's is actually a mix of prescription and description. That's why it's quite hard to understand often.*

It can be hard to understand, because Dworkin said on the one hand here's an ideal for judging, and then he said on the other hand that this ideal has to be present and operating wherever there's judging, even when judges are doing badly relative to it. That's quite a complicated thought, isn't it? It is a thought about the real, non-ideal world that depends on a thought about the ideal world.

Why don't we clarify the matter by focussing on one of the concrete cases that Dworkin discusses, relating to the chap who murders his grandfather to inherit under the latter's will.

Yes, good idea. So what does Dworkin have to say about that? At the time of the case, one could imagine—indeed there were—two conflicting views about what should happen. On the one hand, you had a law of inheritance which said that the will is to be honoured—I'm simplifying, but something like that. On the other hand, you had the thought, which hadn't yet been applied to such a case but which had emerged in some other legal contexts, that nobody should profit from their own wrong. The question which arose for the court was how to go forward with a case like this. Dworkin argues that the way to do this is to take the cases that you have and see if you can come up with principles that, so far as possible, unify them, and that are also morally acceptable, and then you know the answer to the new case that comes before you. I suspect that Hart, on the other hand, would just have said this: "There's a legal conflict between the rule about honouring wills and the rule about not profiting from wrongs and somebody has to decide what to do—I, Hart, have no idea how. Somebody else has to write that book—maybe Dworkin!". So you can see how the cross-purposes infect even this example. Hart never actually discussed the case, so I don't know—I'm obviously putting words into his mouth.

I'd like to touch on something with which I always struggled. My research, broadly in this area, was to do with how you could computerise the law and legal reasoning, and so I was naturally sympathetic to an approach to the law which could actually break it down into rules that could then be processed. That was one of my key interests. And sometimes, when I read Dworkin's work, it seemed to me that he would have thought that kind of rule processing would be absolutely incorrect while, on other occasions, I thought he might concede that, yes, you've got to have a go with rules first of all, before you find out, or can find out, that there is a need for some kind of further reasoning, say, about principle or purpose.

Your predicament is a very common predicament, and many of my doctoral students today struggle with a similar thought. To see why it's difficult, let me reconceptualise this as a cultural problem. Dworkin came to Oxford from Yale, and from an American tradition of law school education. The debates that flourished in Britain were debates of quite a rarefied kind compared to the ones that flourished in America. In America, it was the job of a law school professor to make a difference to the law, and the big debates in the American law schools had been not about, not really about, the nature of a legal system, but about the thinking and the functions and the purposes of judges and lawyers. Going back before Dworkin, there had been a really major debate about this, which hadn't just afflicted trained philosophers of law, but every law school professor. Do we think of the law as a sort of autonomous discipline which contains all the material needed to answer all its own questions? Or do we think of the law as really just a sort of sugar coating for a lot of material that's borrowed from outside—a bit of economics, a bit of psychology, here's some morality, you stir it all all together, and then you put some legal icing on top. The "legal formalists" were the people who said, "it's our discipline, it's special, you come to law school and you learn a different and autonomous intellectual discipline with us—it's not psychology, it's not morality, it's not economics." The "legal realists" were those who said, "hah, law school, that's just a way of providing the sugar coating for all those other materials that are really supplying the nutrional value".

Dworkin is a fantastic hybrid character in that debate. On the one hand, he stands with the formalist tradition in saying that the law can answer all of its own questions. The answers are all to be found in the law. You'll find them if you look deep enough behind the cases to the principles that justify them, and those principles are part of the law already; you don't need an official to tell you that, they're already there. So that's a formalist instinct. On the other hand, he has a legal realist instinct, which is to say that those same principles answer to political morality. They're not only legal, they come into the law using moral argument, and judges therefore have to engage in moral argument. Law is not an autonomous discipline in the way that the formalists hoped, and law schools therefore have to provide a moral education. So Dworkin's at the junction of those two traditions. A fantastically original set of ideas, as everyone can agree. The problem is that, in a move that history will I think come to regard as bizarre, Dworkin superimposes all these amazing ideas on a completely different and almost entirely unrelated set of philosophical puzzles that had intrigued Hart. These other philosophical puzzles tend to seem unimportant to an American law school professor because they don't have pay-offs for how lawyers, or anyone else, should behave. They don't make and aren't intended to make a difference to the way that any court should decide any case. In the UK, we have a different intellectual tradition in the law schools, with nothing analogous to the historic struggle between the realists and the formalists. That's probably because we have nothing remotely like the American Supreme Court, and people don't spend all their nights awake worrying about the legitimacy of the Lord Chief Justice or the question of whether the next judge to be appointed will be a Democrat or a Republican.

Let's lead from that, quite naturally I think, to the question of judges and jurispru-
dence, because one of the main preoccupations of jurisprudence, and we've touched on
this already, is, on the one hand, to seek to describe and explain how it is that judges
as a matter of fact go about making their decisions and, on the other hand, to prescribe,
to recommend a particular methodology or approach. What fascinates me is the extent
to which this theoretical thinking actually has impact on judges. I was listening to
Radio 4 one day and Lord Bingham, who's sat in the Gresham interview seat in the
past, was on the programme, as indeed you were, alongside another jurisprudence
expert and another judge, as I recall. Clive Anderson was conducting proceedings. It
was a rather bizarre discussion, because the other jurisprudence expert seemed to be
saying, actually to real judges, that no matter what you think about how you go about
your judicial decision-making, here is actually (a) how you do do it, and (b) how you
ought to do it. They seemed rather flummoxed by this. In fact, it seemed to me that that
legal theorist was speaking a different language from the judges.[3]

I think that's true. Compared with the picture Dworkin paints of the Herculean judge, most judging, at least in the UK, is less self-conscious and less ambitious about what it's for and what justifies or legitimates it. One of the questions that you have to think about if you're a philosopher of any subject is to what extent you trust the appearances, to what extent you take the practices you are analysing at face value. On one view, you should normally trust the appearances. People make mistakes, but if you look closely enough at exactly what they are doing and how they interrelate with what they are doing, you will be able to understand their mistakes in their own terms, without imposing a whole new scheme. At the other extreme, some think that we are all blighted by false consciousness. Nothing we think about anything can be trusted to be free of self-deception and pathological delusion. Now, it's a general problem when you study a subject: to what extent do you take things as they seem? Personally, I tend to veer towards trusting the appearances. When somebody asks me about judges, I tend to look at the way judges themselves articulate their own work when they are doing it, so I take seriously categories that judges themselves use, like "overruling" and "distinguishing". A judge says, "I overrule another judge", and I think to myself, "That's interesting. What's that all about? How is that possible? What sort of rules do there need to be to make that possible?". But Dworkin is more inclined to think that what meets the eye isn't most of what there is to it and that one should go behind categories like "overruling" and "distinguishing" and replace them with other categories. In the end, he replaced almost every category with the category "interpretation", which is such a big category it could cover everything, he thought. But it's not in fact what judges think they're doing all the time. Judges know they do interpretation sometimes: sometimes they have to interpret a statute, sometimes they have to interpret another case, sometimes they have to interpret a whole body of law. But often they do other things, like make decisions, overrule old decisions, and so on. But Dworkin thought, in the end, that one could really understand all of that in terms of interpretation, and it is a huge

---

[3] This radio programme is also discussed by Lord Bingham (Ch.7). Judicial decision-making is also discussed by Lord Woolf (Ch.1), Lord Bingham (Ch.7), Dame Elizabeth Butler-Sloss (Ch.11) and Cherie Booth (Ch.12).

shock to somebody who does this for a living to discover that what they thought was just part of their job is now supposed to be, according to some philosophers, the whole of their job.

I am sceptical about that Dworkinian reconstruction of the subject in terms of interpretation, as was Lord Bingham on the radio programme you mentioned. In fact on that occasion, in my view, Lord Bingham was being more philosophical about his work as a judge than was my colleague Stephen Guest, who was standing up for the reconstructed Dworkinian view. But I would naturally say that, wouldn't I, because of the respect that I think philosophers should give to the self-understanding of practitioners.

Discretion. That's a subject, certainly at undergraduate level, that's discussed a lot. And I've asked a number of judges here to what extent they feel they have discretion. Perhaps you might just give some insight into the jurisprudential debate here; the point being that judges face enormously difficult decisions, and the question being whether they are more or less constrained by the law in the decisions they reach.

Yes. Well, there's no general answer to that because it depends on how much law there is. On some subjects, there's a lot, and on some subjects, there's only a little. But there is a philosophical question underlying it, which you have to begin by thinking about in these terms: you have to ask "what do you mean by discretion?". Now, one way to think about discretion is just to think that there's discretion whenever the law doesn't settle the case, and that happens whenever there's a conflict between two legal doctrines, and that in turn happens most days in most courts, because on most subjects, you have conflicting material from different legal sources, none of them more authoritative than any other. There's no way to decide between them just by asking the question: "Which one is the law?". The answer is they are all part of the law, and the question is which one you are going to follow, and that's, relative to the law, a kind of discretion. But it doesn't follow that the way to proceed is just do what you want or what you fancy, because of course there's lots of reasoning to be done still about what would be the best way for the law to go, and that reasoning can be informed by moral considerations. It can also be informed by other legal considerations, for example attempting to create a form of harmony with another area of law by analogising. That's an important sort of consideration as well. Judges work with all these considerations in these cases involving conflict to provide a new resolution. Now, that's discretion in the sense that it means deciding a case that wasn't already decided for them by the law, but it doesn't mean arbitrariness; it means thoughtful, deliberative judgment. And so if the word discretion implies arbitrariness, then it's a libel against most judges to use it in connection with them, but if the word discretion implies thoughtful, deliberate judgment about how to take the law from here, then it's not libellous to use it, and that's where the problems come from. People think of discretion in a way that straddles the two implications.

Before we discuss your own work, let's just touch one other old chestnut in the jurisprudential world, and that's the relationship between law and morality. It is a vast subject so why don't you cherry-pick.

Well, I already touched on something there, which is that legal reasoning is often a kind of moral reasoning because it involves using legal materials in combination with moral considerations to arrive at a new legal ruling. I use moral there in a broad sense to include what lawyers sometimes like to call policy considerations. Lawyers prefer to talk of policy considerations rather than moral considerations; philosophers prefer to talk of moral considerations rather than policy considerations. We shouldn't care about that; the point is that legal reasoners use considerations that are not themselves legal considerations, in combination with legal considerations, to generate new law, and that's a connection between legal and moral life. We could sum it up, as I just summed it up, by saying that a lot of legal reasoning is moral reasoning. It's also legal, because you need to use legal materials.

Of course, this is not the only issue that people fight about under the heading of the relationship between law and morality; there are plenty of others. One which has preoccupied people, really going right back to before Aristotle, to before Plato, is the question of whether the law is morally binding—whether the law binds in conscience, to use the Thomist phrase. You can see how it might be tempting to think that it always does. Many people who believe that the law is always morally binding will present you with an alternative, which is a world of terrible disorder, and they'll say, "Look what happens when people aren't morally bound by the law", to which I always reply this: "The people who are creating all this disorder aren't very interested in morality, and they're not very interested in their moral obligations. Why should you think that they would be interested in their moral obligations to obey the law? So why do you think that their having a moral obligation to obey the law would make the world a better place?". That line of thought forces us to start thinking about the bindingness of the law, not on delinquents who don't care about morality any more than they care about law, but on people who do care about what they should do morally. For them, the problem is really rather the opposite. It's not that without law there's going to be disorder. They're going to be very orderly. What they're worried about is the way that the law impinges on their judgment. Here they are, morally well motivated people trying to do the best for the world, and here comes a silly law that says to them, "Stand on your head for 10 minutes every morning or you'll be locked up", and they say to themselves, "What could possibly be morally binding about that? In 10 minutes, think of all the good things I could do!". And that does rather change the dynamic of the debate, if you think about these conscientious people instead of the delinquents as the object of the debate about the obligation to obey the law. The real question is not: "Why should we prefer people obeying the law to people doing the morally wrong thing?", the real question is: "Why should we prefer people obeying the law to people doing the morally right thing?".

There are some perplexing questions here, aren't there? For example, whether Nazi law was really law. If the content of some legal provision seems so abhorrent, can it really be law? Is it part of the definition of law that its content must be morally acceptable and, if so, to whom? And if the content of the law is morally unacceptable, does that then mean that the obligation to obey the law is thereby withdrawn?

Yes. There's also that debate. I find it hard to understand how somebody could ask the question: "Is Nazi law really law?", when they just describe it as Nazi law, and they clearly thought it was law when they described it that way, and two words later, change their minds or raise some doubt about it! I also have a similar puzzle with the famous expression, the famous claim, attributed to Aquinas: "Lex injusta non est lex"—an unjust law is not a law. How could that possibly be true? It's an unjust law, isn't it? Of course it's a law. It can't be an unjust law unless it is a law. Now, you may say that's just word play, but I'm not guilty of it; the people that I'm talking about are guilty of it. They're messing around with the concept of law for some other purpose that I don't understand. Nazi law is law because it's Nazi law. Then there's the question whether it's unjust and should be defied, to which the answer is often yes, and that just helps to reinforce my previous thought that we shouldn't really be taken in by the claim that generally there is a moral obligation to obey the law.

Okay. Let's move onto your own thinking then. What are you working on just now?

Just now, today, I was working on complicity.

Go on!

I should say, first of all, that I don't work mostly on those topics that we've just been discussing. A lot of people working in my field, in the philosophy of law, are interested in those general questions, and those are the ones that we teach undergraduates. But I tend to work on particular philosophical problems that arise in particular areas of the law, and quite a lot of my work has been about problems about criminal responsibility and compensation for accidents, what are called torts by lawyers. I'm interested in responsibility in general, and just lately I've been thinking about an area of criminal law which is about accomplices—that's the law of complicity. It's about the wrongs that people do by contributing to other people's wrongs. So, a simple scenario would be where I supply a crowbar to somebody whom I know to be a suspicious type that assists with breaking into somebody else's house. The primary wrong here, the wrong committed by the person that lawyers call "the principal", is the wrong of burglary. I'm an accomplice to burglary by providing the crowbar. There are lots of interesting philosophical puzzles about that.

One question that is very interesting is whether there's a general principle that, all else being equal, accomplices are less blameworthy than principals. The law has tended to make that its working assumption, although it's not by any means without exceptions, but in fact it's easy to see that it's a silly assumption. After all, the Krays in gangland East London were mainly accomplices to murders committed on their instructions by their henchmen, and their henchmen were mainly the principals. But would we think of the Krays as less blameworthy than their henchmen? To take an even more extreme case, there are cases in which terrorists use duress to get innocent people to carry bombs for them; the people carrying the bombs are the principals, and the terrorists are the accomplices. It would be a far-fetched idea that across even those cases, the accomplice is to be regarded as, at least presumptively, less culpable than the principal. So that's one area of discussion that interests me.

Another question is: why have the distinction between principals and accomplices at all? Couldn't you just say that people who cause death are murderers? Quite a lot of accomplices cause death, even though they do it through other people, so why don't we just think of them as murderers too? Why do we need this convoluted and complex idea that they're murderers at one remove, that is to say accomplices to murder, because they commit the wrong of contributing to somebody else's murder? Why not just say, "No that was murder to begin with"? In some jurisdictions, and indeed in some cases in this jurisdiction, that's been the direction in which the law has gone. Some courts have started to think that the law of complicity is an unnecessary spare wheel that could be abandoned, because really you could cope with all of this just by thinking about these people as murderers themselves, under the normal rules. I tend to think that this view is wrong, that the distinction between principals and accomplices remains morally and legally important. But why? That's quite an interesting problem too. These are some of the things I've been working on.

When we have chatted in the past, you mentioned an interesting case study of the chap in the jungle. That would be a useful one to tell us about.

Yes, I could tell you about that one. There are lots of relevant cases that are not legal cases—they are invented by philosophers or they are found in the history books—that help us to think about complicity as a moral problem rather than a legal problem. I'll give you two. One of them is a case that's invented by a philosopher, and the other one is a real case from history.

The case invented by a philosopher is known as Jim in the Jungle. It was invented by a wonderful moral philosopher called Bernard Williams, who died in 2003. In Jim in the Jungle, we have a backpacker in some South American country torn by civil war, and he treks across the jungle and finds himself in a village where the militia are about to execute 10 villagers as a collective punishment for some protection that the village has given to some rebels. Jim, who's a highly moralistic type, explains to the militia that exacting collective punishments is quite immoral, and the militia commander, who's no fool, replies to Jim, "You're quite right, and we won't do it, on the condition that you kill one person for us and you decide who it is going to be". Jim doesn't want to be the one who pulls the trigger, and he doesn't want to be the one who makes the choice. Is this disinclination reasonable? This example serves lots of purposes, and it served a different purpose for Bernard Williams from the purpose it serves for me. The purpose it serves for me is a purpose connected with complicity. You might think the problem Jim is faced with is a no-brainer—ten killings to one, of course he should do it! He is just being squeamish when he shows reluctance. But one way to interpret his reluctance is that he prefers to be an accomplice to 10 killings than a principal in just one. He's an accomplice because he fails to prevent the 10 killings when he could. Now, some people say that just failing to prevent something that you could prevent is not a way of being an accomplice to it, to which I reply, "well it is if Jim should prevent the killings". His reluctance is, in a way, a reluctance to get his hands dirty, and if the correct answer is that he should get his hands dirty and shouldn't allow the 10 people to be killed, then allowing the 10 people to be killed is a kind of complicity in their deaths. So it is, once you see it that way, a straight choice between being a principal in one death and being an accomplice in ten. You can see why, if you thought about it for a while, that might lead you to think that it's better to be an accomplice than to be a principal, or worse to be a principal than to be an accomplice. You might think that the reason why Jim feels reluctant about pulling the trigger is that it's worse to be a principal than to be an accomplice. In fact, it has to be more than 10 times worse, doesn't it? Because he's an accomplice to 10 killings if he refuses to pull the trigger. Of course you can reply that Jim shouldn't feel that reluctant, but if we want to defend Jim's reluctance at all, then in my view that's how we have to think about it. That's one interesting case.

Another case, with a different lesson to teach us, is a real case. This is the case of the bombing of Dresden in the Second World War. Now, this case is interesting because there is no individual principal. If you think about it, there's no one person who set fire to Dresden. There's a collective principal, which is the RAF or Britain or the Allies—I don't want to make a final determination on which of these collective bodies it is, but it's one of them. And all of the individual pilots, if they have any case to answer individually, it must be as accomplices, accomplices to the act of the collective agent of which they were part; because if you said to any one of them, "Did you burn Dresden?", they'll say, "No, if I had been sick that day, it wouldn't have made any difference. Suppose I hadn't been able to go? Dresden would still have been burnt. It would probably have been burnt in exactly the same way, at exactly the same time, to exactly the same extent". In other words, "it wasn't me, govn'r" would be the obvious answer. So, that's a way for an individual pilot to defend himself against the charge that it was he, as the principal, that burnt Dresden. The question which is interesting is: is that also a way of defending himself against the charge that he was an accomplice? Suppose you now say, "But weren't you complicit in the bombing of Dresden because you played your part in it? You were like the person who provided the crowbar to the burglar". To which the individual pilot can again reply something like this: "No, I wasn't like the person who provided the crowbar. My assistance could have been dispensed with. The bombing could have gone on without me. I wasn't even an accomplice". This makes me think—I don't know what it makes you think—but it makes me think that the test "would I have made any difference" isn't the correct test for complicity, that it must be possible to be an accomplice even though you wouldn't have made any difference. Because otherwise it's too easy to be exonerated, isn't it, from collective war crimes? It's too easy for the individual players who were entirely dispensable to say, "It was nothing to do with me", even at the level of complicity, and that result seems to me to be morally unacceptable. We must think about the doctrine of complicity in a way that allows people in that position still to be accomplices, assuming of course that they have the right intentions and that they know what they're doing and so on.

Does this not lead into another area in which you're interested—the question of causation? Because it seems to me that while some could argue even if I didn't pull the trigger, even if I didn't release the bomb, the result would have been the same, the fact is that they did and they were part of the causal chain. Now this is one of your specialities, so perhaps you could explain a little about causation. Causation in five minutes please!

Well, I'm not sure I can give you the answer, but I can give you a sense of the puzzle about causation. Here's an example that was set to me when I was applying to university to study law, but it's actually a philosopher's example. It's got something in common with the Dresden fire-bombing. I'm setting out across the desert and I have one water bottle. I'm at camp the night before I go, and I fill my water bottle because I'm always prepared. In the middle of the night when I'm asleep, my first enemy comes and adds a drop of poison to my water, thinking that when I'm out in the desert, I'll poison myself. A few hours later, still during the night, unbeknown to me and unbeknown to the first enemy, a second enemy comes and punctures a tiny hole in the water bottle. I'm dead in the desert 24 hours later. The question is: who killed me? Now, you can see straightaway what the puzzle is, can't you? Because if someone says to enemy number two, who punctured the hole, that he deprived me of my water and that's why I died, he'll say, "No I didn't, I just deprived you of some poison that would otherwise have killed you sooner". And if someone says to the first enemy that he did it, he'll say, "No, no, no, I didn't pour away any water, I just put a drop of poison in. If it had been me, he would have died of poisoning not of thirst".

Philosophers call this a case of over-determination: too many causes, and therefore you might think none. The result of having too many seems to be none, and that's because we apply this test: "if it hadn't been for that, would the person still have died?". Normally, the answer to that question gives you the answer to the question: "Who caused the death?", but in this story, it gives you the answer: "Nobody caused the death. The death was just a miracle". And so that shows, most people think, that there's something wrong with the test. So some of us mess around with that test and try to find other ways of understanding causation that don't link it in that way to the question "but for" or "if it hadn't been for that". You can see how that would feed back into the problems about complicity, about the Dresden bombing. Remember that our hypothetical Dresden bomber pilots were saying, "If it hadn't been for me, the fire bombing would still have happened", to which I might answer, "That's a bit like the case of the water bottle in the desert, isn't it? Too many poisoners, too many killers, means there's none. That doesn't seem to be a credible answer. There must be a different test". But don't ask me to tell you what exactly the test is, because it's extremely convoluted and not suitable for presenting without a text!

In terms of your working method, how do you operate? Do you simply sit down at your desk pondering?

Yes, that's right. I always feel a little embarrassed, because in today's universities you get a form every year or so that says what research have you done? I always want to say, "Sorry, I haven't done any research. I do a lot of thinking, and quite a lot of writing, but none of it was research". How would you research these problems? You have to know a few things, you have to know a bit about the law, you have to know a bit about what other philosophers have said, but once you know that stuff, well you know it, and now the question is what are you going to do with it? And I spend my life doing things with it. That mainly involves, yes, sitting and thinking, sitting and writing, sitting and deleting—I do more deleting some days than I do writing, because I find that I've taken a wrong turning. It's all very individualistic, and the rules are very unclear, even to me. Sometimes I start with a bit of law and I see what philosophical problems it throws up. Sometimes I start with a bit of philosophy and see if there are any legal cases that are connected. And sometimes I wonder whether I'm perpetrating some stupendous fraud!

Well let's talk about—well, not about the fraud, but . . .

I'm sure all academics think that they're charlatans some days. I'm not unique!

I don't think that's just intellectuals—most of honest humanity fall into that category! But there will be some people in the audience thinking: "does any of this change the price of fish? Does it really matter?". And I'm not talking specifically about your work, but about legal theory generally. What impact does it have? What difference does it make? Is it worth pursuing?

There are several different chains of influence. Personally, I always think about this in terms of my students. Most of my students don't become philosophers of law. They do all sorts of other things—they go and work for the Cabinet Office, or they become lawyers. Some of them sail round the world. They do all sorts of things. But generally, I feel my influence when I see what my former students do rather than what I do. I think to myself, "The approach to such-and-such that I'm now seeing emerging from the Law Commission reminds me of an approach we developed in class". And that's a nice feeling. That's a lot more influence than I would have if I went and wrote a letter to the Law Commission myself!

So, to jump in, you're equipping them with the ability to analyse and clarify concepts?

I hope. That's the kindly way of putting it. The ruder way of putting it would be that I'm making new versions of myself and dropping them like cluster bombs!

Okay, you're shaping young minds!

That's very much my vocation. I am from a family of teachers and it's far and away my favourite part of what is by any standards a very varied job. There are other ways in which one can leave one's mark through this job, and some people have a much more direct aim with their work. I work very closely with a very influential legal scholar, Tony Honoré, who's now in his 80s, and he has always addressed at least some of his work directly to lawyers and had a great deal of direct influence on the development of doctrine. He has a different writing style, it's less self-consciously philosophical. It raises all the same issues, but it presents them as issues that would be immediately applicable. As a legal academic, one could also leave a mark that way. Personally, it interests me less than leaving my mark as a teacher.

Just to interrupt again, isn't it interesting that Professor Honoré, who really is a giant in academic legal circles, and both in this jurisdiction and in South Africa as I recall, that someone of his age is still so productive. I think the same also of some judges who are in their early 70s. They are actually at the peak of their powers.

Yes, it's quite true. I always want to know what the secret is of Tony's intellectual longevity. I think he has some elixir, because he still teaches, and he still writes, and he's still just as innovative as he ever was. It's a remarkable career.

But philosophers don't tend to retire, do you? You don't suddenly switch off and say: "Well, I'm not going to be thinking deeply any longer"?

It's hard to retire when you don't really work! Sorry, I'm putting a bit of a self-deprecating spin on this, because in fact I spend a ridiculous amount of my time working, mostly filling in forms and managing small corners of the university, which I hope I won't have to do when I'm Tony's age. But as for the scholarly work, should we really count that as work? I sometimes think it's an amazing privilege that I get to think about things that I find interesting, I get to write about them, I don't really have to answer to any particular political pressures in how I write about them, and yet somebody pays me to do it. I won't retire from that in a hurry!

I should now ask you a closing question really. In fact, I ask everyone who sits in that seat a similar question. If a student said to you that they were considering a career as an academic lawyer, how would you respond? Encouragingly or discouragingly?

I'd be giving a mixed message. If I were talking to someone exceptionally brilliant, I would suppress the downside a little, because I hate to lose exceptionally brilliant people to some other line of work where their brilliance probably won't be valued so much. But the downside of becoming any kind of academic in Britain now is that the amount of bureaucratic hogwash that you have to deal with has grown ridiculously—the regulation is completely out of proportion to the risk. And the teaching is much more routine or standardised. It's more and more like being a schoolteacher for those in relatively junior jobs. I'm not saying anything against schoolteachers, of course. I have schoolteachers in my family. But most people who wanted to be academics wanted to do something different, and nowadays it's harder and harder to do it in this country.

On the other hand, insofar as you do get time to work on your ideas, what I said before applies. Nobody's asking you to tailor your ideas to a particular audience or a particular political purpose or even to make them socially acceptable. Journalists do have to tailor their ideas, and policy-makers have to tailor their ideas, and even lawyers have to tailor their ideas to the politics of their audience—I don't mean the party politics, but the interests of their constituency or their clients. Academics in the humanities, by and large, don't have to do this at all. That's an amazing form of liberation. It's close to being a novelist or a poet. When my graduate students

265

abandon it, which sometimes they do for better money or for less bureaucracy, that's the thing they most often miss. They think to themselves, "Now I have to write things which people are going to agree with or find a use for, whereas before I could write things that were just exciting and interesting". I tell my most academically-oriented students that this would be the most important thing they would lose, and probably miss, if they left the profession.

John Gardner, thank you very much.

The Rt Hon The Lord Mackay of Clashfern
Lord Chancellor, 1987–1997

Tuesday March 9, 2004

Before I introduce tonight's guest, Lord Mackay, I would like to extend my thanks to the Mercers' for hosting this evening in this marvellous hall. The Mercers', as many of you will know, is one of the two sponsors of Gresham College (along with the City of London Corporation), and we're extremely grateful for all the support they give us.

In introducing Lord Mackay, I'd like to take you back, if I may, to a very rainy Glaswegian night, in about 1982. I was a law student about to publish my first article. I had an appointment with the editor of the journal of the Law Society of Scotland, who lived about a mile from my home, and I decided, so valuable was the document, that I would deliver it by hand. I wandered down the road through the persistent rain, knocked on the editor's door and was welcomed in. I wasn't in a rush to leave so we started chatting about the law and the state of the Scottish legal system. As a law student, I was interested to know who were the great lawyers of our time, so I posed this question to the then editor: "Who is the most influential and the most outstanding Scots lawyer of our time?". He didn't skip a beat; he said immediately, "The man to watch is James Mackay," he says, "that man will go extremely far". Well, we have James Mackay, Lord Mackay, with us this evening, and he could scarcely have gone further, having been Lord Chancellor for 10 years. Just by way of background, I think it's interesting to know that Lord Mackay started his professional life as a mathematician before turning to the law in the 1950s. In 1955, he was admitted to the Faculty of Advocates (advocates being the Scottish equivalent of English barristers). Ten years later he became a QC. His meteoric rise through the profession then followed. He was Lord Advocate. He was a judge in the Court of Session. He became a Law Lord, a Lord of Appeal in Ordinary, in 1985, until 1987, when he was appointed Lord Chancellor in the last Tory Government.

Lord Mackay, it's a great pleasure to have you with us, not least to help us think through these turbulent times in which we live. Just yesterday there was the major debate in the House of Lords over the Constitutional Reform Bill. Indeed I thought we should launch straight in and discuss that first of all, because we are living, as I say, in very, very changeable times for the legal world. Can you give us a flavour of what it was like in the House of Lords yesterday?

Well, it was an occasion; it felt like an occasion, and there were very many speeches—44 I think speeches before the wind-up, so that would be 47 altogether. It was supposed to start about three o'clock; it started just after three o'clock, and then there was an intimation of a statement, and this statement was of course about the Penrose Report. Lord Penrose, George Penrose, was a pupil of mine, so it was quite an exciting day for me in that respect. Of course, statements last for a bit of time, and it took quite a bit of the time that otherwise would have been available for the debate.

Anyway, as it happened, as you know, in the Lords there's a speakers' list, with the order given so that nobody calls anybody; you just get up when your turn comes. As it happened, the break for the statement about Lord Penrose's report was just after Lord Woolf and just before me. They had put me down immediately after Lord Woolf, for some reason—maybe for no reason, just like that. Anyway, the interval came just between us, so I found myself starting again immediately after Lord Penrose's report was dealt with, and the debate went on until almost midnight. Really, to my surprise—because nobody can tell in the Lords, the Lords at least is exciting from the point of view of votes; you know roughly what's going to happen if it's a vote in the Commons, most times, not always, but most times these days, but in the Lords it's very hard to tell. Well, to my surprise, the motion that Lord Lloyd of Berwick moved to send the whole thing to a select committee was approved by quite a substantial majority, and I gather the Government were indicating yesterday morning that they were going to withdraw the Bill if that happened, it was being wrecked and so on. I gather—I may be wrong—but I gather up till now anyway, they seem to be setting up arrangements for the select committee, so it looks as though they're going to accept that. I'm not absolutely certain of that. We may see tomorrow morning a different thing, because they're not always absolutely consistent from day to day . . . ! The whole episode may be an example of that in a way.

Let's take a step back. On June 12th last year, unilaterally really, the Government announced major constitutional reforms, including the abolition of the role of the Lord Chancellor and the establishment of a new Supreme Court. There had been little or no consultation with judges, and there's been controversy every since. Am I right in saying there were three major issues in the Constitutional Reform Bill, as debated yesterday: the Supreme Court, the abolition of the role of the Lord Chancellor, and the setting up of a Judicial Appointments Commission? These were the three focuses of concern?

That's right.

Shall we pick off each in turn and you can talk us through the background and the context to each and give us your thoughts? It must be difficult for you, in many ways, having held the office for a decade, but should we talk first of all about the role of the Lord Chancellor and the practicalities and the realities of abolishing the role?[1]

---

[1] The role and the future of the role of the Lord Chancellor are also discussed by Lord Irvine (Chs 6 and 13), Sir Hayden Phillips (Ch.15), Lord Falconer (Ch.18), Professor Bogdanor (Ch.19) and Lord Woolf (Ch.20).

Well, Lord Elwyn Jones, who was the Labour Lord Chancellor from '74 to '79, says in his autobiography that he spent his time as Lord Chancellor trying to ensure he wasn't the last. So the idea of abolishing the Lord Chancellorship is not a new one; it's not a very startling, original idea. To abolish things on the whole is fairly easy. I remember my father saying to me long ago that someone had said to him that any fool can knock down a house, it takes a wiser man to build one, and I think that has been shown on this. It's easy—the Lord Chancellor, as you all know I think, was the Speaker of the House of Lords, he was the President of the Supreme Court of England and Wales, he was the Chairman, if he sat, in the Appellate Committee of the House of Lords and in the Judicial Committee of the Privy Council, and he was also a member of the Cabinet. Now, some people have thought that these were contradictory roles. Personally, I don't share that, but then I saw it from a somewhat different point of view. It's true that from time to time there are conflicts in the role, but I think these are conflicts that are much the same as any minister has. The Minister of Health, for example, is anxious to do the best he can for the National Health Service and the services related to health, but there's a limit to the amount of money he can get. The resources available to him are not infinite, and therefore he is constrained by the general Government policy about the amount of taxation that's going to be levied on the population. And the Lord Chancellor's difficulties are really of that kind: he wants to do his best for the courts and for legal aid and all the rest of it, but there's a limit to what he can do. Now, I don't think that's very special in relation to the Lord Chancellor, but I think the Lord Chancellor's role is to try to ensure that the rule of law is respected and that the judges are looked after as best one can in the circumstances and, generally, to be a kind of buffer between the—maybe buffer in more ways than one—but to try to take the pressures out of the relationship between the judges and the Executive. There are bound to be pressures, bound to be, in the nature of things, and in a sense some degree of pressure is probably good, otherwise it might be thought that the judges were not protecting the ordinary people against the ravages of Executive power. But on the other hand, too much pressure I think would damage, because it's supposed to be a single Government after all. We have three branches to the Queen's Government: the Executive, the Judicial and the Legislative, and they should work together for the common good, but there's certain tensions between them certainly, and it's the job of the Lord Chancellor I think to reduce these.

And of course he was Speaker of the House of Lords, and that is a job which, now that they've examined it as a separate job, isn't much of a job at all, because the House of Lords is self-regulating. As I mentioned in connection with making speeches, you have a list, and you get up when your turn comes and you sit down when you're finished and hope that you don't last too long. These are self-regulating arrangements, so the Speaker of the House of Lords, the Lord Chancellor, doesn't have much to do in that respect.

There are certain office things to see to. I think also he has quite a strong representative role. I used to find myself visited, to my surprise, by Heads of State that came to the United Kingdom, which is really quite something for a minister not the Prime Minister, and that I think was due to the judicial responsibility of the Lord Chancellor and the fact he was a Speaker of the House of Lords. Heads of State would go to visit the Speaker of the House of Commons, and I think it's partly due to that. I think that on the whole that gave the Lords a certain degree of being known in the world that otherwise they might not have.

269

Would you have been comfortable keeping the Lord Chancellor's role as it has always been?

Yes. I wouldn't have thought it needed to be abolished. I think that the role of appointing judges has become more and more complicated as the years pass. It used to be done by the Lord Chancellor with a small staff. Gradually, difficulties have arisen. One of the problems is trying to get the sort of diversity that people want. Now, it's not easy to get that, and it's very difficult to convince some people that it isn't easy, but it requires developments in the profession, and indeed going wider than the profession itself. Appointing is the third element in the package, is a Judicial Appointments Commission, and I think there's very little controversy over that—it's a good thing, provided it's set up properly, and the Lord Chief Justice and the present Lord Chancellor have come to an agreement, in considerable detail, about what that should be, and the judges and the Judges' Council I understand are quite satisfied with that. Therefore, so far as I am concerned, the main proposals in relation to the Judicial Appointments Commission are perfectly reasonable.[2]

You are suggesting that reforming judicial appointments is relatively uncontroversial, in that some kind of modernisation and separation is needed. That was the second reform discussed yesterday, the first being the abolition of the Lord Chancellor's role. The third reform is the establishment of a Supreme Court. Could you introduce us to the background to this proposal and at the same time to the current function of the Appellate Committee of the House of Lords?[3]

I think it's fair to say that the Lords of Appeal in Ordinary, who put in a memorandum about the constitutional reform, were unanimous in the view that the office of Lord Chancellor is an important factor in the constitution. It's preserving the separation of powers insofar as the independence of the Judiciary requires that, and that office has enshrined values which are very important. I think that was a unanimous view of the Lords of Appeal in Ordinary, and therefore they say, "If the Lord Chancellorship is abolished, you have to put some arrangements in its place to secure these values", and the Government has attempted to do that in the earlier clauses of the new Bill.

So far as a Supreme Court is concerned, as you know, the present ultimate court of appeal in the United Kingdom is the House of Lords, as a judicial body. The House of Lords' functions as a judicial body are discharged by the Lords of Appeal in Ordinary, who are the full-time lords, and other Lords of Appeal who are qualified—those who have held high judicial office and are members of the House of Lords—are entitled to sit according to requirements in dealing with these appeals. One of the features of the present arrangement is that we were able to have

---

[2] The appointment of judges is also discussed by Lord Bingham (Ch.7), Lord Irvine (Ch.13), Sir Hayden Phillips (Ch.15), Lord Falconer (Ch.18) and Professor Bogdanor (Ch.19).
[3] The judicial work of the House of Lords and the possibility of a new Supreme Court are also discussed by Lord Bingham (Ch.7), Lord Saville (Ch.14), Sir Hayden Phillips (Ch.15), Lord Falconer (Ch.18) and Lord Woolf (Ch.20).

for a number of years sitting as a judge in the House of Lords Lord Cooke of Thorndon, who was an eminent judge from New Zealand who was latterly the President of the Court of Appeal of New Zealand. He was a member of the Privy Council and he was given a life peerage during my time as Lord Chancellor and he became eligible to sit as a judge, and I think those who have studied these matters over the years that he sat would agree that he has made a very substantial contribution to the development of English law during that time, and Scots law too. He has taken part in some Scottish appeals as well.

Now, the Judicial Committee of the Privy Council is the body of the Privy Council that deals with appeals from overseas. It dealt with appeals from New Zealand until recently. They are mainly appeals just now from the Caribbean. They also did, until recently, appeals from for example the General Medical Council's disciplinary procedure. They also dealt with devolution questions from Scotland. Now, the reason for that as I understood it at the time of the Scotland Act was that there are no appeals to the House of Lords from Scotland in criminal matters. The Scottish criminal system is rather different, very different, from the English in a lot of its concepts and the way it has developed, with very little . . . interference I was going to say—that's not perhaps a very respectful word—with very little adjustment by Act of Parliament. So it's a very different system from the English, and as I say no appeals were competent from Scotland on criminal matters. But when devolution came along, it appeared that human rights issues could arise, which were devolution issues if they arose in Scotland, and they could arise equally in criminal and in civil matters. In fact, as it's turned out, most of them have arisen in criminal matters, so since there was no criminal appeal to the House of Lords from Scotland, it was thought wise to put them to the Privy Council, because there's no argument about that particular aspect of the matter.

The Lords of Appeal in Ordinary were appointed as judicial members of the House of Lords. They were the first life peers. They were appointed for life. They have a qualification in their Letters Patent that they enjoy their office so long as they shall well behave themselves therein—a qualification not imposed on any other life peerages given since 1958. I don't know what that implies exactly, but anyway that's the way the Letters Patent are framed.

Now, if you look very theoretically at the situation, it could be thought that the Lords of Appeal in Ordinary and the other Lords of Appeal are legislators and therefore, the argument goes, not independent in the sense required by, for example, the Human Rights Act or the European Convention on Human Rights. There's a difference of opinion about that amongst the Law Lords themselves.

Can we be absolutely clear here: the fact that the Law Lords sit in a legislative chamber of Parliament and therefore, at least in principle, have a legislative role, this is potentially inconsistent with also having a judicial role?

That's the argument. The Law Lords have, in fairly recent years, adopted a self-denying ordinance saying that they wouldn't vote in matters of party political controversy or they would seek not to give their opinion in matters that might come before the House at a later date. Now, obviously that's a matter of formal expression as to how they're going to conduct themselves from the time of the declaration onwards. I have some difficulty with that view about matters which may come before the House and which they shouldn't express an opinion about, for this reason: that anyone who is going to be a judge at that level is going to be a person with opinions. A judge at that level without opinions would be a very extraordinary individual, and on the whole I think probably unsuited for getting to that place. If he got there without any opinions, he probably was there by mistake, which would be the Lord Chancellor's fault. But on the other hand, I think that a judge at that level should have the sort of mind that on listening to argument may well change his opinion, whatever opinion he's had about these matters. It's the openness of mind to receive argument and alter one's opinions in accordance with the argument or in accordance with the arguments to make one's judgments that's really important.

Some years ago, I was invited to a conference organised by the Advocates of Ontario. They had invited also the Chief Justice of the United States, William Rehnquist, and the then Chief Justice of Canada—who has since passed away, but Bill Rehnquist is still Chief Justice of the United States—and myself. We had a discussion, as part of the conference, about the appointment of judges, and the American system and so on, and the way in which they were examined. I think we reached, or at least I reached a formulation, which I think was generally accepted: that judges in the United States were appointed for their opinions. In the Senate Judicial Committee, they're examined very closely about all that they've written and what sort of views they have about this, that and the next thing—abortion and all the current issues—whereas I think that judges in the United Kingdom are appointed for their ability to frame opinions in the light of the argument which is presented to them. So I don't really personally go along with this particular restriction, although it's a matter for the judges themselves. Anyone who wants to serve with that restriction, well that's up to him or her.

The judges themselves, as you say, or maybe you haven't said, they're divided as to whether or not there should be a Supreme Court to replace the House of Lords, or at least partially replace the work of the House of Lords. Well, the real debate on that had taken place on the previous occasion, on the 12th of February, before the Bill was introduced. Lord Nicholls of Birkenhead, who is the senior Law Lord from the point of view of length of service—he's not the Senior Law Lord, that's Lord Bingham at the moment, he was appointed to that from being the Lord Chief Justice of England and Wales, but Lord Nicholls is the Law Lord, the Lord of Appeal in Ordinary, who is longest serving in that capacity—made quite a detailed defence of the present supreme court system. One of the things he said, which I hadn't really thought of properly before, was judges are usually, are often, accused of being in an ivory tower, you know, away, gathered away from everybody else, and they're unaware of what's going on in the real world. In fact, he said, all his time until he came to the House of Lords he had served in a building and in a place which was judge-orientated. But when he'd come to the House of Lords, it wasn't like that. It wasn't judge-orientated. The Ordinary Lords, if I can call them that, are much greater in number, and he felt that the judges, the Law Lords, profited from being in a building which wasn't dedicated, as it were, to judges. His speech is well worth reading, for anyone who has interest in these matters. Now, Lord Bingham of Cornhill, who is the Senior Law Lord, has taken the opposite view.

I think, I may be wrong about this, but I think the views of the Law Lords have crystallised somewhat since they gave evidence to the Wakeham Commission. I think this point is strengthened with the passing of the Human Rights Act. This particular point has become somewhat sharper than it was before and, accordingly, the views have been differentiated perhaps more than they were in the times past. But that's the essence of the argument I think, and of course there are various practical considerations. The Government has not yet found a building for the new Supreme Court, and they have given some estimates about how much it would cost, and by comparison with the Scottish Parliament it's absolutely minimal, but one's experience may be that estimates are not always carried out fully in practice. Even on the basis of their present figures, they estimate that the fee income would have to be 10 times the fee income presently taken in by the House of Lords, which I think means that the fees that litigants will have to pay for going to the court—not the counsels' fees but the fees, the court fees—will be 10 times those which are presently charged by the House of Lords. And what's more, in addition, there will be an extra cost spread over all the civil courts in the country to help fund the new Supreme Court.

And that's caused considerable concern over the last couple of weeks.

Yes, it has.

So where do we go from here? We have this very controversial Constitutional Reform Bill. The House of Lords has expressed its view last night. What are the potential courses of action?

Well, I think the Lord Chief Justice has said with considerable deliberation that once the Lord Chancellor was knocked out by the decision that the Prime Minister took, it might be difficult to re-instate. There was some interesting debate going on on the 12th of June as to what was to happen, because I don't think it was fully appreciated that the Lord Chancellorship was so deeply embedded in statute, and I think it was thought possibly that the Prime Minister could abolish the Lord Chancellorship as he might abolish the Secretary of State for Transport. It wasn't quite as easy as that.

For example!

That's right, and when the dust settled, there emerged Lord Falconer of Thoroton as the Lord Chancellor and as Secretary of State for Constitutional Affairs for the first time. As far as I know, it's the first time that a Lord Chancellor has been a Secretary of State as well, and the judges felt that inappropriate. I think Lord Woolf was really saying that it's very hard to put Humpty Dumpty together again, if I can use that description to mirror that of the Lord Chancellor. Once that's been lost, it's very hard to put it back again. I mean it's interesting to see how this developed. In the Cabinet, the Lord Chancellor was always given fairly high seniority in the list. There's a list of the Cabinet starting with the Prime Minister and the Deputy Prime Minister and so on. The Lord Chancellor was never I think much below number five or something of that sort. Certainly when I went there first, which was in 1987, I was higher in the Cabinet than I expected to be by quite a margin, and gradually moved up as people went out, and by the time I finished up I was number two in the Cabinet, next to the Prime Minister. Now, when Lord Falconer was appointed Secretary of State and Lord Chancellor, it was in that order, and lo and behold the first Cabinet list that came out showed the Lord Chancellor at the very end of the Cabinet list, after all the Secretaries of State and after the Chairman of the Party, who is a Cabinet Minister. So he's right at the very end of the Cabinet list, which was quite a fall for Humpty Dumpty, and I think that's a significant fact.

I was interested—the Lord Chancellor issued a paper shortly after his appointment about the other matters that he was doing apart from the judicial matters. He was to discuss the judicial matters with the Judiciary, but he issued a paper about other matters, and one of these was his ecclesiastical patronage, because the Lord Chancellor appoints a number of priests in the Church of England—round about 500 livings I think are in the Lord Chancellor's gift. In this paper it said the question is whether it is appropriate at this time for a senior Secretary of State to appoint such people or to carry out these functions. So, having read this, I wrote a little letter to Lord Falconer to ask him on what basis he described himself as senior Secretary of State, having regard to the fact that at that time in the Cabinet list he was the most junior of all!

Did he respond?

Well, I wrote the letter on the 23rd of September. The response came on the 12th of December. So the issue was one of some delicacy. His answer was that the precise position in the Cabinet was for the Prime Minister to decide. Traditionally, the Lord Chancellor had been high in the Cabinet, having regard to the nature of his duties. The reason he was described by himself as a senior Secretary of State, was because he was to have duties in relation to the Keepership of the Great Seal and also in relation to the Judiciary, which marked him out as a senior Secretary of State. The letter didn't help me to see where and how that seniority was recognised by anyone apart from himself . . . but I have no doubt that in due course something will occur in that connection. There is just—I hope I'm wrong about this, I very much hope I'm wrong—but there is just a feeling that all of this is not entirely aimed at elevating the Judiciary as a whole in our Government arrangements.

So there are now two schools of thought. On the one hand, and I think Lord Woolf now falls into this category, there are those who were I think disappointed at the lack of consultation in relation to the abolition but now accept that it may be best if the Lord Chancellor's role no longer exists. And, in fact, last week in Lord Woolf's Squire Centenary lecture in Cambridge, he outlined five or six reasons why he thought it was inappropriate to continue with the Lord Chancellor's role in its current form.[4] On the

---

[4] Lord Woolf, "The Rule of Law and a Change in the Constitution" (July 2004) 63 *Cambridge Law Journal* 317–330.

other hand, there are those who are of the view that the role can and should be pre-
served and indeed they're putting up a fight for preservation. Now, you said Humpty
Dumpty can't be put together again. You can't put the toothpaste back in the tube, as
they say. Just as a matter of realistic politics, how is this likely to end up?

I think it's likely that the view will prevail that the Lord Chancellorship should be
split up and that the Lord Chancellor's part—I am hoping that perhaps even yet the
title, which is a very old title going back to before the Norman Conquest and in its
present form, Lord High Chancellor of Great Britain, dates from just after the
Glorious Revolution from the time of Queen Anne, it's a Letters Patent of Queen
Anne that settles the title as the Lord High Chancellor of Great Britain; it's an old
title, and if you have a sense of history it might be good to adapt it rather than
abolish it, but at the moment, it looks to me as though the role of the Lord
Chancellor, anyway, whatever happens to the title—the role of the Lord Chancellor
with which I was familiar will be abolished. And indeed, what Lord Woolf is saying
is that for practical purposes it's been abolished already.

As regards the Supreme Court, though, and you can surely separate out these issues,
it's conceivable, isn't it, that the Government could push forward with its plans to
abolish the Lord Chancellor's office, but they may backtrack on setting up a new
Supreme Court, having regard perhaps to the cost and the practicalities and the views
of the Law Lords?

They might. My, if I had to—as Alistair Cooke said, if he was asked to decide
between Genesis and the Big Bang at the point of a pistol, at the end of the barrel
of a gun, he would go for Genesis rather than the Big Bang—if I had to answer,
I think I would say that the likelihood is that ultimately we will have a Supreme
Court and an abolished Lord Chancellor's office.

Why don't we move on from one controversial Bill to an arguably more controversial
Bill, namely the Asylum and Immigration Bill, clause 11 of which is causing a great
deal of concern within and beyond the Judiciary. Could you introduce this topic and
track us through the issues?[5]

Yes. The asylum and immigration system, particularly from the point of view of
asylum, has been a very difficult system to operate, and great concern has been
expressed about it for some considerable time. One of the difficulties, and perhaps
the main difficulty, is that in the nature of the claim for asylum, it depends on ascer-
taining the facts about the person who comes to this country seeking asylum, and
that investigation can be quite complicated. Apart from anything else, it depends
primarily on facts existing in other countries—quite difficult to investigate. The

---

[5] Asylum and immigration are also discussed by Oliver Letwin (Ch.10).

person coming may be traumatised as a result of his or her experiences, without any papers of any kind, because fleeing from persecution on the whole you may have some difficulty with papers. So, it's a difficult issue, and systems have to be set up to examine these issues, and they take time. And then in relation to the complete disposal of the matter, quite difficult questions of law may arise, and the result is that the procedures that have been used can sometimes continue over quite a considerable period, and successive Home Secretaries have been anxious to try and speed these up. Various countries have adopted systems for trying to speed them up. None of them can completely eliminate the need to examine the particular facts of the applicant's situation.

Now, the present Bill seeks to streamline the system by removing a layer of appeals. There used to be an appeal to an adjudicator, then another appeal to a tribunal. They are now proposing a single tribunal to hear appeals from the Home Office decisions, and it will be a tribunal of lawyers, as I understand, headed up by a president who would be a judge of the High Court. Now, in addition to that, under the present system, when the ultimate tribunal had dealt with the case, they could apply—the applicant could apply—for judicial review. Now, a judicial review is simply the exercise by the ordinary courts, the High Court and above, of its historic jurisdiction to supervise the inferior courts and tribunals, and in particular it would be in the habit of considering applications from asylum seekers who had been turned down on appeal. These cases have tended to come quite frequently to the courts and also to take some time to resolve, and in the course of considering what to do, the Government has proposed this Bill, which as I say takes one tribunal out of the previous arrangements, and secondly, takes away this right of supervision or this jurisdiction to supervise the tribunals' work.

In 1969 the House of Lords had to consider a case in which the Parliament had provided that the decisions of the Foreign Compensation Commission were completely protected from interference by the court. The court was not allowed to interfere or adjudicate upon a determination of the Commission. Some people would have thought that was that, but it wasn't exactly, because what the Lords of Appeal concluded was that what was protected by that clause were the determinations of the Commission, and not everything the Commission did could be regarded properly as a determination. One of the examples they gave was that if the tribunal in the course of its discussion or process had neglected to give the applicant the benefit of the principles of natural justice, then Parliament would certainly not consider that a determination. Parliament would assume that the applicant had been given the proper protection of natural justice, and if he hadn't, or she hadn't, then it wasn't really a determination at all, and wasn't protected by the exclusion clause in the Act of Parliament. Well, that persuaded me for a long time that it wasn't possible for Parliament to legislate to obliterate judicial review, but this clause that's now proposed is an attempt to do exactly that, and what it does is to say that even if, for example, it's alleged that natural justice was breached by the tribunal, even then the court will not intervene. So it's requiring Parliament to affirm that even in a case where manifest injustice has been wrought because the rules of natural justice have not been followed, even in that case, the ordinary court, the High Court and above, the ordinary courts are precluded from intervening. Now, the judges I think until now have assumed that Parliament would not affirm that proposition. It seems a very strong proposition to affirm, that if manifest injustice is evident in a case, the court cannot intervene to correct it. That's the clause 11—I think it's getting a new number, there are more and more clauses added; that's the nature of Bills, they attract new clauses as they go along; I think it's now maybe clause 14—anyway, that's the clause that's caused a lot of difficulty.

There's another interesting thing about the clause. The Secretary of State has certified that the Act, the Bill, is to conform to the Human Rights Act, but yet in the clause there's a provision that says: "Section 7 of the Human Rights Act is to be understood in the light of the provisions of this clause", which I would have thought, if it was consistent with the Human Rights Act, wouldn't be necessary; but maybe I'm wrong about that. The Secretary of State is required to certify that the Bill does not infringe Convention Rights and that is subtly different from the way I have stated it.

How fundamental is this? I've spoken to a number of judges who are exceptionally concerned. Deploying the thin end of the wedge argument, if the Government can seek to eliminate judicial review in this context, one must ask what protections are in place to prevent analogous reductions in the applicability of judicial review across many other areas of life?

I think that is the question. In the proceedings in the Standing Committee of the Bill in the House of Commons, the minister was claiming that this was a very special area of the law where delay suited the applicant, and therefore anything that caused delay was attractive to the applicant, and therefore this is a special reason for taking it out in this particular area. But I would have said personally that there may be one or two other areas of the law where delay is not altogether to the disadvantage of one of the parties, and so if that's an argument, it's not a particularly strong one, specialising or bringing out this area as a special case.

This comes at a remarkable time, because this is a time when the judges, in light of the constitutional reforms, are uneasy about their ongoing independence, and it seems insensitive, at least to me, that the Government should seek at such a controversial time to be reducing the powers of the Judiciary, albeit in a confined area.

Well, I think you might think that that was wise to be careful at this particular juncture. I think I'm right in saying, I haven't got the words in front of me, but Lord Woolf yesterday in the Lords said that they had pointed out, the Judiciary through him had pointed out to the Government that this was not wise; they thought it was contrary to rule of law, and yet the Government have gone ahead with it. I have the impression that that has made the Judiciary anxious about the present situation. In a time of flux, suddenly to be faced with a particular illustration of a Bill or a provision in a Bill which the judges said was, they thought, unconstitutional, for the Government to go ahead with it is quite an anxious feature.

And, I think, most controversially, Lord Woolf last week suggested this could be the beginning of a step towards having a written constitution. Can we change subject

277

altogether now? We'll still stay with judges, but we'll move away from controversial Bills. Let's turn to judicial inquiries. These have attracted a huge amount of interest over the last few years and, in your own time, you set up a number of such inquiries. I wonder if we could reflect on the purpose of a judicial inquiry, in light of recent inquiries, and whether or not it's appropriate to have judicial inquiries in certain areas of social life. Perhaps we could talk about a few of the inquiries that you launched.[6]

Well, first of all, can I just make the general point that some parties—the Liberal Democrats in the House of Lords—were making the point in relation to the Bill that we've been—the first Bill we were considering, the Constitutional Reform Bill—that they thought it inappropriate that judges should be invited, that sitting judges should be invited to conduct inquiries where there was any kind of political content. There are very few inquiries that haven't got some form of political content. Some may have more than others. My impression has been that whatever politicians and the public tend to say from time to time about judges seeking to detract from their authority, when it comes to a real matter of dispute about factual situations, everyone regards the judges as the supremely independent and reliable tribunal to go to. Occasionally as you know, they've had tribunals under other people. The present inquiry under Lord Butler is an example of that. But very often, in cases where there's intense dispute about the facts and so on, the appointment of a judge, or sometimes more than one, has been resorted to because Parliamentarians generally respect the Judiciary as independent and unlikely to be influenced in favour of any party or in favour of the Government of the day.

These have two effects. One, the judge is taken out of his ordinary business for a time, and that is to the detriment of the ordinary system and the job which he normally would have to do. The second point is that it does put the judge, sometimes, into an area of quite considerable party controversy. Now, during my time, as you say, there were quite a number of judicial inquiries. One of the most notable I think was Lord Scott, as he is now, his inquiry into arms for Iraq. That was an area which required investigation. The Prime Minister felt that it was a matter that required to be looked into, and was, as I understood, very anxious that nobody could suggest that the resulting inquiry was a whitewash, because that's sometimes the allegation that's made one way or the other, and you sometimes hear it occasionally still in relation to some. The appointment of the Vice Chancellor as the judicial inquirer in that case I think certainly produced a result that couldn't be regarded as a whitewash. He took a good long time for it. Lord Penrose—his inquiry was set up by the present Government and it took quite a long time as well.

It's I think quite an important theoretical consideration whether judges should take part in inquiries of that kind. They have traditionally done so and I think it's a useful and proper way for a judge, on being invited, to employ his or her time.

However, it is hard, given the very nature of some of the inquiries, for judges entirely to avoid political controversy. This seems to me to be especially so of both Lord Hutton

---

[6] Judicial inquiries are also discussed by Lord Irvine (Ch.6), Lord Bingham (Ch.7), Dame Elizabeth Butler-Sloss (Ch.11) and Lord Saville (Ch.14).

and Lord Saville's inquiries. Indeed, Lord Saville was a past guest of ours at Gresham and we talked about how he is managing his inquiry. But what we do know, surely, is that there are two quite different bodies of opinion in relation to the focus of his inquiry, and the likelihood is that whatever view he comes to, there will be a large body of people who will be dissatisfied. I suppose this must be true if one's investigating a set of facts that surround a major controversy.

Yes, that's true in a way, but on the other hand, you have to keep in mind that judges spend all their time, or nearly all their time, in the ordinary course of their work dealing with matters in which there are two sides at least to the question, and there aren't many judges who are able to satisfy both sides with their judgments in every case. There may be an occasional time when both sides are satisfied, but these cases are rather infrequent. So judges are accustomed to seeking to analyse the dispute and come to an independent, rational judgment as to the proper outcome on the facts presented to them. I think where there's hot political controversy, as for example in relation to the arms for Iraq, the idea is that the judge will present the facts and the arguments and come to conclusions which are independent of the views that the parties have taken—the then Conservative Government on the one hand, or the Opposition on the other. On the whole, I think they've tended to respect these judgments. Lord Hutton's Inquiry, which is perhaps one of the most recent to report—Lord Penrose I suppose was more recent still, but Lord Hutton for the Government of the United Kingdom in recent times has been a very important inquiry. It's different in a way to some of the earlier ones in that the terms of reference used were pretty narrow. I think if you've read Lord Hutton's report, you will see that he adjudicates between the arguments that were put to him. Some people have been—commentators, especially the press, have been—expressing sometimes a degree of surprise at his views, but I think if you read the report, the views are compelling, because he was adjudicating on the arguments that were put to him, some of them quite extreme. I think these reports do tend ultimately to settle the dispute, maybe not immediately; there's often some sort of reaction, but very often they settle the disputes.

Now, during my time, although I wasn't responsible for the appointment, Lord Cullen did the inquiry into the Piper Alpha disaster in the North Sea, a very complicated, technical matter—a huge accident, certainly a sad disaster, but very technical in its nature—and he also did the inquiry into the Dunblane shootings. These attracted very little political controversy when he ultimately came out with the findings, so it varies according to the circumstances. If the Government has been closely involved, as for example in connection with the circumstances leading up to Dr Kelly's death, then there's likely to be more political controversy after the findings are given than if the inquiry is related to something in which the Government or the political parties haven't had an active role prior to the occasion for the inquiry.

So you're saying, first, that you believe that judges are both well placed to conduct that form of public inquiry given the respect that's generally held for them in relation to their fact finding skills and, second, you think that this is normally a good use of judicial time, even though, for many judges, it may take them out of mainstream judicial work for years.

Well yes, that's right, and of course there's always a question for the individual judge whether that's a sacrifice that he wants to make. It's the same for counsel, advocates, barristers, if they find themselves in an inquiry that goes on for many years. Their practice may not recover once that's finished. It depends on the nature of the inquiry, but it can have quite an effect in disrupting relationships between you and the solicitors who would instruct you and so on.

There are quite different uses of judges for inquiries. We can contrast an inquiry into a hugely significant event or series of events—for example, Lord Hutton and Lord Saville's inquiries—with, say, Lord Woolf's work when he undertook, at your request, his Access to Justice Inquiry,[7] or Lord Justice Auld when he conducted his investigation of the criminal justice system,[8] or Sir Andrew Leggatt when he reviewed the tribunal system.[9] I would assume you support these latter uses of judicial time, where there's a fundamental appraisal of a key set of legal issues or legal processes to be undertaken.

Yes I think so. Lord Woolf's inquiry into the civil justice system was something that was very much concerned with the processes of justice and grew out of a previous inquiry really, which was set up by Lord Hailsham into the civil justice system. There were a number of findings of that earlier inquiry, but one of them was that if you're going to have proper flexibility between the courts, the civil courts at different levels, you need some kind of uniform set of rules. It's really inquiring into that, as the starting point, that generated the Woolf Inquiry with the very considerable changes that have been introduced; and I believe, so far, these have been generally pretty successful.

Alas, we've almost run out of time. Can I ask one final question? It relates to Scots law. Many people do not understand the distinction between English law and Scots law. Can you, very briefly, give a flavour of Scots law and its distinctive character?

Well I think that the best way I can put the distinction in a few moments is that some of the Scots in the times of civil insurrection and disturbance in Scotland in the time of the Stuarts—when they came to England, they became troublesome to the Scots, which sometimes happens I suppose—they went to the low countries and studied the Roman law, as it was practised by that time in the low countries, in the Netherlands particularly. One of them, Viscount Stair, came back and wrote a very large volume which was supposed to incorporate the whole of the principles of the law of Scotland in the Institutes, and there were others later who did

---

[7] Lord Woolf, *Access to Justice—Interim Report* (Woolf Inquiry Team, June 1995) and *Access to Justice—Final Report* (HMSO, July 1996). Also available at *www.dca.gov.uk*

[8] Lord Justice Auld, *Review of the Criminal Courts of England and Wales* (The Stationery Office, London, October 2001). Also available at *www.criminal-courts-review.org.uk*

[9] Sir Andrew Leggatt, *Tribunals for Users: One System, One Service, Report of the Review of Tribunals* (The Stationery Office, London, March 2001). Also available at *www.tribunals-review.org.uk*

somewhat the same. The Scots law developed primarily from these, whereas the English law, although there were people who wrote systematic treatises, on the whole English law has developed from the case by case evaluation, which is its genius.

Lord Mackay, thank you so much for joining us this evening.

CHAPTER EIGHTEEN

The Rt Hon The Lord Falconer of Thoroton
Secretary of State for Constitutional Affairs and Lord Chancellor

Thursday April 22, 2004

I am delighted to have with me as my guest this evening Lord Falconer, who is the Secretary of State for Constitutional Affairs and the Lord Chancellor. He went to school in Scotland, which was of course a good thing. He then went to Cambridge, was called to the Bar in 1974, took silk in 1991, in 1997 became a life peer, and that same year he was appointed Solicitor General. Since then he has occupied a number of roles as a Minister of State in Transport, in the Cabinet Office and at the Home Office. Last year, in June, under quite dramatic circumstances, he became the first Secretary of State for Constitutional Affairs, and, as we will hear tonight, the last Lord Chancellor.

Lord Falconer, welcome to Gresham College. Why don't we jump straight in and talk about the abolition of the role of Lord Chancellor? In a sense, you are currently overseeing the demise of your own role.[1]

In discussing the abolition of the role of Lord Chancellor, I think it is quite important that we try and focus on the arguments in favour and the arguments against the abolition of the role of Lord Chancellor. Quite a lot of the debate has got intermingled with the circumstances in which it was announced, which plainly weren't the best in the world. I think we should try and focus on what the arguments are. The Lord Chancellor as an office, and it is a great historical office, has been in existence for 1,400 years. The office of the Lord Chancellor has only quite recently, say in the last 60 to 100 years, developed to the point that it is at now, with the Lord Chancellor as the Speaker of the House of Lords, the head of the Judiciary and a judge, and also a Cabinet Minister, with special responsibility for the rule of law and the independence of the Judiciary. Until about 30 years ago, what people in my position did was spend quite a lot of time sitting on the woolsack, as Speaker, and significant amounts of time sitting as a judge as well. And that was really the bulk of their job. Now—not because of any change that has been announced—the Lord

---

[1] The role and the future of the role of the Lord Chancellor are also discussed by Lord Irvine (Chs 6 and 13), Sir Hayden Phillips (Ch.15), Lord Mackay (Ch.17), Professor Bogdanor (Ch.19) and Lord Woolf (Ch.20).

Chancellor has a Department of State that spends about £3 billion, and the question has arisen, and it has arisen over quite a long period of time: can you be a minister with that degree of responsibility and be a judge and be Speaker of the House of Lords? I don't think he can be any more. There are constitutional principles involved, separation of powers for example, but if the system was working I don't think the pure constitutional issues would justify the change, because as people have said it had worked quite well. But I think each of the three jobs—Cabinet Minister (with the independence of the Judiciary and rule of law role), head of the Judiciary and Speaker of the House of Lords—all of them would be performed better if they were done by separate people. So for example I think the Cabinet Minister responsible for a £3 billion budget should be somebody the Prime Minister can choose as the politician he thinks is best to do that job, whereas currently the Prime Minister has to pick a senior lawyer who is in the House of Lords. I think the head of the Judiciary in this day and age should now be somebody who is genuinely a judge and is able to provide leadership for the judges as a judge, and again that is not the same person whom the Prime Minister might choose to be the £3 billion departmental head. I think the Lords should now choose their own Speaker, rather than having as the person who is their Speaker somebody who in effect is chosen for them by the Government.

That is a very useful summary of the background. Why don't we now focus on one particular subject: the judges. There has been, understandably, some nervousness amongst the judges in relation to the abolition of the Lord Chancellor and related reforms. However, there are some tensions in their own thinking: on the one hand the judges, rightly, hanker after independence, and on the other hand I think there is some concern that they will no longer have a seat, as it were, around the table. Indeed I think one of the most common sources of judicial anxiety is this worry about how it is that the judges' needs, concerns and interests will be best represented at Cabinet level.

I think when you say hanker after independence, I would put it completely differently. I think that our constitution utterly depends upon the independence of the Judiciary. The independence of the Judiciary secures for the citizen the rule of law. Only if you know that the judges will look at the issues independently do you know that your rights under law are absolutely safe. The difficulty I think that has grown up after the last few decades is that having a Cabinet Minister who has got responsibilities to the public for spending £3 billion, and also to the political party of which he forms a part, and the role of the judges, increasingly come into conflict. Let me give an example. The judges might take one view in what sorts of evidence you admit into court whereas the Government, with overall policy, might take an entirely different view. You can't have the same person taking the Government's view and the judges' view. Recognising the need to separate doesn't in any way undermine the independence of the judges. How do you preserve that? I think in two ways. One, by making the Lord Chief Justice the head of the Judiciary you give the judges an independent voice and an independent leader, separate from the politician, which I think greatly strengthens their independence; but secondly, you place a statutory duty, which is what we are doing, on all ministers, on all people involved in the administration of justice, to preserve the independence of the Judiciary. Now, there was some very impressive evidence given by Lord Bingham to the Select Committee in the House of Commons about the independence of the Judiciary and he said the independence of the Judiciary comes not so much from the role of the Lord Chancellor, he said, but from the fact that it is absolutely embedded in our political and Governmental culture. I think we have got to reflect that in the statutory arrangements we make. We have got to reflect that in the important position we give to the Lord Chief Justice. But I don't think that independence, which is critical, depends upon the Lord Chancellor sitting in the Cabinet.

But we do need, I think, to unpack the notion of judicial independence. I think it is clearly vital and uncontroversial that judges should be independent, in the sense of impartial in the decisions that they make. But it is naïve—and I know you are not suggesting this—for anyone to suppose that judges can be operationally separate from the current Executive, in the shape of the court service, as currently conceived. It has always been the case that the Judiciary has worked very closely alongside the court service, not least in relation to resources, court buildings and technology; and certainly judges and the officials who are running the court service have had to collaborate on an ongoing basis. But I suppose one of the concerns now is that if the head of the court service, in the shape of the Lord Chancellor, is not a judge, then the same lines of communication may not be in place. In turn, this could have impact on some of the decisions of the court service; decisions that bear directly on the day-to-day running of the context in which judges operate.

I entirely agree with your premise. We have to unpack what independence means. Independence means being absolutely free, directly or indirectly, to decide a case on its merit; but freedom to do that isn't just about not being bribed or threatened, it is also about having enough resources to be able to do it. What we have sought to do as well as making sure there are statutory protections for independence is we have also sought, in the new arrangements that have been made, to embed the Judiciary much more in the practical management of the courts. Let me give you two examples. Part of the arrangements that have been made with the Lord Chief Justice involve putting two senior judges on the board of the Constitutional Affairs Department. They have got some say in the running of our department. Another example is that the judges become involved in the budgeting process for the courts, because currently what happens is they are not always involved in administrative things, and as you rightly say, there needs to be a partnership in which they are working closely with the Executive.

So you are arguing, in fact, that in the new world there will be greater transparency, a better working relationship and greater—certainly not less—independence.

Very much so, and I think there is a practical aspect to this. The current position is that the Lord Chancellor is both a judge and a minister. But as far as the Judiciary is concerned, he is primarily a judge. Traditionally, and I include myself in this, he has always been part of the Judiciary, rather than focussed on the running of the department. That has got to change, I think, because the partnership that you refer to between the judges on the one hand and the Executive on the other—providing them with buildings, providing them books—it is very important. The judges need to be much more engaged in those particular issues. Quite legitimately, some of them won't want to be, because if you became a judge, you didn't become a judge in order to become a building manager. But there needs to be a pretty intense partnership, I think, to make the thing work well.

Tell us a little in this context about the "constitutional settlement" and the "concordat". What do these terms mean and how enforceable are these arrangements? What is their status?[2]

The concordat, which I think is a very important part of the arrangements, arose out of very detailed discussions that took place between myself and the Lord Chief Justice, after the announcement of the abolition of the Lord Chancellor, to work out what functions the Lord Chief Justice would do and what the Secretary of State for Constitutional Affairs would do once you had abolished the role of Lord Chancellor. Take two issues that the concordat deals with: the Lord Chancellor currently disciplines the judges; that is acceptable to the judges currently because the Lord Chancellor is himself a judge. It would not remotely be acceptable, quite rightly, to the judges that an ordinary minister, off his or her own bat, could discipline a judge. That would plainly affect the independence of the Judiciary. So the Lord Chief Justice and myself have made agreements about how disciplining will be done in such a way that absolutely ensures independence. What is the status of that document? The document has been published and its provisions are reflected in the Constitutional Reform Bill. Another example is deployment of judges. The Lord Chancellor can say of an individual judge, "I don't want you to sit in Leeds, I want you to sit in Newcastle". It is a bad theory that the Executive has that power. It has not been abused in recent times. So one part of the concordat has been that the deployment of individual judges will be dealt with by the judges themselves, rather than by the Executive. The concordat in fact represents quite a lot of steps forward in terms of what people would regard as a sensible arrangement between judges and the Executive.

And much of it will be enshrined or, as you say, reflected in the statute.

In the statute, exactly.

Just before we leave that subject, is it emotional or irrational to regret the passing of the great office of Lord Chancellor?

---

[2] The constitutional settlement and the concordat are also discussed by Sir Hayden Phillips (Ch.15), Professor Bogdanor (Ch.19) and Lord Woolf (Ch.20).

No, it is not. For me, it is a fantastic honour to be Lord Chancellor, my predecessors have included people like Thomas More, like Lord Shaftesbury, like Lord Clarendon, like Lord Mackay who was an excellent Lord Chancellor, and like Lord Irvine who I think was also an excellent Lord Chancellor. The office represents the values of the rule of law. It carries the power of history. But change is necessary, to reflect the need no longer to be the head of the Judiciary and the Speaker of the House of Lords. These two roles and the Cabinet Minister, I fear, are not best delivered by one person doing them. In the last 60 to 70 years the nature of the change in the job has been huge, and although many people say, "Well, if it ain't broke, don't fix it", but the corollary of that is to wait until it is broken before you fix it. And the standing of our judges, the perceived independence of the Judiciary, the really high quality of justice in this country is something that has got to be preserved at all costs. And to wait until the arrangements are in danger would be a very bad idea I think.

And to have preserved the role for just one of the three that you mention would have been to dilute it, to water it down?

I think you recognise that as time has gone on, the ministerial function has become the prevailing function of the Lord Chancellor. But even if one went back to, say, 1970, which is 34 years ago when Lord Hailsham was first appointed Lord Chancellor, he would spend lots more time sitting as a judge than any of my immediate predecessors, lots more time sitting as Speaker of the House of Lords. In effect, when he was Lord Chancellor, that was primarily what he did to start with. But then he got responsibility for the courts through various Acts of Parliament, he quite rightly appointed a lot of Deputy Speakers to put a Speaker in the Lords, and his successors then began to sit less, both on the woolsack and as judges, and got more and more drawn into the very demanding role of the ministerial responsibilities they had.

Do you have any personal regrets, if you are able to say so, about not yourself being able to sit as a judge, as Lord Chancellor, just once or twice?

Huge personal regret at not being able to. I could think of nothing more challenging and enjoyable than sitting in the House of Lords Judicial Committee, but I don't think it is appropriate. Lord Bingham gave evidence to the House of Lords Select Committee this afternoon on the abolition of the role of Lord Chancellor and he said, not commenting on any individual Lord Chancellors, one can see that over the last 40 to 50 years the particular skill for which most Lord Chancellors have been appointed was not their skills as judges. In a way, there is something inappropriate about having not been appointed because of your qualities as a judge, then suddenly finding yourself chairing the highest court in the land.

And, I suppose, not having travelled through the judicial hierarchy and gaining all the experience along the way.

I should say there have been two occasions since the war—Lord Mackay of Clashfern and Viscount Simmonds—where the person who was appointed to be the Lord Chancellor was in fact a Lord of Appeal in ordinary, so I don't think what I have said applies to them. But it has not been the norm.

Let's move on to another, equally contentious constitutional reform: the Supreme Court. First of all, can you give us the context to the debate on the proposed reforms?[3]

The context is that the final court of appeal in legal cases at the moment is the Appellate Committee of the House of Lords. The people who make up the Appellate Committee of the House of Lords are senior judges from Scotland, England and Wales, and when they are appointed to be a member of the Judicial Committee they are appointed to be a member of the Legislature, as a member of the House of Lords. It is for largely historical reasons that this has happened. So we have this rather odd circumstance where in order to be made a member of the final court of appeal you are appointed to be a Legislator. From time to time attempts have been made to change that, the last time it happened being in the late 19th century, because as Lord Bingham the current senior Law Lord says, it must be right that our constitutional arrangements should reflect reality. People should be able to see and understand that the people who are on the final court of appeal are in fact judges and not Legislators. I think that is right. And again, referring to Lord Bingham's evidence, he said that it must be the minimum requirement of a sensible liberal democracy that its final court of appeal is identifiably separate from its Legislature, and that is what we are trying to give effect to.

And that of course is fundamental to one set of arguments in relation to the proposed Supreme Court. Lord Bingham, while our guest at Gresham College in October 2002— that is, before the announcements of June last year—was supportive of a new Supreme Court. But it is also the case, isn't it, that about half of the Law Lords have thought otherwise? The late Lord Hobhouse was particularly forceful in this connection—in a supplementary document to the Law Lords' response to the proposals for a Supreme Court, ran the argument, and it is not one I have read before, that what is important in the separation of power is not that judges should not be directly involved in legislating but that judges should not be directly involved in the activities of the Executive. So there are those who run that argument and say that they accept, in respect of the Lord Chancellor for example, that it is inconceivable that a judge and a member of the Executive should be one and the same person, but there can be good practical reasons for having judges involved to some extent in legislative activities, withdrawing only where there are any conflicts of interest. Now I am not here to defend or propose such arguments, but I am interested in your views.

---

[3] The judicial work of the House of Lords and the possibility of a new Supreme Court are also discussed by Lord Bingham (Ch.7), Lord Saville (Ch.14), Sir Hayden Phillips (Ch.15), Lord Mackay (Ch.17) and Lord Woolf (Ch.20).

The evidence which Lord Bingham gave, which was given in public today, concluded with him reading a memorandum that Lord Hobhouse had sent him shortly after he arrived as a Law Lord. And you are right, that Lord Hobhouse, who was a brilliant Law Lord and a very, very impressive man, spoke out strongly against the Supreme Court proposals in the Lords in the debates that took place in February of this year. But Lord Bingham read this memorandum at the end of his evidence this afternoon in which Lord Hobhouse had said, "I am writing to you before you are 'captured' by the place; what we need is our own building, our own arrangements, entirely separate from the House of Lords". And in this memorandum that Lord Bingham read, Lord Hobhouse was arguing strongly for a Supreme Court.

In any event, there is an issue here of identity, I would have thought. The man on the Clapham omnibus is not intuitively going to know what the Appellate Committee of the House of Lords is all about. Even the term "Law Lords" can confuse. Why are Lords judging, it might be asked? It must all seem pretty vague if you are not a lawyer or you have not been trained in legal matters or in some way exposed to our upper courts. So I can see, simply for the sake of clarity, that actually having a Supreme Court, with separate judges, might be much clearer for the lay person to understand. But to raise another issue and to quote Lord Hobhouse again, his first argument in the paper that I mentioned was that he could not see the "business case" justifying the Supreme Court. This is ironic coming from a judge, incidentally, because such remarks about business cases, are usually directed by officials at judges when the latter are proposing various expenditures. In any event, what is the business case for the Supreme Court?

Lord Hobhouse has tragically died since he made his speech, so he won't be able to take the argument forward. But as far as the money is concerned, as again was said this afternoon, we are something like the fifth biggest economy in the world, and the idea that the fifth biggest economy in the world can't afford a Supreme Court building seems to me to be, with respect, complete nonsense. And the idea that one asks oneself the question, if one spent, say, between £6 to 32 million on building it—and that is the range we're currently looking at—and then maybe it cost £10 million per annum thereafter to run, would that be value for money? Of course it would be value for money for our country to be able to say, "There is the final court of appeal, it is identifiably a court", and I believe we would also be able to say it is the best court in the world.

That has to be right and I agree with that. But I think there is real concern about how it is to be funded. There is an indication that some of the expense would have to come at least partially out of court fees. I want to talk a bit about that. It has to be right that the United Kingdom can afford a Supreme Court costing £50, 60, or 70 million. But it doesn't seem to me to be reasonable that that should actually be funded by the limited number of people who happen to pass through the courts.

I agree, and we are not proposing that it be funded by fees in House of Lords cases. If private litigants use, or indeed Government litigants, or local Government litigants use the courts in civil cases, they should pay a fee. You pay a fee, everybody does. Very, very many people who start litigation never get to court because the case settles. Very very many people who start litigation never get to the Court of Appeal, because they don't appeal a case. But it is not wrong that in looking at the fees that you charge for civil litigation, which are quite small, a small proportion of that fee should go partly to the first instance courts, partly to the Court of Appeal and then partly to the final court of appeal.

So has it been suggested that it is purely funded out of court fees?

It is suggested that a significant proportion of the civil cases heard by the Supreme Court be paid out of civil fees. Criminal cases—which are entirely different because it is on the one hand the Crown that is the Prosecutor, and on the other the defendant has not necessarily chosen to be in court in that way—these cases are dealt with in a separate way. They, the criminal cases, will be funded by the State.

So where is it going to be? Have you identified that site yet, and would you tell me if you had done?

We have got a shortlist of sites. They are all in central London, because London is the capital of the United Kingdom, and I think the Supreme Court should be where the capital of the country is. We have agreed a set of requirements for this with the Law Lords, and it has got to be a prestigious, well appointed building, suitable for housing the Supreme Court of the land.

Which is about 50 people, with three hearing rooms.

Exactly. I have targeted something over 3,000 square metres including a library.

We are in danger now of sounding a bit like estate agents!

But another aspect to this is that there are very few members of the public who actually go and watch the Appellate Committee of the House of Lords in action. It is not easy to come to the Lords to see a Judicial Committee in action; it is possible, it is open to the public, but very, very, very few come. See how the Lord Chief Justice describes what happens in Court Four in the Strand, which is the Lord Chief Justice's Court. He sees people trooping through all the time— members of the public from this country and people from abroad—and quite rightly so, because it is the Chief Judge of England and Wales sitting, and the court is easily accessible. I think public access is important when you are dealing with the final court of appeal.

Do you think, although this may be just a detail, that the judges of the proposed Supreme Court should sit, as Law Lords do today, in lounge suits? That would look and feel very different from the Lord Chief Justice's Court for example. Will that change? Will the Supreme Court be more stereotypically court-like?

It is entirely a matter for the Law Lords, or the Supreme Court Justices, to determine the form in which they would sit. From speaking to them, their inclination would be to continue to sit in lounge suits; their inclination would be to continue to sit in arrangements whereby, instead of being up on a dais, which is where a judge in a more conventional case sits, they would be sitting in a horseshoe shaped room, and it being a low key discourse rather than a very formal discourse. But I don't think that in any way detracts from the proposition that people would be keen to see them operating in action.

Yes, and it is perhaps trivial to make this observation, but as a spectacle, a visit to the Lord Chief Justice's Court is a bit of an outing actually and it is everything that one would expect and more.

I think if you went to see the House of Lords Judicial Committee in action, that is still an outing. Remember the advocates wear wigs and gowns, they look completely terrified all the time, and that is very visible. And, the debate is at a very, very high level.

Which is the key point in all of this.

If you went to the Supreme Court in the United States of America, which does in fact have a raised dais for the Justices to sit on, it is visited regularly and it is an identifiable understandable centre of the justice system in America and I think that is important.

Well of course they didn't have their own court building, I think, for about 146 years. They sat in Capitol Hill.

They were in the basement in the legislative building until 1926.

We wouldn't have that here?

They are on the first floor of the legislative building.

In his Squire Centenary lecture in Cambridge, Lord Woolf said, and I need to be careful in the way I quote this, but he talked about the proposed Supreme Court being a "second class Supreme Court".[4] I think this is worth clarifying. What is your reaction to that claim, given that it may not be suggesting what it appears to be imply?

He referred to it as being a "second class Supreme Court" and I think that the point that he was trying to make was that the Supreme Court in America has the ability to actually strike down legislation. That is because America is a federation that came together at the end of the 18th century on the basis that states only joined the federation on the basis that there were certain principles that legislation couldn't affect, and therefore you have a written constitution that is superior to any ordinary piece of legislation that Congress can pass. So the Supreme Court in America frequently strikes down legislation as being unconstitutional. Lord Woolf was saying it might appear to some people that our Supreme Court would be second class because it couldn't strike down legislation. Now I unequivocally disagree with that. I think people would regard the quality of what our current final court of appeal, the Law Lords, do as second to none in the world. Nobody would regard it as second class simply because we, unlike a federation like the United States of America, have a rule of Parliamentary sovereignty, but as a legal body it is second to none, and I have got absolutely no doubt that when the move to the Supreme Court occurs in this country it will continue to be regarded as a first class court.

I am sure Lord Woolf was not casting any doubt on the likely quality of arguments or the quality of judgments. I think he was suggesting that the term "Supreme" might reasonably be interpreted as belonging to a court with much broader powers than are in fact envisaged. Happily, Lord Woolf will be with us at Gresham in a few weeks' time,[5] so I will ask him then what he meant and we will let you know. Can I turn now to the third big constitutional reform issue in debate just now. I don't want to spend too much time on it, because I think it is unexceptional. I am referring to the subject of judicial appointments. Can you give us a quick overview of the issue and then we can have a chat about it?[6]

The Lord Chancellor appoints nearly all judges. That doesn't mean just the High Court judges and the circuit judges, it means a whole range of judicial officers—for example the Chairman of Mental Health Tribunals, and the Chairman of Employment Tribunals. My predecessors in 1950 were appointing about 50 judicial figures a year. The vast majority of those people they were appointing as judges, they were appointing from the Bar, and they would know not just the people that they were appointing as judges, but also the pool from which the selection is made. Putting aside magistrates, whom I also appoint, I currently appoint about 900 full time judges

---

[4] Lord Woolf, "The Rule of Law and a Change in the Constitution" (July 2004) 63 *Cambridge Law Journal* 326.
[5] See Ch.20.
[6] The appointment of judges is also discussed by Lord Bingham (Ch.7), Lord Irvine (Ch.13), Sir Hayden Phillips (Ch.15), Lord Mackay (Ch.17) and Professor Bogdanor (Ch.19).

a year. The vast majority of the judges that I appoint I don't know before I appoint them. It seems to me in those circumstances it must be sensible to get a proper methodical system of appointing judges in place involving proper methods of appointment, proper scrutiny, identifiable and transparent methods, that not just the people who are judged but also the people who apply to be judges can see is fair, rather than being dependent on just one person. A Judicial Appointments Commission is a way of doing that. It still involves the Executive to some extent, because as you said earlier on Richard, there needs to be a partnership between the two. But the Executive can only have a very limited role, it seems to me, and we have proposed that a name can only be rejected once. But broadly the aim is to set up a proper and rigorous and transparent appointments system that gives people confidence that it is done both independently, which already is done, but also methodically.

And apolitical, by definition, then?

Totally apolitical. And I should say, and it is important to make clear, that the appointment of judges by me and all of my immediate predecessors has been done on a totally apolitical basis. We have scrupulously sought to appoint judges on an objective basis. But it becomes harder and harder, not to do it on an apolitical basis, but harder and harder to do it on a proper methodical basis if you are dealing with such a large number of appointments.

But the comparison with the US is interesting. We have not had a US Supreme Court Justice here at Gresham—that would be marvellous at some stage—but I think the contrast would be remarkable, not least in how political is the process by which Supreme Court Justices are appointed.

But that is something we very much do not wish to emulate here. Supreme Court Justices in the United States of America are questioned in public by legislators about what their views on abortion are, would they uphold the current law on abortion, what their views on capital punishment are . . .

The reality is that many of their decisions are political in nature.

Because they are making constitutional decisions which are superior to the Legislature, they are in effect making decisions that we in this country would regard as political. I think that our Judiciary would be fatally undermined if people were interested in what their particular views on particular political issues were, because I think people want the position to be as it is currently—that you are appointed as a judge, not remotely on the basis of your political views, but entirely on the basis of your quality as a lawyer. That should continue. In order for that to continue there should be no public, or indeed private, examination of the judges' political views—political with a small p, that is.

293

One thing I wanted to touch on in this context arose in your lecture to the Law Society last year at their annual conference. You talked then about the challenges of trying to ensure that ethnic minorities and women were well represented in the law. In the short and medium term, how can this be achieved without some form of positive discrimination? I know it is not going to be within your portfolio to decide this, but I wondered what thoughts you had. For the reasons you mentioned, a significant percentage of women, by the time they come to be of judging age, have left the legal profession. So how can we deal with this?

Point number one: it has got to be clear that appointments to the Judiciary must continue to be made on merit, and merit as a lawyer. There cannot be any arrangements that involve positive discrimination. Having said that, you can dramatically increase the pool from which you select people to be judges if you are more willing to look at for example more varied sorts of lawyers. Currently the appointments to the Circuit Bench and the senior Judiciary come almost exclusively from the Bar, although there are some appointments from the solicitors' profession. One can first of all be more willing to appoint from the solicitors' profession, but I think it goes further than that, I think we should be looking as well at seeing whether or not you can appoint from people who are employed as lawyers; employed as lawyers whether by private sector organisations or by public sector organisations. For example, would somebody who had been a CPS prosecutor be somebody who might be capable of being a judge? Would somebody who had done lots of family law cases for a local authority be capable of being a judge? Would somebody who had been working in a law centre, or in a not-for-profit provider of advice, be capable of being a judge? In principle I believe the answer is yes. Not everybody of course, and you would need to make sure that they had appropriate judicial qualities, particular personal qualities, and also legal knowledge and appropriate training. But you can change the mix by widening the pool, without diluting merit, which I think is incredibly important. Now it will not happen overnight. We have a precedent in relation to this. In I think it was 1970 or 1980 Jean Chretien, who subsequently became the Prime Minister of Canada, was then the Minister of Justice in Canada, and he committed himself strongly and firmly to a more diverse Judiciary; said, as I say, it can't happen overnight, said, as I say, it can't be done by positive discrimination and must be done in a way that doesn't in any way give people cause to be fearful that merit has been diluted. In the autumn of last year the Chief Justice of Canada came over, a lady called Beverley McLachlin. She said that political commitment, which was accompanied as well by a Judicial Appointments Commission, has delivered change over a period of 10 years. I think it is important that we do deliver something in relation to this because I think every part of the State is under much more examination than it ever was before—politicians are much more examined by the press, legislators are much more examined by the press, and so judges will be. Representativeness of society will become more important than it is now.

We have talked about the role of the Lord Chancellor, the Supreme Court, judicial appointments. These reforms are all in the Bill. What is the current status of the Bill? We know that the House of Lords responded strongly. Could you summarise the response, what it means in practice, and when you anticipate the Bill becoming law?

I started by saying let's consider these proposals on their merits, let's not judge them on the basis of the way that they were first announced. The way that they were first announced gave rise to anxiety in a number of quarters. The Bill to give effect to these changes was introduced in the Lords in March of this year. It was given a second reading by the Lords, which means that the principles were debated. Normally the next stage after that would be a committee of the whole House. Instead what the Lords decided very unusually was it should go to a Select Committee of the House, which means evidence would be taken on it, that Select Committee can amend the Bill. Then the next stage is a committee of the whole House. So they have added unusually a stage in its consideration. Now we opposed that extra stage at the time because we thought it might be a way of trying to kill the Bill. That has not happened and it is providing a forum for the detail of the provisions to be looked at, and I hope that will very much help in both validating many of the provisions, and also making people feel more comfortable about the process. When will the legislative process be finished? On current estimates, by March of next year it will have become an Act.

It seems to be an example of how dissatisfaction and concern with process can actually affect views on the substantive issues. The fundamental merits or otherwise of a new Supreme Court, for example, are not affected by the fact that in the middle of June 2003 announcements about reforms were not fabulously handled. Although, your Permanent Secretary, Sir Hayden Phillips, when he was with us at Gresham and we talked through the announcement process, he made it all sound rather fine actually.

He always does!

Why don't we move on to something entirely different, and that is the subject of QCs and their possible abolition. Again, if you can outline the context for us first of all, we can then go on to discuss the issues.[7]

For a very long time the State has, on application by senior members of the Bar and also solicitors, awarded the rank of Queen's Counsel, which is an indication by the State that it accepts you as a particular expert advocate. The last time this was done was the year before last. My predecessor, Lord Irvine, indicated he was suspending the process of the appointment of Queen's Counsel, in effect for two reasons. The process by which Queen's Counsel was appointed was perceived particularly by Sir Colin Campbell, Chairman of the Judicial Appointments Commission, as potentially not being fair—that if you didn't have a sort of running assessment of whether or not you are good enough to be a QC, but instead it was basically done on the basis of self-selected consultees, you might not be

---

[7] The future of QCs is also discussed by Lord Irvine (Ch.13), Sir Hayden Phillips (Ch.15) and Lord Woolf (Ch.20).

getting a fair competition. Another part of Government said not just the process of appointment is wrong but also it might be uncompetitive. The question was asked: why should the State give a status to senior lawyers, there is no Queen's doctor, or there is no Queen's estate agent, why should there be a Queen's Counsel? It is giving an unfair advantage and the only effect of doing that is to allow—and this is the cynical view put forward by various bits of the world—the status the Government bestows, it allows the lawyer to charge more so it is not good for the market. Now we have looked at all those arguments. The contrary argument seems to me to be it very much helps the State that lawyers feel that if they behave well they might become QCs. There is a huge international prestige to QCs which brings trade into the country. Which arguments are right? Is it right that the Government shouldn't advantage somebody and that the process is too flawed to be saved? Or, is the argument right that it helps the nation that there is a proper management of leading advocates, and that it helps international trade? I can't tell you, is the answer to that, because I will make an announcement in the next few weeks in relation to that.

So when are you making an announcement?

In the next few weeks.

A couple of thoughts arise from what you have said. I see a big difference between the relationship between a senior barrister and the Government and, say, a doctor and the State. It seems to me that the Judiciary, most of whose number are taken from the Bar, is one branch of Government. As for QCs, I am never entirely sure—although I should know this—whether or not they are, strictly, officers of the court, but certainly if they are, and even if they are not because of their involvement with the administration of the law, there is some ground for saying that the State has a justification in being involved in their appointment in a way that would not make sense in relation to doctors. In any event, I am always troubled when people speak of "QC" as a quality mark. It seems to me this is rather to demean the notion of Queen's Counsel. It is a bit like saying that being appointed a Fellow of the Royal Society or of the British Academy is to be the recipient of a quality mark. Quality marks in industry, where they really come from, are normally about conformity with some process. But with QCs (as with FRSs or FBAs), the honorific is in respect of something far more substantial. So, I think to question, as others have, whether or not the State should confer a quality mark is a rather tendentious way of putting it, because it does not fully convey or capture the nature of the appointment.

I accept that, and I also think however one does it, there are various aspects of the State's relationship with lawyers, for example, in legal aid, where there is bound to have to be some differentiation between senior advocates and junior advocates, if only for the purpose of pay. So there are other as it were tangential benefits that come from having a pretty bona fide system of distinguishing between junior counsel and leading counsel.

But under another system, as in Ireland, you could be an SC (Senior Counsel) rather than a QC and that could be conferred presumably by the Bar Council. Could that not be done?

Yes, you could have a system whereby it was the profession, but for it to be valid you would need the way that the profession did it to be acceptable from the point of view both of the State, as represented by the judges, and the State as represented by the publicly funded paymaster.

There are a strong set of arguments in favour of involving the State, given its weight and gravitas.

You could, I am just throwing out ideas here, but you could have something that the professions were doing, but done in accordance with particular parameters set by the State.

Hypothetically, if the end is nigh for QCs, would the reform be implemented retro-spectively? Would people who are currently QCs no longer be QCs, or would there be a body of people who were still QCs, and other people who might be SCs, or indeed might be nothing? Because it seems to me that a lot of the mischief would actually be maintained unless you could retrospectively remove the suffix QC from people's names. If you can't, it is still there and would be for a generation hence.

Yes, we raised that in the consultation paper. I myself, it is very difficult for people not to be able to indicate that they once held the rank, so to be Charles Falconer QC (ex) would be . . .

Or a wee line through it maybe?

Have a red line through it to indicate it had gone. However, it is possible constitu-tionally to remove the rank of QC and it does get removed automatically. For example, when you become Lord Chancellor you are no longer a QC. But instinc-tively I understand the point you are making. But it seems neither practical nor sen-sible to try and strip from those people who have already got it, the office.

In which event, you are left with the issue for at least another 20 years. Let's move on. Freedom of information. I have never talked about freedom of information in any of my Gresham discussions and it is actually a development of huge significance. I am conscious of time, so—a quick overview and then some quick analysis.[8]

---

[8] Freedom of information is also discussed by Professor Bogdanor (Ch.19).

For years and years and years, Governments have both promised a Freedom of Information Bill and also promised that they would be more open in the information that they gave. No Government delivered one until we delivered one in 1999. Prior to that there had been, and there is, a code of practice in Government which is published which sets out the circumstances in which information will be provided, if asked. There has been lots of debate as we passed the Freedom of Information Bill through Parliament about whether it went far enough, whether it would actually change anything. I have got absolutely no doubt that it will radically change things, because for the first time you have a statutory scheme in effect that is enforceable in front of a tribunal or the courts, and that will determine what information comes out, and inevitably the process of what information is disclosed will over time get determined by people outside Government. But however keen you are to be open, if it is a code of practice that is ultimately supervised by people within the Government machine, that is a totally different process from one where you have courts or independent tribunals doing it. The inevitable and inexorable process will therefore be that more and more information gets out, and our culture, I believe, over time will change. That isn't about the precise terms of the Freedom of Information Act, which has been incredibly contentious, but about the fact that you set up an independent legal or quasi-legal structure which makes the determination.

But it will also change culturally in the sense that with this far greater transparency will come an awareness on the part of everyone working in the public sector that, in principle, their material will be available for scrutiny in a way that was never so before.

It has got to be done sensibly.

Can I just jump in and clarify, because I think there is a confusion here, even amongst specialists. We are not talking about offering general access to personal information, which is very much the domain of data protection law. These matters overlap considerably, but what we are talking about here is offering access to public sector information of a non-personal sort.

Though from the point of view of people, particularly ministers, the two could overlap to a considerable extent. So who is in my diary, who I see as Lord Chancellor every day, should that become public under Freedom of Information? My own view is that it probably shouldn't, on the basis that you must give ministers some space in which to conduct the ordinary business of Government, because quite a lot of what we do shouldn't be as it were done in the glare of publicity, it should be done on a private basis. There is a balance to be struck between sensible openness, which means for example making it clear that all pure policy material comes out, it should also be clear that once stuff has got no relevance to how you conduct your business today it should come out, but equally you need to be sure that you don't end up in such a situation, which you do in some bits for example of the American Government, where everything is conducted on the telephone so that there can be a free exchange of views. And we all know that when we are trying to come to a view on things, a moderately open textured discussion in which you express views that you would have regretted expressing as a thought process being exposed, you don't want to become too limited and inward looking in the way that you express things.

"Please don't minute that" as is sometimes said at a meeting—that kind of thing? But what I always want to claim is that there must be a private space created and protected, into which others won't be able to intrude. There are analogies here with data protection law, when it was originally introduced in this country in the early 1980s. At that time, when it seemed only to apply to electronically held material, the way around the law, if you didn't want someone to find out what information was held about them, was to store it manually, in a filing cabinet, on bits of paper. Now the law was changed, so that individuals have rights of access to personal information about them, whether or not it is stored in electronic form. But, of course, people are quite ingenious in trying to avoid the demands of the law. It is early days for the freedom of information regime and so the impact of its implementation remains to be seen. What I am interested to know from you, however, is the extent to which you think its scope and thrust is sufficiently appreciated across the public sector, because it really is quite fundamental.

It applies to central Government, it applies to local Government, it applies to parish council organisations, so I can't speak for the whole of Government. I can tell you, because my department is responsible for freedom of information, that as far as my Cabinet and political colleagues in Government are concerned, they are extremely aware of it. Because if the judgment I make is correct, and I believe that it is, that it will have an effect on the change of culture, we have got to be looking now at setting up arrangements as to how we can comply with our obligations, and I think one has got to become much, much more aware of what the sensible space in which policy is perceived is, and what is going to become available to the public. So are my political colleagues aware? They most certainly are. Is the senior civil service aware? They most certainly are. And there are mixed views, I can tell you.

I think I should move now to my final question. And it is a question, or a variant of a question, that I ask of everyone sitting with me at Gresham College. You can see that there are some school pupils and young students in the audience this evening. If one of them approached you and said he or she was considering a career in law and/or politics, what would you advise?

Speaking entirely personally, I can think of no better career than a career in the law, save possibly a career in politics.

In that order?

My father and my grandfather were both lawyers, I always wanted to be a lawyer. I was at the English Bar from 1974 to 1999 when I ceased to be Solicitor General.

It was the most engaging, most worthwhile profession one could possibly imagine. Engaging, because it was extremely difficult—you were dealing with people's problems. Worthwhile, because whatever you may read about lawyers in the press, they are ultimately, the vast, vast majority of them, engaged in seeking to help people through difficult times. And the moment you get engaged in that, that is what you focus on, not the caricature or stereotype of lawyers who are only interested in money. I deeply, deeply wanted to stay at the Bar in 1997 when I became a Government minister. But the last seven years have been utterly engaging and compelling as well, and of course you move from helping individuals to helping a wider public, or at least you believe you do. So both jobs I strongly recommend.

Lord Falconer, many thanks indeed.

CHAPTER NINETEEN

Vernon Bogdanor CBE FBA
Professor of Government, University of Oxford

Tuesday May 11, 2004

I am delighted tonight to welcome as my guest my successor as Gresham Professor of Law, Professor Vernon Bogdanor. Just a little bit of biographical detail: Vernon is Professor of Government at Oxford University and he's a Fellow of Brasenose College. He is an acknowledged expert on constitutional matters, and we read him regularly in the popular press as well as in academic writings. His speciality of Government and constitutional issues is particularly relevant for my series of discussions, because those of you who have been with us will recall that we have had many judges and politicians discussing the impact of a number of vital constitutional reforms, including a new Supreme Court, the abolition of the office of Lord Chancellor, the introduction of freedom of information legislation, human rights legislation, and so forth. Together, these changes constitute a major set of changes—it's a seismic shift, if I can put it that way—in the constitutional landscape of this country, and what I'm hoping to do tonight is discuss some of these matters in depth with Professor Bogdanor.

But I wonder if I could start on a more general point: what does the Professor of Government at Oxford do? How do you divide your time?

I am an academic, and, as Professor of Government, I teach and lecture on systems of Government. My own speciality lies in the Government of Britain, the Governments of Western Europe, and also that of the United States. I am interested in how modern democracies work. I ask why there are differences between different systems of Government, and what the consequences of these differences are. For example, why does United States have a presidential system, while we have a cabinet system? Different countries have different electoral systems. Most countries on the Continent have proportional representation, while we stick to first past the post. I try to isolate the differences between different systems, and of course when one asks why these differences exist, one has to look into historical factors. As you imply, it is an interesting and challenging task.

I suppose you can be involved with some intensely practical issues as well as matters of high theory. To focus on the latter, are you interested in and do you work on

301

fundamental issues such as the nature of authority, the nature of legitimacy, the rule of law, and so forth?

I have always had a predilection for questions that can be answered. It is perhaps a characteristic of philosophical questions that they can't really be answered in any final sense. Philosophers are asking many of the same questions that they asked in the time of Plato and Aristotle. If one asks a question such as: how did Britain come to have a Cabinet system? One feels that one can, in principle, answer it. But if one asks a philosophical question such as: what is reality or what is legitimacy? There is a danger that, at the end of one's life, one does not know very much more than one did at the beginning. So I tend to stick to questions which can be answered. I am an unapologetic empiricist.

Good, because I think, by and large, our audiences like concrete answers to concrete questions, so let's focus on some of the practical issues. I gave a hint at my view as to how radical, collectively, the various changes since 1997 have been. I would like to get a more rigorous and systematic account of the changes from someone who actually specialises in these areas, because we have had, as I have said, various comments and observations from a variety of guests who are personally involved, but you can take a step back and take perhaps a more objective view. In the first instance, then, can you give us a snapshot of the range of constitutional reforms that we've seen since the current Government came to power?

You are absolutely right. The period since 1997 when Tony Blair came to office has seen a huge amount of constitutional change. Perhaps it has not been as much noticed as it ought to have been. In the very first week of the Blair Government there was an extremely radical constitutional change, which surprised many people, when the Government made the Bank of England constitutionally independent. The changes since then have been fairly continuous. In a month's time, in June 2004, we will have the chance to vote in local elections—elections for the Mayor of London and the London strategic authority and elections for the European Parliament. There was, however, no Mayor of London before the Blair Government came to power. The legislation providing for a Mayor of London and a London strategic authority was passed by the Blair Government. There were of course elections to the European Parliament before 1998 but these were held under the first past the post system. In 1999, however, Parliament passed legislation providing for proportional representation in these elections. So the voting system for these elections is quite different from what it was.

That leads me on to talk about something else that has not perhaps been as much noticed as it should have been. We have elections for the House of Commons and we have elections for local Government. There are also a number of other bodies—the London strategic authority, the Scottish Parliament, the National Assembly of Wales, the Northern Ireland Assembly. All of these bodies are now elected by proportional representation, as is the European Parliament. Proportional representation is almost wholly new in Britain, another radical, rather unnoticed change.

Of course, the Scottish Parliament, the National Assembly of Wales and the Northern Ireland Assembly are themselves new institutions, a result of the Government's devolution programme. Moreover, these bodies, as well as the London Mayor, were established following referendums. The people were consulted, and the Prime Minister has promised further referendums on joining the Euro and on the European Constitution. We have come perhaps to take this idea of popular consultation for granted, just as we are perhaps beginning to take proportional representation for granted, but I am old enough to remember a time when that wasn't so. Our first and so far our only national referendum was in 1975 when we were asked whether we wished to stay in the European Community, as it was then called. But there had been a huge argument before 1975 about whether the referendum was constitutional or not. That issue now seems to have been settled.

It is easy to see that the referendum is an instrument of great importance. Let us suppose that it was still regarded as unconstitutional in Britain. Then we would probably now be using the Euro, because Tony Blair, and the Government as a whole, would like us to join the Eurozone. In fact, however, the Government cannot join until it secures the approval, not just of Parliament, but also of the people, which will not be easy because every single opinion poll so far has shown a majority in the country *against* the Euro. But if the referendum had never been invented, we would almost certainly be using the Euro.

These are just a few examples of the radical constitutional changes that have occurred and how they have affected us.

Let me now make a further point. If one looks at previous periods of radical constitutional reform, for example the great Reform Act of 1832, one can see that there was tremendous popular pressure and agitation. The public were storming the barricades demanding the vote. So were the Suffragettes at the beginning of the 20th century. Women were throwing themselves under racehorses, chaining themselves to railings, getting sent to prison, in order to secure the vote. Today, however, although there have been pressures for reform—particularly perhaps in the case of devolution for Scotland—there has been hardly any popular agitation in favour of reform. Nobody is chaining themselves to railings demanding proportional representation, or more devolution. All the evidence we have from survey research shows that— sadly for the sale of my books!—constitutional reform is a very low priority for most of the electorate. Bob Worcester, the well-known head of Mori, the polling organisation, did a survey in 1997 of the relative importance of various issues. There were 14 issues and constitutional reform came 14th!

Can I interrupt and ask, and I don't mean this in a patronising way, is this apparent lack of interest because people are unclear as to the nature of the issues that come under the heading of constitutional reform, or is it the case that they're simply not interested in such matters?

People simply do not think that they are very important. In 1997, I had what I thought was a bright idea of writing a guidebook to the various reforms. But my publisher said that he would take it on two conditions. The first was that I kept the word "constitution" out of the title, because that would stop it being sold; the second was that I added a chapter on the monarchy, because that, my publisher said, was the only issue that really interested the public. There simply is very little public pressure for constitutional change. It is a distinctly minority interest.

But the reality is, if you combine your set of observations there with the various changes I mentioned as well, that we are going through a period of very radical change. In relation to these changes, do you sense there is some kind of constitutional master-mind or puppet master who is bringing the whole thing together with a vision as to how it's all going to end up, on the one hand, or are we experiencing a series of piecemeal, perhaps even knee jerk, reforms by a Government that is concerned perhaps more with appearance than substance? There are four or five questions there, I know!

It is perhaps equally surprising that there is no overall plan as to what ought to be done and where we are to go. The Government has been responding, for better or worse, to what it sees as practical demands. For example, the Government took the view that, if Scotland was not given a degree of self-Government, she might seek to break away from the United Kingdom entirely. The Government took the view that in London there was some pressure to restore an elected authority—the Greater London Council had been abolished in the 80s—and a directly elected Mayor. It took the view that people would not be willing to enter the Euro without a referendum, and it has just accepted, under some pressure from the press, that we should not adopt the European Constitution without a referendum.

All this has been attacked as just mindless pragmatism, but there is a defence. One may say that the task of Government is precisely to respond to practical problems. There is no popular demand for a new blueprint, but there are pressures. From this point of view, the pragmatic and piecemeal approach is a strength and not a weakness.

Can we dip into this subject in a different way now, by your taking us through the basic concepts in the first instance? We have, as is often said, no written constitution in this country. Are we by default moving towards that? If we had had a written constitution, would these constitutional reforms have been possible? Can you talk us through the distinction between a written and an unwritten constitution?

It is often said that Britain hasn't got a written constitution, but that is a slightly misleading statement. It is certainly true that if one is in the United States or France or Germany, one can go into a shop and buy a copy of the constitution. The American Constitution is the oldest still existing, dating from 1787, and one of the best. One can read it through in about half an hour and get a fairly good idea of how America is governed. The same is true of France or Germany. France, however, is very different from America. There have been no less than 16 constitutions since the French Revolution of 1789. The last one is fairly recent, it dates from 1958, 46 years ago, but it is the second longest lasting since the French Revolution. There used to be a joke in France that someone went into a shop and asked for a copy of the constitution, but the reply was, "we don't sell periodicals here"!

We in Britain do not have a document of that kind. That does not mean to say that we do not have a constitution. There has recently been some controversy on the precise question of what a constitution is. People may have followed the debate about the European Constitution, in which Michael Howard, the Opposition leader, implied that only States have constitutions, and so if the European Union gets a constitution, it will have become a State. Yet, golf clubs, tennis clubs etc. have constitutions. One meaning of "constitution" is simply "the rules of the organisation". Every organisation, almost by definition, must have rules that tell you who runs it, how those who run it are to be chosen, what their powers are and so on.

We in Britain have rules regulating Government—who holds power, how they are chosen, what their powers are etc. Moreover, these rules are written down. To say that they are unwritten implies that they are passed on, as it were, from generation to generation by word of mouth. That would be absurd. Our Governmental rules are, of course, written down. They can be found, for example, in statutes. For example, habeas corpus is part of our constitution, the rule that one cannot imprison someone without charging them. The Parliament Acts which limit the powers of the House of Lords are also part of our constitution.

But the difference between Britain on the one hand, and the United States, France etc. on the other, is that there is no single document in which one can find all the rules of the constitution gathered together. It would therefore take a long time to find them—one would have to go through various statutes and judicial decisions, and there would also be some controversy over which particular rules should be considered part of the constitution and which should not. Our constitution, therefore, is not codified—the various rules have not been brought together in a single document. It is uncodified.

Why is it that we are almost unique amongst democracies in not having a codified constitution? The fundamental reason is that in Britain, Parliament has traditionally been seen as sovereign. This means that it could do what it liked. Someone in the 18th century said that Parliament could do anything except turn a man into a woman, or a woman into a man. But, if Parliament said that in future, from the point of view of the law, a man is a woman and a woman a man, the legal status of men and women would have been changed. If, however, Parliament could do what it liked, then there would be no point in having a constitution, because a constitution is a kind of higher law above Parliament.

Our peculiarity is that we do not have a codified constitution because Parliament is sovereign; although some might say that Parliament was no longer sovereign since we entered the European Community, as it then was, in 1973, for Parliament then arguably bound itself to observe a higher law: European law.

And of course this is crucial from the judicial point of view because the Supreme Court in the United States can judge the Legislature's output as unconstitutional by reference to this definitive single document in a way that our Supreme Court will not be able to. So it's not simply a question of it all being in one place; it's the very status of that document once assembled.

That is a very important point. Some countries, and, as you say, the United States is a good example, have what is called judicial review. This means that if the

Legislature exceeds its powers, a court—the Supreme Court in the case of the United States—can strike the offending law down. Let me give an example. The American Constitution declares that Congress shall pass no law restricting or abridging the freedom of speech or religion. During the Second World War, there was a very interesting case brought by Jehovah's Witnesses, who objected to a requirement to salute the flag in schools. They said that this requirement was a breach of the clause providing for freedom of religion, since their religion forbade the saluting of the flag. This case went up to the Supreme Court, caused a great deal of controversy, but in the end the Court agreed with the Jehovah's Witnesses, so that the law requiring people to salute the flag was ruled unconstitutional, and struck down—it became void.

Clearly, we in Britain do not have a system of this sort. If Parliament is supreme, it can make what laws it likes, and however unjust the law the courts could not, in my opinion, strike it down. Parliament could pass a law providing that all red-headed people are going to be executed next Monday, and that would be the law of the land. Of course, Parliament would not do this, but nevertheless the example does show that Parliament has a great deal of power; some would say unlimited power. That is why some people in Britain say that it is high time that we had a constitution of the American type.

The American Constitution was in fact an innovation in human affairs. There had been codified constitutions since the time of the Ancient Greeks. Aristotle, for example, had written about the constitution of Athens. These constitutions of the ancient world were rules about the organisation of Government and these rules restricted what Government did. But the American Constitution was an innovation in the sense that it restricted what the people themselves could do. The First Amendment to the Constitution, for example, declares that Congress shall pass no law abridging the right of freedom of speech or religion. This means that even if we, the majority, want the Jehovah's Witnesses to salute the flag, we simply do not have the constitutional power to do so. For we, the democratic people, have deliberately limited our power. The American Constitution combats what has been known as the tyranny of the majority. Majorities will not necessarily respect the rights of minorities, but the American Constitution requires that they do.

Some people now argue that we too should have something similar to the American Constitution to protect minorities, although others say that we have not done too badly without such a constitution in the past, and that minorities have, on the whole, been well protected in Britain; better protected perhaps than black people were in the United States, an example which shows that constitutions are not necessarily always successful in protecting individual rights.

And this is particularly current. Indeed I'll be speaking to Lord Woolf about this in a couple of weeks' time here at Gresham. For now we can note, however, that in his recent Squire Centenary Lecture in Cambridge, he focused on this point in a number of ways.[1] One of the points he has been quoted on was his observation that any Supreme Court we might have, he said, would be a "second class Supreme Court". Now, I don't think he

---

[1] Lord Woolf, "The Rule of Law and a Change in the Constitution" (July 2004) 63 *Cambridge Law Journal* 317–330.

meant that in the sense that its output would be of poor quality, but he did mean it wouldn't have the spread of powers that, for example, an American Supreme Court has— in the way you've suggested. Another issue, I suppose, is that of judicial review: some people might say judges can review the decisions and the activities of the Executive, but of course they're simply reviewing whether or not the law is actually being applied appropriately in a particular case, not whether or not the law itself is acceptable by reference to some higher instrument. Do you have any thoughts on these matters?

Lord Woolf has gone even further, because in a lecture he gave in Israel, shortly after the Squire Lecture, he declared that we ought to have a codified constitution of the American type. He was, I believe, so annoyed with the provisions of the Constitutional Reform Bill, in particular with the way the Government had abolished the office of Lord Chancellor, that he said we now need what most other democracies already have: a codified constitution.

Yes, Lord Woolf actually commented on this in Cambridge as well. The thing that he was particularly agitated about, as indeed most judges and many other knowledgeable people were, was the Government's proposed Immigration and Asylum Bill, whose clause 14 or 11 (the number changed, as it progressed through Parliament) eliminated any right of appeal or judicial review from decisions of the appropriate immigration tribunals. This was unprecedented in our justice system. At Cambridge, Lord Woolf said that that single clause introduced by the Government could actually precipitate a move towards a written constitution because we need to be protected from that kind of erosion of basic constitutional entitlements. Since then, the Government of course stepped down on that issue.

I am very glad that you have raised this issue since I wrote an article in *The Times* on this very point. As you say, this attempt to exclude the courts was unprecedented, and it offers a good illustration of the powers of Government in our system. In the original form of the Bill which was concerned with asylum seekers, the Government had, as you say, taken away the right to appeal to the courts against an adverse decision by a tribunal. That clause has now been withdrawn, I am glad to say. Nevertheless, it was unprecedented and it does show how our rights and liberties are at the mercy of the goodwill of those in Government. That provides a powerful argument in favour of a codified constitution.

But it also shows how the ability of commentators and specialists such as yourself to influence public thinking can be crucial, and it further demonstrates, it seems to me, how important the Law Lords, those judges who sit in the House of Lords, have been, or can be, in influencing Parliament's views. And of course, and we'll perhaps go on to this later, under the Government's proposed reforms you will no longer have senior judges in the House of Lords. They may find other channels for communicating their views, they indeed may write in the press as well, but it does show that there currently are quite effective mechanisms and safeguards, even if not so formal, in place to influence Government policy, even when they have a majority.

Yes, that is so. Nevertheless, any political system has to resolve fundamental questions which often affect very small and perhaps unpopular minorities. The example I gave a few moments ago, of the Jehovah's Witnesses in the United States, is very relevant here. They were a very small and not particularly popular minority, especially in wartime. Not many people would go to the barricades on their behalf. Similarly, asylum seekers are not always popular in Britain, and not many people would be prepared to go to the barricades on their behalf either. So there is a powerful argument to the effect that one needs some sort of institutional protection, such as is provided by a codified constitution, for minorities who find it difficult to get into the electoral process. If a minority is large enough, it will be listened to. Obviously the Scots are listened to, and the Welsh are listened to, but when we come to much smaller groups, safeguards may be needed in addition to that provided by the electoral process, to secure fair play.

Can we just go back to the constitutional reforms? It seems to me that there are at least two dimensions here. On the one hand there's the process by which a reform is effected, and on the other hand there's the substance of the reforms. In many ways, a lot of the controversy over, for example, the abolition of the Lord Chancellor's office, has been more about the process by which this office was abolished or is being sought to be abolished, rather than whether or not its abolition is a good idea. Some months ago, we had Sir Hayden Phillips sitting in your chair. He is Permanent Secretary of what was the Lord Chancellor's Department and is now the Department for Constitutional Affairs. I asked him about the way in which these changes came about, and he made an eloquent and valiant defence of the process. Lord Falconer, who was my last guest, actually said that the circumstances surrounding the announcement of the reforms "plainly weren't the best in the world". Can we dwell on the process by which constitutional reform can and ought to be effected?

I am sure that some ministers would privately concede that the method by which the reforms had been carried out left something to be desired. But perhaps they might also say that if they had spent a great deal more time consulting, there would have been a lot more opposition and hostility and they would never have achieved anything. In a sense, however, that is but a restatement of the problem, for it is one of the characteristics of most countries with codified constitutions that it is more difficult to change the constitution than to change an ordinary law. If one looks, for example, at the constitution of Ireland, one will find that it cannot be changed without a referendum. In the United States, the Legislatures of three-quarters of the states or specially elected Conventions in three-quarters of the states must agree to changes in the constitution. It is not surprising that there have been only 27 constitutional amendments since the constitution was promulgated in 1791, and that most proposals for amendment fail. In France, the constitution may be changed only by a referendum or by three-fifths of the members of both legislative chambers sitting together. So the procedure for changing the constitution is more difficult than the procedure for changing the law. What is the point, after all, in having a constitution if constitutional rules could be changed as easily as an ordinary law can be changed?

There are some people in Britain who say that a change such as the abolition of the office of the Lord Chancellor should not be made just on the whim of the

Government, with a temporary majority. Might that not be potentially dangerous? Suppose a Government decided, for example, to alter the electoral system in its own interests? Do we not really need a constitutional umpire of the kind possessed by most other democracies?

And indeed one key concern of the judges has always been the extent to which the independence of the Judiciary might be eroded by the whim of a Government in power. Can I just jump ahead, because we will shortly discuss the constitutional reforms relating to the Judiciary, but the solution that seems to be emerging has been expressed by Lord Woolf as a "constitutional settlement". The mechanism used so far to achieve this settlement is a document that is being called a concordat. This formally decrees the independence of the Judiciary and indeed, as I understand it, imposes an obligation on each and every Government minister to uphold the independence of the Judiciary. But my question to you, in light of what you were just saying, is whether it will be as easy to change the law that establishes that independence as it is to change the law on any other subject? What does a constitutional settlement mean?[2]

That is a very difficult question to answer. The whole notion of the independence of the Judiciary is more complex than it appears at first sight. We all agree, of course, that judges should not be swayed by political considerations when making decisions on major issues, such as, for example, asylum seekers. Yet, when we are dealing with these very difficult questions, it is rather different from dealing with purely technical areas of the law, such as, for example, taxation law; since, on matters affecting individual rights, judges might legitimately take different views, not because one judge is a good judge and the other is not but because they hold different philosophies of the law. One judge may tend towards a more liberal viewpoint and the other judge may tend towards a more conservative viewpoint. The question is whether one should take account of that when appointing senior judges. Should one have a balance between judges of different viewpoints? Then, of course, there is a question which is much exercising the present Government as to whether there should not be more women and members of ethnic minorities amongst the higher Judiciary. At present there is only one female Law Lord, and none from the ethnic minorities, and so it would be difficult to have fewer! One may argue that when one is dealing with matters such as abortion or stem cell research, it is very important that a female voice be heard, that the experience of women be heard. When one is dealing with matters connected with racial discrimination or asylum seekers or similar matters, is it not important that the viewpoint of ethnic minorities be heard in the Supreme Court? So, we cannot simply say, appoint the best person, whatever that means. One is not dealing with a purely technical question. One is dealing with an issue where the philosophy of the judge may come into play. The question, then, is what is the best way to appoint judges? That is a very complex question which the Government is endeavouring to grapple with.

---

[2] The constitutional settlement and the concordat are also discussed by Sir Hayden Phillips (Ch.15), Lord Falconer (Ch.18) and Lord Woolf (Ch.20).

Well let's focus on one aspect of that: the issue as to whether or not you feel the Law Lords should actually also be part of the Legislature. Currently they sit in the House of Lords, although by custom they participate in a very limited number of debates.

A good way to approach the answer is to imagine oneself advising a new democracy on its system of Government. Let us imagine that one was called in by, for example, Uzbekistan and told, "We are just recovering from Communism, we want to set up a democratic constitution, how should we go about it?". Would you say to them, "Look, we've got this wonderful system by which our top judges are also members of the Upper House of our Parliament, so as well as being judges, they've got the right to speak and vote on legislative matters. Of course they don't exercise that right; by convention, they don't do it, but nevertheless, it's a wonderful system". And when someone says, "But isn't that bringing the judges a bit into politics perhaps?", you may say, "Well, in theory I can see you might say that, but in practice, it doesn't happen. And we've got this other wonderful arrangement which you might consider, because the head of the Judiciary in our country is also a member of the Cabinet and he's the Speaker of the Upper House. He does three things at once. We think this is a splendid idea and you should adopt that!". Now, I think that you probably wouldn't recommend that to other countries, and I think if you did, they might say, "But under Communism, the judges were far too political. We don't really want that again. We want a separation of powers". So I think one response to those who now find enormous virtues in the office of Lord Chancellor and the Law Lords, is to ask whether they would recommend this system to anyone else. The answer, I am sure, would be no.

That's very interesting. Can I go back to the earlier question? Does the constitutional settlement that establishes or declares the independence of the Judiciary enjoy special status as a piece of legislation? What mechanisms are there for enshrining this independence in a way that is in some sense superior to conventional legislation?

This is now being discussed, and it is an extraordinary difficult problem. The Government has proposed that there should be a Judicial Appointments Commission, which will recommend names to the Secretary of State for Constitutional Affairs.[3] He will then pass them on to the Prime Minister who will advise the Queen whom to appoint. We have to remember that our courts are the Queen's courts and our judges are the Queen's judges. Nevertheless, in a constitutional monarchy, the Queen cannot herself decide on who should be a judge. She therefore acts on the advice of a responsible minister. That protects the Queen from criticism. One can blame the minister, not the Queen, if something goes wrong. But, for the advice to be meaningful, there must be some sort of discretion. So the solution, which I think the Government is moving towards, is to say that although the minister will have discretion, by convention it will not be used. A similar convention

---

[3] The appointment of judges is also discussed by Lord Bingham (Ch.7), Lord Irvine (Ch.13), Sir Hayden Phillips (Ch.15), Lord Mackay (Ch.17) and Lord Falconer (Ch.18).

is used with the appointment of peers. The Prime Minister has discretion, but he has said that he won't question the nominations by the Opposition leaders. If the Conservatives say, "These are our five choices", Tony Blair has said, "I will by convention accept this recommendation even though I could, constitutionally, reject it". That is one way of getting round the problem of reconciling ministerial discretion with the need for a non-political appointments system.

But, some would argue that the Appointments Commission should have guidelines. That would be a controversial proposal. Should it be required to appoint a certain number of women or a certain number of non-white people, to get a more diverse bench? The vast majority of top judges have been to Oxford and Cambridge, many are from public schools, and they are very unrepresentative of British society. Does it matter? There is the well-known joke about the judge who asked, "Who are The Beatles?". Do we want more diversity on the bench, and if so, how do we get it?

Does all of this not mean, though, that you could have a Government in majority who could say, "We have a Judicial Appointments Commission but we are now using our majority to push through legislation that abolishes it, and we are going to appoint judges again ourselves and, not only that, we are also inclined to appoint judges who lean towards our political way of thinking"? I can't see where the protections come from.

You are absolutely right. There are no institutional protections against that, and it is fair to say that we have recently seen a period of judicial activism. The judges are getting more involved in decisions which affect politics, particularly perhaps in the asylum and immigration area, and the more that happens, the more politicians will start to worry about who the judges are. When the judges were just dealing with technical legislation, it did not seem to matter so much who the judges were, but now it is beginning to matter. In the Pinochet case, at the end of the last century, *The Times* did a survey of which judges were liberal-minded and which were more conservative-minded—profiles of judges, familiar to those who follow the United States' Supreme Court. The great danger and, as you say, there are no institutional mechanisms to check it, is that the more judges get involved in decisions which affect politics, the more politicians will want to get their sticky fingers on the appointments process. They will want to ask who are the judges, are they sympathetic or reliable people? Perhaps we do now need institutional checks against that.

We have a Home Secretary just now who is unhappy with a lot of judicial decisions. I'm not for a second suggesting he's calling for inquiries into judges' political leanings, but I think we are seeing unprecedentedly outspoken criticism of judicial decisions by the Home Secretary.

That is true. It relates largely to the issues of asylum and immigration. Politicians say that they have to face voters who, to put it crudely, do not like asylum seekers, but, politicians would argue, the judges are preventing them from carrying out policies to restrict asylum in line with popular opinion. It arises also in the area of crime, because the politicians say, "Our constituents, particularly perhaps our less well-off constituents on the housing estates, face a daily menace of crime, and the judges are not taking strong enough measures to deal with it". Now that is partly based on a misconception. Survey evidence has shown that when people are asked whether they thought the judges were too lenient or too strict in sentencing, almost everyone said that they were too lenient. Then the same people were given specific examples of sentencing, for particular offences, and they said in each case either that the judge was too strict, or that the sentence was about right. So people take a different view when they are talking in generalities and when they are talking about specifics. It is the same when people talk about MPs. They say that in general they are a dreadful lot, but they tend to exempt their own MP from this criticism, saying, "My own MP is actually rather good. I saw him recently about a problem and he dealt with it quite well". Nevertheless, these two areas—asylum and crime—do arouse conflict, the kind of conflict I talked about earlier, which is in a way the stuff of a constitutional democracy, between the pressures from the majority and the need to protect the constitutional rights of minorities.

There's a third area that I find even more challenging, and that's in relation to terrorism and the so-called protective state that is being set up. A key question here is the extent to which we can or should tolerate in respect of individuals who are suspected of terrorist activities a diminution of their human rights. Of course on the one hand you will have judges by and large defending the individual rights of people no matter who they are, and on the other hand the Government will be saying that we really have to put protection in place when it takes the view that the situation is so critical or the threats are so grave that there needs to be a different balance. I suspect we'll see, over the next few years, considerable conflict over that issue.[4]

Yes, but the example of terrorism does show the limits of what can be done with a constitution. For, although we don't have a constitution, we don't have any people in the equivalent of Guantanamo Bay. The constitution tells us what is in the shop window, not whether we can buy the goods. So we don't need to have too much of an inferiority complex about those societies which do have constitutions, such as the Americans! But as you say, the question is a powerful one, and it is one of those philosophical questions which perhaps you like more than I do, since there is no obvious formula by which one can determine where to draw the balance. However, an American Supreme Court Justice once said that a constitution is not a suicide pact; one does have to find effective measures to deal with terrorists.

There was an interesting example in the Second World War, where Parliament passed a regulation, 18B, which in effect allowed the Government to detain anyone whom it believed to be a threat to national security. The prospective detainee did, however, have the right to put his case to a tribunal. Under that provision, in 1940, Sir Oswald Mosley and other leaders of the British Union of Fascists were detained, but they were later released when the danger of invasion had passed. However, in

---

[4] Human rights are also discussed by Lord Woolf (Ch.1), David Pannick QC (Ch.3), Lord Bingham (Ch.7), David Lock (Ch.9), Oliver Letwin (Ch.10) and Cherie Booth QC (Ch.12).

1940, when there was a genuine danger of invasion, people said, "Look at the damage that Fifth Columnists have done in other countries. We can't afford to leave Fascists free". I think probably the right balance was struck. In a time of extreme national danger, civil liberties had to be curtailed, and we couldn't afford to take the risk of leaving potential traitors free. But, once the immediate danger had passed, there was a good case for releasing Mosley and the other Fascists, obnoxious though their views were. So we did, I think, manage to achieve a reasonable balance, even without a constitution.

I'm sympathetic to some of the observations of politicians in this context, because many of them say that it will only be after some tragedy or some serious assault on our soil that people's opinions on the balance will shift.

People will panic. That happened in America. There is an interesting example from the wartime period in the United States during the Second World War. The Americans decided after Pearl Harbor to deport those of Japanese origin, living in California, away from the coast, away from their homes, and the Supreme Court did not rule against that. The Court said that it was constitutional in the special conditions of wartime. Many now regard that decision, on the part of the Court, as illiberal. But, as you imply, it is difficult to understand the psychology of the Americans when we ourselves, fortunately, have not had to face the problem of 9/11. I think that the psychology of the United States, which felt itself invulnerable, was radically changed by September 11th. It will be interesting to see whether our own civil liberties come under threat as the fear of terrorism grows in this country.

We have been touching for the last few minutes on human rights, and of course human rights legislation is another fundamental reform. Just as people have said over many years that we don't have a written constitution, we've similarly said we don't have a written Bill of Rights. But what is the difference now between having European human rights legislation implemented in this country and having a single document that's called a Bill of Rights?

Most constitutions do have what the Americans pioneered—a Bill of Rights saying that Governments can't do certain things, even if the majority want them to be done, such as, with the First Amendment in the United States, that Congress shall pass no law abridging freedom of speech or religion. We have never had anything similar. Our own Bill of Rights of 1689 is quite different. It protects the rights of Parliament against the monarch, not the rights of the people against Government, for the American idea of the Bill of Rights is incompatible with the sovereignty of Parliament, the notion that Parliament can do what it likes. But we did agree in the 1950s to commit ourselves to a document called the European Convention on Human Rights. This often causes confusion amongst press and public, for it has nothing whatever to do with the European Union. It is an emanation of a quite different body, the Council of Europe, entirely distinct from the European Union. The press, perhaps deliberately sometimes, tends to confuse the two organisations.

We agreed to abide by the European Convention on Human Rights, as adjudicated by the European Court of Human Rights, which meets in Strasbourg. The Court of the European Union, on the other hand, meets in Luxembourg. It was, however, difficult for the ordinary litigant to go to Strasbourg to vindicate his or her rights—it was time-consuming and expensive. The Blair Government wanted, therefore, to, as it were, domesticate these rights, so that one could ensure them without going to Strasbourg. But it faced a problem, a fundamental problem, since we could not, because of the principle of Parliamentary sovereignty, say that Convention rights were superior to Parliament. The Government dealt with this problem in a fairly ingenious way. They said that each Bill when it comes to Parliament has to be certified by a minister to say that it is in accordance with the Convention on Human Rights, the European Convention. The courts are required to interpret every statute, if they can, so that it is in accordance with the Convention on Human Rights. If they can't do that, they must issue a Declaration of Incompatibility, declaring that the relevant statute is not compatible with the European Convention on Human Rights. So, if Parliament were to pass a law saying that all red-headed people are to be executed next Monday, the courts would say, "This is not compatible with the European Convention on Human Rights". The courts cannot, however, do what the American Supreme Court can do—strike a law down—and the offending statute remains part of the law. Nevertheless, there is a special fast track procedure for altering the law in such situations, and it is hoped that this will be used to repeal or amend the offending statute. So we have preserved what seem like two incompatible principles. The first is that of Parliamentary sovereignty, that Parliament can do what it likes; the second is that basic rights should be recognised. All that is in the Human Rights Act of 1998, which came into force in England and Wales in the year 2000. This was, in my view, a fundamental alteration in the constitution, because we now have in effect a kind of Bill of Rights, and we are becoming more like other democracies than we were.

Another subject, one that I'm extremely interested in, is freedom of information—yet another major reform, but one, I sense, about which many people have little real awareness and understanding, both within and beyond Government. Once exposed to the topic, however, it is easy to recognise that this is something fairly fundamental. Would you like to talk us through this?[5]

We do now have a Freedom of Information Act, although most of its provisions will not come into effect until next year. The Act is very feeble, in my opinion, because it provides for too many exemptions. In particular it exempts the advice given by civil servants to ministers. Such information would help Parliament and the people to determine who is responsible when something goes wrong, for example the abuse of prisoners in Iraq; whether it is the minister, in which case, the minister should resign, or whether civil servants are to blame, in which case they should be disciplined. Under our system, it is almost impossible to find out because officials cannot speak out, only the minister can speak out. The minister, therefore, can blame his

---

[5] Freedom of information is also discussed by Lord Falconer (Ch.18).

officials and the officials can't reply in terms of the advice which they gave. The freedom of information we really need to have is to know what advice officials gave to ministers, because then we can tell when something goes wrong whether the minister is to blame or whether a civil servant is to blame. It is too easy, under our system, for ministers to blame civil servants. Under our constitution, the convention of ministerial responsibility provides that ministers take the credit when things go right and they take the blame when things go wrong. The trouble is, however, that most ministers accept only the first part of the principle!

You're saying what is going to be implemented at the beginning of next year is feeble?

I believe that many people will be disappointed when the Act does come to be implemented.

Are you most worried therefore about the various exemptions and exceptions?

The exemption of policy advice is, I think, a mistake. Its consequence will be to protect politicians, and to enable them to blame civil servants for their own mistakes.

There is an argument, as with data protection law when it came in 1984 and there were those who were saying that it didn't go far enough, that it's better to get to the first rung, as it were, and it will evolve and extend, as indeed that piece of legislation has done. So it may well be with freedom of information—we're seeing the beginning rather than the end of a set of changes.

I can understand that. I think that, in the area of freedom of information, we want to work towards the principle that the onus should be on the Government to say why something should not be released, rather than on us, the people, to say why something should be released. In my opinion, one could release the minutes of Cabinet meetings tomorrow without damaging our system of Government, and indeed, much of the discussion in Cabinet does get into the press in some way, often in garbled form. Interestingly enough the minutes of the Cabinet of the Welsh National Assembly are publicly released six months after each meeting without any obvious ill effects. Politicians like to think they have important secrets that can't be revealed to the rest of us, but I think that the real reason for non-disclosure is often to protect themselves rather than for any deeper constitutional principle.

It may be of interest and relevance to know that I chair a public body called the Advisory Panel on Crown Copyright.[6] Formally, it's known as a non-departmental

---

[6] This body is now known as the Advisory Panel on Public Sector Information—*www.apssi.gov.uk*

public body. Its focus is on the re-use of public sector information. On this subject we are going to see further legislation or regulation, again derived from Europe—from the European Directive on Public Sector Information. And the implementation of this directive could well necessitate a change in the culture of the public sector in respect of official information. There is a view that there is great value in Government information and this value should be maximised. But there is disagreement over the way in which it might be maximised by Government. So here is another new and potentially fundamental source of change. Taking this into account, although I agree with you I think that the current freedom of information legislation could go further, I am quite confident we are indeed at the beginning of a set of changes rather than at the end.

Can I conclude and ask you a question that I ask of all people in your chair, as it were? If a student approaches you and says that he or she is considering a career, an academic career, perhaps in politics or law, what message would you pass along from your own experience?

People should only consider becoming an academic if they wish to take a vow of poverty! The universities face very serious problems and need radical changes in the way they're organised. The decline of our great universities has not been sufficiently noticed because it is stepwise each year, but the cumulative effect is very great. The Government is now proposing that students pay more for their education. The question which the universities must face is whether the Government's proposals are sufficient. I think no one can foresee the outcome of the current debate. What is clear is that our universities are competing with American universities as great international universities. In the modern world, there aren't many great international universities outside the United States, but many of them are in Britain. The question is whether we are prepared to pay, either through taxation or if not through taxation in some other form, to preserve our great universities.

If people were to say that our football clubs aren't doing very well internationally—Manchester United and Arsenal keep losing matches against Continental teams—the response would be that this is shocking, and something should be done about it. But people don't say that about our great universities!

To take another example, if people said of Manchester United, "we don't want just the best footballers at Manchester, we should also choose footballers who aren't quite so good, so that we get a social mix", the response would be that we could not do that. In the case of the universities, on the other hand, people seem more prepared to dilute quality. They are less robust when it comes to education. That seems to me rather worrying.

Thank you for joining us, Professor Bogdanor.

The Rt Hon The Lord Woolf of Barnes
The Lord Chief Justice of England and Wales

Monday May 24, 2004

My guest tonight is Lord Woolf. There is a pleasing symmetry to this because Lord Woolf was my first guest 19 guests ago and so I have both started my Gresham law discussions and will be ending them tonight with the Lord Chief Justice.

Last time when we spoke, Lord Woolf, when we sat in these very chairs, it was the 30th of October 2001. We spoke a lot about terrorism and human rights. We spoke about the civil justice system and its reform. These issues are still very much alive, but since we were last together, a whole new set of challenging issues have arisen, not least the constitutional reforms currently before our country. I wondered, just by way of warm-up, if we could touch on the reforms; and, first of all, the announcement of the reforms on 12th of June last year, on how you came to hear about them. Then we can go on to discuss the substance of the reforms themselves. First, though, can we cast our minds back to almost exactly one year ago?

It is not controversial now, but the way the reforms were announced was not a model which should be followed by a Government embarking upon a large programme of constitutional reform. However, I have thought it much better to look forward than look back, and to accept the fact that the reforms were announced in the way that they were, and what is important is that if there is to be this programme of reform, we get the right result in consequence of it. From a personal point of view, if there had not been the initiative from the Government, I would not have been going round saying let's have reforms on this scale, but the reforms having been announced and the matter having been the subject of considerable public discussion, the judges having determined what they would like to see in consequence of those reforms, I now believe the whole process has been positive. The announcement was a catalyst, but what we have now realised is that there were areas where our system prior to the announcement was not in the state it should have been in order to have a Judiciary which is in its position to play its role in relation to the public that it should be in.

The reason I was wanting to focus on the process is this: that those who worry about the ease with which fairly fundamental constitutional change can come about may

317

similarly worry about the durability of the new constitutional settlement you are currently helping to put in place. I think it is understandable that many would ask: "well, just as the role of the Lord Chancellor was swept away with little consultation and through the issue of a press release, then what guarantees do we have that any settlements agreed upon now will not similarly be laid to one side by a future Government?". That's something I'd like to talk about a little later when we talk about the nature of the reform; but that's why I raise it at this stage.

And you're right to do so, and it was the very fact that reforms of this scale could be announced in the way that they were that focused attention on the fact that although there was a longstanding convention, or conventions, which supported our constitutional settlement prior to the reforms, that was not a sure foundation when there was reform in the air, as it has been under this administration, which is a reforming administration.

Indeed. In fact, my last guest—who is to be my successor as Gresham Professor of Law—Professor Bogdanor, who is Professor of Government in Oxford, discussed this with us. As he pointed out, since 1997, there has been a vast range of constitutional changes. Some of these we've discussed here and, in coming years, he'll be looking at them in more detail. But two that we focussed upon and that I thought we could also discuss today, and indeed that I've also discussed with Lord Mackay and Lord Falconer, are the following: (a) the proposed new Supreme Court, and (b) the proposed abolition of the role of the Lord Chancellor. So can we focus on each of these now, in any order that you please?

I am more involved in the reform of the Lord Chancellor than I am in the Supreme Court. Why I am more involved with the Lord Chancellor is because he has a direct and an immediate relationship with the Judiciary of England and Wales. The Supreme Court also has a direct relationship with that Judiciary, but it also has a relationship with the Judiciary of Scotland and Northern Ireland, so it affects all three jurisdictions. We have judges who are regular members of the Supreme Court, at the present time the House of Lords, of which I am not one, and so I really am concerned primarily with the Judiciary below the House of Lords.

Is that today or are you looking forward to the new role of the Lord Chief Justice?

Both today and looking forward. I mean if I achieve what I would like to achieve then I will still be able to sit from time to time, or to be more accurate my successor will be able to sit from time to time, in the new Supreme Court, if and when it is established, in the same way as I sit from time to time in the House of Lords. When I sit in the House of Lords, I am, so to speak, a visiting judge, rather than a member of the permanent panel who sits regularly there, but I do so because I think it is very important that someone who is performing my present role is, so to speak, linked into the Lords of Appeal in Ordinary, and from time to time is spending time with them so that I have an added insight as to how they are thinking. It also gives me a clearer impression of how the law is developing, and that can be relevant to my main and principal job, which is to be in charge of the Judiciary below the House of Lords.

Can I jump in, for the sake of non-lawyers here, because this is a peculiarity of our system here. You were at one stage a Law Lord. Indeed, when you did your Access to Justice Inquiry in the mid-1990s, you were a Law Lord, but when you were appointed then to be the Master of the Rolls, you moved away from sitting on the Judicial Committee of the House of Lords.

I moved from Westminster back to the Strand.

Indeed. But that's not necessarily the standard route, if I might put it that way. Many others have come along a different route.

Lord Bingham went the other way.

Yes. So, we have spoken a bit about the current and future role of the Lord Chief Justice. Can we turn now to the abolition of the office of the Lord Chancellor? In your Squire Centenary Lecture in Cambridge[1] in March of this year, you said you had come round to the view that the abolition of that role was a good thing, and one of your final comments was that you can't turn the clock back—once an announcement had been made about the reform, a full body of opinion and Government machinery rolled into action, such that it would be very hard to stop that momentum. But, leaving aside that argument, I wondered if you could outline why it is, if you've had a change of heart, that you have had?[2]

I think the role of the Lord Chancellor has changed, quite apart from the reforms. The size of the department has grown remarkably. The amount of work that is involved in running that department means that even if there were not other difficulties, it would be extremely difficult for the Lord Chancellor to be more than a nominal judge. One of the roles of the Lord Chancellor is to be Head of Judiciary, but you cannot find it stated anywhere in a statute that he's Head of the Judiciary. The nearest you get to anything in the statute is the statement that he's President of, this is confusing, the Supreme Court, by which it is meant the courts below the House of Lords.

---

[1] Lord Woolf, "The Rule of Law and a Change in the Constitution" (July 2004) 63 *Cambridge Law Journal* 317–330.

[2] The role and the future of the role of the Lord Chancellor are also discussed by Lord Irvine (Chs 6 and 13), Sir Hayden Phillips (Ch.15), Lord Mackay (Ch.17), Professor Bogdanor (Ch.19) and Lord Falconer (Ch.18).

Could you just dwell on that for a short while? It was something I was going to ask you later, because there already is, and this is massively confusing, something called the Supreme Court. Could you just clarify exactly what the current Supreme Court is as against the new proposed final court of appeal?

It is confusing, but it is, funnily enough, a model that was taken round the Commonwealth, and explains the setup in the different countries, such as India or Canada. The traditional judges of England and Wales were the Queen's or King's judges who can trace their line back historically right into medieval times. They were travelling out to provide justice and hear petitions, very much on behalf of the monarch, and therefore they had a sort of supervisory role to deal with grievances in addition to being judges, as we would understand it today. Because of that, what is called a High Court and the Court of Appeal, which is a statutory body, whereas the High Court was a body which was a common law institution, has always had prerogative powers which it had inherited from the monarch, and there is a relationship between the High Court and inferior courts, and it was "supreme" because it supervised the courts below, long before the House of Lords, in its present form as the final court of appeal of the United Kingdom, had developed. So it has always been called Supreme Court, and if you go to the Supreme Court in India, just as people can here go direct to the High Court, so, they can go direct to the Supreme Court of India. The same thing, for example, is true in Israel. And having that direct jurisdiction is something which sometimes in modern times is an embarrassment, because it means they have to do many cases. But it has meant, for example, that the Indian Supreme Court can play an absolutely critical part in Indian society, which it could not do otherwise. I think that, as part of my role of Chief Justice, it is much better that I am a Chief Justice in, so to speak, the middle tier, because I can go and sit as a judge of First Instance, I can go and travel the country, which a Supreme Court judge in the normal way cannot do. It is very important, having a leadership role and having an understanding of the system as a whole.

But coming back to what your original question was, with regard to the Lord Chancellor, he ceased officially in June last year to act as a judge, and once he had made that decision, his natural position as a leader of the Judiciary, I would say, was fatally flawed. There are suggestions that we should keep the Lord Chancellor. People feel it is an office of great antiquity and historic importance and we would lose something if we got rid of the office; and they are saying, "Well, we will keep it in a different form". But none of those who are in favour of keeping the office of Lord Chancellor say he should continue to be a judge, and if he cannot be a judge then it seems to me he cannot be the Head of the Judiciary. Now, as you know, the Select Committee of the House of Lords is considering that question at the moment, and there has been talk in the Select Committee that we will have two heads of the Judiciary: we'll have the Chief Justice, who will be the professional head, and we will have the Lord Chancellor, who will be a constitutional head. Again, I emphasise this is a matter really for my successor rather than myself, and so I have no personal axe to grind, but I think that sort of suggestion is mistaken, that is my personal view, even though if all the reforms had not been announced I would have thought we were in a very fortunate position in having our Lord Chancellor. It made my job much easier, because although I still had a lot to do in the way of leadership, he was there to go and fight battles which in future I am afraid the Chief Justice is going to have to fight. So there were benefits, but I do not think you can, or should, have a leader of the Judiciary who is not a judge, because to an extent the judges should be separate, the judges will not have the same respect for a person who is not one of their number. You cannot be sure that anybody who does not have the protection of his independence, which a judge has, can perform his duties, as they say, without fear or favour, unless they are a judge. The Lord Chancellor, if he's not a judge, in my eyes, he's just like any other minister. He could one day be Lord Chancellor, next day Home Secretary, or he could be Home Secretary and Lord Chancellor; I mean, if the Prime Minister so decided. And the one thing I am sure is that we do not want for our court system and the Judiciary to be in a position where they're subservient to the Home Secretary. Not because of personalities or anything of that sort, it is just not a desirable arrangement.

That almost happened at one stage, did it not?

It did!

Would you like to expand upon that?

I think that I've said enough!

Moving on then, what we're now seeing is the Lord Chief Justice taking on a number of the tasks that hitherto were the province of the Lord Chancellor. This leaves a concern, I know in many judges' minds, about how it is that the independence of the Judiciary can be maintained if, as it were, the Lord Chancellor is not sitting around the Cabinet table, or indeed, historically, as the Lord Chief Justice once sat round the Cabinet table, if there is no one sitting round the Cabinet table representing the judicial branch of Government. This has led, amongst other factors, has it not, to you working with Lord Falconer in putting together what is called a concordat, which is in part to try and clarify and lay down the constitutional independence of the Judiciary? Could you talk us through the nature of the concordat, what kind of document it is, how it will be implemented, and what its main features are?[3]

Yes well, the difference that will take place, if in fact the legislation which is now before Parliament is enacted, is there will be in statute legislation which actually sets out the basic needs of the Judiciary for independence. And I again repeat it, the Judiciary do not want it for themselves, but they want it so that they can do their job as judges properly. So it is going to be in statute. It will be like any other statute. It can be repealed, but there is a huge difference in having to come to Parliament to

---

[3] The constitutional settlement and the concordat are also discussed by Sir Hayden Phillips (Ch.15), Lord Falconer (Ch.18) and Professor Bogdanor (Ch.19).

make changes of a constitutional nature, and merely announcing them by a press announcement, as happened in June. I think that is an improvement.

When we got over the shock of what happened a year ago, it seemed obvious to us that there needed to be a public debate as to what form the settlement should take. Although the consultation papers which were issued by the Government did not actually deal precisely with this, the Judiciary, through the Judges Council which I chair, brought out their response, which included the recommendations as to what should be the responsibilities of the Judiciary. In the new situation there is a mass of detail to be considered. What happened thereafter was negotiations took place between myself, on behalf of the Judiciary, with the Lord Chancellor and Secretary of State Lord Falconer, and between a committee of judges with civil servants, with a view to finding where the divide should be drawn. We identified a series of principles. Then having identified the principles, we looked at the detail and decided how they fitted in with the principles. In this way, we have been able to reach a package where the Judiciary, who I represented—and this was a matter which was consulted upon fully throughout the Judiciary, not only High Court judges, but down to district judges and magistrates, because they were affected as well—could sign up and say that, as a package, this is what we would like to see for the future. I understand that although there's a controversy as to whether we should have a Supreme Court, and there is also controversy as to whether the Lord Chancellor should remain in some form of modified capacity, there is generally acceptance that the concordat does what it sought to achieve: produce a fair balance. You do not want judges to have, and the judges were not asking, for them to have unlimited power. They did not want the Government cut out of a lot of things they are doing. But what was wanted was to ensure that things that the Judiciary should have control of, they had control of. Responsibilities that it was proper for the Government to have control of under our system, the Government would have control. The grey area, in the middle, is a difficult area when the detail becomes important. Here, either consents were needed from both the Lord Chancellor and myself if there was going to be any change made, or if there was a situation where one or other of us had to consult the other. It was necessary to preserve the partnership which has been built up during my judicial career—over the 26 or 27 years that I've been a judge—between the Judiciary and the civil servants, for the management of the court system. We have a very large court system now. It is not so large in numbers, but it is a large system, and it has to be managed.

So, the Executive and the Judiciary have to work alongside one another, and so the notion of there being entire independence is fictional in any event. It is independence in your decision-making and in the management of various aspects of your affairs that is crucial.

What is important is that when a judge is making a judicial decision he can take it without concern, so that it does reflect his or her honest opinion of what is required in that particular case.

And part of the concordat is that there will be a ministerial duty to uphold judicial independence, which is new.

That is going in statute as well, and there is a clear statement already in the Courts Act of last year as to the duty of the Secretary of State to provide an efficient and effective court service to support the court system, and there's schedule after schedule in the Act containing these points of detail. Some of them are really just of historic interest now, but they had to be catered for and they are.

You've touched on this, but I think one of my biggest concerns about this is the nature of the document, the statute, that enshrines the ideas you're talking about. Will this be a regular Act of Parliament?

There is talk before the Select Committee—it was a suggestion of two of the members of the Court of Appeal, Lady Justice Arden and Lord Justice Thomas— that it should have some extra significance because it involved the protection of the independence of the Judiciary. It would be said in the statute that this independence was something that had to be taken into account in construing any other statute. You must not construe that statute in a way which would interfere with the independence. That would be some protection. In addition, our law is developing so that we are distinguishing between one statute and another statute. This is a technical point but there are statutes, the Human Rights Act is an example, which are clearly of constitutional importance of which our case law now is saying have greater importance and it will not be so easy for them to be impliedly repealed. Now, can I explain implied repeal?

Please do.

Implied repeal is: if you have an Act of 1st of January and you have an Act of the 30th of January which conflicts with the Act passed on the 1st of January, the normal principle is that the 30th of January Act impliedly repeals the 1st of January Act insofar as it is inconsistent with the 30th of January Act.

Here's my big concern, and I talked to Professor Bogdanor about this as well. It is really a matter, I suppose, of the nature of constitutions. We don't have a written constitution, of course. But linking back to my earlier comment about the ease with which, frankly, the current Government swept away the role of the Lord Chancellor, what added protection, what safeguards are there in place, in relation to the constitutional settlement that establishes the independence of the Judiciary, such that another Government, or indeed this Government, at any stage could not simply announce that it's decided, for example, that there will no longer be a ministerial duty to uphold the independence of the Judiciary? Does this statute have any special constitutional status?

Well the statute is there, and a Prime Minister, no matter how powerful he may be, cannot change the law as laid down by Parliament without going back to Parliament and getting Parliament to change the law, so that is the added protection.

Why is that added protection over and above the protection, for example, that was hitherto afforded to the role of the Lord Chancellor?

Because there was no legislation.

Although the Lord Chancellor was mentioned in hundreds of different pieces of legislation?

Yes. As I said, it was only convention that he was Head of the Judiciary. The Lord Chancellor was a central figure who had a well-defined position which was different from that of any other minister. Once you have him as Secretary of State for Constitutional Affairs and Lord Chancellor, already you're knocking his unique position within our informal constitution. Once he ceases to be a judge, you're knocking this away further. There was nothing in writing, but we depended on our unwritten constitution and the checks and balances that have been built up over the years to provide our security. The fact that you could reform it in this way was always possible, but nobody had ever contemplated it would ever happen like that.

And presumably that's one of the sets of arguments that people bring to bear when they say that we should perhaps have a written constitution, because it's precisely that kind of . . .

That would give greater security, but on the other hand, it would produce greater inflexibility. I mean the American Constitution can be amended, but it is virtually impossible to amend it, and one of the virtues of our system hitherto is that we have been able to have a constitution which evolves as the needs of society change, and I think that was a great virtue, but time will tell. It could be, when you put it like that—I've got no reason to say so and I am not suggesting the time has come—when the public would say we think we should have a written constitution. There's talk of a European Constitution. It is said that will change the way we do things in this country. We do not have the counterbalance of a written constitution here.

But you're comfortable just now with the settlement and the various safeguards by convention and practice that are available?

I very much hope that the settlement that we've reached is now reduced into legislation. Anything can happen within the political process and it might not happen, but

I think I would feel much more comfortable for the future if we had the legislation which is now contemplated.

Can you just clarify further, where is it just now, the legislation?

It is in the Select Committee, which is an unusual committee, of the House of Lords, where they're looking at the legislation with great care, and they're taking evidence from all sorts of people. Tomorrow, the Chief Justice of New Zealand is giving evidence. There has been a whole range of witnesses giving evidence, including distinguished academics and judges.

Can we turn now to the Supreme Court? We've talked a little about it. We've already mentioned that there is actually a confusion over the very name of the court.[4]

Nobody's said what the existing Supreme Court is going to be called if you have another Supreme Court. That is a difficulty which has yet to be overcome. There's also a difficulty as to, if we have a President of the new Supreme Court, the President of the Family Division will say, "Hoi! That is my title! I've been known historically as the President of the Family Division. Nobody asked me about losing my title". And she feels very proud and fond of her title.

There are quite a few title problems.

These are very important matters! Because Law Lords have been called Law Lords or Lords of Appeal in Ordinary for some time, the judges in the House of Lords. It is not settled what they would be called in a Supreme Court.

They may be like the American members of the Supreme Court—Associate Justice Woolf. I am not sure that I would not be happier being called by my present title, Lord Chief Justice! It does not sound quite as good to be Associate Justice! But there we are, they're very distinguished people.

I can see that Lord Chief sounds better than Associate. But talking about the Supreme Court, again in your Squire Centenary Lecture in March I think eyebrows were raised when you mentioned that it would be, and I think this is worth clarifying, a second class Supreme Court. Clearly, you weren't meaning the quality of justice, but you were referring to the extent to which it is supreme in the sense that other courts have power to strike down laws of their Parliaments as unconstitutional. Would you like an opportunity to talk about that?

---

[4] The judicial work of the House of Lords and the possibility of a new Supreme Court are also discussed by Lord Bingham (Ch.7), Lord Saville (Ch.14), Sir Hayden Phillips (Ch.15), Lord Mackay (Ch.17) and Lord Falconer (Ch.18).

It is very, very kind of you to give me this opportunity, because I have been rightly teased over my comment. I think some of my colleagues in the House of Lords were not very happy about my calling it a second class Supreme Court, which is understandable on reflection. But what I really meant was it would not be the final court of appeal for criminal matters for Scotland, although Scotland is one of the countries to which it applies, or that is my understanding at any rate. The Scots would be very unhappy if it were to take over jurisdiction in relation to criminal appeals from Scotland.

Can I just clarify that? Just now, and I say this as a Scots lawyer, the final court of appeal on civil matters is the House of Lords, but it's not the final court of appeal in Scottish criminal matters.

Secondly, and much more important, most Supreme Courts around the globe can overrule statutes if they contravene the constitution. Well as we have not got a written constitution, we do not have that power, and the new Supreme Court, as I understand it, would not have that power, except in a limited area in relation to devolution matters or in situations where the statute conflicts with legislation from Europe. Where there's European legislation, that takes primacy over domestic legislation. So that is again why it would not be what I would call the normal model of a Supreme Court, like that of United States, Canada or India.

Leaving aside the name though, can we talk about the notion of taking top judges out of the Legislature and putting them—and I want to talk about the relocation in a second—in a new court? Specifically, how do you now feel, on reflection, after all the debate, about the difficulties and perceived conflicts between being a judge part of the time and potentially involved with legislating at other times?

I listened to the debate which took place, and a number of members of our existing House of Lords, the Appellate Committee of the House of Lords, gave speeches in which they explained how they saw their role being diminished by not being so close to the Parliamentary process, and I was impressed. It is not a fundamental issue. On any change of this nature, there's going to be things that are on the plus side and there's going to be other things which are on the deficit side. But they identified a number of reasons, which seemed to me to be quite persuasive, for saying they would be diminished by being taken away from the House of Lords. One of the reasons I made the remark I did was there is only one body anywhere in the world quite like our final court of appeal at the moment in the House of Lords. It is a body which has huge prestige because of the quality of its judgments over the years; it has earned its reputation by its excellence. It is almost like a brand name, and I wondered whether it was a good idea to lose the brand. Looking at the matter as a whole, I can see great advantages.

There is another matter that I think caused me concern, and perhaps again it is not a real concern. The whole ethos of the present final court, of which I was a member, will be changed if you put it in a building elsewhere with the label Supreme

Court above it. We have always had a relationship with Parliament, which again depended upon convention, where we expected the Legislature to respect the position of the courts, and the courts, on the other hand, respected the position of the Legislature. Now, somehow, the very fact that you were all in the same building helped that sort of arrangement to work. Very difficult to define, it is easy to mock and make fun of this and say, "Well it is really not that important", but again that is just something that just causes me concern. It may be that it is because I am probably, in some ways, not in all ways, conservative with a small "c".

The branding issue is an interesting one. My intuition as you spoke there was to agree, but that's partly because I'm a lawyer, and on day one as a law student you hear about the House of Lords and so forth. But I have no idea what the average non-lawyer thinks about the final court of appeal being called the Appellate Committee of the House of Lords, a court where top judges don't sit in robes but they actually sit in lounge suits. It's quite hard to explain, and I wonder . . .

Certainly clarity will be produced by what is proposed. It will be much clearer, and people from overseas will understand our situation. It will be easier, when you're setting out on a legal career, to understand the system. But you know, those things, we manage now. When you make these changes, it is always in one direction. You can never go back. You cannot go back. I think that is part of the reform of the Lord Chancellor. Once you've made an announcement there is not going to be a Lord Chancellor, and you also call him Secretary of State for Constitutional Affairs, and his department sees itself as a frontline ministry, a vehicle of Government policy, it is very difficult to change the culture back again.

Yes, the Rubicon has been crossed. You've anticipated one of the questions I was going to ask, but I'll ask it anyway in a different way. It was about the building, because there was a story in a recent newspaper about the possibility of not having found a building for the Supreme Court and that this might lead to putting the plans for the Supreme Court on ice for a while. The Lord Chancellor denied that that was the case, and I don't want to discuss that particular story, but I do want to ask you, and you've hinted at this, if you think it's vital to have a new building if there is to be a new Supreme Court? I understand the benefits you were saying of being housed in the same building if you are indeed the Appellate Committee of the House of Lords, but if you are actually creating this new brand, do you think we need to wait?

I think if we are going to have a Supreme Court, it should be housed in its new quarters and we should wait until the new quarters are ready until it moves.

There are others of course who say that it was 146 years until the Supreme Court in the United States had its own home, until it was moved out of the basement of Capitol Building, but I suppose that's different from the current context of setting up a new one.

I think it is different. I must say that . . . This is probably an unworthy thought, but having indicated that I am going to say it, I will go on to say it!

We're allowed to have unworthy thoughts at Gresham!

Yes. I think if they were to stay there as squatters, they would lose their ability to exercise leverage to make sure that they have a new building, whether it is in an old, existing building or brand new building, started from scratch, which is worthy of the Supreme Court. If we are going to have a Supreme Court, it must be properly resourced and it must have proper accommodation. I mean we have to be very careful not to give the public the impression that we do not value our court system. One of my concerns, right from the start, about the whole concept of the Supreme Court has been that it is agreed there is to be no new resources for it, and I am afraid I know just how tight are the resources at the present time. There are many aspects of our court system which could be improved if the resources were available. They're not available. I do not complain about that, because I recognise that the Government has to have priorities, but if you cannot have resources for some of these matters which are critical for the everyday running of the courts, then I wonder whether this is the right time, unless it really is a convincing case, and that is a matter for the judgment of Parliament, to have a new Supreme Court. I cannot tell you how much it is going to cost, but I am sure it is going to cost a lot of money by the time it is finished.

The proposal is, is it not, to fund it largely out of increased civil court fees?

That is for its everyday running. I do not approve of that.

Why don't we put the constitutional reforms to one side and touch on another few issues. Firstly, QCs and the potential abolition of what some speak of as this "quality mark" (I don't personally like the phrase). You are personally in an interesting position to comment, are you not, because of the career path you took? You didn't take silk. You did not become a QC. That's worth explaining because it's an interesting quirk of the system, and I say that by way of preface because I think it allows you to be particularly impartial on the issue.[5]

Well yes, because of the job I did, the only way the Government could get a barrister to do the job was by saying well at least at the end of it, you've got the security of knowing you'll become a High Court judge. It is the Standing Counsel to the Government. It is a tremendous privilege to have filled this role, because you do

---

[5] The future of QCs is also discussed by Lord Irvine (Ch.13), Sir Hayden Phillips (Ch.15) and Lord Falconer (Ch.18).

really most of the interesting cases. I always say that administrative law in this country was built up on the cases I lost before Lord Denning as Master of the Rolls. I was regularly appearing in really interesting cases, and so for a barrister who wants to argue interesting cases, it is a marvellous job to be able to have the privilege of doing. In those days, you did not get paid at all well, so I never had any substantial earnings, which I read about some barristers having now. But by no means all of them do and many of them have very modest earnings. But you did have the interest of the work, and it did mean that when I finished the job I had served my sentence and I was then entitled to become a High Court judge, and did.

And with that background in mind, what are your thoughts about the future of QCs?

The reason we have reached the situation we are now in was the selection process was proving totally unmanageable. The Bar, during my legal lifetime, has grown tenfold. Most QCs, but not all QCs, come from the Bar. QCs can now be solicitors with higher rights of audience. So if you're going to have a system which has a special rank of QC, which brings privileges with it and can result in higher earnings, then you have to have a fair and proper system for appointing of QCs. The Judiciary, at my level, plays a very significant role in advising the Lord Chancellor as to who is to be QC, and he had the final decision. The system worked alright with the people who were obviously either to get it or not get it, but there was a rump in the middle which I was concerned about, because the system we had, although everybody strived to make it fair and open, did not work as it should, and there were people who should have got silk who did not get it, and there may have been, but I think this is much less likely, people who got it who should not. I think it is much more the former than the latter. Quite a number of people were unfairly discriminated against.

We brought in, which was a good idea, Sir Colin Campbell and his Commission to overview the system so that he could advise us and identify examples of unfairness. The result of that was the system, as it was, was doomed, because he was, quite properly, insisting on proper paper trails to support the conclusions we came to. We were just drowning under the weight of the system. My job is to be a judge and to do other things that the Chief Justice was doing. There would be 14 lever arch files, would come into my room in the law courts before we started the selection process. There would be guidance provided by civil servants, but if we were going to take responsibility for this, we had to do it ourselves and go through all this mass of material that was collected. To try and distinguish one person from another to decide who should get this quality mark and who should not was, in the grey area, impossible. When you knew the person, as used to be the case in the past, it was all very straightforward. You knew from your experience in court who were the good people. But there are barristers now who are of the highest quality, and solicitors, who never see a High Court judge, but they certainly deserve silk because of the specialist nature of their practice. I was very uncomfortable about this, and Lord Irvine eventually said, well enough was enough, because we'd all tried our best and we were being criticised, but we did not know how we could make the system so that it could not be criticised. Now that is one aspect of it. Some other way has to be found of doing it. But if you could find some other way of doing it properly, then I would be all in favour of keeping silk, because I think it is a real advantage having a system where one knows that if you have a very difficult case, you want a counsel who is of high standing, the initials QC help to identify suitable candidates.

In addition, you need to have silk for the overseas market. We earn a lot of money from the provision of legal services to the countries overseas, particularly in the commercial field, and the City would like to see QC established because they know that this is a source of invisible earnings. Our QCs can have rights of audience in many jurisdictions where they would not let ordinary solicitors or barristers have rights of audience because they know QCs are outstanding lawyers who are probably more skilled at court presentation work than any equivalent body in any jurisdiction. If you talk to the judges, as I have, of the European Court of Human Rights, and they say the way the English silks present cases is better than the competition, and so it would be very sad to lose this. I hope we won't lose it. I hope a method will be found. I think the answer is for the profession to take control of identifying the people, rather than the judges, but the judges having, so to speak, the right to veto.

I was going to make a similar point. To a large extent, what you are arguing for is the maintenance of the quality mark, but whether or not it should be State-conferred is a different matter.

Different, yes.

Can we turn now to prison reform, because I know that this is an issue close to your heart? It's perhaps not something that you've been associated with over the last decade, but I know it's something you've done a great deal of work on and, I think, non-lawyers associate you more with civil justice and reform. But I think it's important that your thoughts on prison reform are more widely understood.[6]

Since I've taken this job, I am closely involved again in what happens within our prisons, and I think it is of the greatest importance. I think Churchill got it right when saying that the quality of our prisons is to some extent a reflection of the quality of our society. One of the main concerns of the public is with crime. Getting our criminal justice system to work in a more effective way than it does at present is one of the things that both myself and many other judges and the Government are striving to do. I think we are actually making considerable progress. One of the problems is that although we are building more prisons and spending more and more money on prisons, they are still grossly overcrowded, and that inhibits our ability to achieve our aims, and somehow we have to break the vicious circle of going to prison, coming out, re-offending again, and going back to prison for longer, coming out, re-offending. We have also to break the vicious circle where we have not enough money for probation officers because we are having to spend so much money

---

[6] Punishment and sentencing are also discussed by Oliver Lewtin (Ch.10).

on keeping people in prison. We all know that sensible and effective community sentences have a lot more to offer in the long-term tackling of criminal behaviour than prisons have. People have to go to prison if they commit serious offences. They sometimes have to go for a very long time. Under our law, as it is at present, they've even got to go there for the whole of their natural life. But that does not alter the fundamental fact, which is clear beyond peradventure, that what is important is to have a criminal justice system which confines the use of prison to those for whom it is really necessary, and ensures that when they go to prison they do so for no longer than necessary, and that outside of prison we have constructive methods of dealing with offending which does not require prison.

Just one issue, and this is a huge issue and I can't expect you to answer it in full this evening, but reading one of your recent lectures, where you talked a lot about prison reform, you laid out your views there, and I have to paraphrase, but you were talking a great deal about offenders not going to prison for the very good reason that you say, that the likelihood of re-offending is increased if they go to prison. You talk about community service and so forth. And as a piece of social engineering, that must make sense. What I always find difficult is, at the level of the individual, the victim, the individual cases, it's terribly difficult for people to have confidence in the justice system, when their house is broken into, their children are assaulted, all manner of offences are perpetrated, and the individuals don't seem to be receiving, in some sense, their just desserts. And of course this is a classic question in the theory of punishment: is it about paying back the offender or is it about protecting society? But I think there are many who don't have full sympathy with your views precisely because in the instant case they don't feel that the result is just.

I think what you say about most peoples' response is true, until you actually sit them down and talk to them. This is a while ago now, but I went and talked to members of an organisation, Street Watch, where people are concerned about protecting their own homes by being part of a national organisation which does that. The organisers were a bit worried when I went there because they thought I might get a very rough ride, and I am quite sure that the size of the audience reflected the fact that a lot of people felt like you were saying. However, it is my experience that if you talk to people, and tell them of somebody who has a drug habit and commits crime to feed his or her drug habit, and then explain to them that all we can do if we send them to prison, because you have to have a graduated scale of prison sentences, is to send them to prison for three years, and then explain what does that really amount to. First of all, after 18 months, they have a right to be released on licence, so they are actually going to spend 18 months inside and then they are going to be released on licence. And then you take into account the fact that under tagging they're going to be in home custody for part of the 18 months they would otherwise stay in prison, because there is not room in prison for them. And then you find out that there is no really effective treatment that can be given for their drug habit in the time that they're in prison, because they're not there long enough for it to be fulfilled, and unfortunately, we have not the situation where we could start the drug treatment and training in prison and continue it in the community. That the alternative is a drug treatment and testing order. You know if a person is addicted, if they want to kick the habit, it is hugely difficult for them to do so. But if, and it won't happen in all the cases, but if in a substantial number of cases you can get them to break the habit, the long-term benefit will be that a lot fewer houses will be broken into by that person. Then again, restorative justice, I know, works in some cases. People whose house is broken into feel defiled by it being broken into. Again, it does not apply in all cases, but sometimes, for the offender, who is often a 16 or 17-year-old, to actually meet the person whose home they've broken into and hear what that person thinks about it and what it has done to them, how they are frightened at night to go to sleep as a result of this, and they can see that this is not just "them", it is a real live human being they've affected, can have much more impact upon that offender and produce a better result. And what's more, it can be much better for the victim, not in all cases, but in some cases, because the victim sees the person who is responsible, and hears how that person came to commit the offence, and above all, they hear them say sorry. And you know, in my job, I see lots of statements by victims, and the one thing they often say is they have never heard a word of regret.

What happens in young offenders' institutions now, one of the things that they're meant to do, is write a letter to the victim—it is not sent—but they want to prepare a letter to explain what they feel about the crime they've committed, now they know what its effect has been. Some of those letters are really, I find, moving and convincing letters, and the terrible thing is they're never sent to the victim because the authorities think it would be wrong to do that, because it may cause them to relive the crime. But you have this mismatch, and I just think this is another example of the way there are different forms of dealing with offenders, which are punishments, real punishments, but they do not involve youngsters lying on their bed for 20 hours, at least, a day and doing nothing constructive day in and day out. I think we should, we can, do things better, but if we're going to do things better, then we need more resources. I understand, you know, it has been public knowledge so I do not mind saying it again, I've had my home broken into and my wife's wedding ring stolen. I know how upset she was. But equally—and she will agree with me, because she's a longstanding magistrate—she knows that in the majority of cases, prison is not the answer. It is the easy solution, it is the popular solution, but it is not the one that works necessarily best.

I wish we had another hour to discuss that in more detail. Sadly, we don't, and in fact we've come to the end. I just wanted to ask you one final question, if I may, just very quickly. You've contributed in so many ways to the justice system—civil, criminal, constitutional now, and of course in your decision-making. For what would you like to be remembered most? Which area do you feel you've contributed most to?

This is a spontaneous answer: I would like to be thought to have occasionally injected a bit of commonsense into the system.

Lord Woolf, thank you so much.

Postscript

On June 17, 2005, it was announced that Lord Woolf would retire on September 30, 2005. His successor as Lord Chief Justice of England and Wales will be Lord Phillips of Worth Matravers.

The Constitutional Reform Act 2005 received Royal Assent on March 24, 2005. The Act makes provision for:

- the modification (but not, note, the abolition) of the office of Lord Chancellor;
- the Lord Chancellor and other Ministers of the Crown (and many others) to uphold the continued independence of the Judiciary;
- the establishment, for the first time, of a Supreme Court of the United Kingdom;
- the abolition of the appellate jurisdiction of the House of Lords;
- the establishment of a body corporate called the Judicial Appointments Commission;

and much else besides.

INDEX